BEARING
—*the*—
WORD

Women in Culture and Society
A Series Edited by
Catharine R. Stimpson

BEARING
—the—
WORD

Language and Female Experience in
Nineteenth-Century Women's Writing

Margaret Homans

The University of Chicago Press
Chicago and London

The University of Chicago Press, Chicago 60637
The University of Chicago Press, Ltd., London
©1986 by The University of Chicago
All rights reserved. Published 1986
Paperback edition 1989
Printed in the United States of America

98 97 96 95 94 93 92 91 90 89 6 5 4 3 2

Library of Congress Cataloging-in-Publication Data

Homans, Margaret, 1952–
    Bearing the word.

    (Women in culture and society)
    Bibliography: p.
    Includes index.
    1. English literature—Women authors—History
and criticism. 2. Women in literature. 3. English
literature—19th century—History and criticism.
4. Women—England—Language. 5. Feminism and
literature—England. 6. Feminist literary criticism.
I. Title. II. Series.
PR469.W65H66 1986   820'.9'9287   85–20960
ISBN 0-226-35107-6 (cloth)
ISBN 0-226-35106-8 (pbk.)

For my parents,
John and Sallie Homans

Contents

Foreword

I n "The Eumenides," the last play of the *Oresteia*, Orestes is on trial for matricide (the translation I am using of the *Oresteia* is that of Richmond Lattimore [Chicago: University of Chicago Press, 1953]). The terrible question is not whether he has cut Clytemnestra's throat, for he admits that he has, but whether the killing is wrong. Casting her ballot for the son, Athena frees him. The Eumenides, the Furies, the guardians of the female, realize that the laws of an older time have been ripped from their hands. "Disinherited, suffering, heavy with anger," they threaten vengeance, until Athena persuades them to accept their defeat and a home with honor in the caverns beneath Athens, the new citadel of civilization.

Nearly twenty-five hundred years after the death of Aeschylus, his narratives still drive dominant Western perceptions of life, death, and power. Lucidly, Margaret Homans examines a modern version of this compelling tale, the "cultural myth" of Lacanian psycholinguistics. Here the father demands that the son leave the mother and their blissful preoedipal union. The son's reward for obedience is passage into the symbolic order, citizenship in the domain of language. Once there, he must regard and guard women only as objects, as matter. He must transmogrify the lost maternal presence into "Mother Nature." Romantic poetry, as Homans so clearly shows, emblematizes this pattern of thought and action.

Yet, as Homans reminds us, some women wish to enter the symbolic order. Despite prohibitions against it, they desire to bear the word as well as the child that culture insists they must first carry and then, if he is male, give up. Powerfully, deftly, often ironically, Homans lays bare the complexities and complicities of such ambition. However, she sees possibilities as well as difficulties in women's writing. Fusing the revisionary sociological and psychological theories of Nancy Chodorow with those of Lacan, Homans suggests that women, because they are daughters, are less fearful than sons of remaining with and identifying themselves with the mother. As a result, women are capable, if they wish to be, of two languages: an original one, the "literal," that they have learned with the mother; and that second language, the "figurative," that they learn under the father. In a brilliant, original series of readings, Homans then shows four patterns of "collision" between the literal and the figurative in women's texts from the nineteenth-century England that ideologies of gender so structured.

Bearing the Word boldly asks if women write differently because they are women. Its subtle, affirmative answer is that they have. However, Homans is the opposite of a crude biological determinist. When women write differently, they do so because their femaleness has meant that they will become mothers and daughters in a culture that separates the roles and needs of father and son, mother and daughter. Women also write differently from each other. If Dorothy Wordsworth accepts her place as the object of the Romantic quest, Elizabeth Gaskell reveals the possibilities of the mother's tongue.

Language, of course, demarcates the ends and limits of culture. Homans persuasively mediates between and reconciles two attitudes about language that have roiled feminist criticism. One declares that language is a neutral medium that is more or less separable from experience. Once women begin to write, they can reasonably represent their experience, including the thematics of their long-muted femininity. The second attitude tends to find the first naive. It declares that no experience exists outside of language and systems of representation. Unhappily for women, those systems cannot exist without devaluing women, without demanding that they serve as a "repressed referent." Homans demonstrates how writers deploy language itself—nothing more, nothing less—to mark their treacherous, liberating moves between repression and expression.

Homans' first book, *Women Writers and Poetic Identity* (1980), was a sophisticated, persuasive contribution to feminist criticism. Now *Bearing the Word* is a major work of literary theory and a series of amazing readings of women's texts. Pregnant nineteenth-century writing has enabled its twentieth-century daughters, among them feminist critics, to wander more freely and boldly in cultural space. In *Bearing the Word*, Athena, that motherless divinity, emerges as a dangerous goddess. However, the mothers she subdued and the daughters she controlled have escaped from her sentences and now form and reform their own.

Catharine R. Stimpson

Preface

This book is about some of the particular ways in which nineteenth-century women writers wrote their relation to language by writing about the relation between women and language. Women writers' representational thematics of women's experiences collides with their acknowledgment of a dominant myth of language according to which women's experiences are unrepresentable and women cannot perform acts of representation. This book examines some of these collisions in order to understand better what it meant for a woman to write in the nineteenth century. In nineteenth-century fiction by both men and women, those experiences that are most specifically feminine—and, in a culture that so fully differentiated between men's and women's roles, that were celebrated as such (for example, childbirth or child care)—are again and again framed as antithetical to women's writing. The writers considered in this book align with this female thematics certain phases of their ongoing writing and revising of the cultural myth of language's process and structure that situates them as the silent and absent objects of representation. Through their representations of women's lives within an androcentric culture, they organize their own thinking about what the very act and art of representation, or of other ways of writing, might mean for them as women. They attempt, in a variety of ways, to reclaim their own experiences as paradigms for writing.

My argument responds to some of the questions raised by the contradictions between the practices of two kinds of feminist criticism and between the assumptions underlying them. On the one hand, one major branch of North American feminist criticism is interested primarily in what has been called "women's culture," the articulation by women of their experiences as women (whether social, cultural, or biological).[1] This criticism makes two assumptions about language: first, that there is a realm outside language called life or experience that can be experienced separately from its articulation as language, and second, that language is a neutral medium through which men and women can articulate their experiences equally well. Within these assumptions, women's access to language, especially to written and to literary language, may be seen to have been restricted in the past, for example, through actual and ideological prohibitions against higher education for women and against women writing for publication, but the language itself is impartial. On the other hand, French feminist criticism (criticism practiced on both sides of the Atlantic but influenced by French psychoanalytic and literary theory) tends to be interested in women in the context of "the feminine" as a position in language. This criticism also makes two assumptions about language. First, it assumes that there is no realm of experience outside of language, that all experience takes place within a system of representation, usually identified as Lacan's symbolic order. The second assumption, given this perspective on language, is that language is not a neutral medium but rather that its very construction is based on presuppositions about gender that devalue women: the speaking or writing subject is constitutively masculine while the silent object is feminine, and the signifier, through Lacan's privileging of the phallus as the primary signifier, is masculine while the fictive or absent referent is feminine.[2]

Widely differing critical practices follow from these two sets of assumptions about the relation of language to experience. On the one hand, feminist critics in the United States interest themselves very much in women writers because they believe women have been able to represent themselves. We might say that this kind of criticism belongs to the mother, as it values the heritage that one generation of women writers can pass on to another. On the other hand, the French feminist critics are relatively less interested in women's writing because, if representation silences women or assumes their silence, language excludes the possibility of a woman who is a subject or a writer. "The feminine" will make its appearance in texts regardless of the signature of the author.[3] We might say that this kind of criticism belongs to the father, as it accedes to the authority primarily of male theorists who themselves adduce an abstract "Law of the Father" as justification for the subordination of women through the repression of "the feminine."

Since I find myself by turns persuaded by each of these points of view, but even more by the view that "female experience" includes "the experience implicit in language,"[4] my critical project in this book is to find out to what extent, and with what effects, nineteenth-century women writers of realistic novels, who wrote about women's experiences on the assumption that they could do so, also subscribed to some version of the cultural myth of women's relation to and subordination within language. The critical contradictions outlined above are in many respects the products or symptoms of the same history that formed the problematics of nineteenth-century women's fiction writing. We are all the inheritors of the same literary tradition, through which cultural values and myths are transmitted, stretching from the classics and the Bible to Milton and the romantic poets. Moreover, the dominant ideology of family structure in industrialized society has not, in its main outlines, changed very much. On these grounds, I would claim both the value of contemporary critical questions for studying the nineteenth century and the relevance of the nineteenth century for addressing today's critical questions. Contemporary women's writing—critical and theoretical, as well as literary—is still playing out the nineteenth century's contradictions. For nineteenth-century women writers, the collision between the urgent need to represent female experience and women's silencing within language and literary history remained a collision, articulated but not resolved. But an analysis of this contradiction might help us to stop repeating the disabling choice of one parent over the other.

My own experience of writing has been a genuine pleasure, thanks to the kindness of many friends and colleagues. Harriet Chessman, Margaret Ferguson, and Patricia Meyer Spacks read and provided detailed and invaluable commentary on the entire manuscript. Christine Froula, Paul Morrison, and J. Hillis Miller read and helpfully commented on substantial parts of it. For stimulating conversation about the book's questions and for important suggestions about specific portions of the argument, I am indebted to those mentioned above, as well as to Jay Clayton, Nancy Cott, Joan Dayan, Gillian C. Gill, Patricia Kleindienst Joplin, Susan Levin, Mary Loeffelholz, Mary Poovey, Julie Rivkin, Gordon Turnbull, Hélène Wenzel, Bryan Wolf, and Patricia Yaeger. Students at Yale, audiences at Dartmouth, Princeton, Rutgers, and elsewhere, and my editors and anonymous readers at the University of Chicago Press all helped me think more clearly about my argument.

I am grateful for the financial support of a Morse Fellowship, an ACLS Fellowship, and of Yale's Griswold Fund for travel and typing. The Keeper of Printed Books at the British Museum very kindly provided me with books during the only week of the year when the reading room is closed. Channing Hughes and Mary Loeffelholz accurately and indefatigably typed and retyped the manuscript. And I thank Gordon Turnbull for proofreading and for disentangling many a syntactic snarl.

For their generous friendship and support during the years when I wrote this book, I wish to thank Harold Bloom, Richard Herzfelder, Ethan Nadel, and Julie Rivkin. Most especially I wish to thank Harriet Chessman, whose writing inspired the best parts of my own and who unstintingly supplied invaluable conversation about every phase of the book's construction. My parents' love and confidence in me receive a small return in the dedication of this book.

1

Representation, Reproduction, and Women's Place in Language

Early in "The Window," the section of *To The Lighthouse* in which Mrs. Ramsay is vividly present, Virginia Woolf mocks the dependence of androcentric culture on the mother's absence. Mr. Ramsay's highly abstract project, "subject and object of the nature of reality," takes up the central questions of Western metaphysics. The artist, Lily Briscoe, baffled by the dry abstraction of these terms, elicits this explanation from his son Andrew: "'Think of a kitchen table then,' he told her, 'when you're not there.'" The narrative goes on through Lily's perspective as she takes a walk:

> So now she always saw, when she thought of Mr. Ramsay's work, a scrubbed kitchen table. It lodged now in the fork of a pear tree, for they had reached the orchard. And with a painful effort of concentration, she focused her mind, not upon the silver-bossed bark of the tree, or upon its fish-shaped leaves, but upon a phantom kitchen table, one of those scrubbed board tables, grained and knotted, whose virtue seems to have been laid bare by years of muscular integrity, which stuck there, its four legs in the air.[1]

Lily's rich and concretizing power of imagination mocks the egotistical speculations that question the existence of objects apart from perception, even though Mr. Ramsay raises this question in an attempt to cross the abyss between subject and object. Like any true romantic quester, Mr. Ramsay does not make his attempt to cross the abyss entirely in good faith. His life depends upon there always remaining some distance to cross. Although he risks the shame of failure in questing toward the letter R, the object of his quest must remain somewhere in the distance, in order that he always have something left to pursue. The abyss between subject

1

and object that so fascinates Mr. Ramsay is constitutively that between a man and an absent mother. Behind the phantom kitchen table that Lily imagines back into existence, so much more vividly than Mr. Ramsay would ever want to, stands an even more phantom woman, the nurturing, maternal woman whose years of scrubbing have laid bare the table's grained and knotted virtue. Western metaphysics, in Woolf's perceptive and mocking portrayal, requires that the mother remain perpetually out of reach in order for Mr. Ramsay and his kind to speculate forever on how to reach her, or to replace her with their own abstractions.

Not all women writers have shared Woolf's ability to toss lightly into the air this central myth of our culture's dependence on the mother's absence. In this chapter, I will investigate why the mother's absence is what makes possible and makes necessary the central projects of our culture, and I will begin to sketch out this book's central concern, the variety of responses nineteenth-century women writers have made to this profoundly troubling myth. We could locate in virtually all of the founding texts of our culture a version of the myth Woolf mocks: that the death or absence of the mother sorrowfully but fortunately makes possible the construction of language and of culture. Christine Froula has recently argued that in Genesis and in *Paradise Lost*, it is the repression of actual maternity in the original scene of creation that enables the myth of a paternal god's monopoly in creation.[2] Similarly, Luce Irigaray has suggested that in Freud's myth, in *Totem and Taboo*, of the founding of human culture on the murder of the father by the primitive horde of his sons, Freud "forgets a more ancient murder, that of the woman-mother (*femme-mère*)," a murder necessary to the establishment of civilization.[3] This more ancient murder, Irigaray suggests, is represented by the myth of the murder of Clytemnestra by her son in revenge for the murder of Agamemnon. The Furies, whom Irigaray characterizes as "insurgents against patriarchal power," drive Orestes mad in revenge for the matricide, but "the matricidal son must be rescued from madness in order to institute the patriarchal order."[4] In the *Oresteia*, under the guidance of Athena, the goddess whose very existence demonstrates how unnecessary mothers are, Apollo asserts that Orestes is innocent on the grounds that, while the tie between wife and husband is protected by law,[5]

> The mother is no parent of that which is called
> her child, but only nurse of the new-planted seed
> that grows. The parent is he who mounts.

Irigaray's notion that the murder of the mother is necessary for the founding of patriarchal culture corresponds to and criticizes Wordsworth's myth of language acquisition, in which the absence and loss of the mother are again necessary.[6] In Wordsworth's account of the child's acquisition of language in book 2 of *The Prelude*, the poet writes that the infant babe is blest, because

> For him, in one dear Presence, there exists
> A virtue which irradiates and exalts
> Objects through widest intercourse of sense.
>
> (2.238–40)

Drinking in the feelings of his mother's eye, connected with the world because he is so intimately connected to her and thus to everything that she sees and feels, the infant

> Doth like an agent of the one great Mind
> Create, creator and receiver both.
>
> (2.257–58)

This creative power closely resembles Coleridge's formulations of the poet's power, except that the baby's creative power is without language. Indeed, Wordsworth summarizes his account of infancy by calling it

> that first time
> In which, a Babe, by intercourse of touch
> I held mute dialogues with my Mother's heart.
>
> (2.266–68)

As the infant matures, these mute dialogues, which take place so happily in the presence of mother and child, give way to the pain of the mother's absence and, simultaneously, to language.

> For now a trouble came into my mind
> From unknown causes. I was left alone,
> Seeking the visible world, nor knowing why.
> The props of my affections were removed,
> And yet the building stood, as if sustained
> By its own spirit!
>
> (2.276–81)

This trouble, which leaves the child "alone, seeking the visible world," whereas previously the visible world was present for him in his mother's eyes, can be interpreted in two ways, which Wordsworth conflates here. The trouble is the acquisition of language; it is also the death of Wordsworth's mother when he was eight years old. This is not to suggest that Wordsworth learned language only after his mother's death, but rather that he connects learning representational language (and discovering some of its implications) with a loss that is equivalent to his mother's death, some loss of her prior to her actual death. This loss feels like the mother's death, and it is, paradoxically, both caused by and the cause of the acquisition of representational language.

But why should language and culture depend on the death or absence of the mother and on the quest for substitutes for her, substitutes that transfer her power to something that men's minds can more readily control? And—most important for the question of women's writing—what does it mean to women writers that the dominant myths of our culture, as embodied in these and other founding texts, present language and culture as constructed in this way?

An investigation of the second of these questions will be the major project of this book. To take up this question very briefly before returning to the first, what is most problematic for women writers about these myths of culture is the way they position women, or "the feminine," in language. For the same reason that women are identified with nature and matter in any traditional thematics of gender (as when Milton calls the planet Earth "great Mother"), women are also identified with the literal, the absent referent in our predominant myth of language.[7] From the point of view of this myth, the literal both makes possible and endangers the figurative structures of literature. That we might have access to some original ground of meaning is the necessary illusion that empowers the acts of figuration that constitute literature, just as it is Mr. Ramsay's belief in the possibility of crossing the abyss between subject and object that empowers his metaphysical speculations. At the same time, literal meaning would hypothetically destroy any text it actually entered by making superfluous those very figures—and even, some would argue, all language acts—just as the presence of the mother's body would make language unnecessary in Wordsworth's myth of language acquisition and just as the presence of the mother's kitchen table would obviate Mr. Ramsay's endless quest for the object. This possibility is always, but never more than, a threat, since literal meaning cannot be present in a text: it is always elsewhere. This positioning of the literal poses special problems for women readers and writers because literal language, together with nature and matter to which it is epistemologically linked, is traditionally classified as feminine, and the feminine is, from the point of view of a predominantly androcentric culture, always elsewhere too. A dualism of presence and absence, of subject and object, structures everything our culture considers thinkable; yet women cannot participate in it as subjects as easily as can men because of the powerful, persuasive way in which the feminine is again and again said to be on the object's side of that dyad. Women who do conceive of themselves as subjects—that is, as present, thinking women rather than as "woman"—must continually guard against fulfilling those imposed definitions by being returned to the position of the object.

Yet another view of the literal, of literal language and of women's identification with it and with nature, is possible if we make the effort to look at the situation from women's perspective. Women might, and do, embrace this connection, not for the same reasons for which androcentric culture identifies women and the literal, but for reasons having to do with women's own development and identity, even though that identity is never entirely separable from culture as a whole. The literal is ambiguous for women writers because women's potentially more positive view of it collides with its devaluation by our culture. I will argue that the differential valuations of literal and figurative originate in the way our culture constructs masculinity and femininity, for if the literal is associated with the feminine, the more highly valued figurative is associated with the masculine. To take something literally is to get it wrong, while to have a figurative understanding of something is the correct intellectual stance. And yet, to the extent that women writers are able to have a view of this situation independent of men's, women may value both the mother and the literal differently and consequently understand their linguistic situation in a way that makes their writing unacceptable to those who privilege the figurative.

Before we investigate particular women's revisions of the cultural myth of women's place in language, it will be necessary to explore in greater depth, first, just what this myth of language is and what its implications are for women, and second, what revaluations and reconceptions of the gender associations of language might emerge from a closer look at the model provided by a recent feminist account of women's developmental history. To represent what I have been calling the dominant myth of language, I will use Jacques Lacan's account of language because he provides the most explicit and compelling contemporary formulation of a myth that was, in its largest outlines, already at the heart of nineteenth-century European literary culture, the myth we have seen at work in Wordsworth and Aeschylus. Lacan's writing originates in Freud's theory of the stages and processes of human development, a theory based on Freud's reading of the myth of Oedipus, which in turn supports and is supported by the androcentric implications of many other classical myths that have always informed Western culture's myths of itself.[8] The Lacanian view of language is not a universal truth, but the

psycholinguistic retelling of a myth to which our culture has long subscribed. I believe that a woman writer could be affected by this myth
without my believing in its truth. I am aware that I am myself taking this
myth literally, in connecting those psychoanalytic or linguistic positions,
"masculine" and "feminine," with the experiences of real women who
wrote. But "taking it literally" is what these writers have learned women
might happily do, or are supposed to do, and it is only by our taking
literally the myth of women's literality that we can find out what is at
stake in the very process of taking it literally. Nancy Chodorow's feminist revision of Freud has obvious but unstated implications for Lacanian
theory, and after reviewing the Lacanian account of language acquisition, we will map the implications of Chodorow's theory for Lacan's as
well as chart the way in which Lacanian terms can transform Chodorow's psychosocial theory into a revisionary myth of women and
language.[9]

In the Lacanian myth, language and gender are connected in such a
way as to privilege implicitly the masculine and the figurative. At first,
according to Lacan, all children, irrespective of gender, are engaged in a
dyadic relation with the mother in which they find themselves to be
whole and unitary, even if that sense of wholeness is "imaginary" or
founded on an illusion.[10] During this period, before language as we know
it has begun, the period that corresponds to Freud's preoedipal stage, the
child shares with the mother what Julia Kristeva calls the semiotic,
consisting of body language and nonrepresentational sounds.[11] During
this time, to quote from Terry Eagleton's useful paraphrase of Lacan,
"no gap has as yet opened up between signifier and signified" because the
child communicates with the mother's presence without mediation, as in
the "mute dialogues" Wordsworth says he "held" with his mother's
heart as an infant.[12] At about the age of eighteen months, however, two
changes occur simultaneously: the child begins to acquire language, and
he (I use the pronoun advisedly here) becomes aware of sexual difference.
(Actually, the timing of these events, as of some important sequels, may
vary widely, but Lacan and Lacanians are engaged in cultural mythmaking.) This Lacanian stage is the mythic equivalent of Freud's oedipal
crisis, both its onset and its resolution. The father, who is discovered to
have all along been in possession of the mother, intervenes in the potentially incestuous dyad of mother and child. Because what marks the
father is his possession of the phallus, the phallus becomes the mark of
sexual difference, that is, of difference from the mother.

The phallus becomes the mark of language's difference as well, which
becomes equivalent to sexual difference. Whereas in the preoedipal
relation to the mother, communication required no distance or difference, now, with the intrusive entry of the phallus, "the child uncon-

sciously learns that a sign has meaning only by dint of its difference from other signs, and learns also that a sign presupposes the *absence* of the object it signifies" (italics his).[13] The phallus, the first mark of difference, will always stand as the primary signifier, for the apparent owner of the phallus, of the marker of difference, is he who speaks. Thus the child leaves behind the communication system he shared with his mother, which required no difference, and enters what Lacan calls the "Law of the Father," or the symbolic order, which is simultaneously the prohibition of incest with the mother, the *non* of the father, and the sign system that depends on difference and on the absence of the referent, the *nom* of the father, that complex of signifying systems and laws that make up Western culture. It is this absence of the referent that Andrew Ramsay sums up in his account of his father's thought: "Think of a kitchen table then, . . . when you're not there." Lacan illustrates this earliest functioning of symbolic language with Freud's story of his grandson's game of Fort!/Da!, with which the child represents and thus controls his mother's absence.

While the phallus is the mark of man's difference from woman, and of language's difference and of the absence of the referent, it is also, paradoxically, the "copula" or "hyphen in the evanescence of its erection" that would restore the connection between children and mothers.[14] Because its use in this way is denied by the father to the child, however, it is perpetually missing. It is, by this logic, because of the lack of the phallus, not its possession, that the child enters with such enthusiasm into the Law of the Father, for it is symbolic language alone that can approximate the bridging of the gap between child and mother opened up by the simultaneous arousal and prohibition of incest. Language promises to cross, even while operating through dependence on, that gap. Thus language becomes what Lacan calls desire. In a simultaneity that can only exist in mythic time, desire comes about through separation, while separation comes about only through the punitive consequences of desire. Lacan defines desire as the difference or gap between "need" or "appetite" and "demand:"

> Thus desire is neither the appetite for satisfaction, nor the demand
> for love, but the difference that results from the subtraction of the
> first from the second. . . . The phallus is the privileged signifier of
> that mark in which the role of the logos is joined with the advent of
> desire. . . . The phallus as signifier gives the ratio of desire.[15]

Replacing the forbidden phallus, language's system of differences and absences ("the phallus as signifier") becomes a system for generating substitutes for the forbidden mother. Renouncing his desire for his mother, the child turns next to searching for substitutes for her that would be permissible within the Law of the Father. That quest is constituted simultaneously by heterosexual desire and by language as desire in a series of substitutions along a chain of signifiers that refer, not to things, but always to other signifiers. As Eagleton puts it, "All desire springs from a lack. . . . Human language works by such lack: the absence of the real objects which signs designate. . . . We are severed from the mother's body. . . . We will spend all of our lives hunting for it."[16] Desire springs also, we might add with Leclaire, from the lack or absence of the "evanescent" phallus, which might have supplied a direct link to that maternal body. Both phallus and mother are lacking.

It is important to note, however, that from the perspective of the symbolic order, this lack is something to be grateful for. Without this lack, there would be no law:

> Freud reveals to us that it is thanks to the Name-of-the-Father that man does not remain in the sexual service of the mother, that aggression towards the father is at the principle of the Law, and that the Law is at the service of desire, which it institutes through the prohibition of incest.
> It is, therefore, the assumption of castration which creates the lack through which desire is instituted. . . . Desire reproduces the subject's relation to the lost object.[17]

"Thanks to the Name-of-the-Father" does not carry quite so strong a sense of gratitude in the original as in the translation (*grâce au* meaning "thanks to" in the sense of "due to"), but the attribution to the mother of a demand for "sexual service" from the "man" amply suggests the revulsion toward the mother that would make the loss of her and of any tangible connection to her a matter for gratitude. I do not detect any irony in Lacan's phrasing. The loss of the mother through the prohibition of incest and the desire, law, and language it makes possible are construed here in a wholly positive way.

It should be clear that neither the Lacanian myth of childhood nor the cultural tradition it summarizes notices that its narrative of the entry into the symbolic order is based on the son's experience of a scene of sexual sameness and difference. It is only for the son, and not for the daughter, that the entry of the phallus marks a difference between the mother and the self. Although the daughter learns sexual difference, too, her difference refers to another figure in the sexual triangle, the father. Because the father's relation to the daughter is not symmetrical with the mother's relation to the son, the very notion of sexual difference has different meanings for the son and for the daughter. The son's search for substitutes for the forbidden body of his mother will therefore constitute, not a universal human condition, but a specifically male desire, the desire of the son who must renounce his mother.

That Lacan's narrative originates in male experience shouldn't necessarily invalidate it as a description of a daughter's relation to sexuality and language. But his narrative depends upon a disingenuous confusion of trope and material condition.[18] On the one hand, "phallus," "masculine," and "feminine" are all argued to be tropes or positions in language, which anyone, male or female, can occupy. On the other hand, he himself applies what he has said about the trope "woman" to actual women, in a remark in which gender has obviously become a material condition: "There is no woman who is not excluded by the nature of things, which is the nature of words, and it must be said that, if there is something they complain a lot about at the moment, that is what it is—except that they don't know what they are saying, that's the whole difference between them and me."[19] While Lacanian language assumes the lack of the phallus, it is only those who can lack it—those who might once have had it, as sons believe their fathers have—who are privileged to substitute for it symbolic language; daughters lack this lack. Lacan's narrative of the origin of figuration authorizes itself by telling the story in such a way as apparently to privilege figuration as a mode, and yet it depends on the literal difference between sex organs.

Before going on to examine what a daughter's experience of acculturation might be, we will need to look more closely at the implications for men's and women's language of the androcentric bias of Lacan's telling of the old story. What the son searches for, in searching for substitutes for the mother's forbidden body, is a series of figures: "someone *like* his mother."[20] At the same time, language is structured as the substitution for the (female) object of signifiers that both require the absence of the object and also permit its controlled return, something *like* the lost object. Figuration, then, and the definition of all language as figuration gain their hyperbolical cultural valuation from a specifically male standpoint because they allow the son, both as erotic being and as speaker, to flee from the mother as well as the lost referent with which she is primordially identified. Women must remain the literal in order to ground the figurative substitutions sons generate and privilege.

In the passage from Aeschylus from which I quoted earlier, the passage in which Apollo astoundingly argues that the mother is "only nurse of the new-planted seed that grows," consider how much depends upon a figure. It is only by comparing the mother to the earth in which a seed grows that the mother's actual part in the growth of her child can be denied. The denial of the mother is produced by a son's invention of a figure, a figure, moreover, that identifies the mother with the earth: with nature, matter, and also with the literal as a position just outside language, the object to which the figure refers but that the figure sanitarily replaces. The symbolic order, both the legal system and language, depends on the identification of the woman with the literal, and then on the denial that the literal has any connection with masculine figurations.

Percy Shelley's *Alastor* provides a fuller example of the gender specificity of all aspects of the myth of the symbolic order. This quest romance typifies the romantic period's articulation of the way in which "we are severed from the mother's body [and] will spend all of our lives hunting for it." The poem proper narrates the story of the hero's quest for an ideal female figure of his own invention, a "fleeting shade" whom he pursues to his death, bypassing the available love of a real woman along the way.[21] That this figure is a figurative substitute for a mother who has been killed (like Clytemnestra, dead for the sake of Athenian law) in order to set the poem's chain of signifiers in motion is suggested by the introduction. Invoking a Miltonic "great Mother," nature, as the muse of his poem, the narrator nonetheless makes it clear that it is her association with death—and therefore I would suggest her death itself—that motivates and makes possible his song:

> Mother of this unfathomable world!
> Favour my solemn song, for I have loved
> Thee ever, and thee only; I have watched
> Thy shadow, and the darkness of thy steps,
> And my heart ever gazes on the depth
> Of thy deep mysteries. I have made my bed
> In charnels and on coffins, where black death
> Keeps record of the trophies won from thee.
>
> (18–25)

As Mary Shelley's reading of this passage will make clear, it is not possible for a male poet both to "make his bed" with a *living* Mother Nature and at the same time to write a poem. Mother Nature must be dead in order for her to "favour [his] song." The process of writing the poem, of generating a chain of substitutive signifiers, is dramatized in, and cognate with, the quest of the hero for a figurative maiden, for to kill and replace the mother is the same as language's search for substitutes for the object.

Lacan's dictum that it is "thanks to the Name-of-the-Father that man does not remain in the sexual service of the mother" rings true in these passages. The symbolic order is founded, not merely on the regrettable loss of the mother, but rather on her active and overt murder. Thus a feminist critique begins by indicating the situation in which women are placed by a myth of language that assumes the speaker to be masculine. But let us go back at this point and start over, looking this time not from the son's but from the daughter's point of view. We will then be in a position to investigate the mother's experience, taking into consideration both that she was once herself a daughter and also that she lives in a culture in which a powerful androcentric myth requires her absence and silence.

When, in the Lacanian scheme, the father's phallus interrupts a mother-child dyad in which the child is a daughter, the discovery of difference acquires a rather different set of implications, both for gender and for language, from when the child is a son. For a daughter, sexual difference and the difference that underlies the functioning of the symbolic order are not the same in the way that they are for a son. The daughter discovers that she is the same as her mother and different from her father, so her relationship to her mother contradicts, rather than reinforces (as in the case of the son), the dependence of the symbolic order on the absence of the mother. The Law of the Father, the *non du père*, is preeminently the prohibition against incest, backed up negatively by the "castration" enacted in that prohibition, and positively by the reward of entry into the symbolic order. The daughter might seem to desire the mother as much as does the son, so that the law would be as meaningful for the daughter as it is for the son. But because difference does not open up between her and her mother in the same way that it does between mother and son, the daughter does not experience desire in the Lacanian sense, that is, as differentiated from a preoedipal merging with the mother. Or if she does experience Lacanian desire, that does not become the whole story of their relationship, as it does with the son. Drawing on the object relations theory developed by D. W. Winnicott, Alice and Michael Balint, and others, Nancy Chodorow argues that a mother experiences "a daughter as an extension or double of . . . herself, with cathexis of the daughter as a sexual other usually remaining a weaker, less significant theme" (p. 109). Because of her likeness to and identification with her mother, the daughter does not need a copula such as the phallus to make the connection, as the son does. She also does not need a phallus, paradoxically, because she is never told she may not use it: in a culture already heterosexual, the father would be unlikely to suspect threats to his sexual terrain from that quarter. Because he does not threaten castration (or, indeed, perform it through his verbal prohibitions as he does with the son), the daughter never needs a phallus. Or to put it the other way around, the father does not threaten castration because the daughter has never been far enough away from her mother to have devised a phallus to wish for. In this circular way, a daughter is never encouraged to abandon her mother in the way that a son is, never needs to replace the lost phallus (which she never wanted in the first place, or lost) with other hyphens, is never given so great an incentive to enter the symbolic order as a consolation for that renunciation. Indeed, as Judith Herman has shown, for the daughter the passing of the oedipal period means, not the end of incest, but its instigation, for while the Law of the Father prohibits incest between mother and son, it authorizes incest between father and daughter.[22]

Thus, because of various consequences of the daughter's likeness to her mother, she does not enter the symbolic order as wholeheartedly or exclusively as does the son. Furthermore, Chodorow argues, because the daughter doesn't share the son's powerful incentives to renounce the mother, a girl's "preoedipal attachment to her mother lasts . . . often well into her fourth or fifth year" (p. 96), that is, in terms of linguistic development, well past the time when she acquires representational language. Since the girl does not experience her father directly as a rival—the father is less likely to intervene between mother and daughter than between mother and son—the dyadic relation with the mother is not, or is not entirely, replaced by the triangular relationship that for Lacan is the prerequisite of the symbolic order. Chodorow agrees with Freud that the girl does to a degree turn away from her mother, but their accounts of her motives differ radically. Freud says that the girl, having seen a penis and having decided in a flash that she wants one, hates her mother for not giving her one and scorns her for not having one herself. She then turns to the father, who will give her, not one of her own, but some restitution through fantasized sexual possession of him or through giving her a baby as substitute. Chodorow, using clinical revisions of Freud to reassess his theory, argues that the girl turns to the father not because she hates her mother but rather because, continuing to love her mother, she hopes that the father will be able to supply her with what she perceives (given a traditionally heterosexual mother) would satisfy her mother's desire. Consequently, Chodorow can argue that the daughter's "'rejection' of her mother, and oedipal attachment to her father, . . . do not mean the termination of the girl's affective relationship to her mother. . . . A girl's libidinal turning to her father is not at the expense of, or a substitute for, her attachment to her mother" (pp. 126–27).

Our recent mythographers, from Freud to Lacan's current explicators, view this continued preoedipal attachment to the mother as the daughter's tragedy because it means she is deprived of the experience they value most highly. Freud argues that a girl's superego is relatively weak because she is wounded from birth and cannot be castrated a second time; because women are thus not susceptible to the threats of the father's law, they lack the well-developed moral and ethical sense of men. A commentator on the implications of Lacanian theory for women has recently written, "The particular tragedy for daughters who identify with their (m)Others along traditional gender/role lines, is that they avoid primary Castration—i.e., difference or psychic separation—and, in so doing, verify the myths which become secondary Castration."[23] And yet from the daughter's point of view, there might be another and more positive way of viewing this continued attachment to the mother. Only in an androcentric culture would it be considered tragic for a girl not to experience pain, if that pain is preeminently a masculine experience.

This alternative story of human development, this story about a daughter's long continuation of her preoedipal attachment to her mother, and of her embracing the Law of the Father so much less enthusiastically than the son, has important consequences for the writing of daughters, for the ways women rewrite the story of language. Although in this new story, the daughter does enter the symbolic order, she does not do so exclusively. Because she does not perceive the mother as lost or renounced, she does not need the compensation the father's law offers as much as does the son. Furthermore, she has the positive experience of never having given up entirely the presymbolic communication that carries over, with the bond to the mother, beyond the preoedipal period. The daughter therefore speaks two languages at once. Along with symbolic language, she retains the literal or presymbolic language that the son represses at the time of his renunciation of his mother. Just as there is for the daughter no oedipal "crisis," her entry into the symbolic order is only a gradual shift of emphasis.

The daughter's retention of this earliest language has profound implications for the differential valuations of literal and figurative, and for women writers' relations to them. The son, as we have seen, will view the mother as the literal, she whose absence makes language both necessary and possible. The literal will be valueless and the figurative valuable because what the son searches for is not the mother herself, the literal that is forbidden by the father's law, but figures for her. For the daughter, however, to the extent that she is able to see differently from the cultural norm set by sons, to the extent that she is only partially within the symbolic order, the whole question of literal and figurative will be more complex. The daughter will perhaps prefer the literal that her brother devalues. Although she does not share Chodorow's view of its continuation past the oedipal phase, Irigaray suggests most compactly the implications of this presymbolic mother-daughter relation for figurative and literal language in our present culture: "Nourir a lieu avant toute figure" (Nourishing takes place before there are any images/ any symbols/ any faces). That is, the mother's and daughter's earliest relation takes place prior to the distancing of one from the other that would give either of them a visible face, and also, most importantly, prior to figuration or to the symbolic order.[24] Unlike the son, the daughter does not, in Chodorow's view, give up this belief in communication that takes place in presence rather than in absence, in the dyadic relation with the mother, and prior to figuration.

Although what she shares with her mother, her presymbolic or literal language, with its lack of gaps between signifier and referent, will resemble the literal from which the son is in flight in that both begin with closeness to the mother's body, they are not exactly the same, and they are valued very differently, because the tie to the mother's body is valued so differently. Many possible avenues of divergence from the model based on the son's experience open up. For example, the daughter might simply not find the opposition of literal and figurative as telling and important as the son might, for it maintains a boundary not sacred to her (the boundary of the prohibition of incest with the mother). Or, recognizing such a boundary, she might nonetheless favor the literal over the figurative. She might also view the operation of language in an entirely different way, not based on the privilege of figuration, and possibly not based on any concept of representation that requires the absence of and covert desire for the object. "Representation" in this daughter's view might indeed mean presence, not absence, since her experience is not one of complete loss in the first place.

Before going on to suggest some of the ways in which this theoretical account of daughters' language will be useful for our study of nineteenth-century texts, I would like to clarify my assumptions about the status of that theory. Like feminist theorists of the French school, I would agree that the Lacanian analysis of acculturation is probably correct, as far as it goes, and that what he analyzes should be changed. But in my view we cannot know how well his analysis applies to women. Had the story of human acculturation been written from the start from the daughter's perspective, it would have been written quite differently. But given that the story is written from the son's perspective, beginning with the earliest examples of Western literature, followed by a literary history that has only reinforced the myth already written, it is scarcely possible to imagine a gynocentric myth, or even a more equitable one, for androcentric myth has, in effect, shaped female experience. Although women writers past and present have made important and bold attempts to give voice to women's silenced story, we will perhaps never know the extent to which such revisionary myths (based on women's "experience") have unintentionally reinscribed the pervasive androcentrism of our culture.[25] Nonetheless, Chodorow's theory, and the readings it makes possible, supply what may be a genuinely different story.

Chodorow's argument derives in large part from her feminist manipulations of the Freudian myth, so that her own writing constitutes mythmaking just as much as Lacan's does. Yet she relies to an equal degree on recent clinical studies of children, which allow her to claim for her argument a greater degree of experiential accuracy than Freud's or Lacan's may contain. These clinical studies were undoubtedly influenced by cultural myths, both Freudian and anti-Freudian, and it is possible that Chodorow's account of human development is just as much a myth (if a more palatable one) as Freud's and Lacan's are. To say that a theory is mythic is hardly to diminish its authority for interpreting culture. And yet I am not wholly satisfied to leave it at that. Chodorow's theory is more accurate than Freud's in that it accounts for more than half of the human race, and I would make this argument on the grounds of the critique of cultural construction of the privilege of figuration that her theory has helped us to make. Since the wish to see all accounts of human life as figures—as myths—derives from the peculiarities of masculine psychosocial development, we would be justified in arguing that to call Chodorow's account only a myth would be once again to exclude the mother's body. Even though in the present context, any way in which I can write about that body frustratingly only contributes to its exclusion, that body is still there, beyond theory. To grant Chodorow's story the status of truth is therefore to begin the process of re-presencing the mother's body, over and against the exclusion of it required by the father's law. It is not simply to reinscribe the mystifications of a unified and phallocratic "truth," although this is how it might appear to theorists of the French school, following Foucault and Derrida, who see "feminism" as simply another form of humanism.[26] (And if this is what I am doing, it is no worse—and at least more self-conscious—than Lacan's conflation of gender as trope with literal sex.) Although at this point I can prove the value of this theory only by recourse to that theory itself, the readings of texts by other women writers that make up the rest of this book will support the contention that Chodorow's account of female life has more explanatory power than Freud's or Lacan's.

At least some nineteenth-century women writing self-consciously as daughters create myths of their own writing that reveal that they hold some variant of the daughterly perspective we have uncovered with the help of Chodorow. The next three chapters, on Dorothy Wordsworth,

Emily Brontë, and Charlotte Brontë, will investigate three such myths, each enacted both as theme and as literary practice. These authors articulate thematically a daughter's bond to and identification with a vulnerable or vanished mother (often figured as Mother Nature); at the same time, their texts' literalizations of figures, in which the literal is sometimes preferred, constitute a linguistic trace of a mother-daughter bond. (The writings of Mary Shelley, George Eliot, and Elizabeth Gaskell share this practice and thematics, though for more complex reasons that we will investigate shortly.) For example, Dorothy Wordsworth self-consciously literalizes several of her brother's most important figures for sublimity and transcendence, figures that she understands rely on the mother's exclusion in just the way we have seen the symbolic order exclude the mother. When Dorothy Wordsworth literalizes these figures, she restores a female presence to life, asserting both through her literaliz-ing style and through her subject matter the value of a language not requiring absence. More ambivalent than Wordsworth, but to differing degrees, Emily and Charlotte Brontë both value the literal and subscribe to the symbolic order's notion of the threat it poses to writing. The first Cathy in *Wuthering Heights* seeks a return to her childhood in nature, which is synonymous with what the novel defines as the dangerously nonfigurative, while Jane Eyre first approaches and then rejects an iden-tification with Mother Nature, an identification that is, again, associated with literalization. These writers, I will argue, are writing and practicing myths of daughters' relations to symbolic language, working out through their writing the conflicts between being a daughter and being a writer. The myths these works reveal can best be understood as variously situated on a scale between the protesting acceptance of the androcentric myth Lacan summarizes and the celebration of the more gynocentric myth Chodorow allows us, for the first time, to read.

While these nineteenth-century daughters write revisionary myths of literal and figurative, they do so more through thematics than through the invention of new representational practices. At the level of language, their disconcertion of the categories of literal and figurative remains relatively limited when viewed from the perspective of the kinds of experimentation with language that, for a variety of historical reasons too complex to consider here, more recent writers have practiced. In order to indicate most vividly what I mean by the practice of a daughter's language based as far as possible on the continued presence of the mother, I would like to turn briefly to another passage from *To the Lighthouse*. This passage provides an extreme case of a daughterly writer's inscription of the way a presymbolic language carries over to become part of a daughter's adult language. At the same time, this passage is also thematically more overt in its claims for the possibility and value of the mother's presence: while in the writings of Dorothy Wordsworth and the Brontës, the mother is only marginally present (and then sometimes ambivalently valued), Mrs. Ramsay is present as a character. Reading Woolf's bolder version of a self-consciously female practice and thematics, like reading Chodorow's even more boldly stated theory, helps us to be alert to what is less easily perceived, but no less important, in their predecessors' writings.

Mrs. Ramsay is in the process of putting her children to sleep after the dinner party. James, who is six, refuses to go to sleep without the phallic horned boar's skull hanging on the wall, while Cam, who is seven, cannot go to sleep because "she could see the horns . . . all over the room" (p. 171). Mrs. Ramsay devises the strategy of covering it up, which satisfies both children's demands, and she then goes to each child in turn to provide the particular form of reassurance each needs in order to sleep:

> She could see the words echoing as she spoke them rhythmically in Cam's mind, and Cam was repeating after her how it was like a mountain, a bird's nest, a garden, and there were little antelopes, and her eyes were opening and shutting, and Mrs. Ramsay went on speaking still more monotonously, and more rhythmically and more nonsensically, how she must shut her eyes and go to sleep and dream of mountains and valleys and stars falling and parrots and antelopes and gardens, and everything lovely, she said, raising her head very slowly and speaking more and more mechanically, until she sat upright and saw that Cam was asleep.
>
> Now, she whispered, crossing over to his bed, James must go to sleep too, for see, she said, the boar's skull was still there; they had not touched it; they had done just what he wanted; it was there quite unhurt. He made sure that the skull was still there under the shawl. (pp. 172–73)

It might seem that Mrs. Ramsay's discourse with her daughter depends on figuration, as she is listing all the things that the wrapped skull might be like, and the relation between the signifier "mountain" and any actual mountain is as distant as it ever is in ordinary figurative representation. However, the aim of Mrs. Ramsay's talk is not to represent mountains or other distant objects, but rather to reassure Cam of her own sheltering presence. There is a gap between the signifier "mountain" and an actual mountain, but there is no gap at all between Mrs. Ramsay's words and her bodily presence for her daughter. Her words do not so much signify the far-off places they allude to as enact the present contact between mother and daughter, a contact emphasized by the way Cam repeats her mother's words. The words matter as sounds, monotonous and rhythmic, issuing from and returning to the body. This is what I mean by a literal language shared between mother and daughter: a language of presence, in which the presence or absence of referents in the ordinary sense is quite unimportant.[27] That this is specifically a daughter's experience of language Woolf indicates by having the whole situation so sexually polarized in the first place. It is Cam's terror and dislike of the phallic horns "branching at her all over the room" that instigates this exchange.

As for James, the language he exchanges with his mother at first seems nonfigurative, especially compared to the elaborate comparisons Mrs. Ramsay evokes for Cam. And yet Mrs. Ramsay uses language in a conventionally representational way with James. The aim of her words is to reassure James of the existence of the object referred to, an object that can and must be named now that it is out of sight, if not altogether gone. And furthermore, the importance of the horned skull for James is in its status as a representation, a substitute for the phallus that would be in turn a substitute for an infant's lost connection with his mother. Language appears to aim at making the phallus and mother present, but in actuality, they serve to keep the mother at a safe distance. Rather than the son "remain[ing] in the sexual service of the mother," this mother makes it clear that she serves him ("they had done just what he wanted"). His fetishization of the phallic object keeps her at a distance, the distance of figuration. Before going to sleep, "he wanted to ask her something more. Would they go to the Lighthouse tomorrow?" This expedition, on which in all probability Mrs. Ramsay would not have been included, would have been a quest after a phallic object that would have repeated James's fascination with the skull. By referring to the lighthouse, he again uses referential language to distance his mother, even this mother whom he loves.

Woolf defines as distinctly female the pleasure Cam and Mrs. Ramsay share in the rhythm and feel of words, which I would argue derives from and constitutes a myth of a daughter's never having lost the literal language she shared with her mother. It is important to stress that this linguistic pleasure differs from what Kristeva calls the semiotic and defines as the central linguistic element in the writing of such modern male writers as Joyce, Celine, and Artaud. Like other Lacanians, Kristeva never wavers in her assumption that the child is male, for she refers to the modern writer's use of rhythms and sounds that violate symbolic "sense" with their sensual "nonsense" as a return of and to the "forbidden" maternal body: "*poetic language would be* for its questionable subject-in-process the *equivalent of incest*" (italics hers).[28] For sons, whose entry into the symbolic order was a response to the prohibition of incest, a return to and of the semiotic is a return of the repressed, and thus for Kristeva best characterized, not only by the rhythmic nonsense of many modern writers, but most particularly by the obscenities that characterize the discourse of Celine. While obscenities commemorate the writer's knowledge that he violates a taboo, I detect no sign of violation, and therefore no taboo, in such passages as the ones I have cited from Woolf. Kristeva's view, furthermore, like that of other Lacanians, is. that too great a prolongation of the mother-child dyad leads to psychosis, or a splitting of the ego; health resides in the success of the paternal metaphor.[29] Although Kristeva celebrates (male) modernism's articulation of the semiotic and defends it by suggesting that "the resistance against modern literature" is "evidence of an obsession with meaning, of an unfitness for such jouissance," and although she argues for the inclusion of the semiotic within contemporary theories of language,[30] the general picture of the mother-child relation, and of such traces of it as carry over into adulthood, is of a situation that must be fled as being dangerous to adult sanity. Only the poets are strong enough to contain and articulate its forces.

If the mother-daughter language I am discussing is continuous from childhood and is therefore, unlike Kristeva's semiotic, neither repressed nor capable of a dangerous return, it is, instead, socially and culturally suppressed and silenced, but silencing and suppression are a very different matter from repression. Elsewhere in Woolf's novels, women's language is represented as devalued and silenced within androcentric culture. For example, in *Between the Acts*, Isa utters her fragments of poetry only silently and to herself, her utterances wedged in between interruptions caused by the demands of her place within her patriarchal family (she must order the fish; she must entertain the guests). Similarly, it would have been possible to cite in Irigaray examples of a nonsymbolic discourse, but wherever such language is identified as a mother-daughter language, it is always also marked by the intrusion, from the start, of androcentric culture.[31] While Woolf does articulate examples of such silenced female talk, and of an unheard mother-daughter language, she at the same time indicates its usual suppression in a curious way, by making it appear to depend on the devaluing and silencing of women's desires and talk. Mrs. Ramsay's soothing exchange with Cam would not have taken place were it not for their culture's privileging of the phallic, and their obligation, as women, to accommodate that privilege. Woolf represents mother-daughter language as dependent on its own suppression because of the peculiar situation her writing (and any woman's writing) puts her in. To write a novel that is ordinarily comprehensible, that is,

decodable according to certain established principles of symbolic signification, is to exclude the literal and the nonsymbolic. To write "literature" is to write within the symbolic order. Thus, in order to include a
nonsymbolic mother-daughter language in her novel, Woolf must represent it symbolically. Because the articulation of the nonsymbolic depends
upon the symbolic, Woolf portrays her women characters' language as
paradoxically dependent upon its silencing by androcentric culture,
when this dependence—if it exists at all—is perhaps no more significant
than the silencing itself.

The pleasure in a nonsymbolic language that Woolf's novels at least
intermittently express does not appear, or does not appear in the same
way, in the works of nineteenth-century women writers. Living in a
culture that even more than Woolf's disparages women's writing of any
kind at all, these writers are all the more dependent on their writing being
legible and acceptable within the conventions of the symbolic order.
Their feeling that to write is necessarily to be, or to impersonate, a man is
suggested most obviously by, for example, Mary Ann Evans's choice to
write under the pseudonym George Eliot. As Elaine Showalter writes in
her indispensable discussion of the contradictions between being a
woman and writing in the mid-nineteenth century, "One of the many
indications that this generation saw the will to write as a vocation in
direct conflict with their status as women is the appearance of the male
pseudonym."[32] As imitation sons, these women writers join in the high
cultural valuation of figuration, transcendence, and other modes of flight
from the literal that is always identified with the mother. And yet at the
same time, they are all interested, if indirectly and pessimistically, in the
possibility of a female discourse, both because of cultural determination
(the belief in separate spheres) and because of what we might like to see
as their own positive choice. While Mary Ann Evans took an unequivocally male pseudonym, the Brontës, Charlotte later explained, took the
pseudonyms Currer, Ellis, and Acton Bell, "the ambiguous choice being
dictated by a sort of conscientious scruple at assuming Christian names
positively masculine, while we did not like to declare ourselves women,
because . . . we had a vague impression that authoresses are liable to be
looked on with prejudice."[33] And both Shelley and Gaskell wrote first
anonymously, then under their own names. The complexity and power
of the works considered in this study derives largely from their authors'
not simply writing as imitation men. Instead, by writing novels that
represent the position of women in societies that do not accommodate
their needs, these authors thematize the position of women's language in
a culture that does not admit it.

Still, these writers seldom mythologize or articulate a nonsymbolic language without making it appear to depend on and accede to the norms of androcentric culture, or without distancing themselves from it as a dangerous or maddening force. Or if they do reveal an interest in such a language, it is as a debased relation, like the one Irigaray laments, to a mother who has already been frozen by androcentric culture into the objectified form of a still and silent mirror, anticipating the Lacanian "mirror stage" in which the mother is no more than that.[34] While Woolf's accommodation of nonsymbolic language to the exigencies of representational form seems to be just that, an accommodation, which is furthermore accompanied by many thematic statements of a protest against women's silencing, the nineteenth-century writers seem to be genuinely ambivalent about the desirability of the female discourse they tentatively explore. Indeed, their attitude toward it resembles not so much that of Woolf as that of Kristeva when she contemplates the semiotic as a force that seems at once fearful and valuable. Likewise, contemporary theorists of daughterhood ranging from Nancy Friday to Irigaray, and including Chodorow, stress the ambivalence of the daughter who wants to preserve her love for and closeness with her mother at the same time that she feels constricted by that closeness and seeks relief in turning to the father's seductive difference.[35] For Chodorow, the daughter who is intensely dependent on and attached to her mother will nonetheless feel ambivalence that makes her oscillate "between identification with anyone other than her mother and feeling herself her mother's double and extension" (p. 138). A daughter's "earliest relationship with a man" includes qualities of "rationality and distance" (p. 198) that appeal to her need for separateness. An adult woman's choice of heterosexual objects, as representations of this "earliest relationship with a man," will preserve this "distance." This choice will partake of the same figurative structure as men's heterosexual choices, and this figurativeness associated with the father becomes a relief for the woman writer whose interest in writing in or about a mother-daughter nonsymbolic language also threatens her ambitions.

Of the writers considered here, Gaskell comes the closest (to risk a melioristic phrasing) to Woolf's sense of the possibility and desirability of articulating a nonsymbolic mother-daughter language, and only then by using the same qualification Woolf relies on, of depicting this language as dependent on its interruption and silencing. Yet it has been necessary to call attention to and examine the possibility of a mother-daughter language (both in theoretical terms and in terms of the example of Woolf) because it is only by being especially alert to its traces, denied or compromised as the case may be, that we can see how nineteenth-century women writers mythologize their view of such a language, and therefore how they situate themselves with respect both to their given place in language and to some other place of their own choosing.

So far we have been looking at language from the perspective of the daughter who grows up to become an author. Indeed, to look at development and the acquisition of language and culture, if not from the daughter's perspective, at least from the child's, is the bias of almost all psychological and psycholinguistic writing. But what if the writer is herself a mother? Her perspective has been largely left out of theorizing about language and culture, probably for a reason that Chodorow hints at: most of the authors of such theories have been men who identify with "the child" (who as we have seen is implicitly male) and with his need to disavow the mother, to have her be silent and absent, in order for his entry into the father's law to be complete.[36] Theories, like literature, are ordinarily part of the symbolic order. A mother is particularly subject to the son's disparaging transformation of her into the literal, and she has also gone through some version of the complex ambivalence towards maternal and paternal languages sketched above. In the nineteenth century, when women's lives were increasingly defined in relation to a standard of motherhood, regardless of whether or not they were of childbearing age, women who wrote did so within a framework of dominant cultural myths in which writing contradicts mothering.[37] Paradoxically, the high value placed on mothering as a vocation for women is entirely consistent with the devaluation of everything women did relative to men's accomplishments. Both Mary Shelley and Elizabeth Gaskell were mothers, and George Eliot, as "Mrs. George Lewes," lived with a man who had once written, "The grand function of woman . . . is, and ever must be, *Maternity*,"[38] and she was "die mütter" and "madonna" to his sons. Charlotte Brontë wrote "Southey's advice to be kept forever" on the letter containing these words: "Literature cannot be the business of a woman's life, and it ought not to be. The more she is engaged in her proper duties, the less leisure will she have for it."[39] Even the staunchly adolescent Emily Brontë seems to have been troubled by the contradiction between women's "proper duties" and writing or using language. Symbolic writing was inappropriate for women, and yet writing in any other way would have been even more inappropriate, as it would have been to articulate what their culture required to be left silent.

In order to clarify the ambiguities attending nineteenth-century women's writing with respect to the relative values of literal and figurative, it will be necessary to continue to follow Chodorow's argument about the differential development of daughters and sons as she extends it to analyze mothering, and to explore the implications of her argument for Lacanian language theory. Having examined the daughter's extended stay in the preoedipal relation to her mother, which is so different from the son's need to separate, Chodorow asks the question, What does a girl's continued closeness to and identification with her mother, which got started in the first place because women mother, have to do with the likelihood that this daughter will grow up to become a mother and her brother will not? Women mother and men do not, she argues, because of the complex asymmetry of the gender situation as she has sketched it for sons and daughters. All adults "as a result of being parented by a woman, . . . look for a return to this emotional and physical union" (p. 199). But while "a man achieves this directly through the heterosexual bond," *representing* his lost oedipal attachment to his mother in the symbolic way suggested by Lacan's view of desire (and by Eagleton's understanding of desire as originating in the quest for substitutes for the mother), women seek to *reproduce* their preoedipal relation to their mothers, and they do this not through heterosexual attachments but in other ways. Women fulfill these needs in part through "deep affective relationships" with other women but far more, given the constraints of a society that is homophobic and that tends to confine women within nuclear families, through bearing children. The father is never an "attachment figure" for the son, and so his sense of the relation to his mother, in the ideal form in which he would wish to reconstitute it, is that it is a dyad, him and her. And so an adult heterosexual attachment will represent, at a suitably figurative distance, the son's recollection of that relation to his lost mother. But adult heterosexual attachments for women reproduce the girl's relation to her father, to whom, as we have seen Chodorow argue, she was never so fully attached as she was to her mother. While a grown daughter will seek figures for the father in much the same way that men will seek figures for the mother, because both the son's relation to the mother and the daughter's relation to the father take place in the symbolic order, this will satisfy her longing only for one parent, the one who came second in her affections. The other side of her emotional life, her deep if ambivalent attachment to her mother, is not satisfied by the father figure she finds in heterosexual relationships. "Thus, women's heterosexuality is triangular and requires a third person—a child—for its structural and emotional completion. For men, by contrast, the heterosexual relationship alone recreates the early bond to their mother; a child interrupts it" (p. 207). Whereas a man may want a child because that is what he learns fathers are supposed to do, "having a child recreates the desired mother-child exclusivity for a woman and interrupts it for a man, just as the man's father intruded into his relation to his mother" (p. 201). Freud long ago speculated likewise that women's wish to reproduce comes from a longing for something lost, but what Freud thought this was is quite different from what Chodorow proposes. The famous equation, baby equals substitute penis, explains that girls grow up wanting babies because, in rage and frustration at not getting a penis from their mothers, they turn to their fathers in the hope that through an incestuous attachment they will get one in the form of a baby. Thus babies are said to still women's penis envy. Lacan and Lacanians also assume that the mother's wish for a baby is really her desire for the phallus.[40] But a much simpler explanation is at hand. The baby, if it reconstitutes for the mother her dyadic, presymbolic symbiosis with her mother, is not a substitute for the phallus (what phallus?) but rather a baby, quite literally, repeating another baby and bypassing the phallus altogether. Insofar as the daughter's continuing relation with the mother takes place at least in part prior to or outside of the state of loss that Lacan would call desire, that daughter's baby will not be a substitute for the phallus, for the phallus comes into being only insofar as the child has already been separated from the mother. If what was lost was not the phallus, which is already a substitute for a more real connection, but that prior relation to the mother, then the baby substitutes, not for the phallus, but for how the mother felt as a child, not for loss but for presence.

In her own revisionary myth of motherhood, Irigaray suggests that preceding the famous trauma of castration (which male theorists are so fixated upon that they project it onto daughters as well as sons) and obscured by its prevalence, lies the trauma of an earlier cutting that we all experience, the cutting of the umbilical cord that literally links mother and child. Like the primordial murder of the mother that makes possible the symbolic order, the cutting of the cord, she argues, must be forgotten by culture in order that it may foreground the severing of the phallus, that figurative and uniquely male connection to the mother the lack of which makes symbolic language a specifically male domain. The substitution of phallus for umbilical cord already privileges the figurative over the literal or the nonsymbolic, for the phallus's way of connecting bodies is figurative and momentary, while the cord's connection is physiological and of many months' duration. "The phallus erects itself where the umbilical cord used to be":[41] the *nombril* (navel) marks the place where the cord was cut to make way for the *nom* that will replace the phallus erected near this spot. "There would have been a risk of fusion, of death, of a lethal sleep, if the father hadn't come to sever this too tight bond with the original matrix. Establishing, in its place, the matrix of his language."[42] That the cord must be cut for daughters as well as for sons emphasizes that all humans must enter the symbolic order, and it emphasizes what Irigaray views as the inevitable appropriation of the maternal by patriarchy. And yet the cord may make graphic for us the way in which other connectives with the mother have existed besides the lost phallus and may be available to the imagination, other connectives that are not founded on an already completed separation: "But where, for us, is the imaginary and the symbolic of life inside the womb and of the first *corps-à-corps* with the mother? In what night, what madness are they hidden?"[43] This more literal connection might be a figure for the literal language I am suggesting may adhere to the mother-daughter relation: like nonsymbolic language, daughters may have repressed this tie less than sons have; indeed, they may recall and reproduce it.

What are the implications for Lacanian language of these feminist revisions of the Freudian account of mothering? If the daughter's preoedipal closeness to her mother is accompanied by a presymbolic language of presence, then when the daughter attempts to recreate her symbiotic closeness with her mother, she is also attempting to recreate that presymbolic language. The reproduction of mothering will also be the reproduction of a presymbolic communicativeness, a literal language. While men are satisfied with heterosexual attachments as figures for the mother because they are replicating a situation existing after entry into the symbolic order, and while, as far as repeating their relation to their fathers goes, women too are satisfied with figures for the father, it would be impossible for the daughter to find the lost relation to the mother in any figure for it, since the preoedipal bond to the mother preceded the entry of the daughter into the world of figures, the symbolic, and thus the preoedipal bond could not be reimagined in symbolic terms. Quite possibly, a new child is just such a nonsymbolic figure. While a man in the nineteenth century ideally married an "Angel in the House," the emphasis in the structure of childbearing is on the materiality of the baby; the point of the myth of the human birth of the son of God is his acquisition of a human body. Furthermore, while the feminine object of a man's desire is a figure for his mother, representation can be seen to work differently in childbirth. The mother is reproducing an entire situation and a relationship (embodied at first in the umbilical cord), and the relationship is virtually the same as hers with her mother, while a heterosexual relationship patently only represents, and differs from it in important and obvious ways, a son's relation to his mother.

We saw that Chodorow's account of the reproduction of mothering would offer an alternative to the Freudian and Lacanian equation, baby equals phallus, to the notion that babies answer women's penis envy. In Lacanian terms, the interpretation of the baby as substitute phallus suggests that what the mother seeks is that hyphen or copula that would figuratively connect child to mother in the symbolic order. Kristeva writes that the process of the "'natural' inducements" toward maternity, which amounts to a return to biology, "that archaic basis," "is quite rightly understood as the demand for a penis. . . . And, as long as there is language-symbolism-paternity, there will never be any other way to represent, to objectify, and to explain this unsettling of the symbolic stratum . . . this event called motherhood."[44] But women's language is not restricted to the symbolic, and women's yearning for the mother is constituted in a discourse different from the one in which the missing phallus would supply the only connection. If the baby helps the mother reproduce her presymbolic relation to her own mother without translation into the symbolic terms of the phallus, then her bearing of a child, very much like the daughter's experience of a presymbolic symbiosis, will take place in and model a nonsymbolic discourse. Although Freud argues that the baby is a figure, a figure for the phallus, much as a man's wife is a figure for his mother, Chodorow's revision would remove the baby from the register of the figurative altogether. The baby is not a phallus, both in the sense that the baby is not a replacement for the lost phallus and in the sense that the baby is not phallic, that is, not a symbol dependent on an absence.

As I will explain at greater length in a moment, I will use the term "literalization" to refer to a series of literary situations and practices each of which has the same structure, in these books by women, as childbearing does in Chodorow's analysis of it and in our new sense of its place in the Lacanian myth of language. Not only is the daughter, whose relation to her mother was one of literality, literally repeated in that daughter's child (daughter), but also the very structure of childbearing, in which something becomes real that did not exist before—or that existed only as a word, a theory, or a "conception"—is a structure of literalization, by which the relatively figurative becomes the relatively literal.

Chodorow's picture of the reproduction of mothering is quite positive. The women in her book derive satisfaction from replicating their early relation to their mothers, and it would seem that the implications for a feminist revision of Lacan would be equally positive. That is, it appears that it would be equally satisfying for women writers to rediscover the presymbolic language shared with their mothers that writing as motherhood, as opposed to writing as the search for symbolic phallic connections, might activate. Yet daughters, as we have seen, may have a complex and ambivalent relation to the idea of the literal, and daughters who became women in a culture that defined all women as potential mothers would have reproduced that complex relation to the literal. Every form the daughter's ambivalence might take, between identification with the male view of the literal and recalling the nonsymbolic language that may resemble it, can be found as well in the mother's view of her reproduction of the nonsymbolic language and the preoedipal relationship, for as we have seen, motherhood is an attempt to reproduce the relation of daughterhood.

The reasons for a woman's ambivalence about writing as a mother also go beyond a daughter's ambivalence. The social imperative to measure all women's activities by their suitability to motherhood results in a taboo against women's writing for being in conflict with women's "proper duties," which in turn results in women writers writing as men, a strategy that causes them to find the idea of a mother-daughter language dangerous to writing. This is the general situation of the Brontës (and Charlotte more so than Emily), who articulate most explicitly women writers' negative or ambivalent views of being identified with the literal and literalization. Moreover, despite Chodorow's optimistic tone, motherhood, especially before the twentieth century, brought with it its own dangers, both physical and psychological. Helene Deutsch argues in her psychology of motherhood that women fear childbirth, and that they fear it specifically as the transformation of the internal into the external, of part of the self into another being. While Deutsch's analysis of the structure of childbirth coincides with Chodorow's, as a structure of what I am calling literalization, what Chodorow sees women embracing, Deutsch sees them fearing. It is this account of motherhood that will be of greatest relevance to my account of Charlotte Brontë's rejection of motherhood as structure and as figure, and of Emily Brontë's ambivalence about it. Chodorow's favorable portrayal of the mother-daughter bond, as well as of the passage from "conception" to physical reality and the privileging of the literal I believe are implicit in it, most closely recalls Woolf's novels. All of the nineteenth-century women writers considered in this book reflect this favorable view of motherhood too, and it is always crucial to their writing, but it makes up only a part (greater or smaller, varying from author to author) of each one's complex relation to motherhood. Deutsch's notion of the fear of reproduction will help to bring out certain aspects of their unfavorable views of motherhood and of a literal, mother-daughter language.

Beyond the fear and denial of motherhood, however, another and more positive strategy for accommodating Victorian ideology was possible, one that the writers who were themselves mothers (or stepmothers)—Shelley, Eliot, and Gaskell—preferred. To define writing as motherhood holds out the possibility of justifying the woman writer's temerity by neutralizing the conflict between writing and motherhood. And yet this strategy, which in fact encouraged these writers' interest in myths of a mother-daughter language, has its difficulties as well, for it falls afoul of a patrilineal culture's appropriation of motherhood for its own purposes. These women writers may value a specifically maternal language either because of cultural pressures or out of their own interests, and yet whichever their reason, they also always mythologize the subordination of this language to the demands of the culture that defined women as mothers in the first place. These writers see that maternal language will always be put to the use of promulgating androcentric culture, with its paternal metaphors, flight from the mother, and all the rest.

This pattern, the appropriation and redefinition by androcentric culture of something once specific to women, emerges from many aspects of women's experience. Not only maternity and mother-daughter language, but also women's identification with nature and the literal, all begin (if we can point anywhere in culture to a distinct beginning) by being distinctly appealing to women who were daughters of mothers. But all are redefined, very confusingly for women, as valueless, precisely for being specific to women, and all are simultaneously appropriated to serve the ends of the culture that denigrates them. Women's version of the literal may look confusingly like that from which male culture is in flight, but the difference is all in their relative valuation.

This situation has relevance, not only for the women's experiences discussed in this book, but also for the theorizing about women of which this book is an example. It is sometimes said, for example, that feminist scholarship, by accentuating historical differences between men and women, simply repeats the invidious nineteenth-century segregation of women that twentieth-century feminism in the United States, with its emphasis on equal rights, has worked so hard to reverse. And yet the perspective from which such enterprises are undertaken makes a tremendous difference. There is all the difference in the world between countless nineteenth- and many twentieth-century "experts" telling women that wifehood and motherhood is their proper sphere and proper duty—pronouncements about women's specificity that appropriate it to the convenience of the expert—and recent studies by female and feminist psychologists, philosophers, and other scholars concerning both the origins and the genuinely positive value, for men as well as women, of such traditional female roles as child rearing and such traditional female values as pacifism. This is scholarship that would restore women's difference to women's own—and probably quite novel—uses. To study gender difference from a woman's perspective is to begin to redress the appropriation of women's lives by androcentric culture.

Although I believe it is crucial to study and to revalue all women's experiences as women, this revaluation seems particularly appropriate for the period covered by this book, since at that time the majority of women's experiences were almost entirely separate from men's. I am arguing for the recovery of historical experience, not for the existence, much less the perpetuation, of any essential difference between men and women. I am not arguing that women should write (or do anything else) as daughters or as mothers, but only that in the nineteenth century women did nothing, including writing, except as women. Women's exclusive mothering, which has not fundamentally changed since the nineteenth century (certainly our myths of parenthood have not changed), is the result of a social system oppressive to women. If there is an enormous appeal to the notion of tapping a hitherto unwritten and devalued mother-daughter language (as there is for Irigaray and other French theorists, for Carol Gilligan, and implicitly for Nancy Chodorow), there is also this disadvantage, that to seek its perpetuation is to seek at the same time the perpetuation of the oppressive sex/gender system it depends upon. Chodorow suggests that were men to participate equally with women in the raising of children (whether in nuclear family settings or elsewhere), then our gendered definitions of subject and object, self and other, and figurative and literal would change radically. Perhaps then what I have been calling a literal or nonsymbolic language would cease to be a female province, or would cease to be altogether; but then that would mean, too, that the symbolic order, with its phallic priority and its denigration of women, would have ceased as well. In the meantime, it is worth finding out what women, in a culture whose definitions of sexual identity were exaggerations of our own, did to explore women's place in language and a women's language.

I wish now to suggest very briefly how the forms of ambivalence about traditional and revisionary myths of language that this chapter has explored are manifested in literary works, for the rest of this book will be concerned with how specific works articulate these ambivalences. Articulations of myths of language, and specifically of their relation to the literal and to literalization, appear generally in the form of four recurrent literary situations or practices, which I designate as instances of "bearing the word." Each instance of bearing the word brings together the thematics of female experience and some aspect of women's special relation to language, whether women's place in the traditional psycholinguistic map or their place in the revisionary map we have sketched with the help of Chodorow and others.

    1. Moments at which a figure is literalized. Because the relative valuation of figurative and literal language, and of figuration and literalization, is at the heart of gender difference in language, we should

expect to find that literary texts concerned with writing and revising myths of the relation of gender and language would locate this project first in the structure of their own language, in their own practice with respect to literal and figurative. And indeed, in the works considered here, the shift from figurative to literal and back again is heavily charged with mythic and thematic significance, for if literalization suggests a move in the direction of a mother-daughter language, figuration suggests a return to the paternal symbolic. In a literary text, the literalization of a figure occurs when some piece of overtly figurative language, a simile or an extended or conspicuous metaphor, is translated into an actual event or circumstance. An important example of literalization occurs in *Adam Bede*. Hetty Sorrel is illicitly and secretly pregnant by Arthur Donnithorne. When he breaks the affair off, the narrator describes Hetty as having had a "new-born passion" which is now "crushed"; and then, the narrator goes on, "came the frightening thought that she had to conceal her misery, as well as bear it."[45] At this point in the novel, we do not know for certain that Hetty is pregnant, nor does she. This language of passion and misery as things that are newborn, or that must be concealed and then born, is thus far only figurative. But these figures are literalized when Hetty's misery takes the physical form of a baby that must be born and then concealed. When Hetty gives birth, all her efforts are directed toward concealing the child. By her account, the baby's death is the accidental result of her concern with concealing it, so that Eliot extends the same language from Hetty's figurative concealment of a newborn but dead passion to her actual concealment of a newborn but dead baby. Such literalizations of figures, especially when connected to female themes, articulate a woman writer's ambivalent turning toward female linguistic practices and yet at the same time associating such a choice with danger and death. These female themes, which either contain or imply a shift from figurative to literal, include the other three kinds of bearing the word.

2. The figure of the Virgin Mary, who gives birth to and is frequently imaged carrying (thus two senses of "bear") a child who is the Word, the embodiment of the Logos. Successor to Eve and to Sarah, each of whom was "the channel through which that illustrious prophecy was carried into effect," Mary is "the instrument of the Redeemer's incarnation."[46] From Mary, in the novels discussed here, despite their having been written by Anglicans and Dissenters, comes the repeated figure of a woman who gives birth to or carries a child who represents language. In *Romola*, this figure takes its most striking form at the end of the novel when Romola is taken quite literally to be the Virgin Mary, with a halo around her head and the Christ child in her arms.

3. The theme of women characters who perform translations from one language into another or from one medium to another, or who carry messages or letters for other people, or who act as amanuenses or as readers for others, usually men: that is, the thematic presentation of women carrying or bearing language itself. This is a typically female theme, partly because of its overtones of the second kind of bearing the word. Like the mother of the Word, the woman who carries language from one place or state of being to another does not herself originate or even touch it, and she gets nothing for her labor, which she performs for others. In terms of specifically literary transmission, one prototype is the figure of Milton's daughters reading Greek to him without understanding it; as Gilbert and Gubar point out, Dorothea in *Middlemarch* wants not only to repeat this task for her scholar husband, Casaubon, but also to enjoy it. Romola likewise serves as amanuensis and reader for her blind father, and her patient performance of these duties makes a large part of her "most lovable womanliness." Countless Gaskell characters carry letters and messages between other characters.

4. Moments when the text itself performs any of these linguistic operations—translation, transmission, copying, and so on—with respect to the language of other (again usually male) authors; when the writer as woman replicates, in her own relation to literary language and literary history, what her women characters do with language within the thematic frame of the novel. The writer may allude to or quote some author, or she may have her own text act out, in terms of plot and character, something that remains figurative or abstract in the earlier text. For example, *Frankenstein* acts out *Alastor*, and Eliot bears Wordsworth's words from poetry to fiction in *The Mill on the Floss* when she has Maggie Tulliver experience in a realistic social context a Wordsworthian childhood in nature that in the original is essentially solitary and also mythic. In a culture that was still essentially patrilineal, or at least that still subscribed to the ideology of patriliny, as mid-nineteenth-century England was and did, women's primary role was to afford the means of the transmission of inheritance from father to son. It became incumbent upon women writers to convert the writing that they nevertheless felt driven to do into a version of these female duties of selfless transmission, just as, mythically, Mary facilitated the transmission of Word into flesh. Eliot's early translations of Strauss and Spinoza and Gaskell's early project to write prose versions of the English poets are both symptomatic of this felt need to convert the unwomanly selfishness of writing into the selflessness of transmission, and their fiction still bears the marks of these beginnings.

The first kind of bearing the word, the transfer from figurative to literal, subsumes the other three, because in all three cases there is a shift from relatively figurative to relatively literal. When an author carries another author's words into her own text, as in the example from *The Mill on the Floss*, it is generally also a shift from figurative to literal. Childbirth, as it is used in these cases, is structured as a transfer from inner to outer, from "conception" to actual form, or from word to being. The example from *Adam Bede* of the literalization of a figure is also and inextricably a scene of childbirth, in which the transfer from the secret interior of Hetty's body to its public exterior is the same as the literalization of the figure of the crushed and concealed newborn. Logistically, the birth or externalization of the baby is what necessitates the literalization of the figurative concealment and murder, but even more important, childbirth and literalization are structurally the same here. Not always do all four kinds of bearing the word occur at once, but they occur together often enough to suggest that each one is about the others and therefore that they may be mapped onto each other.

To recapitulate my argument from psycholinguistic theory, the reason that all these instances of bearing the word are characterized by an ambivalently valued shift from figurative to literal derives from the central place of, but differential valuations of, figurative and literal in the two differing myths of gender and language these writers write and revise. On the one hand, women's place in language, from the perspective of an androcentric literary tradition (and the psycholinguistic theory it generates), is with the literal, the silent object of representation, the dead mother, the absent referent, so that within a literary text the shift from figurative to literal connotes a shift from the place of the signifier, the place of the speaking subject, to the place of the absent object. On the other hand, and this is the feminist revaluation of linguistic positions we have looked at with Chodorow and Irigaray, women's memory of and wish to reproduce the nonsymbolic language they shared with the mother takes the form of a literal language that looks like (or even really is, given that these writers acknowledge their appropriation) an embrace of the very position to which male theory condemns the feminine. These differing versions of—or differing valuations of—the literal will collide with each other and especially with women writers' wish to write in the symbolic order where literature has traditionally taken place. Even though the novel in question always keeps on going in the symbolic order, because the actuality that these borne words become is only relatively closer than the figurative to the literal, these are moments nonetheless in which there is an implicit contradiction between the novel's continuous representation of female experience and the text's seeming suddenly to become aware that the implication of such representation is, from the perspective of the symbolic order, the silence and objectification of women. In a literary culture dominated by the symbolic order and its values, the word that women writers and their female characters most often bear is the word of their own exclusion from linguistic practice, even if they take up this bearing in the (unconscious) hope of bearing their inclusion in another linguistic practice. In carrying language from the relatively figurative to the relatively literal in these various ways that are connected to the thematics of female experience, the women writers and their women characters dramatize at once the way in which the relation of women as women to symbolic language is continually in jeopardy and the hope that the father's law might cease to be the exclusive language of literary culture.

In the context of both traditional language and the feminist revisions of it we have surveyed, I wish to turn now to a passage that reveals some of the tensions inherent in a nineteenth-century woman's attempt to write as a subject in the symbolic order and at the same time as a mother in the literal. The literal is composed here of a collision between women's placement as the silent object in the traditional male view of language and a mother's more positive wish to reproduce the nonsymbolic language of infancy. The passage is from a letter written by Elizabeth Gaskell when her family was just beginning (she eventually had four daughters) and about ten years before she started to write seriously for publication. Thus it is written before she has any tangible stake in the notion of a woman's being in possession of literary subjectivity or in the position of the figurative. But in this letter, she is also indirectly exploring the possibility of formal literary writing, and so it is of importance because it reveals a tension between the wish to be in the place of the writing subject, the pleasure of not bothering, and the wish to write from the place of the mother.

> We are up with the birds, and sitting out on the old flag steps in the very middle of fragrance—'far from the busy hum of men,' but *not* far from the busy hum of bees. Here is a sort of little standard library kept—Spenser, Shakespeare, Wordsworth, & a few foreign books, & we sit & read & dream our time away—except at meals when we *don't* dream over cream that your spoon stands upright in, & such sweet (not sentimental but literal) oven-cakes, and fresh butter. Baby is at the very tip-top of bliss; & gives a happy prospect of what she will be at your Aunt Holbrook. There are chickens, & little childish pigs, & cows & calves & horses, & *baby horses*, & fish in the pond, & ducks in the lane, & the mill & the smithy, & sheep & baby-sheep, & flowers—oh! you would laugh to see her

going about, with a great big nosegay in each hand, & wanting to
be *bathed* in the golden bushes of wall-flowers—she is absolutely
fatter since she came here, & is I'm sure stronger. I suspect I'm
writing a queer medley, for I have had a walk in the heat, & my
hand trembles & I think my brain trembles too—I ramble so. . . .
The house & walls are over-run with roses, honeysuckles &
vines—not quite in flower, *but all but*—Betsy is quite in her element, and teaches baby to call the pigs, & grunt just like any old
sow. I have brought Coleridge with me, & am *doing* him &
Wordsworth—*fit place for the latter*! I sat in a shady corner of a
field gay with bright spring flowers—daisies, primroses, wild anem-
ones, & the 'lesser celandine,' & with lambs all around me—and
the air so full of sweet sounds, & wrote my first chapr of W.
yesterday in pencil—& today I'm going to finish him—and my
heart feels so full of him I only don't know how to express my
fullness without being too diffuse.[47]

The letter from which this passage is excerpted was written to Gaskell's sister-in-law, in May 1836, from the country home near Manchester of the family of Gaskell's dead mother. The baby is Gaskell's first and
at this point only child, her daughter Marianne, who is here about twenty
months old. When at the end of the letter Gaskell alludes to "doing"
Wordsworth and Coleridge and says that she wrote her first chapter of
Wordsworth yesterday and will finish him today, not much is known of
this project beyond what she says in this letter. Two years later her
husband, William, gave at the Working Mens' College, a night school for
men who worked in Manchester factories, a series of lectures on "The
Poets and Poetry of Humble Life," and Elizabeth Gaskell took some part
in his research for these lectures. And in January 1837, the couple
published in *Blackwood's* an imitation of Wordsworth (in the mode of
"The Old Cumberland Beggar") that she describes as the first in a
projected series of "sketches among the poor" and as an example of what
was meant by the poetry of humble life, that is, the aesthetic and
emotional appeal of that life itself. The project Gaskell refers to in the
letter doesn't seem to be a poetic imitation of this kind, however, but it
might have been some kind of prose commentary or perhaps a paraphrase of selected poems.

At the beginning of the passage from the letter, the writer plays
repeatedly with the literalization of metaphors and takes pleasure in the
literal generally, that is, in the immediacy of the mother's and especially
of Baby's contact with flowers and animals. This part of the letter is in
this respect a celebration of woman's traditional place, both in the
thematic sense that a woman's place is in the home, with her children,

and in nature, and also in the psycholinguistic sense that a woman's place is with the literal. The "little standard library" and the project of reading, that is, of experiencing the distance from nature and objects that symbolic representation entails, are balanced against Gaskell's account of a participation that is as direct as possible in nature: "We are up with the birds" and sit "in the very middle of fragrance." As for the literalizations of metaphors, the metaphoric and literary "busy hum of men" becomes the literal hum of bees, the metaphoric dreaming that describes their mental state while reading in such an atmosphere becomes a literal dreaming that is further literalized by their not dreaming, and the sweetness of the oven cakes is not sentimental, or figurative, but literal. In these juxtapositions of figurative and literal, the literal always takes precedence as a tangible good, on the basis of Baby's criteria of excellence: as a result of all this literality, "Baby is at the very tip-top of bliss."

At this point, the letter simply becomes a catalog of names of animals and other things: chickens, pigs, cows, calves, and so on. Gaskell again is writing as literally as possible within the frame of symbolic language, pointing outside of language as much as it is possible to do so while still using language. Baby reappears as part of this catalog of natural creatures. If there are "childish pigs," "baby horses," and "baby-sheep," Baby herself has become animalish, even if her humanness is demarcated by the momentary withdrawal of the letter's perspective to an absent scene, when she is reintroduced ("oh! you would laugh to see her going about, with a great big nosegay . . . "). Baby's relation to natural objects is unmediated, or as unmediated as possible. She is not quite one of or with the flowers but rather picks them and desires them. Still, as a mirror image of the "childish pig," this happily piggish child is "absolutely fatter" as well as stronger.

Baby can have this mainly unmediated relation to nature, in which she is almost a part of it, because, unlike her letter-writing mother who spends time in the library, her language is presymbolic. Her nurse, Betsy, "teaches baby to call the pigs, & grunt just like any old sow." The mother who is writing has a more complex relation to the natural scene and to language's mediation of it. While she celebrates the literal, Baby's and her own merging with nature, this participation is very difficult to sustain while writing at the same time. Her own venture out into the landscape, her "walk in the heat," makes her hand and brain tremble as she writes. She can either write or be in nature, but not both, with any degree of comfort. Hoping to combine these two mutually exclusive activities, in the next passage, Gaskell arranges her writing as an analogy to Baby's way of communicating with nature: while Baby learns "to call the pigs, & grunt just like any old sow[,] I have brought Coleridge with me, & am *doing* him & Wordsworth—*fit place for the latter!*" It's a wonderfully impudent and irreverant moment, with its antiliterary implication that Wordsworth and Coleridge might best be "done" by speaking like the pigs, by reproducing Baby's nonsymbolic language, but the irreverence comes only from Gaskell's training in viewing the literal favorably. Wordsworth and Coleridge can't be made the same as nature, despite Gaskell's wish to identify nature and language (for example, in her wish that "the poetry of humble life" exists in the slums without the mediation of language). She discovers about herself, in fact, what she also discovers about the poets, which is that she too must write at a slight remove from nature's intensities. Her walk in the heat has taught her to stay out of it, and so while Baby seeks to be bathed in flowers, the mother sits "in a shady corner of a field gay with bright spring flowers" to write her chapter.

The flowers she catalogs in that field include the "lesser celandine," a perfectly ordinary flower whose name needs no quotation marks, unless the one she has in mind is not the biological plant species but the one mentioned in one of three Wordsworth poems on that particular flower. In fact, from there to the end of the passage, her writing is permeated with allusions to Wordsworth's poetry, mainly to his "Ode: Intimations of Immortality." As she becomes more absorbed in the poet and in writing, she moves further from nature and from her version of Baby's nonsymbolic language, to the extent that her descriptions of nature become quotations, overtly literary figures for nature in place of the relatively literal naming of nature and participation in nature claimed earlier in the letter. To be writing an imitation of or commentary on Wordsworth is to be in the place of the speaking subject, which is to remove herself from her pleasure in "woman's place" in the object world. Once she turns to writing, she can no longer take the same pleasure in the identification with the literal that was perfectly acceptable from the point of view of the mother, because, from the point of view of the writer, that would silence her.

But Gaskell tries to reconcile her writing with her identification with the literal, by making her writing a compromise between two positions. As she describes it, her project is not first to write Wordsworth but to be *"doing"* him, and also humbly to take on the woman's role of passive transmission by putting Wordsworth into language accessible to, say, her husband's working-class students. But because such a project is ultimately self-cancelling—what she is bearing here is the word of her own silencing—what appears in the letter is not so much a compromise as a tension between the two contradictory aims, on the one hand to be a writer, to write like Wordsworth, and on the other hand to remain part of the nature he writes about. That this tension is at work can be seen in allusions to the Intimations Ode, which resonates through the final lines of the letter. In stanza 3 of the Ode, for example, "the birds thus sing a joyous song," and "the young lambs bound / As to the tabor's sound."[48] Gaskell's phrasing, "lambs all around me—and the air so full of sweet sounds" picks up the "bound/sound" rhyme from the poem, as well as the images of bounding lambs and bird song.

For her use of the first part of stanza 4 of the Ode, it is worth quoting at length:

> Ye blessed Creatures, I have heard the call
> Ye to each other make;
> . . . .
> The fulness of your bliss, I feel—I feel it all.
> Oh evil day! if I were sullen
> While Earth herself is adorning,
> This sweet May-morning,
> And the Children are culling
> On every side,
> In a thousand valleys far and wide,
> Fresh flowers; while the sun shines warm,
> And the Babe leaps up on his Mother's arm:—
> I hear, I hear, with joy I hear!
>
> (36–50)

The stanza goes on to articulate the poet's sense of loss, which already appears in the first part of the stanza in his excessive protestations, such as "The fulness of your bliss, I feel—I feel it all" or "I hear, I hear, with joy I hear!" The sense of loss comes first from the poet's sense that nature's pleasure is self-contained: it consists of a series of interchanges between natural objects that do not include the poet, and to which he is merely a spectator and auditor. Gaskell picks up this aspect of the lines, but for her the situation is more complex. Like Wordsworth, Gaskell hears "the call" that "blessed Creatures . . . to each other make," as, for example, in her account of the blissful baby who calls to the pigs; and like Wordsworth she sees a child culling fresh flowers. But while for Wordsworth "the Babe [who] leaps up on his Mother's arm" is another example of those interchanges within nature from which the speaking poet is separated, when the writer is also the mother, her position in the scene becomes divided, between on the one hand her traditional role as part of a group of natural objects that the poet looks at and, on the other, her identification with the writer, the speaker of the poem, who sits to one side, as indeed Gaskell pictures herself writing while sitting out of the sun

in the corner of a field, observing the scene but not participating. Wordsworth's pain comes partly from the fact that, as a poet, he can never be in
the same place as nature, but Gaskell finds, perhaps even more painfully,
that she is in both places at once, which creates in her an almost
unbearable tension.

This division between two positions reappears in Gaskell's allusion to
Wordsworth's lines about his feeling "the fulness of your bliss"of the
"blessed Creatures." About Wordsworth, Gaskell writes, "my heart feels
so full of him I only don't know how to express my fullness without being
too diffuse." Instead of claiming to feel (but not really feeling) the fullness
of the bliss of some other creature, as in the Ode, here it is Gaskell herself
who is "full." Exactly as with her divided identification both with the
mother of the babe in nature and apart from the mother with the poet
outside of it, here at the end of the passage she is both in the position of
the blessed creatures and in the position of the writer who feels the
fullness and is made anxious by that feeling. As she translates Wordsworth's account of nature into her letter, she bears Wordsworth's word
of her own status as a silent natural object. But as she does so and as soon
as the question of her own speaking subjectivity within an androcentric
literary tradition is raised, her identification with the literal, with nature,
becomes distressing, in contrast to the pleasure it clearly gives her in the
part of the letter governed by a mother-daughter nonsymbolic language.
Writing and finishing her chapters on Wordsworth provokes anxiety
because it makes it clear what identification with the literal means within
literary tradition, and it forces her to discover that to be at once a mother
and a writer is to be divided in two.

This, then, is the contradiction in which the woman who would write
as a mother is caught. It is out of a sense of women's "proper duties" that
she takes up the project to serve as Wordsworth's amanuensis. Like
Mary, she incarnates a paternal word in another form. And yet because
in this motherly way she makes herself so susceptible to Wordsworth's
definition of the choices available to men and women—that one can be a
speaker or a mother but not both—she is prevented from writing a myth
of the writer as mother. She is caught between two myths: the received
myth of her own silencing within symbolic language and her own
pleasurable revision of that myth, in which what seems from the point of
view of symbolic language to be silence is in fact a rich, nonsymbolic
language. She is caught between these myths because the literary culture
she would enter appropriates that nonsymbolic language and redefines it
in turn as silence. This dilemma of the woman writer, caught between her
own interest in a literal mother-daughter language and her desire at once
to placate and to enter the symbolic realm of literary language, is the

dilemma shared and articulated by all the authors considered in this book. This letter, written without the constraints imposed by the expectation of a literary audience, reveals a more positive view of the attempt to write in and from the literal than most of the other texts we will be considering. In the other authors, and in later Gaskell texts, the tension we have been tracing often has a gloomier outcome as thematized in the fates of heroines, or it is resolved in the end only by a conciliatory turn to the father's figurations. Only Dorothy Wordsworth, who alone writes entirely without the thought or hope that she is writing "literature," takes unadulterated pleasure in writing in a language that is as literal as possible and that literalizes. By not seeking to be the speaker of a symbolic language, she does not experience the conflicts and tensions of the other writers, whose literary ambitions place them at odds with literature's ambitions for them. Her writing of another and as far as possible nonsymbolic language also includes a criticism of symbolic language, one that could only be made from a position outside of the desires it provokes. It is to her work, as an illustrative exception, and as an end point on a spectrum of responses to women's complex situation with respect to language, that we will now turn.

articulated by a male writer —

recognizes its limitations

2

Building Refuges: Dorothy Wordsworth's
Poetics of the Image

When nineteenth-century women writers bear through their own texts the words of a prior literary tradition, it is most often romantic poetry that they are carrying. The major literary movement of the beginning of the century, romantic poetry also states most compellingly the traditional myth, as transmitted through literature, of women's place in language as the silent or vanished object of male representation and quest. For example, Percy Shelley's *Alastor* has for its major female figures a "great Mother," nature, who is most readily found in "charnels" and a "fleeting shade" or ideal maiden who exists only as a dream. For a living woman only the role of unthanked handmaiden remains.

What was the experience of women readers of such texts; what was their relation to the female roles available in them? The role of handmaiden was indeed taken up by those who were quite literally the first readers of romantic poetry. Catherine Blake assisted her husband in printing and coloring his poems and prints, yet her silence within literary history remains complete. Dorothy Wordsworth took up the handmaiden's role in a way that offers much more for our analysis. Not only did she read, transcribe, and take down at dictation most of her brother William's output as a poet, she also wrote journals and poems that respond to the overwhelming demands that she remain an amanuensis and that she enact another role given to her and other female figures in Wordsworth's poetry, the role of the object of representation. Unlike a later first reader of a later romanticism, Mary Shelley, who overtly criticizes Percy Shelley's positioning of women, Dorothy Wordsworth largely accepts and literalizes this romantic role, allowing her writing to be appropriated by it. She can write from the perspective of the literal because (unlike Mary Shelley) she does not seek the position of the subject in a literary discourse. Paradoxically, however, this acceptance of her brother's authority necessitates to a certain degree her amending of it. Writing from the perspective of the literal requires that she revise her brother's works, because to write from this perspective is to make audible what is for her brother undifferentiated silence.

It may seem farfetched to speak, with respect to such unselfconscious texts as these journals, of literary revision. But precisely that which enables Dorothy to hear and to amplify what is silent in her brother's work is what enables us to perceive an operation of her texts that has hitherto gone unnoted. Dorothy's attentiveness to the silent objects of her brother's representation derives from her identification with them as female; and it is reading from a woman's perspective that now makes possible an adequate account of certain features of Dorothy's writing, those moments in which she writes as a woman reader.

In order to investigate this first paradigm of a woman writer's rewriting of romantic myth, it will be necessary first to look more closely at the nature of that myth, to see why it demands of its female readers the kinds of responses Dorothy Wordsworth and women writers after her produce. We will first read critically Wordsworth's version of the myth of language side by side with the psycholinguistic reading of it by Thomas Weiskel, one of Wordsworth's most important recent interpreters. Weiskel's reading both brings out and replicates the Lacanian implications of Wordsworth's myth of language, including its silencing of women. We will then turn to Dorothy Wordsworth's revision of that myth, her voicing of what the silent woman says.

As we have seen in chapter 1, the dominant myth of Western languages has their operation structured as a quest romance, based on the boy's postoedipal renunciation of the mother and his quest for substitute objects of desire. As a structure of difference and absence, language is modeled on sexual difference, the boy's difference from and renunciation of his mother. The referent of language is always absent; indeed, the word necessitates the absence of the object. That this is the governing myth of language for Wordsworth is nowhere more clear than in his central account of the acquisition of language in book 2 of *The Prelude*, a passage we have already considered briefly and that I would like to review in greater depth here. In this passage, the "infant Babe" is "blest" because he "Drinks in the feelings of his Mother's eye!" (2. 237).[1] What the baby "drinks" is his mother's love of nature. Because her "Presence" "irradiates" nature, and because he loves everything connected to her, the baby's love for his mother grants him "The gravitation and the filial bond / Of nature that connect him with the world" (2. 243–44). Empowered by the feelings he drinks in from his mother, the infant "Doth like an agent of the one great Mind/Create, creator and receiver both" (2.257–58), but his creation is without language: "by intercourse of touch/I held mute dialogues with my Mother's heart" (2.267–68). Very like the semiotic body language that, according to Julia Kristeva, precedes and is repressed by entry into the symbolic order, these mute dialogues achieve creation without any loss of the unity of signifier and referent or of child and mother.

But the entry into the symbolic order causes a "trouble":

> I was left alone
> Seeking the visible world, nor knowing why.
> The props of my affections were removed,
> And yet the building stood, as if sustained
> By its own spirit!
>
> (2. 276–81)

As we have seen, Wordsworth here equates the acquisition of representational language with a loss that feels like his mother's death, most likely the growing boy's oedipal renunciation of his most intimate bond with her.[2] The baby's earliest feeling of connectedness with his mother and with the natural world that he drinks in through her requires no language, indeed excludes language, for nature is present to him, and language would imply a distance between the speaker and the objects to which language refers. Language would violate the immediacy that the mother's presence guarantees. But now the child feels "alone," and that he is "seeking the visible world" suggests that that feeling of immediacy and presence has been replaced by a feeling of loss and absence, an absence that is both the absence of the mother's connecting presence and the absence that language at once assumes and creates. Ironically, the child discovers that he can overcome this crisis with the aid of what has precipitated the crisis: language and personal autonomy, life without the mother, can still support a relation to nature, even if it is not the same relation as before. He now depends, however, on language to bridge the distance between self and nature, to fill the gap left by the departure of the mother, the very distance that language has helped to create.

Wordsworth is very much disturbed that language originates and functions in this way. He fears that language depends upon and therefore necessitates death, the death of the referential object that is always also the death of the mother, and his project is to forestall the determinate meaning of words so that the object need not die. In Thomas Weiskel's formulation, which refers to a passage in *The Prelude* in which "Ye

Presences of Nature" have "Impressed upon all forms the characters / Of danger or desire" (1. 464–75), "when 'forms' begin to assume the shape and function of 'characters,' Nature's significant absence (or 'negative presence') is already presupposed, for characters are symbols standing in for something no longer immediately there. Behind every symbol is an absence, the death of the thing (form or image) whose place the symbol takes."[3] Wordsworth, Weiskel argues, seeks to halt "at the point where the image is . . . on the verge of turning into a 'character'" (p.173). Weiskel terms this halting "a resistance to reading" and identifies it with visionary power and with "what Wordsworth calls imagination" (p.175). Imagination then would be the faculty that preserves images from being killed, from becoming characters or symbols, the faculty that holds off the moment when language absents its referent. It is important to note here that in Weiskel's reading, Wordsworth has in mind, not an undoing of the linguistic system that depends on the death of the object, but only an indefinite deferral of that fatality, an extension of significa-tion's quest. The visionary imagination makes, and stands for the priv-ileging of, transcendent meaning; Wordsworth's hope is to achieve trans-cendent meaning without the absences symbolic language requires.

As his first example of this project to block the completion of the process of signification, Weiskel cites a passage from book 2 of *The Prelude* that comes directly after, and in my view depends on, the passage about the origins of language in infancy. The child's earliest experience of visionary power is connected to a language that does not signify but defers signification:

> for I would walk alone,
> Under the quiet stars, and at that time
> Have felt whate'er there is of power in sound
> To breathe an elevated mood, by form
> Or image unprofaned; and I would stand,
> If the night blackened with a coming storm,
> Beneath some rock, listening to notes that are
> The ghostly language of the ancient earth,
> Or make their dim abode in distant winds.
> Thence did I drink the visionary power.
>
> (2. 302–11)

This language, Weiskel points out, is as nonreferential as possible, first because the mood it creates is "by form / Or image unprofaned," and second because this language is so indefinite and distant. The notes are the ghostly language of the ancient earth and make their dim abode in distant winds. Nature's language, unlike human language, does not refer: it is "a pattern of signifiers without signifieds" (p.173). The passage continues:

> the soul,
> Remembering how she felt, but what she felt
> Remembering not, retains an obscure sense
> Of possible sublimity, whereto
> With growing faculties she doth aspire,
> With faculties still growing, feeling still
> That whatsoever point they gain, they yet
> Have something to pursue.
>
> (2. 315–22)

The sublime is constituted here as a quest that must never be fulfilled, as the feeling that there is still something to pursue. This deferral of the quest is identical to the deferral of meaning involved in the shift from the "what" to the "how" of the soul's feeling. Just as the visionary power earlier in the passage comes from the displacement of language as a "ghostly language" that comes from long ago and far away, the language of the sublime defers determinate signification indefinitely.

That this visionary power, and the forestalling of signification it depends upon, is connected to the ambiguous presence and absence of the mother is suggested by Wordsworth's use of the word "drink" (line 302) to describe how he derives "visionary power" from "ghostly language." This drinking recalls the baby who "drinks in the feelings of his Mother's eye" (line 237). Both drinkings are figurations that at once refer to and repress the mother's body, from which the baby drinks milk. Wordsworth "drinks" visionary power for the same reason that he seeks a way to defer language's signification. To drink visionary power is to suggest that the ghostly language of the ancient earth somehow reconstitutes his lost relation with his mother. For words to signify in a determinate way is a constant reminder of the loss of that presence that once connected him so intimately to nature. But to defer or displace signification, to substitute for determinate meanings indeterminate ones, to hear and speak a ghostly language, is to put off repeating that death, if not to recover that lost presence. Yet at the same time, this procedure depends upon an act of figuration that represses the very bodily presence Wordsworth purportedly wishes to recall. The metaphoric drinking of visionary power, even of the mother's feelings, is just the kind of determinate use of language that requires the absence of its referent, which is in this case the mother's body.

I would argue, then, that what Weiskel calls Wordsworth's "resistance to reading" is based on a wish to recover, or not to reenact the death of, the mother. Yet our discovery that gender difference matters to this project coincides with the discovery that Wordsworth does not undertake it wholeheartedly. Of the passages Weiskel cites as examples of Wordsworth's resistance to reading, I wish to review two that are of particular importance for Dorothy Wordsworth's reading of her brother's project. Both passages are about the role of women in preserving the image from the death required by representational language, and in her journals, Dorothy Wordsworth literalizes both passages as a way of carrying out in complete sincerity the project of preservation that Wordsworth himself undermines even while appearing to practice it. Her literalization criticizes his ambivalence.

The first of these passages is the first of the "spots of time," those passages in book 12 of *The Prelude* in which, Weiskel argues, Wordsworth demonstrates the drama of resistance to reading. In this passage the child, Wordsworth at perhaps age five, is riding on the moors, but he loses the servant in charge of him, dismounts, and descends a hill to a "bottom" where a murderer has been hung. On the turf, as memorial of that hanging, "monumental letters" are inscribed, the murderer's name, "and to this hour / The characters are fresh and visible." The child flees upon glancing at them:

> Then, reascending the bare common, saw
> A naked pool that lay beneath the hills,
> The beacon on its summit, and, more near,
> A girl, who bore a pitcher on her head,
> And seemed with difficult steps to force her way
> Against the blowing wind. It was, in truth,
> An ordinary sight; but I should need
> Colours and words that are unknown to man,
> To paint the visionary dreariness
> Which, while I looked all round for my lost guide,
> Invested moorland waste, and naked pool,
> The beacon crowning the lone eminence,
> The female and her garments vexed and tossed
> By the strong wind.
>
> (12. 248–61)

The writing in the earth, Weiskel argues, signifies death, and the boy's terror comes from his realization that "recognition of a signifier = the intimation of death" (p.178). The sight of the naked pool, the beacon, and the girl with the pitcher rescue the boy from his terror because "an extended seeing replaces reading in this flight; it is a 'backward' displace-ment or regression from the order of symbol to that of image, and it functions to defend the ego against the death which has been signified" (p.179). We notice that the elements of the scene retain an irreducible particularity: when the poet, after having once described common, beacon, pool, girl, and wind (lines 248–53), wishes to refer to them again, he names them each all over again instead of substituting for their particularity a pronoun or collective noun (lines 258–61), and this situation is repeated a second time a few lines later (lines 264–65). While the characters inscribed in the turf signify death because of the very fact that they signify determinately, the images the boy encounters, because they remain images untranslated into metaphors, symbols, or significa-tion of any definite sort, counteract the effect of the characters and promise the possibility of a seeing that does not initiate death because it does not make determinate meaning. As Weiskel points out, the scene includes a drama of resistance that is a synecdoche for the boy's resis-tance to reading: while the pool is already "naked," the girl resists stripping, "her garments vexed and tossed / By the strong wind," but not altogether removed by it. She dramatizes the boy's own struggle "against the fact that things may come to signify" (p.180). As Weiskel describes the process and result of this struggle, "the symbol—the image as symbol or signifier—is glimpsed, and the power of the subsequent visionary state depends upon the repression of the signified, which reappears, as by a profound logic or economy, in the protective domain of things seen" (p.185).[4]

What Weiskel does not bring out in this scene, but what our investiga-tion of the connection between the baby's drinking and the boy's later drinking of visionary power demands that we see, is the crucial role of gender difference in the scene. In the first version of the scene, Words-worth notes that the murderer (whose name is not inscribed in the turf until the later version) was hanged for the murder of his wife.[5] Although the final version calls attention only to the relation between the inscribed characters and the death of the hanged man, the passage originally called attention as well to the first death that lies behind the murderer's death and has set the whole sequence of deaths in motion. The wife is, then, effaced in the final version. Wordsworth is actually conflating two local legends: one in which a man murdered his wife and one in which a different murderer was hung in the open with his initials carved next to the gibbet. But what matters here is that first Wordsworth thought it worthwhile to revise the original stories to introduce the death of a woman, who was a mother, behind the death of the man and the death implicit in the letters of his name.

If we read the two versions of the passage together, the characters in the turf refer, not just to the man's death, but also to the woman's. The death of the husband is the carrying out of the law, which is also what we would now call the symbolic order. That the operation of symbolic language requires the death of the man as the referent of the characters exactly repeats the law's execution of him. The characters do not refer directly to the death of the woman but to the law's decree that the murderer shall die, and yet the law's interest in punishable crime requires a female victim, a requirement that duplicates the necessary effacing of the woman in the operation of symbolic language. The first murder victim is necessarily female, for the same reason that it is the renunciation (or effacement) of the mother that makes the symbolic order possible and necessary in the first place. The symbolic order, both as the law and as language, requires the unmarked death of the woman.

Wordsworth's text adds a third effacement of the woman to this sequence when he revises her out of the poem in the later versions of the passage, so that the dead woman and the characters she makes possible never appear together. Her death is not marked, either by the characters depicted in the poem or by the words of the poem itself. Wordsworth enacts, in leaving her out, the process of her effacement that his poem would have exposed; he duplicates the primordial murder of the mother that he would seem to wish to undo. His poem does accidentally expose this effacement and murder only because manuscripts remain of the poem's first version, manuscripts in the handwriting of Dorothy Wordsworth and Mary Hutchinson. Wordsworth is protesting the operation of the symbolic order, as Weiskel shows, in the story of the boy's flight from the scene of its initiation, and yet because the procedure of his own verse repeats that operation of the symbolic, we must doubt the authenticity of his flight from it.

The girl forcing her way against the wind revives the woman effaced by the operation of the symbolic order. If the symbolic characters depend on the unmarked death of a woman, then it follows that the recovery of the image would require the return, not just of any image, but specifically of the image of a woman. And yet it is not a wife and mother who returns, but a girl carrying a pitcher. If according to Lacanian theory the renunciation of the mother leads to a quest for a series of metaphoric substitutions for her—in the form, according to Judith Herman, of younger, less powerful women—then the substitution of this living girl for the dead woman would constitute just such a move along the chain of symbolic substitutions. The fact that her sexuality is signified by her pitcher, an ostentatiously symbolic object, would contribute to making her a symbol herself. If this is so, then, as suggested earlier by the figurative use of the word "drink" in book 2, Wordsworth's turn away from the symbol toward the image is more ambivalent than it at first seems. There is ambivalence even in Weiskel's formulation: that the referent is repressed in order to be protected raises the possibility that as much fear as love is working here.

Central to Weiskel's demonstration of Wordsworth's resistance to reading is the passage in book 6 of *The Prelude* on crossing the Alps at Simplon Pass and descending Gondo Gorge on the other side. We will need to consider this passage's implications for the place of gender in Wordsworth's myth of language, for it is this scene that Dorothy Wordsworth most prominently literalizes in her journal, in combination with the "spots of time" passage. Weiskel argues that Wordsworth's disappointment at having "crossed the Alps" without having met with the sublime scenes he expected at the top is a screen memory for the truly disturbing experience of descending Gondo Gorge and seeing nature's variousness as "Characters of the great Apocalypse." Descending Gondo Gorge, the travelers first see an extraordinary range of natural phenomena:

> The immeasurable height
> Of woods decaying, never to be decayed,
> The stationary blasts of waterfalls,
> And in the narrow rent at every turn
> Winds thwarting winds, bewildered and forlorn,
> The torrents shooting from the clear blue sky,
> The rocks that muttered close upon our ears,
> Black drizzling crags that spake by the way-side
> As if a voice were in them, the sick sight
> And giddy prospect of the raving stream,
> The unfettered clouds and regions of the Heavens,
> Tumult and peace, the darkness and the light—
>
> (6. 624–35)

This landscape is self-contradictory and seems to be engaged in something like the drama of resistance Weiskel observes in the girl's struggle with the wind in book 12: winds thwart winds. The landscape also includes instances of indeterminate speech, in which the emphasis, as in book 2, is not on the "what" but on the "how" of signification: the rocks mutter, the crags speak, the stream raves, but it is not known what they mutter and speak. The scene presents both the image in "the protective domain of things seen" and instances of indeterminate speech that, like the "ghostly language of the ancient earth" of book 2, resist the determinate or symbolic signification that would necessitate the death or withdrawal of the object.

It is difficult to see, then, in Weiskel's view, in what sense this landscape can be

> like workings of one mind, the features
> Of the same face, blossoms upon one tree;
> Characters of the great Apocalypse,
> The types and symbols of Eternity,
> Of first, and last, and midst, and without end.
>
> (6. 636–40)

Whereas the emphasis in the landscape is initially on its irreducible variety and its resistance to symbolization, here those very qualities are aligned with oneness and singleness and with determinate signification, with language in which words—and not just words, but the Word—signify something: Apocalypse, Eternity. As Weiskel writes, "The aspect of Eternity checks and supersedes the evidence of things seen, so that the image of process, change, or motion evokes and indeed signifies its supratemporal contrary. . . . Nothing in the self-thwarting winds or in 'Tumult and peace, the darkness and the light' conduces perceptionally to oneness" (p. 197). The very fact that natural objects mean anything supranatural implies the death or withdrawal of those objects, a death of nature that is doubly determined by the fact that what these characters mean is Apocalypse, the end of all things natural.

Before this passage, in between the discovery of having crossed the Alps and the descent into Gondo Gorge, Wordsworth inserts a passage on something that happened, not at the time of the journey, but at the time of writing in 1804, as the 1805 version of the poem shows.

> Imagination!—lifting up itself
> Before the eye and progress of my song
> Like an unfathered vapour, here that power,
> In all the might of its endowments, came
> Athwart me. I was lost as in a cloud.
>
> (6. 525–29)

Weiskel argues that Wordsworth defines the imagination here as that which interrupts and would forestall the passage from image to symbol that the poet's mind knows will soon take place, in the writing of the passage on the characters of the Apocalypse. As the passage continues, it defines the imagination in a way that recalls the account in book 2 of the sublime as the condition of always having "something to pursue," as a quest that can never be fulfilled, a quest modeled on the deferral of language's meaning. When the imagination manifests itself in book 6,

> Our destiny, our being's heart and home,
> Is with infinitude, and only there:
> With hope it is, hope that can never die,
> Effort, and expectation, and desire,
> And something evermore about to be.
>
> (6. 604–8)

In both situations, the imagination, or the soul's sense of sublimity, is the power to slow down the passage from image to symbol, from thing to meaning, from indeterminate to determinate signification. The quest figure that Wordsworth uses in both cases, the figure of desire and pursuit, is connected in book 2 with the loss of the mother and the constitution of language there as a never-ending quest for substitutes for her, so that the visionary power that the boy may "drink" substitutes for the drinking in of mother's feelings and mother's milk. In book 6, although the rising up of imagination expresses the wish not to transform natural variety into characters and symbols, but rather to leap directly to infinitude without the aid of characters, the figure of the imagination as desire suggests that it is nonetheless a symbol-making power, since all quests have already been defined as quests for symbolic substitutes for the lost mother. Thus the situation is like that in the "spots of time" passage, which equivocates as to the status of the girl: image on the one hand and yet, as a girl who replaces a dead mother, a symbol.

Some pages before the Simplon Pass passage, Wordsworth invokes the presence of his sister in a way that is significant for the question of desire and symbolism in the later passage. Quite out of place in terms of the time scheme of book 6, which covers his last years at Cambridge, Wordsworth describes a summer vacation prior to his entering Cambridge, the vacation during which he was reunited with Dorothy after a separation of many years. As he explored various lovely places in northern England, he was

> blest
> Between these sundry wanderings with a joy
> Above all joys, that seemed another morn
> Risen on mid noon; blest with the presence, Friend!

Of that sole Sister, she who hath been long
Dear to thee also.

(6. 195–200)

Dorothy's function in this passage is to restore the poet to a more
appreciative and receptive attitude toward nature:

that river and those mouldering towers
Have seen us side by side, when, having clomb
The darksome windings of a broken stair,
And crept along a ridge of fractured wall,
Not without trembling, we in safety looked
Forth, through some Gothic window's open space,
And gathered with one mind a rich reward
From the far-stretching landscape, by the light
Of morning beautified, or purple eve;
Or, not less pleased, lay on some turret's-head,
Catching from the tufts of grass and hare-bell flowers
Their faintest whisper to the passing breeze,
Given out while mid-day heat oppressed the plains.

(6. 211–23)

This relatively nonsymbolic account of nature as seen in Dorothy's
company identifies Dorothy with images not killed into meaning. It is
interesting to note that these uninterpreted images are seen, in both
instances, from the perspective of a ruined castle: a defense that offers
"safety" and yet that is itself partially destroyed. The scene recalls
Weiskel's formula of "the repression of the signified, which reappears, as
by a profound logic or economy, in the protective domain of things seen"
(p. 185). The "oppressed plains" here suggest the repression of the
referent, while the smaller details Wordsworth notes suggest its reap-
pearance in the protective domain of things seen. The defense works by
not entirely working, for the castle is more valuable as a ruin than as a
defense.

Why does Wordsworth remember these moments with his sister at
this point in *The Prelude*? I think the answer lies in his knowledge of
what he is about to write, the crossing of the Alps with its annihilation of
the image in the accidentally successful quest for apocalyptic meaning.
For Wordsworth to refer to Dorothy as a "presence"—"blest with the
presence, Friend! / Of that sole Sister"—is to identify her with the poet's
mother, to whom he refers in book 2 as the "one dear Presence" who
"irradiates and exalts / Objects through widest intercourse of sense,"

and in whose presence the babe is "blest." "Blest" again by Dorothy's maternal presence, the poet recalls that time when signification did not require the absenting of the referent, when the absence of neither the mother nor the referent was necessary to signification. He invokes Dorothy as a proleptic defense against the apocalyptic language of the later passages. Dorothy is not herself the mother, and her preservation of images, depending as it does on the castle's mediation, is not as immediate as the (hypothetical) mother's. Where Gothic windows frame the view, language already distances the object, but it at least returns "in the protective domain of things seen." Like the girl in the "spots of time" passage, Dorothy acts a double role. She makes restitution for the lost or repressed mother and maternal relation to language, yet because she makes this restitution only by virtue of being a figure, her symbolic nature cancels some of the presence restored.

Wordsworth's aim is not the preservation of images in itself, although this is important, but the pursuit of infinitude and eternity, which he hopes may be undertaken without the deaths of images that ordinary signification necessitates. Of the imagination's intervention before the "characters of the Apocalypse" passage, Weiskel writes, "This is the unmediated path of imagination, from sight to the invisible without the necessity of a signifier. Phenomena can drop away without first becoming signs: Eternity without types and symbols, apocalypse without the characters" (p. 204). Dorothy Wordsworth as reader of her brother's poems, however, finding herself identified with the aspect of the project concerned with "the protective domain of things seen," makes her writing preserve images, but not for the sake of the invisible or the eternal. Taking up the women's projects William gives her, at once to be his amanuensis, to defend against the apocalyptic reading of nature's images, and to replace the mother, Dorothy literalizes his words about images in such a way as to enact his equivocal wish to keep the image present. But she does this more effectively, because less ambivalently, than he does, or than he might wish. Thus, paradoxically, at the very heart of the most dutiful of literary projects lies the most generous of subversions.

We will turn in a moment to some instances of this reading, but first it is important to note that Dorothy's concern with the preservation of images originates in her own interests as much as or more than in William's picture of her. Indeed, in so complex a situation of mutual familial influence, it is difficult to distinguish between his influence on her; the influence on him of his image of her, constructed in the image of their mother; and her quite considerable influence on him, which might be responsible for his concern for the preservation of images in the first place.[6] Many aspects of their textual relationship suggest her authority over him, and in her earliest journals, she invents a mode of figuration that is also a myth of language that does not demand the distance or absence of the referent. Unlike lyric poetry, which is expected to transform its objects, the form of the journal is conducive to a nonsymbolic discourse, for journal writing carries an implicit guarantee that what the journalist writes was once really observed.

In February 1798, in the Alfoxden journal, Dorothy herself uses the image of a fortification to write one of her own defenses of nature as insubordinate image, in a passage that takes on Coleridge instead of William as the romantic who would impose his vision on nature. Dorothy and Coleridge walk together over the hills between their houses:

> We lay sidelong upon the turf, and gazed on the landscape till it melted into more than natural loveliness. The sea very uniform, of a pale greyish blue, only one distant bay, bright and blue as a sky; had there been a vessel sailing up it, a perfect image of delight. Walked to the top of a high hill to see a fortification. Again sat down to feed upon the prospect; a magnificent scene, *curiously* spread out for even minute inspection, though so extensive that the mind is afraid to calculate its bounds. A winter prospect shows every cottage, every farm, and the forms of distant trees, such as in summer have no distinguishing mark. (p. 8)

In Coleridge's company, she sees at first in a Coleridgean way: the act of gazing transforms the landscape. "Loveliness" is achieved only by the "more than natural," and her wish to add a sailboat suggests that she sees an inadequacy in the landscape. But when they climb to the hill fort—an Iron Age earthwork that emerges almost naturally at the top of the hill, like Brougham Castle, a naturalized defense—Dorothy's defenses against this romantic way of seeing come to the fore. Now the scene whose beauty had depended on their gazing is "magnificent" in itself and requires "minute inspection" of each of its particulars. Nature itself takes the active role in showing forth its features. That "the mind is afraid to calculate [the scene's] bounds" suggests that for her the fort is the locus of nature's defense against human impositions. Indeed, later in the passage, she describes the moon "on the tops of the hills, melting into the blue sky"; instead of a Coleridgean gaze melting the landscape, the moon melts on its own. And in later journal passages, this strategic reversal recurs. For example, in June 1802, she and William, just as she and Coleridge did in the earlier passage, "lay upon the sloping Turf. Earth and sky were so lovely that they melted our very hearts" (p.139). If nature here is doing the melting, then she can show her brother and her friend that nature can do what they credit only to the human imagination. Nature is the active agency in these passages, while the human heart is the field on which nature acts.

This discourse that is resistant to symbol making is apparent almost everywhere in the Alfoxden and Grasmere journals of 1798–1803. Instead of the relation of symbolism, which suggests a hierarchical ordering of two terms, she presents nature gratuitously working in tandem with the human mind. Since she guarantees that she never imposes meaning on nature, we trust that details that appear to be symbolic of events in the writer's life are actually just the register of nature's free paralleling of human life. To say that she erases entirely the traces of her own creative act would be to suggest incorrectly that her mode is merely covert symbolism; she makes us doubt that there ever was a creative act. No rhetorical term fully conveys the insubordination of these free parallels between human and natural, in which there is no order of hierarchy. Her parallels have meaning only if nature has as full a value as the human experience, and it can have that full value only if it is not portrayed as subordinate to the human.[7]

For example, in June and July 1802, the period just prior to her brother's marriage to Mary Hutchinson, Dorothy's journal entries follow the history of a pair of swallows who build a nest in her window. She writes that she has read to William her letter "speaking to Mary about having a cat. I spoke of the little Birds keeping us company" (p. 136). The swallows, she writes in the same entry, "twitter and make a bustle and a little chearful song hanging against the panes of glass, with their soft white bellies close to the glass, and their forked fish-like tails" (p. 137). Ten days later: "I looked up at my Swallow's nest and it was gone. It had fallen down. Poor little creatures they could not themselves be more distressed than I was" (p. 142). She records her fascination with them: "I had watched them early in the morning, in the day many and many a time and in the evenings when it was almost dark I had seen them sitting together side by side in their unfinished nest both morning and night. . . . I watched them one morning, when William was at Eusemere, for more than an hour. Every now and then there was a feeling motion in their wings, a sort of tremulousness and they sang a low song to one another." Ten days later, they have rebuilt their nest. In her last entry before departing on the journey that will conclude in the marriage, she writes: "The Swallows I must leave them the well the garden the Roses, all. Dear creatures!! they sang last night after I was in bed—seemed to be singing to one another, just before they settled to rest for the night. Well, I must go. Farewell.—" (p. 146). It could perhaps be argued that Dorothy is here making the swallows into a figure for William and herself, with the cat associated with Mary. In this reading, the fall and recovery of the nest would be a wishful allegory of the recovery of their happy domesticity after an interruption. Yet the low song the swallows sing to each other could equally suggest William and Mary. That the parallel is so inexact shows that she does not shape the incident to be symbolic of any of these relations. She convinces us by her long and minute observations of their behavior that the swallows have their own life quite apart from hers. She sympathizes with them, not they with her.

The case for not subordinating the natural to the human appears as well in other early postromantic texts by women—Mary Shelley's *Frankenstein* and Jane Austen's *Persuasion*, for example—if not as an attribute of the writing itself, at least as a theme. In *Frankenstein*, it is the scientist's usurpation of nature's priority that brings disaster, and this usurpation is exemplified by Frankenstein's disregard for natural beauty. He tells Walton, "while, with unrelaxed and breathless eagerness, I pursued nature to her hiding places, . . . the summer months passed. . . . It was a most beautiful season; never did the fields bestow a more plentiful harvest or the vines yield a more luxuriant vintage, but my eyes were insensible to the charms of nature."[8] Although Frankenstein here criticizes his own romantic subordination of nature in the past, the fact that he claims to be able to describe the "charms" that he also claims not to have seen suggests that even now he is not seeing nature but is constructing it as a symbol of his own morality.

In *Persuasion*, Austen's narrator mocks her heroine in this way: on a walk with Captain Wentworth and her rival, Louisa Musgrove, Anne Eliot entertains herself by "repeating to herself some few of the thousand poetical descriptions extant of autumn." Distracted by overhearing the troubling conversation of her two companions, "Anne could not immediately fall into a quotation again. The sweet scenes of autumn were for a while put by—unless some tender sonnet, fraught with the apt analogy of the declining year, with declining happiness, and the images of youth and hope, all gone together, blessed her memory."[9] Since Anne will in the end be restored to hope and happiness, the analogy is wrong, yet an "apt analogy" of any kind would in any case be wrong. As the walk continues, the strollers pass fields "where the ploughs at work, and the fresh-made path spoke the farmer, counteracting the sweets of poetical despondence, and meaning to have spring again." Although "to have spring again" fits nature once again into Austen's figurative scheme, less obtrusively if also less ironically (and I do not claim for Shelley or Austen the same scrupulousness of method that I claim for Dorothy Wordsworth), Austen nonetheless mocks the presumption with which romantic poets and their readers assume nature's subordination to the exigencies of human symbolism.

For our purposes here, what is important is not just Dorothy Wordsworth's own project to retain for nature the status of an equal, both in her rhetoric and as a theme, but most especially her practicing this project as a part of reading and literalizing or enacting her brother's words. While she would write this way in any case, she also puts her texts at the service of his compelling demand, letting his texts appropriate hers for the completion of their own design (in much the same way that I have suggested maternity is usurped by patrilineal intentions, both historically and, as we shall see in later chapters, textually). And yet, because she enacts his words so much more faithfully than he does himself, she covertly transforms this passive female duty back into her own project, which is, implicitly and intermittently, critical of William's apocalyptic tendencies. Showing him that meaning can take place when both signifier and referent are present, she speaks for the literal nature that is most often silent within his texts. Literalizing his words and being with the literal and speaking a literal language are, as we saw in chapter 1, aspects of the same female history, even though in this case no pointed references to mother- or daughterhood appear: literalization reproduces the literal language of daughterhood, of the mother's continued presence, and to be a woman of any age is always to be in danger of objectification.

In the summer and autumn of 1820, the Wordsworths—William, Dorothy, and Mary—made a tour through France, Switzerland, Germany, and Italy, part of which retraced, but in the opposite direction, William's and Robert Jones's route through the Alps in 1790. In writing about the trip in her *Journal of a Tour on the Continent*, Dorothy frequently refers to William's account of his trip in book 6 of *The Prelude* in a way that corrects, while carrying out, his ambivalent wishes for the protection of natural images from apocalyptic language.[10]

As the travelers approach Gondo Gorge and Simplon Pass, they have already crossed the Alps once (at the pass of Saint Gotthard) and descended into Italy as far as Milan before turning north again. All along, Dorothy has noted the difference between the mule-tracks William traveled on thirty years ago and the broad, well-graduated road Napoleon had built since then, which "smooths every difficulty" for the modern traveler (p. 259). As they near the approach to Gondo Gorge, they encounter "an immense column of granite" lying by the road, intended by Napoleon "for his unfinished triumphal arch at Milan" but abandoned en route when he was overthrown. Dorothy comments, "I wish it may remain prostrate on the mountain for ages to come. His bitterest foe could scarcely contrive a more impressive record of disappointed vanity and ambition" (pp. 256–57). The notion of fallen ambitions recalls Wordsworth's "hopes that pointed to the clouds," as indeed throughout the journey Napoleon's roadway has literally been layered over William's way. As the passage continues, Dorothy makes an even more devastating connection between the two. "W. who came after us, said he had named it the 'Weary stone' in memory of that immense stone in the wilds of Peru, so called by the Indians, because after 20,000 of them had dragged it over heights and hollows it tumbled down a precipice, and rested immovable at the bottom, where it must forever remain" (p. 257). The Wordsworth family was in the habit of naming and marking rocks and other places near their home, yet this act of naming seems gratuitous. As Dorothy points out, the stone is quite conspicuously the perfect monument to Napoleon's failed ambition to tame nature and humanity to his will. William's need to see it as referring to some other failed ambition, much longer ago and farther away, suggests that he is attempting to avoid the association between Napoleon's ambitions and his own. He hopes, by making the rock a signifier, not for Napoleon, but for an altogether different overreacher, to dislodge the rock's implications for himself. And yet by this very act of naming, William exactly repeats the error that produced the overreaching he wants now to correct, especially as, arriving after Mary and Dorothy, he aggressively preempts their prior interpretation ("said he *had* named it"). His way of imposing on the landscape of the Alps was not to drag a column over them but instead to force a meaning on them, to see crags and waterfalls as "types and symbols of Eternity," to name nature with reference to something not there, to make it signify something at a distance. Wordsworth's act of naming Napoleon's column after the Peruvian stone has the same structure as his naming crags and waterfalls as the Apocalypse: both reveal a language that operates by distance and absence. Wordsworth is just as willing to impose his word on nature now as thirty years previously, to recuperate his lost hopes by once again imposing meaning on the landscape and thereby making it disappear, even though what he names would seem to suggest he had learned the lesson of excessive ambition.

But if Wordsworth unknowingly repeats his past mistakes as he repeats his past itinerary, Dorothy does not. Self-consciously repeating Wordsworth's route, she continues:

Ere long we come to the first passage *through* the rocks [i.e., like Gondo Gorge, though they are not yet there], near the river's bed, and "Road and River" for some time fill the bottom of the valley.

... Here is no want of variety. We are in closer neighbourhood
with the crags; hence their shapes are continually changing and
their appearance is the more commanding. . . . The very road itself,
however boldly it may bestride the hills or pierce the rocks, is yet
the slave of nature. (p. 257)

That she alludes so unnecessarily to the Gondo Gorge passage—"The
brook and road / Were fellow-travellers in this gloomy strait" (6.621–
22) ("gloomy pass," 1805)—suggests that Dorothy reconstitutes Gondo
Gorge here, in advance, and that what follows in her description revises
the Gondo Gorge passage itself. The phallic road bestrides hills and
pierces rocks, yet nature is its master. Especially if Napoleon's road is
already a revision of Wordsworth's way, this aggressive road's enslave-
ment to nature reverses Wordsworth's subordination of nature to meaning. The variety and the continually changing shapes of the crags that
Dorothy celebrates specifically recall the variegated and internally con-
flicted landscape William describes, including "black drizzling crags." As
she continues, she recalls the crucial close of the Gondo Gorge passage:
they come to "a small ruined Convent on the right—the painting on the
outside nearly effaced by damp." If in *The Prelude* nature's variety is
misinterpreted as Eternity and Apocalypse, here a religious meaning—
the painting on the convent wall—is effaced by nature's process. Immediately following this overturning of the apocalyptic by nature,
Dorothy describes a scene even more like that of Gondo Gorge, as if the
way has been cleared for the writing of unenslaved images: "We come to
the second passage or gallery, through the rocks. It is not long, but very
grand, especially viewed in combination with the crags, woods, and
river, here tumbling in short cascades—its channel strewn with enormous ruins" (p. 257).

   Throughout their passage of the Alps, the Wordsworths have encountered crosses and oratories erected at roadside, as well as the chapels and
churches of the villages they traverse. At the top of the pass of Saint
Gotthard, for example, they find "an oratory" devoted to "thanksgivings
. . . for preservation from dangers encountered on a road which we had
travelled, so gaily."[11] These oratories mark an apocalyptic presence in the
landscape in two ways. First, they testify to the life-destroying power of
the mountains: just before the oratory of Saint Gotthard, a fellow
traveler shows them where six travelers were killed by an avalanche the
previous winter. Second, they indicate belief in a deity who destroys or
preserves according to a system that transcends nature. But as the travelers continue their ascent toward Gondo Gorge, they encounter a slightly
different sort of edifice: "We pass several places of *Refuge*, as they are

named, the word *refuge* being inscribed upon their walls in large characters" (p. 258, italics hers). These refuges, unlike the oratories, are the
work of Napoleon, constructed along with the new road. The travelers
can detect the old road by observing "an Oratory above our heads that
turned its back towards us, now neglected and facing the deserted track"
(p. 258). Where an oratory is replaced by a refuge, an apocalyptic reading
of nature has been replaced by a relatively literal one. A refuge still
imposes human projects on nature, but to build a refuge assumes that
nature's meaning is immanent, a merely physical force that can be
avoided. By contrast, the building of an oratory assumes that nature's
meaning is transcendent and that human safety is not in human but in
divine hands. Even more significant, however, is the way in which
"refuge" is inscribed on the side of the shelter, in "large characters" that
recall the "characters of the great Apocalypse" of *The Prelude.* "Characters of the great Apocalypse" create meaning by absenting the natural
object, not only because "apocalypse" means the end of nature, but also
because it defines the structure of language as requiring the absence of
nature. By contrast, the large characters of the word "refuge" which,
coexist with the object to which they refer and which indeed require the
presence of the object (the wall on which they are inscribed) in order to be
seen at all, offer another model of language. Dorothy's noting here an
instance in which word and referent are one counters William's fear that
language makes nature disappear.

Right after seeing the self-naming refuges and the oratory, the travelers come to a spital (another highway refuge) at the base of Gondo
Gorge. Just as when they encountered Napoleon's column, Mary and
Dorothy get there first, but when William arrives he confers on it a
significance deriving from another time. William "who had been lingering behind" "pronounced it to be the very same where he and his
Companion had passed an awful night" (pp. 258–59). Of course the
building gains significance for Dorothy, too, from its relation to an
absent time, and yet, as with Napoleon's column, that she has already
described its particular present appearance (she gives quite an elaborate
account of its architecture) before William confers on it its absent meaning suggests that her writing privileges the literal meaning inherent in
appearances over symbolism that requires absent signification. This
"wildest of all harbours . . . seemingly fitted to war with the fiercest
tempests" (p. 259) calls to mind the refuges they have just passed, in
which word and referent are one. Within the allusive frame of Dorothy's
text, William's refusal to enter this refuge constitutes, like his naming of
it, his further insistence on a model of language requiring absence.
(Dorothy writes, "[I] had a strong desire to see what was going on within

doors for the sake of tales of thirty years gone by: but could not persuade W. to accompany me.")

Dorothy next repeats from *The Prelude* William's account of the night they spent thirty years earlier. Where William describes the spital as standing at a point "Where, tumbling from aloft, a torrent swelled / The rapid stream whose margin we had trod," and writes of being "deafened and stunned / By noise of waters, making innocent sleep / Lie melancholy among weary bones" (6.643–48), Dorothy writes: "Unable to sleep from other causes, their ears were stunned by a tremendous torrent (then swoln by rainy weather) that came thundering down a chasm of the mountains on the opposite side of the glen." Despite her adherence to his route, Dorothy does not often follow William's words as closely as she does here, and her choice to paraphrase these lines in particular is suggestive. Directly following William's vision of the landscape as characters of the Apocalypse, the torrent's sound gives the lie to the poem's myth of language as absence. As sound supersedes sight, as present voice supersedes absenting visual character, the ambivalence of William's commitment to presence, so recently exposed, might well have returned to him in a painful way. The attention Dorothy pays to this sound recalls her myth of language as presence, especially since her attentiveness takes the form of a repetition of William's words. The act of repetition calls attention to words themselves and privileges the "refuge" model of language as sameness over the "apocalypse" model of language as difference.

It is important to recall the special significance for the Wordsworths of a refuge, or other defense in a landscape. Sitting in a hill fort near Alfoxden, Dorothy substitutes, for a Coleridgean "melting" vision of the scene, a "minute inspection" of "every cottage, every farm, and the forms of distant trees." It is from the ambiguous "safety" of ruined Brougham Castle that William and Dorothy look at the far-stretching landscape of the Lake District, and on a "turret's head" that they catch "from tufts of grass and hare-bell flowers / Their faintest whisper," in the part of book 6 that precedes the journey across the Alps. In looking at these passages, we noted how closely they anticipate Weiskel's account of how the referent is repressed and then reappears "in the protective domain of things seen." At Brougham Castle nature is presented, not only as uninterpreted and "protected" visual image, but also as speech: Dorothy and William listen as the grass and harebells "whisper to the passing breeze." Later in book 6, Wordsworth both defends and defends against natural images: they are at once protected (by the passage on imagination) and annihilated (by the "characters of the great Apocalypse" passage) in the account of crossing the Alps. The spital, the dreary mansion full of sound, concludes this sequence of passages with a distinctly negative image of language as present sound, confirming by echoing it only the defense against images introduced by the ambivalence of the Brougham Castle passage. In Dorothy's text, as in the passage from the Alfoxden journal, the refuges and the spital resume this role as defenders of language as presence, but for Dorothy, this defense is wholly positive.

Leaving without entering the spital, the travelers enter Gondo Gorge itself.

> Skeletons of tall pine-trees beneath us in the dell, and above our heads—their stems and shattered branches as grey as the stream of the Vedro, or the crags strewn at their feet. . . . We sate upon the summit of a huge precipice of stone to the left of the road—the river raging below after having tumbled in a tremendous cataract down the crags in front of our station. On entering the Gallery we cross a clear torrent pent up by crags. (p. 259)

Three features of this passage rehearse and then revise William's account of the very same gorge. First, Dorothy's description recalls (perhaps inevitably) his descriptive language. Her "river raging" echoes his "raving stream"; the "tremendous cataract" and the crags recall William's waterfalls, shooting torrents, and drizzling crags; and the "torrent pent up by crags" faintly echoes the "narrow rent" where winds thwart winds as well as the "torrents shooting" from the sky. Second, whereas William's "sick sight / And giddy prospect of the raving stream" indicates his sense of the precariousness of the viewer's position, a precariousness emphasized by his not explicitly identifying himself or his position in the passage, Dorothy specifies "our station"—"We sate upon the summit of a huge precipice"—and thus decreases the sense of dizziness. Third, she sees a curious uniformity: the tree skeletons' "stems and shattered branches [are] as grey as the stream of the Vedro, or the crags strewn at their feet." Because she has been at pains here and throughout the journal to note as much natural multiplicity as possible, this detailing of the uniform greyness of trees, river, and rocks must be faithful to observation, yet paradoxically, it seems also a manifestation of what in William's description erases natural variety: "Were all like workings of one mind, the features / Of the same face, blossoms upon one tree." The oneness and sameness in William's passage are transcendental, imposed from the realm of eternity that would force natural variety into oneness in order that it signify. Because the sameness of coloring in Dorothy's passage is actually observed, it literalizes and thus renders nonsymbolic the transcendental oneness of William's passage.

Dorothy's literalizing of William's language in a way that naturalizes his antinatural language appears elsewhere as well. Much earlier in the trip, at the falls of the Reischenbach, Dorothy echoes the Gondo Gorge passage and then goes on to observe a perceptual oneness in the scene. "The roaring stream was our companion," she begins, recalling "The brook and road / Were fellow-travellers," and continues: "the substance and the grey hue still the same, whether the stream rushed in one impetuous current down a regularly rough part of its steep channel, or labored among rocks in cloud shaped heavings, or in boisterous fermentation" (Knight, p. 461). She also remarks about this "tremendous" cataract that it inspires "astonishment, and awe—an overwhelming sense of the powers of nature for the destruction of all things, and of the helplessness of man." But what matters here is that she separates out both the literal oneness and the literal destructiveness of the falls from the apocalyptic mode and content of signification with which William has identified such forces in the Gondo Gorge passage. Because she observes the uniformity of its grey tone, as she observes the uniform greyness of Gondo Gorge itself, because she observes the destructive potential of the falls, she is not imposing, as William is, oneness and apocalyptic destruction onto nature. Because her prose promises literal description, the relative oneness of signifier and referent in such a mode of writing corrects William's apocalyptic gap between signifier and referent, the gap that absents and kills the referent. She literalizes his figurative seeing; and what she literalizes is about closing the distance between the mind and nature. His vision both enacts and is about the divide between natural observation and meaning, while in her literalization of it, the same scene, with her calm description, comes to be about the lack of distance between object and meaning, signifier and referent. She assures William that what he envisioned—oneness—he could just as well have observed, and therefore that he is wrong to think that meaning derives only from violating observation. Meaning can be in things, literally.

The famous path that misled Wordsworth and Jones into thinking they were still ascending the Alps, when in fact their "future course was downwards," follows directly upon Gondo Gorge in Dorothy's account. From the new road, however, the turning appears far below. The encounter with this path repeats what happened when they encountered Napoleon's column and also when they reached the spital. Mary and Dorothy are already looking at the path, and Dorothy has already described it in some detail, when William catches up to them and explains its significance, not as an object or image interesting in itself, but with reference to another time and another register of value, as a type and symbol of poetic imagination.

The Bed of the River—far below to our left (wide and broken up by torrents) is crossed by a long wooden bridge from which a footpath, almost perpendicular, ascends to a hamlet at a great height upon the side of the steep. A female crossing the bridge gave life and spirit to a scene characterized in comparison with *other* scenes, more by wildness than by grandeur; . . . less impressive, and less interesting to the imagination than the narrow passes through which we had been travelling. [They continue walking.] Our eyes often turned towards the bridge and the upright path, little thinking that it was the same we had so often heard of, which misled my Brother and Robert Jones in their way from Switzerland to Italy. They were pushing right upwards, when a Peasant, having questioned them as to their object, told them they had no further ascent to make—"The Alps were crossed!" The ambition of youth was disappointed at these tidings; and they remeasured their steps with sadness. . . . W. was waiting to shew us the track, on the green precipice. It was impossible for me to say how much it had moved him, when he discovered it was the very same which had tempted him in his youth. The feelings of that time came back with the freshness of yesterday, accompanied with a dim vision of thirty years of life between. (pp. 260–61)

Just as at the spital, Dorothy says that the path's significance for her derives from its history, and indeed it is unlikely that she would have described just any path in such detail. Yet her description of the bridge and path precede, in the order of her writing and therefore in her phenomenal picture of the scene, the significance Wordsworth brings to it. She presents as objectively as possible the image of the bridge, the steep footpath, the hamlet, and the woman crossing the bridge, and she emphasizes that her eyes and Mary's were often drawn to the path before its historical significance added any reason to look at it, beyond its inherent interest as an image. She sees before she reads. And what she sees is of particular importance for her program to correct, by enacting William's poem, his tendency to obliterate the image in favor of meaning. The woman crossing the bridge, in a scene notable for its wildness, recalls (but without appearing to do so intentionally) the girl in the first "spots of time" passage, whose irreducible particularity as an image and whose resistance to the visionary wind affirm William's desire there to resist reading the landscape as characters signifying death and to find nature unharmed by apocalyptic meanings. Dorothy's observation and inclusion of just such a woman reminds William silently that the image, which is constitutively female, may come before, and survive, meaning. While William has refused to enter the self-naming refuge of a language that would defend against the subordination and destruction of the image by the word, Dorothy's text would recall him, its first reader, to those moments when he has himself placed images "in the protective domain of things seen." But paradoxically, while the value of the woman on the bridge derives from her relation to William's text, she cannot be an allusion, for Dorothy's point is precisely that she was there to be observed, not a meaning imported from elsewhere, but an instance of nature's gratuitously paralleling without being subordinate to human meaning.

After repeating William's recollection of the place, Dorothy writes that they traced the path together with their eyes "till [it was] hidden among the cottages, where they had first been warned of their mistake." She then goes on to note that whereas in Gondo Gorge they had seen no living creatures, animal or human, "At this spot we watched a boy and girl with bare feet running as if for sport, among the sharp stones, fearless as young kids. The round hat of the Valais tied with a coloured riband, looked shepherdess-like on the head of another, a peasant girl roaming on craggy pasture-ground, to whom I spoke" (Knight, p. 497). These children, without any self-consciousness on the part of the writer, recall Dorothy and William playing together as children and the later addition of a second girl, Mary, and they fulfill something of the same function as the woman crossing the bridge to the path. Although they constitute a silent allusion to another time, place, and text, what they refer to is a time before signification's depredations, and they constitute genuine images, really observed, that add something not predicted to the all too determinate scheme of William's allegory of the imagination and reading. Their appearance counters, much as does the woman on the bridge, William's tendency to collapse variety into symbolic oneness.

It is important to recall here why it is necessarily a female figure who, in the "spots of time" passage, counteracts the effect of the characters signifying death. In the early version of that passage, the murderer's execution by the law depends on his having murdered his wife, who, in the story Wordsworth has in mind, was also a mother. This scenario images what we would now identify as the Lacanian view that the operation of symbolic language depends on the death of the mother. The girl on the common makes figurative restitution for the murdered mother, as a restored image but also as a symbolic equivalent for the mother. Dorothy would recognize in this girl the role she herself is given in William's poetry, as for example in the passage on the reunion of brother and sister in book 6 that precedes the tour of the Alps and that shows William learning from Dorothy how patiently to look at and hear nature without dominating it. As a "presence" in that passage, Dorothy is the equivalent of the mother whose disappearance makes symbolic language possible in the first place. And as we see in the journals themselves, Dorothy accepts the role William gives her, allowing his text to appropriate hers. Dorothy's apparently accidental addition first of a single woman and then of a mixed group of children would then be her text's way of inserting femaleness into William's own text, femaleness as it has come to stand both for her own and for William's belief in her and other females' ability to resist the symbolic absenting of the object by the word. Both the act of literalizing his words and what she literalizes call attention to his words' connectedness to an observable nature he thought and thinks they banish.

In the journal passages we have been examining, Dorothy Wordsworth embraces the linguistic project of literalization and a personal identification with the literal, which go beyond William's definition of her as symbolic equivalent for the lost mother, where her being a symbolic equivalent counteracts some of the effect of her being an equivalent. She represents the least ambiguous case of a woman reader's acceptance of the female role specified by romantic poetry, for she overgoes even William's expectations for her. And yet the operations Dorothy's writing performs on William's texts also contain an implicit criticism. Her text points out, as it generously corrects them, his equivocations about trying not to have language require the death of the object; her writing reveals how limited is his understanding of the position of the other. In a much earlier literalization of a Wordsworth poem, her speaking with and for the poetic object indicates why she makes such a critique, by indicating what is at stake for her, at once personally and textually, in William's significations.

The poem is "A Slumber Did My Spirit Seal," and the occasion, in the entry in the Grasmere journal, is the wedding of William and Mary. In entries leading up to this wedding, beginning with William's decision to marry about six months earlier, Dorothy covertly records her anxieties about the changes this event will make in her life with him. She is ill during most of their stay at Mary's home, where the marriage takes place. While waiting for them to return from the church, she writes, "I kept myself as quiet as I could," but when she sees Mary's brothers "coming to tell us it was over, I could stand it no longer and threw myself on the bed where I lay in stillness, neither hearing nor seeing any thing"(p. 154).[12] Obliged to rouse herself, she "moved I knew not how straight forward, faster than my strength could carry me till I met my beloved William and fell upon his bosom." In writing this scene, she speaks in the voice of the silent, subjectless poetic "thing" in William's poem. Sealed in a "slumber" that suggests his unconsciousness of all otherness, the poet does not know whether this "thing" is dead, alive, or immortal: "She seemed a thing that could not feel / The touch of earthly years."[13] After the stanza break, she vanishes beyond his knowing, into what according to his perceptions is silence and death:

> No motion has she now, no force;
> She neither hears nor sees;
> Rolled round in earth's diurnal course,
> With rocks, and stones, and trees.

Dorothy, by writing from the position of this object, questions the limitations of the speaker's perspective. Because her reading and reversing of the poem take place in a scene about desire, she questions the functioning both of William's textual and of his biographical desire. In the poem, "she" is the object of the speaker's desire, and yet desire constituted as the speaker's idealization obliterates her otherness, and so, her. In the journal, Dorothy is not the object of desire, but her position is the same. The functioning of desire in both cases requires the absence of the object and in its place a quest after substitutes. Mary may replace Dorothy, but Dorothy was herself already a representation of the Wordsworths' mother. In terms of psycholinguistic myth, the speaker's representational language, which is desire, depends upon the disappearance of the referent. Leaving the realm of language, "she" joins the "diurnal course" of the original of all referents, Mother Earth, whose objectification constitutes the origin of language. Although Dorothy herself lives on past the end of the plot of William's poem, she identifies herself with this vanished referent, who is also the vanished object of desire, and who is endangered by William's limitations. Perhaps even more than the scenes of effaced mothers in *The Prelude*, this text justifies and explains Dorothy Wordsworth's motives for protecting what become the objects of androcentric textual desire with a language that puts no distance, no necessary death, between itself and what it names.

Dorothy Wordsworth's freedom to explore a myth of a literal and literalizing language that not only acknowledges but requires her gender depends in large part upon her having given up, or never entertained, the ambition to be the writing subject of a publicly literary text. Asked by friends in 1810 to publish a narrative she had written about a local tragedy (the deaths of the parents of a large family), she writes: "I should detest the idea of setting myself up as an Author," on the grounds that publication might harm the real referents of her writing. While she originally wrote and circulated the narrative in order to collect money for the orphans, publication would "bring the children forward to notice as Individuals, and we know not what injurious effect this might have upon them."[14] She circulated her journals among family members and her closest friends, but she did not intend them for publication. For this reason, she is willing to write descriptions that seem genuinely not to impose a literary vision on nature, and for this reason too, she can write from the position of the silenced female object—a position from which, as we saw in chapter 1, Elizabeth Gaskell finds it stressful to write when she is being self-consciously literary, even in the informal context of a letter. Women readers of romanticism who aspired to write "higher" literary forms than Dorothy Wordsworth's respond to the given identification between women and nature, or the uninterpreted natural image, with even greater complexity than she does. The next two chapters will explore how for Emily and Charlotte Brontë writing depends upon the repression of the literal natural image, especially when it is identified with the feminine, for like any novelists, they must value more highly than does Dorothy Wordsworth traditional modes of figuration and symbolic language.

3

The Name of the Mother in
Wuthering Heights

Emily Brontë understands the problem of her own writing in relation to the dominant myth of language that excludes the possibility of women writing, and she writes her own relation to this myth, and her enabling revisions of it, by writing about the relation between her female characters and their language.[1] *Wuthering Heights* is organized around two contrasting stories of female development, the stories of Catherine Earnshaw and of her daughter, Cathy Linton. With these stories, I will argue, Brontë writes two contrasting myths of her own possible relation to language, or rather, one myth of the ambivalence of her relation to language. The first Cathy's story is about a girl's refusal to enter something very like the Lacanian symbolic order, while the second Cathy's story revises her mother's, by having the girl accept her entry into the father's law. These two stories chart differing possibilities for the woman writer. The kind of language of which the first Cathy's story is a myth, a relatively literal language, would not serve very well as a paradigm for writing fiction; the language her daughter's story mythologizes works somewhat better, but at a cost to the woman in the novelist. Lacan's and Chodorow's terms will make explicit the novel's implicit, ambivalent interaction with the traditional plot of the son's revulsion from the mother and his subsequent quest for figures for her, the plot we traced already in Aeschylus, Wordsworth, and in Woolf's Mr. Ramsay.

As we have seen, it is through nature that texts in our dominant literary tradition articulate both the female and the literal in language, and representations of nature will be the starting point for this discussion of *Wuthering Heights*. We might begin by observing a contrast between the way the narrator, Lockwood, represents nature and the way Cathy does at the start of the novel. The choice of a male narrator, like the use of a pseudonym, allows Brontë to write as a son, which is to say, it allows her to enter the realm of discourse in which nineteenth-century fiction had to be written. Lockwood's representations of nature follow the Wordsworthian and Lacanian pattern of a son's language as desire, as a quest for a series of substitutes or figures for the mother and for the literal. At the start of the novel, Lockwood tells the story, a sort of parody of male romantic desire, of his interest in a "most fascinating creature, a real goddess," whom he encountered at the seaside.[2] The moment she began to respond to his interest—that is, the moment any kind of real relation between them became possible—he says, "I . . . shrunk icily into myself." Lockwood's subsequent flight to the desolation of Wuthering Heights means that his entire narrative is predicated on romantic desire's endless oscillations of approach and avoidance. Seeking to be free of womankind, Lockwood inevitably develops an interest in the first available object of desire, the second Cathy, whom he meets at Wuthering Heights.

Just as, erotically, Lockwood never wants to come to the end of a series of substitutes, one woman for another, linguistically he never wants to refer in a determinate way to nature. It is a notable feature of the narrative that although it creates the impression of taking place in the presence of the Yorkshire moors, very few scenes are actually set out of doors.[3] With a few exceptions, the crucial events take place in one or the other of the two houses, Wuthering Heights or Thrushcross Grange. Although Nelly Dean asserts about Cathy and Heathcliff as children that "it was one of their chief amusements to run away to the moors in the morning and remain there all day" (chap. 6), they are never represented on the moors, together or apart, either in Lockwood's narrative or in any of the narratives that his encloses. We can observe the narrative bending its attention away from nature in a scene such as the one in which Heathcliff disappears into a raging storm after hearing Cathy say it would degrade her to marry him. Nelly briefly describes Cathy going out to the road in search of him, but while Cathy remains outside, the narrative returns indoors, so that most of the storm is described in terms of how it feels and sounds from inside: the effect of a falling tree limb is measured by the clatter of stones and soot it knocks into the kitchen fire.[4]

Instead of directly representing nature, Lockwood uses figuration as a way of displacing and postponing any immediate relation between his language and things. The reason for this avoidance of the direct representation of nature, and the substitution for it of figures from nature, is his fear that the literal, or nature, will undermine and destroy the figurative structures of his representational language. We can see this fear at work in his very first encounter with nature. Attempting to walk back to the Grange from the Heights, where he has been delayed overnight by a snowstorm, Lockwood finds that the snow covers the moors so as to eradicate all traces of the human marking of nature:

> The whole hill-back was one billowy, white ocean, the swells and falls not indicating corresponding rises and depressions in the ground: many pits, at least, were filled to a level; and entire ranges of mounds, the refuse of the quarries, blotted from the chart which my yesterday's walk left pictured in my mind. (chap. 3)

The danger to Lockwood's life is the equivalent of a threat to symbolic reading. Previously, the path to Thrushcross Grange was marked by stones daubed with lime, but the storm has covered the ground so deeply that, "excepting a dirty dot pointing up here and there, all traces of their existence had vanished." Nature successfully combats the human attempt to make it legible, for the scarcity of those wordlike dirty dots (which even the smallest amount of snow would have made illegible, as they would be white against a white background) causes Lockwood to founder in his reading of nature, a reading on which his life might depend.[5]

After this episode, Lockwood is ill and housebound, and Nelly Dean stays indoors with him, to entertain him by narrating the story he records. Although Nelly is a woman, as a servant (Lockwood refers to her as "my human fixture") she must identify her interests with those of her male employer and of the patrilineal family. Regardless of whether nature might in other moods appear more benign, Lockwood and Nelly believe that literal nature entering the realm of textuality would be as fatal to their vulnerable narratives as the snowstorm nearly was to Lockwood's life. Both narrators distance actual nature and defend against the interruptions it threatens by turning it into a source of figurative language.[6] For example, when Nelly says of Cathy's choice between Linton and Heathcliff, "The contrast resembled what you see in exchanging a bleak, hilly, coal country, for a beautiful fertile valley" (chap. 8), she subordinates even such relatively literal nature as could be represented within a novel to the priority of human meaning. Such figurative uses of nature, which have seemed to most readers to bring real or unorganized nature into the novel, instead provide a matrix for abstract order, for distinguishing categorically between the worlds of the two houses.[7]

Moreover, what may appear to be representations of nature for its own sake are usually instead symbolic landscapes mediating the distance and difference between the two houses. In the scene just before Heathcliff's return after his three-year absence, during which Cathy marries Linton, the landscape hovers on the edge between relatively literal and overtly figurative description. Nelly observes Cathy and Edgar Linton gazing out at twilight at a "wondrously peaceful" landscape whose main feature is the "long line of mist" that describes the axis of the two houses but does not quite connect them. The line of mist symbolizes proleptically the incomplete reconnection of the two houses, because, although the hills called Wuthering Heights rise above the vapor, the house that takes its name from them "was invisible—it rather dips down on the other side" (chap. 10). The passage intends a vision of repose before Heathcliff's disruptive arrival, yet nature is never reposeful here because it is always radiating significance. Cathy and Edgar think they are looking out at the unconscious beauty of nature, but they inhabit a veritable book of instruction.

Symbolic landscapes like this one recur and become increasingly explicit as the novel proceeds. Even in a passage about nature's obliviousness to Heathcliff's grief over Cathy's death, a symbol for tears lurks in the image of "the dew that had gathered on the budded branches, and fell pattering round him" (chap. 16). Toward the end of the novel, Heathcliff himself epitomizes this tendency of the narrative by not merely perceiving the landscape as symbolic but, more than that, seeing Cathy's spirit replacing the landscape: "I cannot look down to this floor, but her features are shaped on the flags! In every cloud, in every tree—filling the air at night, and caught by glimpses in every object by day, I am surrounded with her image!" (chap. 33). Days before his death, Heathcliff seems really to see Cathy's ghost, and the boy who sees "Heathcliff and a woman, yonder, under t' Nab" (chap. 34) after Heathcliff's death confirms that the human spirit actually fills the landscape. The presence of ghosts in the landscape takes to its furthest limit the narrative's tendency to render the landscape symbolic and thus to make it vanish. Heathcliff and Cathy may be dead, but in dying they become transformed into a symbolic meaning that, projected onto nature, renders nature itself ghostly. Put another way, it would seem that the defense of language against nature only reproduces the danger of death against which it purports to defend.

Figures derived from nature and symbolic landscapes constitute defenses against the threat, as perceived by Lockwood, that the literal, or nature, would bring meaning and life to a close. Brontë compares Heathcliff to "an arid wilderness of furze and whinstone" (chap. 10) in order not to show him in an actual wilderness, a scene that would, according to Lockwood's prediction from his experience in the snow, threaten the novel's continuing intelligibility. To recur to the psycholinguistic terms with which we began, we could say that according to Lockwood, the too-powerful mother, or literal meaning, must be killed, or removed from textuality, and replaced by substitutes that resemble the original but without its threatening power and independence. This is not to say that literal nature is thematically maternal or feminine in the novel constituted by Lockwood's narrative.[8] Yet because the literal's threat to textual life originates in its structural similarity to the mother, and because figuration comes about as a solution to the literal, in the same way that heterosexual romantic desire comes about as a solution to the son's forbidden desire for the mother, literal nature does occupy the position of the necessarily repressed mother.

The use of figures and symbolic landscapes that distance and subordinate nature constitutes the paradigmatic language use of a son. Within Lockwood's narrative, however, appears one brief example of how a daughter writes, the fragment of Catherine Earnshaw's diary that Lockwood finds in her room at Wuthering Heights, sketched in the margins and a blank page of the Reverend Jabes Branderham's "Seventy Times Seven, and the First of the Seventy-First." In this diary, Cathy too leaves out the direct representation of nature, but for reasons opposite to those of Lockwood. Oppressed by patriarchal law, not speaking for it as Lockwood does, Cathy begins her narrative with an account of her brother Hindley's tyranny in locking her and Heathcliff indoors. Unlike Lockwood, who chooses to stay indoors in order to avoid the threat to life and intelligibility posed by nature—that is, in order to narrate—Cathy regards writing merely as an antidote to boredom, and she prefers to go outside. She writes:

> I have got the time on with writing for twenty minutes; but my companion is impatient and proposes that we should appropriate the dairy woman's cloak, and have a scamper on the moors, under its shelter. A pleasant suggestion . . . (chap. 3)

She then breaks off her writing to go outside. Lockwood leaves a space in his account and then writes, "I suppose Catherine fulfilled her project, for the next sentence took up another subject." What follows is clearly an account of the painful consequences of their rebellion ("How little did I dream that Hindley would ever make me cry so!"), and yet Cathy never alludes directly to the "scamper on the moors" itself. The adventure takes place in the space between the two fragments. Cathy avoids writing nature, I would argue, not as a defense against it or in flight from it, as in Lockwood's case, but out of love for it, out of her preference for being in it. To write about nature and to scamper on the moors are mutually exclusive activities. From Cathy's perspective, nature does not need to be recorded and might, indeed, be diminished by being represented. For reasons that will be explored more fully at the end of this chapter, Cathy, like Dorothy Wordsworth, wishes to preserve nature from the effects of symbolization, which, as Wordsworth learns from her brother, requires the death of the object. While Dorothy Wordsworth achieves this aim by naming nature in a language that she insists is not symbolic, Cathy achieves this aim by not naming nature at all.

But for Lockwood, writing is intrinsically valuable, far more so than nature is. Fully invested in the symbolic order, Lockwood understands the antithesis in symbolic language between word and referent and makes his choice for language. Cathy, an outlaw from patriarchal law, also understands that antithesis, but makes her choice for nature, the literal, and therefore implicitly for the unnamed mother. While Brontë obviously approves of Cathy as a character more than she does of Lockwood, the problem is that a novel could never be written following Cathy's principles of writing; whereas a novel can be written, in fact is written, according to Lockwood's and Nelly's principles. Indeed, their narratives are synonymous with the novel *Wuthering Heights*. In juxtaposing the language use of an uncivilized girl to that of an overcivilized man, the novel traces Brontë's own problem as a woman writer. Brontë must transform herself from wild girl to male writer if for a woman to write is for her interests to become merged, like those of a female servant, with the interests of androcentric culture. And yet because the novel frames this transformation so disjunctively, because Cathy will never grow up to become Lockwood, it appears that the wild girl never comfortably becomes the adult writer, and that Brontë's voice, and her motives for not representing nature, may be divided between those of Cathy and those of Nelly and Lockwood. In the significant differences between the motives of her child and adult narrators, Brontë dramatizes something like the conflict sketched in the introduction to this book between, on the one hand, the tremendous appeal of the literal and, on the other, the threat that the literal poses to articulation within the symbolic order. We might say that Brontë shares Cathy's, and Dorothy Wordsworth's, aim to preserve literal nature from symbolization, and that she achieves it by speaking through the voice of a character like Cathy. Yet the existence of Cathy's interrupted narrative depends upon the framing narratives of those who care much more about narrative itself than she does. Unlike Cathy and Wordsworth, Brontë must privilege writing itself, if she is to write and publish a novel in which she questions the value of writing.

This conflict, between the desire to be within the law and to remain outside it, is mediated in the novel's second, revisionary story of female development and language use, that of the second Cathy, who negotiates the passage from lawless childhood to adulthood within the symbolic order far more successfully than her mother does. When she is about sixteen, young Cathy takes a walk with Nelly that shows precisely how a daughter is to achieve this difficult process. At this moment in the narrative, Cathy is coming to terms with her father's impending death. Since her father's absorption in his grief over the death of his wife has made Nelly virtually Cathy's only parent, Cathy associates her father's death with Nelly's: "What shall I do when papa and you leave me, and I am by myself?" (chap. 22). She is also coming to terms with the real character of Heathcliff, of whose existence she has been kept in ignorance during her childhood, but whom she now views as a threatening and arbitrary lawgiver. He has accused her, earlier, of stealing his moorhens' eggs, and her father has told her more recently of Heathcliff's "blackness of spirit that could brood on and cover revenge for years, and deliberately prosecute its plans, without a visitation of remorse" (chap. 21). We know that Heathcliff is in the process of achieving his ends by manipulating the law, primarily the law of inheritance. Since the reader knows that once her father is dead, Cathy will be in Heathcliff's legal power, Cathy's experience at this time, translated into the terms of the Lacanian myth of maturation, is of being on the verge of losing her mother and entering the father's law. Appropriately, it is at this time that Cathy begins to discover what Lockwood and Nelly's narratives have known since the scene of the snowstorm, which is that the landscape must be made symbolic.

Describing their walk by a particular bank of trees, Nelly begins with her memory of the same place on other days:

> In summer, Miss Catherine delighted to climb among these trunks, and sit in the branches, swinging twenty feet above the ground; and I, pleased with her agility, and her light, childish heart, still considered it proper to scold every time I caught her at such an elevation, but so that she knew there was no necessity for descending. From dinner to tea she would lie in her breeze-rocked cradle, doing nothing except singing old songs—my nursery lore . . . half thinking, half dreaming, happier than words can express. (chap. 22)

In this retrospect of Cathy's childhood, the "law" of the mother is no law at all; the point of Nelly's scolding is to reassure Cathy, not to forbid her pleasure. This language is for the purpose of reenacting the pleasure of

the child's intimacy with her nurse, not for the purposes of representation, which would distance those pleasures (Cathy is "happier than
words can express"). Thinking of this passage in connection with the
omission of representations of nature in the first Cathy's diary, we might
say that girlhood is a time when the daughter has no wish to transform
nature into a text, to give it transcendental significance, or to name the
mother within symbolic language. Adulthood, however, as we see as
Nelly describes Cathy, is an initiation into symbol making, and into
banishing the mother altogether. Cathy is sad; Nelly, trying to cheer her
up by recalling her to her childish ways, points out a last bluebell
remaining under the roots of one of the trees and suggests that she climb
up and pick it. Cathy stares at it a long time, then gives it a meaning, as
adults do: "No, I'll not touch it—but it looks melancholy, does it not,
Ellen?" Reading nature thus begins with loss, with the anticipation of the
time "when papa and you are dead." Directly after this incident, on the
same walk, Cathy encounters Heathcliff when she is accidentally locked
outside of the park gates without Nelly's protection. Separated from the
mother, she is forced to defer to the Law of the Father. It is during this
encounter that Heathcliff tells Cathy how much his son Linton misses
her, and by doing so begins the process of seducing Cathy into the
domain of his law.

By the end of the novel, the second Cathy is indeed quite comfortably
incorporated within patriarchal law as a woman happily engaged to be
married. To sum up the difference between the two Cathys' stories—
which are at once stories of female development and stories of daughters'
relations to language—we might say that while the first Cathy's story
represents an uncompromising choice to remain with the mother outside
the law, with the sacrifice of intelligibility that that choice entails, the
second Cathy's story represents the compromise that results when the
daughter agrees to be incorporated within the law. An adult relation to
language appears to require a shift from both Cathys' early privileging of
nature (seen in the first Cathy's diary and in her daughter's love of sitting
in trees singing nursery songs) to a Lockwood-like privileging of language, especially of figurative language. While the second Cathy moves
more or less successfully if sadly from the maternal and nature to the
world of adulthood governed by paternal authority, the first Cathy
refuses to. And at the end of her life, this refusal of the symbolic order
becomes something positive. Temporarily, she names the mother, and
names her outside the symbolic order. We need at this point to turn to the
end of the first Cathy's story, to see what its final implications are for the
story of the daughter's relation to language and, finally, to see why
Brontë replaces the first Cathy with the second. If Brontë dramatizes

through the second Cathy the normal course of a daughter's development as an acquiescence to the symbolic order, she dramatizes through
the first Cathy both the cost and the powerful appeal of women's language remaining outside the law.

I have argued that the first Cathy omitted representations of events in
nature from her diary, not to distance them defensively as Lockwood
would, but because such representations would be superfluous and
perhaps destructive to nature itself. Yet later on, it is Cathy herself who
speaks some of the novel's most striking examples of the symbolic use of
nature. After Nelly compares Heathcliff and Linton to a coal country and
a fertile valley, Cathy produces her own metaphors for her two lovers:
"My love for Linton is like the foliage in the woods. Time will change it,
I'm well aware, as winter changes the trees. My love for Heathcliff
resembles the eternal rocks beneath—a source of little visible delight, but
necessary" (chap. 9). When describing Heathcliff's bestiality for the
benefit of her sister-in-law, Isabella, Cathy recurs to and extends her and
Nelly's original metaphor for Heathcliff and develops the metaphor of
vulnerable natural creature for the Lintons: "Tell her what Heathcliff
is—an unreclaimed creature, without refinement, without cultivation; an
arid wilderness of furze and whinstone. I'd as soon put that little canary
into the park on a winter's day as recommend you to bestow your heart
on him!" (chap. 10). It would seem that just like her daughter later,
she participates in the linguistic practices, the defenses against the literal,
that constitute the father's law.

And yet at the end of her life, Cathy yearns deliriously to return to her
childhood and to an unmediated merging with actual nature, in such a
way as to suggest that her attachment to nature was never fully rejected,
merely suppressed:[9]

> 'Oh, if I were but in my own bed in the old house!' she went on
> bitterly, wringing her hands. 'And that wind sounding in the firs by
> the lattice. Do let me feel it—it comes straight down the moor. . . .
>   I wish I were out of doors—I wish I were a girl again, half savage,
> and hardy, and free. . . . I'm sure I should be myself were I once
> among the heather on those hills.' (chap. 12)

She seeks a literal relation to nature such as the one she shielded from
representational language by omitting it from her diary, a relation in
which nature would be present to her, and she to it. But how does she
change from the girl who loves nature for its own sake into the adult who
uses figures to defend against nature, and how does she change so quickly
from that woman into the delirious figure at the window embracing
nature as immediately as she can?

While the novel represents the second Cathy's entry into the symbolic order, it omits from the narrative any account of the first Cathy's change. All we know is that after her initial five weeks' visit to the Lintons, she is transformed from the "wild, hatless little savage" who could run with Heathcliff barefoot and without stopping from the Heights to the Grange the night of her capture by the Lintons into the "very dignified person with brown ringlets falling from the cover of a feathered beaver" (chap. 7) who now begins using nature for figuration. Her transformation takes place between two chapters, too abruptly to be represented, or indeed, credited. She appears on her return to have forgotten entirely her former pleasures in the out of doors and in her former state of "savagery." Shaking hands decorously with Heathcliff, who now looks to her "odd" and "dirty," "she gazed concernedly at the dusky fingers she held in her own, and also at her dress, which she feared had gained no embellishment from its contact with his" (chap. 7).

The difference between this transition into the symbolic order and the second Cathy's may be due in part to the fact that although they both as children love nature more than language, for the second Cathy, nature is bounded within the walls of Thrushcross Park and within her father's prohibition against going out too far unaccompanied. Whereas the first Cathy and Heathcliff run wherever they wish on the moors, and run to the Grange if they like, the second Cathy does not even know of the existence of Wuthering Heights or of her mother's favorite haunts until the age of thirteen, when in her father's absence, she runs away to Penistone Crags and is sheltered at Wuthering Heights when she gets lost in returning. The second Cathy has not so far to go to get into the father's law. That for her this transition can be and is represented in language, while for her mother it is not, underscores the instability of the first Cathy's entry into the symbolic order, of her acceptance of the substitution of representations for real but unrepresented things. It becomes clear, from the perspective of her final illness, that the period of her life in which she used figuration defensively was only a temporary and superficial excursion into the symbolic order, even if her figurations of nature participated in the defensive work required of Lockwood's narration. She has only suppressed her love both for Heathcliff and for the unmediated nature with which she associates him, and his return brings a resumption of precisely the same mental strife between her two loves that she experienced before and just after he went away. When she becomes ill as a result, what returns is a longing for the childhood in nature that she denied along with Heathcliff—a literal repetition of it, not a new form of it.

Both her relation to Heathcliff, as Leo Bersani indicates, and her relation to nature have been motivated by a desire to obliterate boundaries between self and other. Cathy does not care to see that within the terms of the literary work she inhabits any lack of differentiation—between self and human other or between playing on the moors and being buried under them—is fatal. The actual nature with which she yearns to be united she perceives as lifegiving; others, however, who live more permanently than she in the domain of the symbolic, perceive it as destructive. After Cathy has cried out to be on the moors again, Nelly refuses to open the window, on the grounds that it would "give you your death of cold" (chap. 12), and when Cathy opens it anyway, Nelly perceives the wind only as a form of violence. She says Cathy "bent out, careless of the frosty air that cut about her shoulders as keen as a knife." Like Lockwood after his encounter with the snowstorm, Nelly perceives the unmediated presence of nature as threatening to her ideas of life, which include symbolic intelligibility.

In the same scene, Cathy recounts an episode from her childhood that is unique in being the novel's only direct representation of any part of the childhood she and Heathcliff shared on the moors. The content of this story, which might even have made part of the "scamper on the moors" omitted in her diary fragment, specifies and clarifies her motives for such omissions, which return now only because of her delirium. Pulling the feathers out of the pillow on which she lies, she finds a lapwing's, which looses a flood of memory:

> Bonny bird; wheeling over our heads in the middle of the moor. It wanted to get to its nest, for the clouds touched the swells, and it felt rain coming. This feather was picked up from the heath, the bird was not shot; we saw its nest in the winter, full of little skeletons. Heathcliff set a trap over it, and the old ones dare not come. I made him promise he'd never shoot a lapwing after that, and he didn't. Yes, here are more! Did he shoot my lapwings, Nelly? Are they red, any of them? Let me look. (chap. 12)

What, on the evidence of what returns, has been repressed? The story exposes, not nature's destructiveness to human meaning, as in Lockwood's omissions of narratives about nature, but one human child's destructiveness toward nature. The episode reveals vividly that Heathcliff was as sadistic in his relatively happy childhood as he is as an adult. It is true that Cathy implicates herself to some degree in the violence she recounts. Her interdict on shooting extends only to lapwings, while, by distinguishing shooting as the one form of killing of which she disapproves, she half admits her attraction to the far more perverse technique Heathcliff did use. She takes pleasure in the episode's verification of her power over Heathcliff. Yet her main concern in the passage is with her protectiveness toward a vulnerable natural world that Heathcliff takes pleasure in victimizing. If Cathy has defenses, they have been, not against nature, but of nature.

There is another element in the story, a structural counterpart to the thematics of Heathcliff's cruelty. What he does to the lapwings is to separate parents from young and to ensure that the little ones die of their being orphaned.[10] This action is a symbolic repetition of what he had himself experienced as a child: Heathcliff was left to starve by his parents, and orphaned again by the deaths of Mr. and Mrs. Earnshaw, he was cruelly neglected by another parental figure, Hindley. Already a symbol maker at this early age, Heathcliff imposes the horrors of his own experience on a helpless world of natural creatures. A ghoulish avatar of Freud's grandson, whose game of "Fort!/Da!" represents and therefore controls the pain he experiences through his mother's absence, revealing for Lacan how language depends upon the loss of the mother, Heathcliff reiterates and thus symbolically controls his own painful loss. Symbol making here both depends upon and reproduces pain and loss, since loss is the motive and since to use nature for a symbol is to kill it. Thus the lapwing story shows Heathcliff committing two simultaneous acts of violence: by subordinating the birds to the production of symbolic meaning, as well as by literally starving them, Heathcliff kills them twice. Instead of being identified with the brute forces of literal nature, as we would expect from Cathy's identification with him as a child, Heathcliff turns out to be for Cathy, as he is later for Cathy's daughter, a proponent of the Law of the Father, someone who not only victimizes nature but who does so specifically through his actions as a symbol maker.

Narrated so disturbingly and with such disturbing effects on the sequence of the novel, this scene of symbol making reveals that when Cathy omitted this or a similar outing from her diary, it was not because she sought to protect nature, but rather because even in childhood she was suppressing the knowledge that she was virtually powerless to protect nature from figurative and literal killing at the hand of the androcentric law. Not only was she preternaturally aware of the effects on nature of symbolization and of writing, but also she knew that she could not help but be complicitous in them, even involuntarily. Cathy's motive is indeed like Dorothy Wordsworth's, the wish to protect nature, but this aim is complicated by the knowledge of its unattainability.

It is in this scene, as if in reponse to the return of the painful memory, that Cathy reinserts the mother into nature, the mother whose death and absence the more civilized speakers require. Right after telling this story, willfully converting Nelly from servant to the patriarchy into a female outlaw like herself, Cathy hallucinates a restoration of the mother, whose death and repression is both the ground and the result of murderous symbolic acts, such as the one she has just narrated.

> I see in you, Nelly, . . . an aged woman—you have grey hair, and bent shoulders. This bed is the fairy cave under Penistone Crag, and you are gathering elf-bolts to hurt our heifers; pretending, while I am near, that they are only locks of wool. That's what you'll come to fifty years hence; I know you are not so now. (chap. 12)

This Cathy's daughter, seventeen years later, will fear the death of Nelly because her own entry into the symbolic order is effectually doing away with Nelly's maternal presence. The first Cathy, however, the speaker of this passage, knows that Nelly will live fifty years to become a "withered hag" with magical powers over nature and culture, a Fury with the power to refute the patriarchal laws of ownership. That Cathy refers to the "withered hag" hurting "*our* heifers" suggests that she still in moments identifies herself with the symbolic order she flees. And yet Cathy insists that although, like herself, Nelly has temporarily been captured into doing the civilizing work of symbolization, she will revert to her ancient life as a presence in nature whose being will undo the symbolic systems that depend on her absence.

But the Cathy who thus envisions a powerful maternal presence in nature is mad and dying. From the perspective of Brontë the author, Cathy's identification with nature's pain is madness; the restoration of the mother's presence in nature is likewise madness from the point of view of Brontë's models for successful writing.[11] The irony of Cathy's attempt to restore this maternal presence and assert its power is that, at the time she speaks these words, she is pregnant, and the premature birth of her daughter will be the immediate cause of her death. In her hallucination, the mother is powerful and she speaks; yet in her own real life, coopted by the constricting terms of the law, Cathy's motherhood is precisely what makes her powerless. Nelly, back in her role of servant to the patrilineal family, mentions the pregnancy rarely, only to indicate its place in patrilineal succession. She syntactically subordinates Cathy to the child, and both to the continuity of the Linton family line. During her illness, Nelly says, there is "double cause to desire" Cathy's recovery, because "on her existence depended that of another; we cherished the hope that in a little while Mr. Linton's heart would be gladdened, and his lands secured from a stranger's grip, by the birth of an heir" (chap. 13). Later Cathy's death and her daughter's birth take place within one sentence: "About twelve o'clock that night was born the Catherine you saw at Wuthering Heights, a puny, seven months' child; and two hours after, the mother died" (chap. 16). Once the identity "Catherine" has shifted to the baby, the first Catherine loses her name and becomes simply "the mother," adjunct to the primary identity of the heir, the new Catherine. Within a text whose symbolic operation mirrors the law of patriliny, it is entirely appropriate to have the mother's death, which includes her death within language (her loss of name), coincide with the perpetuation of the law, for the operation of the symbolic order has all along required the mother's absence. The production of the heir makes the mother not just superfluous but impossible, without identity because unnameable.

Reinforcing this disturbing aspect of Cathy's motherhood are the stories of Hindley's wife, Frances, who dies of consumption shortly after giving birth to Hareton, and of Isabella, who vanishes from the story once she is pregnant and who dies once the story is ready for the appearance of her son, Linton. By contrast, the fathers—Linton, Hindley, and Heathcliff—all outlive the mothers and function, after the births of their children, in other ways than just as parents. At one point during Cathy's illness, she is shocked by the sight of herself in the mirror; imagining that she is a child, she is alienated from the image of her adult self. It takes Nelly a moment to persuade her that it is indeed herself, and when she understands, " 'Myself, she gasped, 'and the clock striking twelve! It's true, then; that's dreadful!' " (chap. 12).[12] The mirror images her death, because it shows her to herself as a mother within patrilineal law (a married woman who lives at Thrushcross Grange and no longer, as she imagines, at Wuthering Heights), whose death will soon be structurally required by a culture that defines mothers, and nature and objects, as dead.

If the heir replaces the mother to the mother's disadvantage within the Law of the Father, it is also true that within Cathy's hallucinatory and extralegal understanding of maternity and childhood, the mother replaces the child. Dying in childbirth, Cathy becomes herself a child; the novel equates giving birth with her return to her own childhood. She has, during her illness, wished to "be herself" by being a child on the moors again, and this has been her desire since the onset of her illness. After falling unconscious from her first quarrel with her husband and Heathcliff, she dreams of being a child: she imagines she is "in the oak-panelled bed at home . . . and, most strangely, the whole last seven years of my life grew a blank! . . . I was a child; my father was just buried, and my misery arose from the separation that Hindley had ordered between me and Heathcliff. I was laid alone, for the first time" (chap. 12). Nelly reports of the moment of her death that "she drew a sigh, and stretched herself, like a child reviving, and sinking again to sleep. . . . Her latest ideas wandered back to pleasant early days" (chap. 16). And it is as a child that her ghost appears to Lockwood during the night he spends at Wuthering Heights, after he reads her diary and spells over the names inscribed in the windowsill. Although the ghost is named Catherine Linton (proving that she is not simply a dream, since Lockwood "had read *Earnshaw* twenty times for Linton" [chap. 3]), and Cathy did not become Mrs. Linton until she was eighteen, Lockwood's "waif" speaks in a child's tone of being lost, and Lockwood reports, "I discerned, obscurely, a child's face looking through the window." The ghost-child haunts her childhood room and window, making her wish—"Let me in!"—an already more than half fulfilled wish to return to childhood.

Dying as she gives birth, she is released to become the ghostly child who appears to Lockwood. If her wish to be a child is fulfilled only by her becoming a mother, if motherhood produces only regression to childhood, then the real child who causes her death and the childhood to which she suicidally yearns to return are the same. Yet with her hallucinatory vision of Nelly, she would reestablish the mother's power, presumably her own as well. Because she has never fully abandoned her allegiance to the mother, never fully entered the father's law, she equates motherhood with a return to childhood, and both with power and life. Cathy's history represents an extremely literal version of what Chodorow would call a daughter's reproduction of her own childhood, and this return through maternity to childhood collides with the devaluation of such a cycle within the symbolic order. It is for this reason that the unbearable shock she receives from her final meeting with Linton and Heathcliff shares the blame as the cause of her death: it is not childbirth alone but male interference in pregnancy's rythms that kills her. And so precisely what she might have expected to give her power and life deprives her of it, since to be a mother in the culture in which she lives is to be the excluded term.

This, then, is what it means for the second Cathy to succeed to the first. The first Cathy, with her refusal to grow up into the symbolic, her allegiance to the mother and nature, and her vision of Nelly as powerful mother, is replaced, with her author's ambivalent reluctance, by the second Cathy, whose entry into the novel as an heir causes her to see Nelly as a vulnerable mother and predicts her greater acceptance of the Law of the Father, an acceptance that makes her a safer model for the author's own practice. Although the first Cathy dies into the literal nature she loves, free to return to childhood from her captivity within the law, merging in her death with the moors, the novel continues past her death, showing, by separating itself from her, just what from its point of view it has to, and can, resist. The very brutality with which the novel passes over Cathy's death is necessary to the text's self-preservation. By having her represent a woman writer's allegiance to the literal and her refusal of figuration, and then by killing her, the text reasserts its own figure-making powers. Brontë probes the psychic and imaginative possibilities that the literal represents, yet in the end she identifies these possibilities as dangers within the only terms in which she can write, and she seals up her novel's defenses against them. Brontë thus identifies her project with Lockwood's, with the son's, and with that of Nelly as the female servant of patriliny, repressing literal nature in favor of figuration. But through her heroine, we glimpse a different view, a different allegiance, through which the oppressive writing of nature, and of the mother, would be forgone.

4

Dreaming of Children:
Literalization in *Jane Eyre*

There was no possibility of taking a walk that day. . . . I was glad of it. I never liked long walks, especially on chilly afternoons."[1] With this opening assertion, Charlotte Bronte founds her novel on her heroine's scepticism about the experiences in nature that her sister's just-completed novel so ambiguously celebrates.[2] In reading *Wuthering Heights*, and in considering Dorothy Wordsworth's journals before that, we have been looking primarily at a range of responses to the potential identification between women writers and a female or maternal presence in nature. Dorothy Wordsworth embraces a sympathetic identification with what her brother identifies as female in nature and organizes her writing to protect nature from the law of the symbolic language that he practices. While Emily Brontë shares Dorothy Wordsworth's interests, she also shares the poet's. *Wuthering Heights* celebrates Cathy's resistance to symbolic systems and to the father's law, celebrating her return to childhood that is a return to nature. At the same time, the novel suggests that nature, identified with literal meaning, threatens the writing of fiction as much as Cathy's regressive love of nature threatens her life. Despite Jane's dislike for taking walks, parts of *Jane Eyre* take place in the landscape of *Wuthering Heights*—the Yorkshire moors—but to different effect. Each novelist transforms the moors into a symbolic system, but while Emile Brontë undertakes this project ambivalently, her sister accepts it far more wholeheartedly. Charlote shares her sister's attraction to a nonlinguistic literal, but she shares to a much greater degree her sister's awareness that this attraction contradicts the aims of the novelist.

As we have seen, the literal is historically associated with nature, and especially in and just after the romantic period, it is against identification with nature that women writers stage their ambivalent defenses against becoming identified with the literal and the object. Projected onto women by masculine texts, internalized and reproduced by women writers, an identification of the mother with nature might seem to offer women access to power, since, taking the form of nature, the literal is the final, maternal object of desire. Yet because the desired object is also so feared by androcentric culture, to accept that identification might be to stop writing and speaking intelligibly within the symbolic order. Both Charlotte and Emily Brontë figure this silence as death, because the mother's place in the symbolic order is to be absent. While *Wuthering Heights* entertains the possibility that the mother's place also has power and value of its own, *Jane Eyre* entertains only in order to defend against it the seductive possibility of a woman's becoming the literal.

Wuthering Heights dramatizes the dangers and attractions, not only of a woman writer's identification with a feminized and literal nature, but also specifically of the role in this process of maternity and of a mother's reproduction in her daughter of her own childhood. In keeping with the novel's ambivalence about women's relation to the law, Cathy's childbirth is both contained within the law of patriliny and outside the law. She gives birth simultaneously to the heir of the Lintons and to the wild and ghostly child-self who haunts Lockwood at the start of the novel, the outlaw, antithetical to everything Lockwood stands for, whose wrist he rubs on the broken window pane "till the blood ran down and soaked the bed-clothes." This chapter will extend our inquiry about maternity to a reading of *Jane Eyre*, in the context of investigating Charlotte Brontë's relation to the literal. Like *Wuthering Heights*, *Jane Eyre* reveals its author's knowledge both that motherhood is implicated in women's culturally imposed identification with the literal and that, as a reproduction of the literal, it models a kind of writing that endangers a text's place within what we are calling the symbolic order. But in keeping with its own greater acceptance of the law, *Jane Eyre* does not share the sense of liberating possibility with which Emily Brontë endows her representation of childbirth.

Jane Eyre presents the fear of the objectification of the self in a variety of ways that make particularly explicit the connection between femininity and objectification. Jane fears that Rochester objectifies her when he wants to dress her in jewels and silks that correspond, not to her individual character, but to his abstract idea of Mrs. Edward Fairfax Rochester.[3] Like Cathy shocked by the alienness of her mirror image, Jane is shocked twice by what she sees in the mirror, in the red room when "the strange little figure there gazing at [her] had the effect of a real spirit," and again on the morning of her wedding, when the mirror's "robed and veiled figure, so unlike [her] usual self that it seemed almost the image of a stranger" represents both the appeal and the threat of having her subjectivity replaced by a beautiful object. This chapter, however, will examine the novel's exploration of the feminine temptation to become an object through two kinds of literalization: the circumstances of childbearing and the gothic literalization of subjective states with which, in the novel, childbearing is often inauspiciously associated. (To draw on an already familiar example from *Wuthering Heights*, which makes a similar association, in Lockwood's "dream" Brontë pairs the apparition of a ghost with what we later learn is the birth of Cathy's child-self.) In both the gothic and in childbirth, what was once internal acquires its own objective reality; and in both situations, the heroine is in a position to become identified with the object world on which her subjectivity is projected.

As Charlotte and Emily Brontë write it, the gothic both acknowledges and protests the place to which women are relegated in romantic myths of subjectivity and transcendence. In gothic novels generally, subjective states are so fully and literally projected into a social framework as to alter physical reality.[4] Specifically, the gothic literalizes the romantic imagination, and it is this literalization that produces its terror. When Heathcliff at the end of his life sees Cathy "in every cloud, in every tree—filling the air at night, and caught by glimpses in every object by day" (chap. 33), the effective projection of his desire literalizes Coleridge's figure for the way the imagination shapes the perceptual world, the "fair luminous cloud / Enveloping the Earth."[5] This pattern of literalization operates in all gothic works, but it has special implications for women, which the Brontës make explicit. The romantic imagination that the gothic literalizes is predominantly a masculine mode: Coleridge defines the imagination so that the poet is the patrilineal inheritor of a distinctly masculine God's self-assertion "I AM." Just as Mr. Ramsay's metaphysical speculations depend upon and produce a feminine "phantom kitchen table" for the puzzled Lily Briscoe, the desiring romantic imagination assumes feminine phantoms of desire. And just as Lily impertinently imagines the table back into existence, the Brontës' female gothic literalizes romanticism's phantoms.[6]

The difficulty, especially as far as Charlotte Brontë is concerned, is that literalization is precisely what female figures embody in romantic myth. A woman writer's practice of literalization, like Lily's, would seem to be a protest against romantic speculation; yet in a larger sense, that protest has already been scripted within what it protests. But if the Brontës' gothic rehearses women's fate within the symbolic order, at least it does so self-consciously and therefore skeptically.[7] It may be that the gothic became historically a predominantly female mode because it lends itself so well to women writers' responses to the cultural identification of "woman" with the literal.[8] It could be that Charlotte Brontë uses the gothic, where all sorts of literalizations occur, not because she is incapable of what her culture would define as a liberating transcendence of the body, but rather because it enables her to criticize the double position in which culture places her. To the extent that a woman writes within what we have retrospectively described as the symbolic order, she accepts cultural definitions of femininity, yet those definitions situate her as a woman outside the symbolic. Because as a woman she has been excluded from the symbolic order, as a writer she feels she must continually confront and defend against that exclusion. While Woolf can celebrate Lily's literalizing imagination (in part because she also imagines other things for her woman artist to do), Charlotte Brontë uses the gothic with ambivalence and uses her ambivalence to protest the objectification of the feminine that the gothic enacts.

We can see this ambivalence at work in the way *Jane Eyre* frequently entertains gothic possibilities, then appears to undermine them with rational explanations, and still later undermines those rational explanations themselves.[9] Ultimately, as we will see, in a final twist, Brontë undermines even that return to gothic literalization. The most familiar example of this pattern is Jane's chastisement both of herself and of her reader when she finds herself wondering about the demonic laughter that issues from Grace Poole's attic room. "Sometimes I saw her; she would . . . go down to the kitchen, and shortly return, generally (oh, romantic reader, forgive me for telling the plain truth!) bearing a pot of porter. Her appearance always acted as a damper to the curiosity raised by her oral oddities" (chap. 12). But the laugh in the attic is only temporarily explained away. Jane errs in denying the gothic's literalization of speculation. That the source of those "oral oddities" has an existence and a history more horrifying than the wildest fantasy demonstrates that her allegiance to "the plain truth" offers no escape from the dangers of subjectivity, for it is precisely in the realm of "the plain truth" that Jane's fears and subversive wishes take their most terrifying form. In Brontë's gothic, terror originates in the heroine's confinement to the world of objects.

This reading is confirmed by Brontë's curious and unconventional emphasis on Jane's fear of any apparition, whether good or bad. Apparitions horrify, not because they are evil, but because they appear at all. This is the case in Jane and Rochester's supernatural long-distance conversation at the end of the novel, but more strikingly in the novel's first gothic instance, the apparition of Mr. Reed in the red room. Thinking of stories about spirits returning to earth to avenge the oppressed, Jane relates, "I wiped my tears and hushed my sobs, fearful lest any sign of violent grief might waken a preternatural voice to comfort me, or elicit from the gloom some haloed face, bending over me with strange pity. This idea, consolatory in theory, I felt would be terrible if realised" (chap. 2). This separation of "theory" and "realization" allows Jane to establish that, for this text, any passage from subjective to objective, or from internal to external, is potentially terrifying. The introduction of these terms widens the implications of the use of the gothic and connects them explicitly to the larger issue of women's identification with the literal.

The gothic's literalization of imaginative or other subjective states often coincides with representations of a rather different kind of literalization, the experience or idea of childbirth. That women bear children and men do not is the simple origin of this complex and troubling tradition that associates women with the literal and with nature, an association that at once appeals to and repels women writers. Both novels foreground a curious connection between their most gothic elements and motherhood. The transitory experience of being a mother is the central and recurring metaphor for the abundant sense of danger in *Jane Eyre* (just as the plot of *Wuthering Heights* turns on the main character's death in childbirth and her subsequent transformation into a ghost). The specific connection between the literalization of subjective states and childbirth's actual passage from internal to external takes place in dreams about children. Like other internal states in the gothic mode, dreams are literalized in the object world, and the ambiguous process of their literalization mirrors and reinforces an ambivalence that is almost always integral to the imagery of childbearing in the two novels.

Neither Charlotte nor Emily Brontë was, at the time of writing, in a position to experience or even to anticipate actual motherhood, but my concern here is with a view of the subject of production that might more likely (though not necessarily) be shared by women than by men. Any literary woman of the nineteenth century would have assumed that marriage and motherhood would end her career. Further, the thought of the event of childbirth itself would have had highly ambiguous connotations for any pre-twentieth-century woman. In the nineteenth century, giving birth was not unlikely to be fatal to the mother or to the child or to both, and to fear childbirth or associate it with death would have been quite reasonable.[10] The commonplaceness of the dangers of childbirth is reflected in its casual treatment in romantic and other nineteenth-century fiction, where a mother's death in childbirth is often merely a convention for producing an interesting protagonist. Women who become mothers in novels tend to die psychically if they do not die literally; survivors usually subordinate their identities to those of their husbands or of their marriageable daughters. Within the conventions of fiction, childbirth puts an end to the mother's existence as an individual. And we have seen how a poetic myth of language such as Wordworth's in *The Prelude* likewise requires the death or absence of the mother.

This negative reading of childbearing is echoed in more recent psychoanalytic accounts that may be suggestive for the nineteenth century. Writing in 1945, Helene Deutsch describes the persistence of fears of childbirth despite medical advances in the last half of the nineteenth century that reduced childbirth mortality "to a minimum." She argues that the fear of actual death had all along been a screen for an expression of psychic fears, particularly of separation. That the unborn child both has and lacks its own identity complicates a pregnant woman's identity. The boundary between her identity and that of the child within her is quite literally permeable, psychically and physically. Her own sense of identity is quite naturally called into question: before birth there is an other, perhaps sensed as parasitical, resident within the self, while after birth a part of the self is gone. Fear of losing a part of the body's content is part of the separation fear, "but it is only one component, among others, of a general fear of separation from the child conceived as a part of the woman's own ego, a fear that assumes the character of the fear of death." This fear of loss of self, Deutsch argues, is augmented by a feeling of powerlessness in relation to the process that has been set in motion: "Whether she wants to or not, she who has created this new life must obey its power; its rule is expected, yet invisible, implacable. Because of these very qualities it necessarily produces fear."[11]

To say that the mother projects into the object world something that was once internal and that now has its own independent existence, and that that projection may produce fear, is also to describe the structure of the gothic (notice how gothic Deutsch's language is). Childbirth, thus construed, almost too vividly figures the gothic pattern in which unconscious projection takes actual form. What the male romantic mind does figuratively, the womb can do literally, and literal self-duplication invites the fear that what one has created will subsequently overpower and eradicate the self.

Jane Eyre establishes a complex series of connectives between danger or trouble and figures of childbirth or of mother-child relationships, comprising the prophetic dreams of children and also the narrative use of such figuration. This series originates in Jane's recollection of Bessie's folk belief that "to dream of children was a sure sign of trouble, either to one's self or to one's kin" (chap. 21), and both Bessie's experience and

Jane's verify the belief.[12] Initially the dream self is Jane, and the child and the trouble it portends are quite external to her, but in successive dreams the sense of self is divided, confusingly, between child and parent figures, or it shifts altogether from parent to child. Introducing this idea, Jane says that "scarcely a night" for a week had passed "that had not brought with it a dream of an infant: which I sometimes hushed in my arms, sometimes dandled on my knee, sometimes watched playing with daisies on a lawn. . . . It was a wailing child this night, and a laughing one the next: now it nestled close to me, and now it ran from me. . . . It was from companionship with this baby-phantom I had been roused on that moonlight night" (chap. 21) by the "trouble" of Mason's outcry at Bertha's attack. Here Jane is clearly distinct from the child, and the trouble external to her. But it is also following this series of dreams that she is called to the sickbed of Mrs. Reed, who deliriously dreams aloud of Jane as a troublesome child: "I have had more trouble with that child than any one would believe. Such a burden to be left on my hands" (chap. 21). Mrs. Reed wished that Jane would die of the fever at Lowood; she hated Jane as a baby "the first time I set my eyes on it—a sickly, whining, pining thing! It would wail in its cradle all night long." From her dream of self as adult and other as child, Jane now becomes the child and the other in someone else's subjective experience. Splitting the sense of self between child and adult, these dreams question and break down the boundary between subject and object, between self and other.

Following this dream inversion of self and other, childbirth enters the figurative structure of the novel as a way of describing the danger that the self will become something other than itself. Returning from Gateshead, fearfully certain that Rochester will marry Blanche Ingram, Jane describes her feelings thus: "And then I strangled a new-born agony—a deformed thing which I could not persuade myself to own and rear—and ran on" (chap. 22). This newborn agony has a twin sister, another of Jane's metaphoric offspring, who at first does not appear to be either as undesirable or as threatening. The morning after her engagement Jane has a feeling of "almost fear" on hearing herself addressed as Jane Rochester, and the night before the wedding she still senses and fears this radical split between her single and married selves. By the next day, she says, she will be on the road to London, "or rather, not I, but one Jane Rochester, a person whom as yet I knew not," and whose name she refuses to affix to her trunks:

> Mrs. Rochester! She did not exist: she would not be born till to-morrow, some time after eight o'clock A.M.; and I would wait to be assured she had come into the world alive before I assigned to

her all that property. It was enough that in yonder closet, opposite my dressing-table, garments said to be hers had already displaced my black stuff Lowood frock and straw bonnet: for not to me appertained that suit of wedding raiment. (chap. 25)

Like Bessie's prophetic dreams of children, this metaphor of a child prophecies danger. As Mrs. Rochester's clothes displace Jane's, so does Jane fear that her desire to love and be the object of love will entirely displace her equally strong wish to maintain her independence. The birth metaphor employed here should not necessarily suggest displacement, as the exchange of one name for another so neatly does; yet apparently for Brontë the image of childbirth connotes primarily loss of self. Jane Eyre will have to die in giving birth to Mrs. Rochester. Especially because the change of a married woman's name is determined by law, the situation corresponds to the aspect of Cathy's childbirth that is within the law, her production of a patrilineal heir who makes her own existence unnecessary. The "trouble" with which all the novel's dreamt and figurative children are associated may originate in this vision of motherhood in which the mother vanishes as the child is born.

Although in fictive time, Jane's two best-known dream children precede her vision of Mrs. Rochester as an unborn child, she narrates these events in reverse order, so that any reading of her dreams is colored by the passage about Mrs. Rochester. In these dreams, Jane is the surrogate mother of a child she seems not to know, but that they almost directly follow an image of birth suggests that the child does belong to the dreamer, who is unwilling to acknowledge it. In the first dream, the dreamer is traveling an unknown road, in the rain and dark, "burdened with the charge of a little child: a very small creature, too young and feeble to walk, and which shivered in my cold arms and wailed piteously in my ear" (chap. 25). Thinking that Rochester is ahead on the road, the dreamer strains to overtake or call to him, "but my movements were fettered" and Rochester vanishes. In the second dream, developing out of the first, Thornfield is a ruin through which the dreamer wanders. "I thought that of all the stately front nothing remained but a shell-like wall, very high, and very fragile-looking. . . . I still carried the unknown little child: I might not lay it down anywhere, however tired were my arms— however much its weight impeded my progress, I must retain it" (chap. 25). Hearing Rochester galloping away in the distance, she climbs the thin wall, frantic for one last glimpse of him; as the wall gives way beneath her, "the child clung round my neck in terror, and almost strangled me." She reaches the windy summit only to see Rochester vanishing, and dreamer and child fall as the wall crumbles. The dream child clearly represents some aspect of Jane's life, but what that might be is not clear. The child may be "Mrs. Rochester," the new self to which Jane pictures herself fatally giving birth at the moment of her marriage; it may be Jane's love for Rochester; it may also represent Jane's own neglected childhood, as suggested by the close parallel with Mrs. Reed's description of Jane as a burdensome and wailing infant; the "new-born agony" that Jane "strangles" may also be present here.[13] However we interpret the child, what is significant is that subjectivity is divided between the dream self and the dream child. That there are several equally plausible readings suggests that what generates the sense of danger is not the particular part of the self the child represents, but that such a representation or division of the self into parts occurs at all. The dreams give Jane an intimation of what it would be like to become other than herself.

These two dreams in which Jane figures as the unwilling mother surrogate for a difficult child-self are complemented two nights later by a third dream in which the child is Jane and the mother is a benign spirit. The threat presented in the first two dreams seems to have been at once fulfilled and avoided. The self has become a child, yet the wedding has failed to take place, and the dream child now is manifestly not Mrs. Rochester. Unable and unwilling to give birth to that troublesome child, Jane regresses to a version of her own childhood. She dreams that she is back at Gateshead, lying in the red room and watching the same ghostly light that once terrified her, but now the ceiling resolves into clouds and that light into moonlight and then into the visionary mother:

> She broke forth as never moon yet burst from cloud: a hand first penetrated the sable folds and waved them away; then, not a moon, but a white human form shone in the azure, inclining a glorious brow earthward. It gazed and gazed and gazed on me. It spoke to my spirit: immeasurably distant was the tone, yet so near, it whispered in my heart—
> "My daughter, flee temptation!"
> "Mother, I will." (chap. 27)

This dream of being the child of a loving and protective mother makes an ambiguous conclusion to the sequence of dreams and figures of children, since so far no child—real, figurative, or dreamt—has given or received anything but trouble. Although the dreamer rejoices, this dream must logically represent the fulfillment of the threat of the previous dreams, with the suggestion that the dream deceives as it soothes.

These dreams of children represent Jane's unconscious investigation of the state of becoming other than herself or of deferring altogether to projections, and the process of this investigation is repeated in the literalization or coming true of the dreams that characterizes the gothic pattern. All the dreams come true in some way, but from one dream to the next they come true in increasingly literal ways. To be prophetic of trouble, according to Bessie's superstition, the dream need only include the apparently arbitrary symbol of the child, and in the original series of dreams that brought out Jane's recollection of Bessie's story, the child represents danger whether it laughs or cries. But in the pair of dreams preceding the wedding, both child and mother are themselves vividly in trouble, so that the dreamt child is not simply an arbitrary symbol but a metaphor. That the dream child appears to represent some feature of Jane's life (and that Rochester riding away from Jane in the dream prefigures their separation three days later) suggests that the child as metaphor would match only Jane's particular situation.[14] Dreams also literalize each other: just as the second of the pair of dreams extends the action and implications of the first, the third dream, in which Jane explicitly dreams of herself as the child, realizes the unpleasant implication of the first two dreams, that Jane is herself the child as well as the mother. Looking further back, the third dream also appears to spell out and explain the morally ambiguous ghost that confused Jane as a child in the red room. Set in the same scene, the more recent vision soothes where Mr. Reed terrified; but the vision of the shining human form "inclining a glorious brow earthward" and speaking words of comfort literalizes what the child had only imagined to be the ultimate terror. Her fear then was that her grief would "waken a preternatural voice to comfort me, or elicit from the gloom some haloed face, bending over me with strange pity," and that is exactly what happens in the dream. The passage from "theory" to "realization" was what was "terrible" in the red room, and the same turns out to be true here, in the passage from the dream to the next few days' actual experience. Jane finds the dream's figures enacted in the object world, and like other literalizations, these threaten her life.

In the waking scenes of flight and wandering that directly follow, the prophetic dream comes true in the literalization of the dreamt mother: "I have no relative but the universal mother, Nature: I will seek her breast and ask repose" (chap. 28). Mother Nature is a mother only figuratively, yet because Jane names the landscape in this way and insists on and extends the figure, the dreamt mother must be connected to this very tangible one. Naming nature "mother," Jane accepts the tradition that identifies the feminine with the object world, an identification that at this point seems very appealing. The visionary mother encouraged Jane to flee temptation, and when Jane wanders into nature after leaving Rochester, the landscape appears maternal because it appears to help on her flight from temptation. This positive view of nature may represent what Nancy Chodorow would identify as the daughter's continued close connection to her mother long past her entry into androcentric culture, a connection that, however, a daughter who is a figure for the novelist, whose main allegiance is to the father's symbol making, finds very difficult to sustain and finally rejects.[15]

As on every other occasion, the coming true of a dream, the discovery in the object world of what was at one time purely subjective, is actually more frightening than the subjective experience itself, even though Jane's tone at first directs us to find it consoling. Mother Nature betrays her daughter, but to be her daughter is dangerous enough, and betrayal is inherent in the relation. In the dream, Jane shifts her identity from adult to child without making the concomitant change from self to other that previous dreams intimated, and being this somewhat regressive child-self is clearly preferable to the loss of self that giving birth to Mrs. Rochester would have represented. It appears now that the transformation of self into other was only deferred: simultaneous with the literalization of her dream, Jane as a child of Mother Nature finds herself in the position of being identified with the literal, first deceived into seeking this identification, then almost forced into it. This experience's close connection with all of the dreams, where Jane has been a mother as well as a child, also suggests an identity between Jane and the mother figure herself, as a continuation of that perpetual shifting between subject and object that the dreams introduce. Either way, being like nature or being nature's child, the danger is the same identification with the literal that jeopardizes both Jane's sense of self and her life.

Just before making this reference to Mother Nature, Jane describes her surroundings. Whitcross, where she alights after her destinationless coach ride away from Thornfield, appropriately signals her entry into a land of literalized dreams, because the name's meaning is as close to literal as any naming can be. Whitcross is not the name of a town but of a whitewashed stone pillar with four arms: a white cross. Like Dorothy Wordsworth's self-naming refuges, Whitcross names only itself. Yet whereas Dorothy Wordsworth's resistance to the symbolic order makes such a discovery fortuitous, Jane's allegiance to that order makes this discovery signal disaster. Jane has neither money, the symbol of symbols, nor any tie to human society, and lacking either a speakable past or an imaginable future, she has, like the self-referential Whitcross, no significance.[16] "Strangers would wonder what I am doing, lingering here at the sign-post, evidently objectless and lost. I might be questioned: I could give no answer but what would sound incredible and excite suspicion" (chap. 28). That she describes her situation in terms of a lack of language explicitly names Jane's experience as literal. To be "objectless" is to cease being a subject. That this passage concerning Jane's reduction to her physical being concludes with the reminder that matter is traditionally female deepens the danger of her position and defines that danger as a particularly feminine one.

Setting out from Whitcross, Jane arrives at a protective place in the heath, a soft hollow sheltered by high banks. As night very gently falls, "Nature seemed to me benign and good; I thought she loved me, outcast as I was; and I, who from man could anticipate only mistrust, rejection, insult, clung to her with filial fondness. To-night, at least, I would be her guest—as I was her child: my mother would lodge me without money and without price" (chap. 28). The curious phrasing of the last sentence here suggests Jane's insight that she is not truly nature's child, but only nature's nonpaying guest. That the passage proposes various images for nature (mother, innkeeper) creates a consciousness of figuration that serves to defend against, while the passage otherwise appears to endorse, the possibility that Jane is nature's child. Even more striking is the doubt implicit in "Nature seemed to me benign and good; I thought she loved me." This doubt is confirmed the next morning when the evening's relative comfort gives way to pressing exhaustion and hunger. Jane no longer refers to the landscape as a mother, the mother having abandoned the child who may have been deluded in imagining herself protected. In becoming actual, what seemed benign as a vision becomes neglectful, even malignant.

Jane discovers here on the moor, as does the dying Cathy in *Wuthering Heights*, that to become part of nature is to die. The solace nature offers is not just an illusion concealing death; that solace is itself death:

> What a still, hot, perfect day! What a golden desert this spreading moor! Everywhere sunshine. I wished I could live in it and on it. I saw a lizard run over the crag; I saw a bee busy among the sweet bilberries. I would fain at the moment have become bee or lizard, that I might have found fitting nutriment, permanent shelter here. . . . Hopeless of the future, I wished but this—that my Maker had that night thought good to require my soul of me while I slept; and that this weary frame, absolved by death from further conflict with fate, had now but to decay quietly, and mingle in peace with the soil of this wilderness. (chap. 28)

Jane's wish to "live in it and on it" echoes Cathy's dying wish to be "really with it, and in it" (chap. 15). That Cathy's "it" refers at once to nature and to a transcendent realm beyond death suggests that Jane's "it," which seems to refer here only to the moor, will soon refer also to the world into which Cathy dies. That there is at this point almost no difference between Mother Nature and her daughter almost completes the dreams' efforts to blur the distinctions between mother and child, subject and object. In the context of the dreams, to become the child is to become an object, while to become part of this mother would also be to turn into an object.

Jane resists the fate that Cathy embraces because she retains her consciousness of difference: she knows that to identify and mingle with nature necessitates dying. Breaking into the middle of this passage, interrupting that tempting continuity, is Jane's recollection that she is not a child of nature but "a human being, and had a human being's wants: I must not linger where there was nothing to supply them." The true child of Mother Nature, one that finds "permanent shelter" in her breast, is the lizard or the bee, never the living woman. Jane's wish that she had died in the night and the temptation as she walks to stop and "submit resistlessly to the apathy that clogged heart and limb" represent nature's residual pressure and conflict with "life, . . . with all its requirements, and pains, and responsibilities," which prevents Jane from yielding. Nature is now a dangerous tempter, in contrast to that mother within Jane's mind who told Jane to "flee temptation." She returns to her starting point at Whitcross, to begin again; soon she is again on the verge of giving in to nature's temptation when she is recalled to consciousness by the chime of a church bell and then by the sight of a village and cultivated fields that, by representing human life, help her resist the literality of the wild moor.

If nature is no longer the mother and Jane no longer the child, she can resist nature's appeal that she become part of the literal. Toward the end of the second day of her wanderings, Jane, having undergone extreme humiliation and physical suffering, finds that she has "once more drawn near the tract of moorland" (chap. 28). In the same location, she seeks a version of the first evening's repose, but here the consciousness of her difference sustains her in her disillusionment with the dream vision's promises. She calls on Providence to guide her, not on Mother Nature to soothe her. Recognizing that she may die, she prefers a death in nature to "a workhouse coffin . . . in a pauper's grave." But in place of her earlier sympathetic identification with nature and her subsequent wish to "mingle in peace with the soil of this wilderness," Jane now images a death in nature as a violent separation from the soil: crows and ravens will pick the flesh from her bones. As if in response to her state of mind, nature now repudiates Jane. Having passed beyond

> a few fields, almost as wild and unproductive as the heath from which they were scarcely reclaimed, . . . it remained now only to find a hollow where I could lie down, and feel at least hidden, if not secure: but all the surface of the waste looked level. It showed no variation but of tint; green, where rush and moss overgrew the marshes; black, where the dry soil bore only heath. Dark as it was getting, I could still see these changes; though but as mere alternations of light and shade: for colour had faded with the daylight. (chap. 28)

Difference is necessary for human signification, and this wild, unvarying sterility represents nature's closure to such meaning. Nature is more than fatal here; it is unwilling to help Jane in any project, even her death. In the earlier "golden desert" vision of this same fatal moorland, in which Jane briefly envies the bee and the lizard, it turns out that nature's vitality was an illusion produced by light, hiding the moor's true barrenness. This last picture of the moorland completes the literalization of the original maternal vision, the metaphor still adhering in "the dry soil bore only heath." This landscape's life-threatening sameness makes it the extreme form of all the novel's literalizations, wherever figural structure gives way to actuality. All literalizations here tend toward death.[17]

Jane survives this confrontation with the fatally literal by means of various kinds of figuration that protect her from psychic and physical death. Directly after her vision of the undifferentiated landscape, the plot offers her a chance of life, a turn of events that appears to be not only paralleled but actually generated by a rhetorical turn from almost literal naming to dense figuration: "My eye still roved over the sullen swell, and along the moor edge, vanishing amidst the wild scenery; when at one dim point, far in among the marshes and ridges, a light sprang up" (chap. 28). This light returns the reader to the complex world of multiple signification that imparts textual life where literal meaning denies it. Cautious now of illusions, Jane at first thinks it is an "*ignis fatuus*"; but what is important about her effort to interpret this sight is that she speculates at such length. If it is not an illusion, it may be a bonfire. When it remains steady, she decides it is a candle in a window, but she subjects even that interpretation to further interpretation. Like Emily Brontë's Lockwood, who cures his flu by substituting tame metaphors for wild moors, Jane rescues herself by making nature into figures. The candle next becomes "my star" of "hope"; finally it repeats an image from one of Jane's visionary paintings, subordinating the actual landscape to a wholly different and entirely internal realm of psychic signification. It is as if, appropriately, Jane were saved by her ability to create figures. Painting herself back into life, she reverses the process of literalization.

From the vantage point of this reading of *Jane Eyre*, I wish to return briefly to *Wuthering Heights* to clarify, by contrasting the two novels, my reading of their structures of literalization and figuration and of their thematics of childbirth. Much as Jane's dreams of herself as child come true in the form of her subjection to nature, Cathy dreams herself as a child, and that dream comes true in the form of the child to which she regresses and later in the form of the ghostly child-self who appears to Lockwood.[18] But Cathy seeks what Jane actively resists: a merging with nature that is also a return to childhood and that is, incidentally for Cathy but crucially for Jane, also death. Jane reverses the process of literalization embodied in the coming true of her dreams, and she resists altogether the literalization embodied in childbirth, while Cathy embraces both.

Jane's almost becoming part of the fatally literal in nature began with her unwillingness to give birth to Mrs. Rochester. When Jane Eyre contemplates giving metaphorical birth to Mrs. Rochester, she justifiably fears that the law will cause the "child" to replace and supersede the "mother." This is exactly what happens to Cathy, when her reproduction of an heir for the Lintons makes her own identity unnecessary within the law. Because childbirth is defined in *Jane Eyre* as entirely within the law, its only meaning is the mother's self-replacement and death. The novel does not acknowledge the extralegal definition of motherhood that in *Wuthering Heights* makes Cathy's reproduction of her child-self a happy restoration. For Cathy, in giving birth, also remains partly outside the law, as we have seen, reproducing the lawless childhood self that she yearns to become again. Similarly, Jane temporarily regresses from being a mother figure to being a child, though for her this occurs through refusing to "give birth" in a way that would perpetuate and subordinate her to the law. Like Cathy (and even more explicitly), Jane becomes a child of Mother Nature; but again because it has no place for the outlaw, the novel presents this return to childhood and the death it would bring with it in nothing like the positive terms of *Wuthering Heights*. The stories of the two heroines, then, because they make different assumptions about the structure and the meaning of childbirth as a form of literalization, conclude in different consequences: while Cathy's production of a child fulfills her desire to be permanently a child, Jane's failure to give birth to her figurative child allows her to survive and grow. In both cases, the potential of motherhood is a transformation of the self or subjectivity into a literal object, a transformation that Cathy desires and Jane at first courts but finally refuses. While Jane comes to understand the danger that to become the child of her dreams would be to merge with objective nature and to transfer the self from subject to object, the view of the same transference expressed by Cathy's situation is almost wholly positive.

The threat that Charlotte Brontë has Mother Nature pose to Jane's identity and existence expresses her sense of the danger to all women of the identification of nature as mother. The temptation to become part of a feminized nature, to become a feminized object like nature, amounts in Brontë's view to a temptation to die, for it would be to join the dead mother, to accept exclusion from what her culture defines as human. By a curiously defensive logic, because Mother Nature is already dead, she might kill the writer who is a daughter, so the writer must kill Mother Nature first. Both Emily and Charlotte Brontë see that a woman, a mother, has been buried in the landscape of romanticism, and both know they have been complicitous in placing her there yet again. In order to assert her allegiance to her culture's dominant myth of language, Charlotte Brontë dramatizes the near-murder of a woman at the hand of Mother Nature. Like Lockwood's snowstorm, this threat justifies Jane's subsequent betrayal of nature. The writer must betray the mother. Emily Brontë may protest this murder by bringing the mother to life again, but she does so only briefly, and only from the perspective of a mad and dying mother. Although the first Cathy in *Wuthering Heights* would view Jane's behavior as a betrayal of Mother Nature, Emily Brontë's view is not wholly contained in the story of the first Cathy. Just as Jane, having almost identified herself with nature's otherness, leaves it by multiplying significations and by thinking of her own figurative art, *Wuthering Heights* continues past Cathy's death to offer a daughter's history more in keeping with the rules of law. Like the story of the second Cathy in relation to the first, Charlotte Brontë offers a correction of a prior story, a story in which the attractions of the mother's place were even more adventurously explored.

5

Bearing Demons:
Frankenstein's Circumvention
of the Maternal

arried to one romantic poet and living near another, Mary
Shelley at the time she was writing *Frankenstein* experienced
with great intensity the self-contradictory demand that
daughters embody both the mother whose death makes language possible by making it necessary and the figurative substitutes for
that mother who constitute the prototype of the signifying chain. At the
same time, as a mother herself, she experienced with far greater intensity
than did any of the authors considered so far a proto-Victorian ideology
of motherhood, as Mary Poovey has shown.[1] This experience leads
Shelley both to figure her writing as mothering and to bear or transmit
the words of her husband.[2] Thus Shelley not only practices the daughter's
obligatory and voluntary identification with the literal, as do Dorothy
Wordsworth and Charlotte and Emily Brontë, but she also shares with
George Eliot and Elizabeth Gaskell (and again with Charlotte Brontë)
their concern with writing as literalization, as a form of mothering. It is to
Shelley's handling of these contradictory demands, and to her criticism of
their effect on women's writing, that my reading of *Frankenstein* will
turn.

Frankenstein portrays the situation of women obliged to play the role
of the literal in a culture that devalues it. In this sense, the novel is
simultaneously about the death and obviation of the mother and about
the son's quest for a substitute object of desire. The novel criticizes the
self-contradictory male requirement that that substitute at once embody
and not embody (because all embodiment is a reminder of the mother's
powerful and forbidden body) the object of desire. The horror of the
demon that Frankenstein creates is that it is the literalization of its

creator's desire for an object, a desire that never really seeks its own fulfillment.

Many readers of *Frankenstein* have noted both that the demon's creation amounts to an elaborate circumvention of normal heterosexual procreation—Frankenstein does by himself with great difficulty what a heterosexual couple can do quite easily—and that each actual mother dies very rapidly upon being introduced as a character in the novel.[3] Frankenstein's own history is full of the deaths of mothers. His mother was discovered, as a poverty-stricken orphan, by Frankenstein's father. Frankenstein's adoptive sister and later fiancée, Elizabeth, was likewise discovered as an orphan, in poverty, by Frankenstein's parents.[4] Elizabeth catches scarlet fever, and her adoptive mother, nursing her, catches it herself and dies of it. On her deathbed, the mother hopes for the marriage of Elizabeth and Frankenstein and tells Elizabeth, "You must supply my place to my younger children" (chap. 3). Like Shelley herself, Elizabeth is the death of her mother and becomes a substitute for her. Justine, a young girl taken in by the Frankenstein family as a beloved servant, is said to cause the death of her mother; and Justine herself, acting as foster mother to Frankenstein's little brother, William, is executed for his murder. There are many mothers in the Frankenstein circle, and all die notable deaths.

The significance of the apparently necessary destruction of the mother first emerges in Frankenstein's account of his preparations for creating the demon, and it is confirmed soon after the demon comes to life. Of his early passion for science, Frankenstein says, "I was . . . deeply smitten with the thirst for knowledge" (chap. 2). Shelley confirms the oedipal suggestion here when she writes that it is despite his father's prohibition that the young boy devours the archaic books on natural philosophy that first raise his ambitions to discover the secret of life. His mother dies just as Frankenstein is preparing to go to the University of Ingolstadt, and if his postponed trip there is thus motivated by her death, what he finds at the university becomes a substitute for her: modern scientists, he is told, "penetrate into the recesses of nature and show how she works in her hiding-places" (chap. 3). Frankenstein's double, Walton, the polar explorer who rescues him and records his story, likewise searches for what sound like sexual secrets, also in violation of a paternal prohibition. Seeking to "satiate [his] ardent curiosity," Walton hopes to find the "wondrous power which attracts the needle" (letter 1). Frankenstein, having become "capable of bestowing animation upon lifeless matter," feels that to arrive "at once at the summit of my desires was the most gratifying consummation of my toils." And his work to create the demon adds to this sense of an oedipal violation of Mother Nature: dabbling "among the unhallowed damps of the grave," he "disturbed, with profane fingers, the tremendous secrets of the human frame" (chap. 4). This violation is necrophiliac. The mother he rapes is dead; his researches into her secrets, to usurp her powers, require that she be dead.[5]

Frankenstein describes his violation of nature in other ways that recall what William Wordsworth's poetry reveals when read in conjunction with Dorothy Wordsworth's journals. Of the period during which he is working on the demon, Frankenstein writes,

> The summer months passed while I was thus engaged, heart and soul, in one pursuit. It was a most beautiful season; never did the fields bestow a more plentiful harvest or the vines yield a more luxuriant vintage, but my eyes were insensible to the charms of nature. . . . Winter, spring, and summer passed away during my labours; but I did not watch the blossom or the expanding leaves— sights which before always yielded me supreme delight—so deeply was I engrossed in my occupation. (chap. 4)

Ignoring the bounteous offering nature makes of itself and substituting for it his own construction of life, what we, following Thomas Weiskel, might call his own reading of nature, Frankenstein here resembles William Wordsworth, reluctantly and ambivalently allowing himself to read nature, to impose on nature apocalyptic patterns of meaning that destroy it. Dorothy Wordsworth herself makes an appearance in the text of *Frankenstein*, if indirectly, and her presence encodes a shared women's critique of the romantic reading of nature. Much later in the novel, Frankenstein compares his friend Clerval to the former self William Wordsworth depicts in "Tintern Abbey," a self that he has outgrown but that his sister remains. Shelley quotes (with one major alteration) the lines beginning, "The sounding cataract / Haunted him like a passion" and ending with the assertion that the colors and forms of natural objects (rock, mountain, etc.) were

> a feeling, and a love,
> That had no need of a remoter charm,
> By thought supplied, or any interest
> Unborrow'd from the eye.[6]

If Clerval is like Dorothy, then Frankenstein is like William, regrettably destroying nature by imposing his reading on it.

When, assembled from the corpse of nature, the demon has been brought to life and Frankenstein has recognized—oddly only now that it is alive—how hideous it is, Frankenstein falls into an exhausted sleep and dreams the following dream:

> I thought I saw Elizabeth, in the bloom of health, walking in the streets of Ingolstadt. Delighted and surprised, I embraced her, but as I imprinted the first kiss on her lips, they became livid with the hue of death; her features appeared to change, and I thought that I held the corpse of my dead mother in my arms; a shroud enveloped her form, and I saw the grave-worms crawling in the folds of the flannel. I started from my sleep with horror. (chap. 5)

He wakes to see the demon looking at him, hideous, but clearly loving. The dream suggests that to bring the demon to life is equivalent to killing Elizabeth, and that Elizabeth dead is equivalent to his mother dead. Elizabeth may have been the death of the mother, but now that she has replaced her, she too is vulnerable to whatever destroys mothers.[7] And, indeed, the dream is prophetic: the demon will much later kill Elizabeth, just as the demon's creation has required both the death of Franken-stein's own mother and the death and violation of Mother Nature. To bring a composite corpse to life is to circumvent the normal channels of procreation; the demon's "birth" violates the normal relations of family, especially the normal sexual relation of husband and wife. Victor has gone to great lengths to produce a child without Elizabeth's assistance, and in the dream's language, to circumvent her, to make her unnecessary, is to kill her, and to kill mothers altogether.

Frankenstein's creation, then, depends on and then perpetuates the death of the mother and of motherhood. The demon's final, and greatest, crime is in fact its murder of Elizabeth, which is, however, only the logical extension of its existence as the reification of Frankenstein's desire to escape the mother. The demon is, to borrow a phrase from Shelley's *Alastor*, "the spirit of" Frankenstein's "solitude." Its greatest complaint to Frankenstein is of its own solitude, its isolation from humanity, and it promises that if Frankenstein will make it a mate, "one as hideous as myself. . . . I shall become a thing of whose existence everyone will be ignorant" (chap. 17). That is, no longer solitary, the demon will virtually cease to exist, for its existence is synonymous with its solitude. But, on the grounds that "a race of devils would be propagated upon the earth," Frankenstein destroys the female demon he is in the process of creating, thus destroying yet another potential mother, and the demon promises,

"I shall be with you on your wedding-night" (chap. 20). If the demon is the form taken by Frankenstein's flight from the mother, then it is impossible that the demon should itself find an embodied substitute for the mother, and it will prevent Frankenstein from finding one too.

The demon's promise to be present at the wedding night suggests that there is something monstrous about Frankenstein's sexuality. A solipsist's sexuality is monstrous because his desire is for his own envisionings rather than for somebody else, some other body. The demon appears where Frankenstein's wife should be, and its murder of her suggests not so much revenge as jealousy. The demon's murder of that last remaining potential mother makes explicit the sequel to the obviation of the mother, the male quest for substitutes for the mother, the quest that is never intended to be fulfilled. Elizabeth suggests in a letter to Frankenstein that his reluctance to marry may stem from his love for someone else, someone met, perhaps, in his travels or during his long stay in Ingolstadt. "Do you not love another?" she asks (chap. 22). This is in fact the case, for the demon, the creation of Frankenstein's imagination, resembles in many ways the romantic object of desire, the beloved invented to replace, in a less threatening form, the powerful mother who must be killed.[8] This imagined being would be an image of the self, because it is for the sake of the ego that the mother is rejected in the first place. Created right after the death of the mother to be, as Victor says, "a being like myself" (chap. 4), the demon may be Adam, created in God's image. Indeed, this is what the demon thinks when it tells Frankenstein, "I ought to be thy Adam, but I am rather the fallen angel" (chap. 10). But it is also possible, as Gilbert and Gubar suggest, that the demon is Eve, created from Adam's imagination.[9]

When the demon takes shelter in the French cottager's shed, it looks, repeating Milton's Eve's first act upon coming to life, into the mirror of a "clear pool" and is terrified at its own reflection: "I started back" (chap. 12). Here is the relevant passage from Milton, from Eve's narration in book 4 of her memory of the first moments of her creation.[10] Hearing the "murmuring sound / Of waters issu'd from a Cave and spread / Into a liquid Plain," Eve looks

> into the clear
> Smooth Lake, that to me seem'd another Sky.
> As I bent down to look, just opposite,
> A Shape within the wat'ry gleam appear'd
> Bending to look on me, I started back,
> It started back, but pleas'd I soon return'd . . .
> (4.453–63)

But the disembodied voice instructs her, "What there thou seest fair Creature is thyself" (468), and tells her to follow and learn to prefer him "whose image thou art" (471–72). Christine Froula argues that the fiction of Eve's creation by a paternal God out of the flesh of Adam values the maternal and appropriates it for the aggrandisement of masculine creativity.[11] Frankenstein revises this paradigm for artistic creation: he does not so much appropriate the maternal as bypass it, to demonstrate the unnecessariness of natural motherhood and, indeed, of women. Froula points out that in this "scene of canonical instruction," Eve is required to turn away from herself to embrace her new identity, not as a self, but as the image of someone else.[12] Created to the specifications of Adam's desire, we later learn—"Thy likeness, thy fit help, thy other self, / Thy wish, exactly to thy heart's desire" (8. 450–51)—Eve is, like Frankenstein's demon, the product of imaginative desire. Milton appropriates the maternal by excluding any actual mother from the scene of creation. Eve is the form that Adam's desire takes once actual motherhood has been eliminated; and in much the same way, the demon is the form taken by Frankenstein's desire once his mother and Elizabeth as mother have been circumvented. These new creations in the image of the self are substitutes for the powerful creating mother and place creation under the control of the son.

That the demon is, like Eve, the creation of a son's imaginative desire is confirmed by another allusion both closer to Shelley and closer in the text to Elizabeth's question, "Do you not love another?" Mary Poovey has argued that the novel criticizes romantic egotism, specifically, Percy Shelley's violation of the social conventions that bind humans together in families and societies. As the object of desire of an imaginative overreacher very like Percy Shelley himself, the demon substitutes for the fruitful interchange of family life the fruitlessness of self love, for what Frankenstein loves is an image of himself. The novel was written when Percy Shelley had completed, of all his major works besides *Queen Mab*, only *Alastor*, the archetypal poem of the doomed romantic quest, and it is to this poem that Mary Shelley alludes.[13] Just before Frankenstein receives Elizabeth's letter, just after being acquitted of the murder of his friend Clerval, Frankenstein tells us, "I saw around me nothing but a dense and frightful darkness, penetrated by no light but the glimmer of two eyes that glared upon me" (chap. 21). This is a direct allusion to a passage in *Alastor* in which the hero, who has quested in vain after an ideal female image of his own creation, sees

two eyes,
Two starry eyes, hung in the gloom of thought,

And seemed with their serene and azure smiles
To beckon him.

(489–92)

In *Alastor*, these eyes belong to the phantom maiden, the "fleeting shade" whom the hero pursues to his death, a beloved who is constructed out of the poet's own visionary narcissism. The girl he dreams and pursues has a voice "like the voice of his own soul / Heard in the calm of thought" (153–54), and like him, she is "Herself a poet" (161). In the novel, the starry eyes become glimmering, glaring eyes, alternately the eyes of the dead Clerval and the "watery, clouded eyes of the monster, as I first saw them in my chamber at Ingolstadt" (chap. 21). This conflation of the eyes of the poet's beloved with the eyes of the demon suggests, even more surely than the allusion to Eve, that the demon is the form, not only of Frankenstein's solipsism, of his need to obviate the mother, but also of the narcissism that constitutes the safety of the ego for whose sake the mother is denied. The monster is still the object of Frankenstein's desire when Elizabeth writes to him, just as its creation was the object of his initial quest.[14] It is this monster, the monster of narcissism, that intervenes on the wedding night, substituting Frankenstein's desire for his own imagining for the consummation of his marriage, just as the visionary maiden in *Alastor* takes the place both of the dead Mother Nature of the poet's prologue and of the real maiden the hero meets, attracts, and rejects in the course of his quest.

That the demon is a revision of Eve, of emanations, and of the object of romantic desire, is confirmed by its female attributes. Its very bodiliness, its identification with matter, associates it with traditional concepts of femaleness. Further, the impossibility of Frankenstein giving it a female demon, an object of its own desire, aligns the demon with women, who are forbidden to have their own desires. But if the demon is really a feminine object of desire, why is it a he? I would suggest that this constitutes part of Shelley's exposure of the male romantic economy that would substitute for real and therefore powerful female others a being imagined on the model of the male poet's own self. By making the demon masculine, Shelley suggests that romantic desire seeks to do away, not only with the mother, but also with all females so as to live finally in a world of mirrors that reflect a comforting illusion of the male self's independent wholeness. It is worth noting that just as Frankenstein's desire is for a male demon, Walton too yearns, not for a bride, but for "the company of a man who could sympathize with me, whose eyes would reply to mine" (letter 2).[15]

It may seem peculiar to describe the demon as the object of Frankenstein's romantic desire, since he spends most of the novel suffering from the demon's crimes. Yet in addition to the allusions to Eve and the "fleeting shade" in *Alastor* that suggest this, it is clear that while Frankenstein is in the process of creating the demon, he loves it and desires it; the knowledge that makes possible its creation is the "consummation" of his "toils." It is only when the demon becomes animated that Frankenstein abruptly discovers his loathing for his creation. Even though the demon looks at its creator with what appears to be love, Frankenstein's response to it is unequivocal loathing. Why had he never noticed before the hideousness of its shape and features? No adequate account is given, nor could be, for as we shall see, this is what most mystifies and horrifies Shelley about her own situation. Frankenstein confesses, "I had desired it with an ardour that far exceeded moderation; but now that I had finished, the beauty of the dream vanished, and breathless horror and disgust filled my heart" (chap. 5). The romantic quest is always doomed, for it secretly resists its own fulfillment: although the hero of *Alastor* quests for his dream maiden and dies of not finding her, his encounter with the Indian maid makes it clear that embodiment is itself an obstacle to desire, or more precisely, its termination. Frankenstein's desire for his creation lasts only so long as that creation remains uncreated, the substitution for the too-powerful mother of a figure issuing from his imagination and therefore under his control.

To return to the terms with which we began in chapter 1, we might say that the predicament of Frankenstein, as of the hero of *Alastor*, is that of the son in Lacan's revision of the Freudian oedipal crisis. In flight from the body of the mother forbidden by the father, a maternal body that he sees as dead in his urgency to escape it and to enter a paternal order constituted of its distance from the mother, the son seeks figurations that will at once make restitution for the mother and confirm her death and absence by substituting for her figures that are under his control. Fundamentally, the son cannot wish for these figurative substitutes to be embodied, for any *body* is too reminiscent of the mother and is no longer under the son's control, as the demon's excessive strength demonstrates; the value of these figurations is that they remain figurations. In just this way, romantic desire does not desire to be fulfilled, and yet, because it seems both to itself and to others to want to be embodied, the romantic quester as son is often confronted with a body he seems to want but does not.[16] Thus Frankenstein thinks he wants to create the demon, but when he has succeeded, he discovers that what he really enjoyed was the process leading up to the creation, the seemingly endless chain of signifiers that constitute his true, if unrecognized, desire.

Looking at *Alastor* through *Frankenstein*'s reading of it, then, we see that the novel is the story of a hypothetical case: what if the hero of *Alastor* actually got what he thinks he wants? What if desire were embodied, contrary to the poet's deepest wishes? That Shelley writes such a case suggests that this was her own predicament. In real life, Percy Shelley pursued her as the poet and hero of *Alastor* pursue ghosts and as Frankenstein pursues the secrets of the grave. That he courted the adolescent Mary Godwin at the grave of her mother, whose writing he admired, already suggests that the daughter was for him a figure for the safely dead mother, a younger and less powerfully creative version of her. Yet when he got this substitute, he began to tire of her, as he makes quite explicit in *Epipsychidion*, where he is not embarrassed to describe his life in terms of an interminable quest for an imaginary woman. Mary starts out in that poem as one "who seemed / As like the glorious shape which I had dreamed" (277–78) but soon becomes "that Moon" with "pale and waning lips" (309). The poet does not seem to notice that each time an embodiment of the ideal turns out to be unsatisfactory, it is not because she is the wrong woman, but because the very fact of embodiment inevitably spoils the vision. Emily, the final term in the poem's sequence of women, remains ideal only because she has not yet been possessed, and indeed at the end of the poem, the poet disintegrates and disembodies her, perhaps to save himself from yet one more disappointment. Shelley was for herself never anything but embodied, but for Percy Shelley it seems to have been a grave disappointment to discover her substantiality, and therefore her inadequacy for fulfilling his visionary requirements. *Frankenstein* is the story of what it feels like to be the undesired embodiment of romantic imaginative desire. The demon, rejected merely for being a body, suffers in something of the way that Shelley must have felt herself to suffer under the conflicting demands of romantic desire: on the one hand, that she must embody the goal of Percy's quest, and on the other, his rejection of that embodiment.

Later in the novel, when the demon describes to Frankenstein its discovery and reading of the "journal of the four months that preceded my creation," the discrepancy between Percy's conflicting demands is brought to the fore. The demon notes that the journal records "the whole detail of that series of disgusting circumstances" that resulted in "my accursed origin," and that "the minutest description of my odious and loathsome person is given, in language which painted your own horrors and rendered mine indelible" (chap. 15). This summary suggests that while Frankenstein was writing the journal during the period leading up to the demon's vivification, he was fully aware of his creature's hideousness. Yet Frankenstein, in his own account of the same period, specifically says that it was only when "I had finished, the beauty of the dream vanished, and breathless horror and disgust filled my heart" (chap. 5). If Frankenstein is right about his feelings here, why should his journal be full of "language which painted [his] horrors"? Or, if the account in the journal is correct, if Frankenstein was aware from the start of his creature's "odious and loathsome person," why does he tell Walton that the demon appeared hideous to him only upon its awakening? If the text of this journal is, like *Alastor*, the record of a romantic quest for an object of desire, then the novel is presenting us with two conflicting readings of the poem—Frankenstein's or Percy's and the demon's or Shelley's—confirming our sense that Shelley reading *Alastor* finds in it the story of Percy's failure to find in her the object of his desire, or the story of his desire not to find the object of his desire, not to find that she is the object.

A famous anecdote about the Shelleys from a few days after the beginning of the ghost story contest in which *Frankenstein* originated lends support to this impression of Shelley's experience. Byron was reciting some lines from Coleridge's *Christabel* about Geraldine, who is, like the demon, a composite body, half young and beautiful, half (in the version Byron recited) "hideous, deformed, and pale of hue." Percy, "suddenly shrieking and putting his hands to his head, ran out of the room with a candle." Brought to his senses, he told Byron and Polidori that "he was looking at Mrs. Shelley" while Byron was repeating Coleridge's lines, "and suddenly thought of a woman he had heard of who had eyes instead of nipples."[17] If disembodied eyes are, in *Alastor*, what are so alluring to the hero about his beloved, eyes in place of nipples may have been Percy's hallucination of the horror of having those ideal eyes reembodied in the form of his real lover. This is an embodiment that furthermore calls attention to its failure to be sufficiently different from the mother, whose nipples are for the baby so important a feature. An actual woman, who is herself a mother, does not fit the ideal of disembodied femininity, and the vision of combining real and ideal is a monster. Mary's sense of herself viewed as a collection of incongruent body parts—breasts terminating in eyes—might have found expression in the demon, whose undesirable corporeality is expressed as its being composed likewise of ill-fitting parts. *Paradise Lost, Alastor*, and other texts in this tradition compel women readers to wish to embody, as Eve does, imaginary ideals, to be glad of this role in masculine life; and yet at the same time, they warn women readers that they will suffer for such embodiment.

It requires only a transposing of terms to suggest the relevance of this reading of *Frankenstein* to the myth of language we traced in chapter 1 in its form as the romantic quest. The demon is about the ambivalent response of a woman reader to some of our culture's most compelling statements of woman's place in the myth. That the mother must vanish and be replaced by never quite embodied figures for her is equivalent to the vanishing of the referent (along with that time with the mother when the referent had not vanished) to be replaced by language as figuration that never quite touches its objects. Women's role is to be that silent or lost referent, the literal whose absence makes figuration possible. To be also the figurative substitute for that lost referent is, Shelley shows, impossible, for women are constantly reminded that they are the mother's (loathed, loved) body, and in any case, "being" is incompatible with being a figure. The literal provokes horror in the male poet, or scientist, even while he demands that women literalize his vision.

That Shelley knew she was writing a criticism, not only of women's self-contradictory role in androcentric ontology, but also of the gendered myth of language that is part of that ontology, is suggested by the appearance of a series of images of writing at the very end of the novel. Once again, the demon is the object of Frankenstein's quest, pursued now in hate rather than in love. Frankenstein is preternaturally motivated in his quest by an energy of desire that recalls his passion when first creating the demon, and that his present quest depends on the killing of animals recalls his first quest's dependence on dead bodies. Frankenstein believes that "a spirit of good" follows and directs his steps: "Sometimes, when nature, overcome by hunger, sank under the exhaustion, a repast was prepared for me in the desert that restored and inspirited me. . . . I will not doubt that it was set there by the spirits that I had invoked to aid me" (chap. 24). He says this, however, directly after pointing out that the demon sometimes helped him. Fearing "that if I lost all trace of him I should despair and die, [he] left some mark to guide me," and Frankenstein also notes that the demon would frequently leave "marks in writing on the barks of the trees or cut in stone that guided me and instigated my fury." One of these messages includes the information, "You will find near this place, if you follow not too tardily, a dead hare; eat and be refreshed." Frankenstein, it would seem, deliberately misinterprets the demon's guidance and provisions for him as belonging instead to a spirit of good: his interpretation of the demon's marks and words is so figurative as to be opposite to what they really say. The demon, all body, writes appropriately on the body of nature messages that refer, if to objects at a distance, at least not a very great distance ("you will find near this place . . . "). Frankenstein, however, reads as figuratively as possible, putting as great a distance as possible between what he actually reads and what he interprets. His reading furthermore puts a distance between himself and the object of his quest, which he still cannot desire to attain; figurative reading would extend indefinitely the pleasure of the quest itself by forever putting off the moment of capture. Just at the moment when Frankenstein thinks he is about to reach the demon, the demon is transformed from a "mark," as if a mark on a page, into a "form," and Frankenstein seeks to reverse this transformation. One of Frankenstein's sled dogs has died of exhaustion, delaying him; "suddenly my eye caught a dark speck upon the dusky plain"; he utters "a wild cry of ecstasy" upon "distinguish[ing] a sledge and the distorted proportions of a well-known form within" (chap. 24). Frankenstein's response, however, is to take an hour's rest: his real aim, which he does not admit, is to keep the demon at the distance where he remains a "dark speck," a mark on the white page of the snow, his signification forever deferred.[18]

At the same time that *Frankenstein* is about a woman writer's response to the ambiguous imperative her culture imposes upon her, it is also possible that the novel concerns a woman writer's anxieties about bearing children, about generating bodies that, as we have seen with reference to *Jane Eyre* and *Wuthering Heights*, would have the power to displace or kill the parent. Ellen Moers first opened up a feminist line of inquiry into the novel by suggesting that it is a "birth myth," that the horror of the demon is Shelley's horror, not only at her own depressing experience of childbirth, but also at her knowledge of the disastrous consequences of giving birth (or of pregnancy itself) for many women in her vicinity.[19] The list is by now familiar to Shelley's readers. First, Mary Wollstonecraft died eleven days after she gave birth to Mary; then, during the time of the writing of the novel, Fanny Imlay, Mary's half-sister, drowned herself in October 1816 when she learned that she was her mother's illegitimate child by Gilbert Imlay; Harriet Shelley was pregnant by another man when she drowned herself in the Serpentine in December 1816; and Claire Clairmont, the daughter of the second Mrs. Godwin, was, scandalously, pregnant by Byron, much to the embarrassment of the Shelleys, with whom she lived.[20] Illegitimate pregnancy, that is, a pregnancy over which the woman has particularly little control, brings either death to the mother in childbirth (Wollstonecraft) or shame, making visible what ought to have remained out of sight, the scene of conception (Claire), a shame that can itself result in the death of both mother (Harriet Shelley) and child (Fanny).

At the time of the conception of the novel, Mary Godwin had herself borne two illegitimate children: the first, an unnamed girl, died four days later, in March 1815; the second was five months old. In December 1816, when Harriet Shelley died and Shelley had finished chapter 4 of the novel, she was pregnant again. With but a single parent, the demon in her novel is the world's most monstrously illegitimate child, and this illegitimate child causes the death of that parent as well as of the principle of motherhood, as we have seen. Read in connection with the history of disastrous illegitimacies, the novel's logic would seem to be this: to give birth to an illegitimate child is monstrous, for it is the inexorable life of these babies, especially those of Mary Wollstonecraft and of Harriet Shelley, that destroys the life of the mother. Subsequently, as Marc Rubenstein argues, the guilty daughter pays for the destruction of her own mother in a fantasy of being destroyed by her own child.[21]

In *Jane Eyre* and *Wuthering Heights*, we saw that the image of childbirth is associated with the uncontrollability of real things. Once a conception has taken objective form, it has the power to destroy its own source, to transform the mother herself into the literal. In the Brontës' novels, childbirth is structurally equivalent to (and indeed also often situated in) the coming true of dreams, which has, like childbirth, an ironic relation to the original conception. Shelley's 1831 introduction to her novel makes a comparable equation of giving birth, the realization of a dream, and writing. As many readers have pointed out, this introduction to her revised version of the novel identifies the novel itself with the demon, and both with a child.[22] She tells of being asked every morning if she had thought of a story, as if a story, like a baby, were necessarily to be conceived in the privacy of the night. And at the close of the introduction she writes, "I bid my hideous progeny go forth and prosper," and she refers to the novel in the next sentence as "the offspring of happy days." The genesis of the novel, furthermore, is in a dream that she transcribes, a dream moreover that is about the coming true of a dream. One night, she says, after listening to conversation about the reanimation of corpses, "Night waned upon this talk. . . . When I placed my head on my pillow I did not sleep, nor could I be said to think. My imagination, unbidden, possessed and guided me." Then follows her account of the famous dream of "the pale student of unhallowed arts kneeling beside the thing he had put together," the "hideous phantasm of a man" stirring "with an uneasy, half-vital motion," and the "artist" sleeping and waking to behold "the horrid thing . . . looking on him with yellow, watery, but speculative eyes." Waking in horror from her dream, she at first tries "to think of something else," but then realizes that she has the answer to her need for a ghost story: "'What terrified me will terrify others; and I need only describe the spectre which had haunted my midnight pillow.' . . . I began that day with the words, 'It was on a dreary night of November,' making only a transcript of the grim terrors of my waking dream." Making a transcript of a dream—that is, turning an idea into the "machinery of a story"—a dream that is about the transformation of a "phantasm" into a real body, is equivalent here to conceiving a child. She makes it very clear that her dream takes the place of a sexual act ("Night waned. . . . When I placed my head on my pillow . . . I saw the pale student."), just as the book idea she can announce the next day substitutes for a baby. The terrifying power of the possibility that her dream might be true encodes the terrifying power of conception and childbirth. In Deutsch's language, "she who has created this new life must obey its power; its rule is expected, yet invisible, implacable."[23]

Despite Ellen Moers's delineation of the resemblance of the demon to the apprehensions a mother might have about a baby, it is the introduction that supplies the most explicit evidence for identifying demon and book with a child. Mary Poovey has demonstrated that this introduction has a significantly different ideological cast from the original version of the novel (or even from the revised novel). Written in 1831, fourteen years after the novel itself and following the death of Percy Shelley (as well as the deaths of both the children who were alive or expected in 1816–17), the introduction takes pains to distance itself from the novel, and it aims to bring the writing of the novel further within the fold of the conventional domestic life Shelley retrospectively substitutes for the radically disruptive life she in fact led.[24] Referring obliquely to her elopement with Percy and its effect on her adolescent habit of inventing stories, for example, she writes, "After this my life became busier, and reality stood in place of fiction." Echoed later by Robert Southey's remark to Charlotte Brontë, that "literature cannot be the business of a woman's life," Shelley's busyness refers largely to her responsibilities as a mother and wife. When she describes her endeavor to write a ghost story she repeats this term for family responsibility: "I busied myself *to think of a story*." This echo suggests that her busyness with story writing is somehow congruent with, not in conflict with, her "busier" life as a wife and mother. It makes the novel, "so very hideous an idea," seem somehow part of the busy life of a matron. It is this effort, to domesticate her hideous idea, that may be at the bottom of her characterizing it as a "hideous progeny." If the novel read in this light seems, like *Jane Eyre* and *Wuthering Heights*, to be full of a horror of childbirth, that may only be the result of the impossibility of changing the basic story of the 1817 novel, the result of assembling mismatched parts.

Thus the novel may be about the horror associated with motherhood, yet this reading seems unduly influenced by the superimpositions of the introduction, and furthermore it ignores the novel's most prominent feature, that the demon is not a child born of woman but the creation of a man.[25] Most succinctly put, the novel is about the collision between androcentric and gynocentric theories of creation, a collision that results in the denigration of maternal childbearing through its circumvention by male creation. The novel presents Mary Shelley's response to the expectation, manifested in such poems as *Alastor* or *Paradise Lost*, that women embody and yet not embody male fantasies. At the same time, it expresses a woman's knowledge of the irrefutable independence of the body, both her own and those of the children that she produces, from projective male fantasy. While a masculine being—God, Adam, Percy Shelley, Frankenstein—may imagine that his creation of an imaginary being may remain under the control of his desires, Mary Shelley knows otherwise, both through her experience as mistress and wife of Percy and through her experience of childbirth. Shelley's particular history shows irrefutably that children, even pregnancies, do not remain under the control of those who conceive them.

Keats writes that "the Imagination may be compared to Adam's dream—he awoke and found it truth."[26] In *Paradise Lost*, narrating his recollection of Eve's creation, Adam describes how he fell into a special sleep—"Mine eyes he clos'd, but op'n left the Cell / Of Fancy my internal sight" (8. 460–61)—then watched, "though sleeping," as God formed a creature,

> Manlike, but different sex, so lovely fair,
> That what seem'd fair in all the World, seem'd now
> Mean, or in her summ'd up.
>
> (8. 471–73)

This is "Adam's dream." But what of "he awoke and found it truth"? Adam wakes, "To find her, or for ever to deplore / Her loss" (479–80), and then, "behold[s] her, not far off, / Such as I saw her in my dream" (481–81), yet what Keats represses is that the matching of reality to dream is not so neat as these lines suggest.[27] Eve comes to Adam, not of her own accord, but "Led by her Heav'nly Maker" (485), and as soon as he catches sight of her, Adam sees Eve turn away from him, an action he ascribes to modesty (and thus endeavors to assimilate to his dream of her) but that Eve, in book 4, has already said stemmed from her preference for her image in the water. Though designed by God for Adam "exactly to thy heart's desire" (8. 451), Eve once created has a mind and will of her own, and this independence is so horrifying to the male imagination that the Fall is ascribed to it.

It is neither the visionary male imagination alone that Mary Shelley protests, then, nor childbirth itself, but the circumvention of the maternal creation of new beings by the narcissistic creations of male desire. While Keats can gloss over the discrepancy between Adam's dream and its fulfillment, Shelley cannot. As Frankenstein is on the verge of completing the female demon, it is for her resemblance to Eve that he destroys her. Just as Adam says of Eve, "seeing me, she turn'd" (8. 507), Frankenstein fears the female demon's turning from the demon toward a more attractive image: "She also might turn with disgust from him to the superior beauty of man" (chap. 20). Also like Eve, who disobeys a prohibition agreed upon between Adam and God before her creation, she "might refuse to comply with a compact made before her creation," the demon's promise to leave Europe. Frankenstein typifies the way in which the biological creation of necessarily imperfect yet independent beings has always been made to seem, within an androcentric economy, monstrous and alarming. Although Mary Wollstonecraft would in any case have died of puerperal fever after Mary's birth, her earlier pregnancy with Fanny and the pregnancies of Harriet Shelley, Claire Clairmont, and Mary Godwin would have done no harm had they not been labeled "illegitimate" by a society that places a premium on the ownership by a man of his wife's body and children. The novel criticizes, not childbirth itself, but the male horror of independent embodiment. This permits us to speculate that the horror of childbirth in *Jane Eyre* and *Wuthering Heights* stems from the Brontës' identification with an androcentric perspective. To a certain extent, as a writer in a culture that defines writing as a male activity and as opposite to motherhood, Shelley too must share the masculine perspective, with its horror of embodiment and its perennial reenacting of Adam's affront at Eve's turning away. For whatever reason, however, perhaps because of her direct experience of the mother's position, Shelley is able to discern the androcentrism in her culture's view of the relation of childbearing to writing, and thus she enables us to interpret her own painful exposure of it.

At the site of the collision between motherhood and romantic projection another form of literalization appears as well. While it is important how Shelley reads texts such as *Alastor* and *Paradise Lost*, it is also important to consider, perhaps more simply, that her novel reads them. Like the Brontës' novels, whose gothic embodiments of subjective states, realizations of dreams, and literalized figures all literalize romantic projection, Shelley's novel literalizes romantic imagination, but with a different effect and to a different end. Shelley criticizes these texts by enacting them, and because enactment or embodiment is both the desire and the fear of such texts, the mode of her criticism matters. Just as the heroes of these poems seem to seek, but do not seek, embodiments of their visionary desires, these poetic texts seem to seek embodiment in "the machinery of a story." For in the ideology of postromantic culture, it is part of a woman's duty to transcribe and give form to men's words, just as it is her duty to give form to their desire, or birth to their seed, no matter how ambivalently men may view the results of such projects. In the same passage in the introduction to the novel in which Shelley makes the analogy between the book and a child, between the conception of a story and the conception of a baby, and between these things and the coming true of a dream, she also identifies all these projects with the transcription of important men's words. Drawing on the ideology of maternity as the process of passing on a male idea, Shelley describes her book-child as the literalization of two poets' words:

> Many and long were the conversations between Lord Byron and Shelley to which I was a devout but nearly silent listener. During one of these, various philosophical doctrines were discussed, and among others the nature of the principle of life, and whether there was any probability of its ever being discovered and communicated. . . . Perhaps a corpse would be reanimated; galvanism had given token of such things: perhaps the component parts of a creature might be manufactured, brought together, and endued with vital warmth.

Directly following this passage appears her account of going to bed and vividly dreaming of the "student of unhallowed arts" and the "hideous phantasm," the dream of which she says she made "only a transcript" in transferring it into the central scene of her novel, the dream that equates the conception of a book with the conception of a child.

Commentators on the novel have in the past taken Shelley at her word here, believing, if not in her story of transcribing a dream, then certainly in her fiction of transcribing men's words.[28] Mario Praz, for example, writes, "All Mrs. Shelley did was to provide a passive reflection of some of the wild fantasies which, as it were, hung in the air about her."[29] Harold Bloom suggests that "what makes *Frankenstein* an important book" despite its "clumsiness" is "that it contains one of the most vivid versions we have of the Romantic mythology of the self, one that resembles Blake's *Book of Urizen*, Shelley's *Prometheus Unbound*, and Byron's *Manfred*, among other works."[30] It is part of the subtlety of her strategy to disguise her criticism of such works as a passive transcription, to appear to be a docile wife and "devout listener" to the conversations of important men. Indeed, central to her critical method is the practice of acting out docilely what these men tell her they want from her, to show them the consequences of their desires. She removes herself beyond reproach for "putting [her]self forward," by formulating her critique as a devout transcription, a "passive reflection," a "version" that "resembles." She inserts this authorial role into her novel in the form of a fictive M. S., Walton's sister, Margaret Saville, to whom his letters containing

Frankenstein's story are sent and who silently records and transmits them to the reader.

Now that we have assembled the parts of Shelley's introductory account of the novel's genesis, we can see that she equates childbearing with the bearing of men's words. Writing a transcript of a dream that was in turn merely the transcript of a conversation is also giving birth to a hideous progeny conceived in the night. The conversation between Byron and Shelley probably represents Shelley's and Byron's poetry, the words, for example, of *Alastor* that she literalizes in her novel. That the notion of motherhood as the passive transcription of men's words is at work here is underscored by the allusion this idea makes to the Christ story. "Perhaps a corpse would be reanimated" refers initially, not to science's power, but to that occasion, a myth but surely still a powerful one even in this den of atheists, when a corpse was reanimated, which is in turn an allusion to the virgin birth. Like the creations of Adam and Eve, which excluded the maternal, Christ's birth bypassed the normal channels of procreation. It is this figure, whose birth is also the literalization of a masculine God's Word, who serves as the distant prototype for the reanimation of corpses. And within the fiction, the demon too is the literalization of a word, an idea, Frankenstein's theory given physical form. As Joyce Carol Oates remarks, the demon "is a monster-son born of Man exclusively, a parody of the Word or Idea made Flesh."[31] The book-baby literalizes Shelley's and Byron's words, the words of their conversation as figures for Shelley's words in *Alastor*, just as the demon-baby literalizes Frankenstein's inseminating words. Christ literalizes God's Word through the medium of a woman, Mary, who passively transmits Word into flesh without being touched by it. Literalizations again take place through the medium of a more recent Mary, who passively transcribes (or who seems to), who adds nothing but "the platitude of prose" and "the machinery of a story" to the words of her more illustrious male companions who for their own writing prefer "the music of the most melodious verse." And yet, as we will see again with Eliot's *The Mill on the Floss*, it is precisely the adding of this "machinery," which would seem only to facilitate the transmission of the ideas and figures of poetry into the more approachable form of a story, that subverts and reverses what it appears so passively to serve.

The demon literalizes the male romantic poet's desire for a figurative object of desire, but it also literalizes the literalization of male literature. While telling Frankenstein the story of its wanderings and of its education by the unknowing cottagers, the demon reports having discovered in the woods "a leathern portmanteau containing . . . some books. I eagerly seized the prize and returned with it to my hovel" (chap. 15). The discovery of these books—*Paradise Lost*, Plutarch's *Lives*, and *The Sorrows of Werther*—is followed in the narrative, but preceded in repre-sented time, by the demon's discovery of another book, Frankenstein's "journal of the four months that preceded [the demon's] creation."[32] Both *Frankenstein*, the book as baby, and the demon as baby literalize these books, especially *Paradise Lost*—the demon is Satan, Adam, and Eve, while Frankenstein himself is Adam, Satan, and God—as well as a number of other prior texts, among them, as we have seen, *Alastor*, but also the book of Genesis, Coleridge's "Rime of the Ancient Mariner," Aeschylus's *Prometheus Bound*, Wordsworth's "Tintern Abbey," Wil-liam Godwin's *Caleb Williams*, and many others. At the same time and in the same way, the demon is the realization of Frankenstein's words in the journal of his work on the demon, a journal that is in some ways equivalent to (or a literalization of) *Alastor*, since both record a romantic quest for what was "desired . . . with an ardor that far exceeded modera-tion." The demon, wandering about the woods of Germany carrying these books, the book of his own physical origin and the texts that contribute to his literary origin, embodies the very notion of literalization with which everything about him seems to be identified. To carry a book is exactly what Mary Shelley does in bearing the words of the male authors, in giving birth to a hideous progeny that is at once book and demon. Carrying the books of his own origin, the demon emblematizes the literalization of literature that Shelley, through him, practices.

I pointed out earlier that Mary Shelley, unlike the Brontës, would not see childbirth itself as inherently threatening apart from the interference in it by a masculine economy. Likewise, writing or inventing stories is not inherently monstrous—witness her retrospective account in the intro-duction of how, before her life became "busier," she used to "commune with the creatures of my fancy" and compose unwritten stories out of doors: "It was beneath the trees of the grounds belonging to our house, or on the bleak sides of the woodless mountains near, that my true compositions, the airy flights of my imagination, were born and fos-tered." Like both Cathys in *Wuthering Heights* in their childhood, indeed, probably like the young Brontës themselves, Mary Shelley's imagination prior to the fall into the Law of the Father—in her case, elopement, pregnancy, and marriage—is at one with nature and also does not require to be written down. The metaphor of composition as childbirth—"my true compositions . . . were born and fostered"—appears here as something not only harmless but celebratory. It is only when both childbirth and a woman's invention of stories are subordi-nated to the Law of the Father that they become monstrous; it is only when such overpowering and masculinist texts as Genesis, *Paradise Lost*, and *Alastor* appropriate this Mary's body, her female power of embodiment, as vehicle for the transmission of their words, that monsters are born. When God appropriates maternal procreation in Genesis or *Paradise Lost*, a beautiful object is created; but through the reflex of Mary Shelley's critique, male circumvention of the maternal creates a monster. Her monster constitutes a criticism of such appropriation and circumvention, yet it is a criticism written in her own blood, carved in the very body of her own victimization, just as the demon carves words about death in the trees and rocks of the Arctic. She is powerless to stop her own appropriation and can only demonstrate the pain that appropriation causes in the woman reader and writer. As we turn now to Eliot's *The Mill on the Floss*, which takes up like *Frankenstein* the question of a woman writer's—and her heroine's—literalization of powerful masculine texts, we will see that Eliot shares much of Shelley's sense of the necessity and the high cost of a woman's literalization, as well as of its power as a criticism of that which appropriates.

6

Eliot, Wordsworth, and the Scenes
of the Sisters' Instruction

wo of Wordsworth's most important lyrics about the growth of
the poet's imagination, "Tintern Abbey" and "Nutting," are also
the scenes of a sister's instruction.[1] Different as these two poems
are, at the end of each the poet turns unexpectedly to his sister
(named either as a sister or, in the case of "Nutting," as "dearest
Maiden"), who enters the poem not in her own right but in answer to the
poet's and the poem's needs. At the end of "Tintern Abbey," the poet
exhorts the sister to "remember me" by living out the stages of youth to
which he himself cannot return.[2] The last three lines of "Nutting" frame
the poet's painfully earned knowledge with the address, "Then, dearest
Maiden," so as to turn that knowledge into instructions:

> Then, dearest Maiden, move along these shades
> In gentleness of heart; with gentle hand
> Touch—for there is a spirit in the woods.
>
> (54–56)

Both sisters exist to receive the brother's wishes, to confirm for him his
hope that what he has gained in the course of the poem will find a
habitation in a consciousness perhaps more enduring than his own. We
do not expect to learn anything from her about how she will use the gift
contained in the poet's words. Her quietude verifies the power of the
poet's performative words: he speaks, and for her to hear his words is,
implicitly, to enact them. To ask what this listening might mean to her is
a question that the text itself excludes; yet for George Eliot it is a real one,
as it was also for the poet's sister. What is the female listener (or reader)
to do with these words that are intended to help her avoid the painful

experiences that have forged the poet's consciousness? What does it mean to follow instructions given, not for the sake of the student, but for the sake of the teacher? The poet implies that the sister he addresses will learn to follow his path if she follows his instructions, but how are they to be followed, and with what results? These are not Wordsworth's concerns, but they are Eliot's.

Mary Ann Evans's remarks on reading Wordsworth at the age of twenty suggest that while, like Wordsworth's ideal sister, her feelings are congruent with his, she also experiences some ambivalence about receiving the poet's instuctions. "I have been so self-indulgent as to possess myself of Wordsworth at full length. . . . I never before met with so many of my own feelings, expressed just as I could like them."[3] She does wish to be instructed: "to possess myself of" admits to a foreign excellence that must be possessed as different, not simply recognized. Yet simply to accept the poet's words would be, like the sister in the poems, to remain silent. That she describes her reading as "self-indulgent" and as a recognition of her "own feelings" suggests that, even though it is done half-jokingly, she needs to diminish Wordsworth's power of suggestion and to make it clear that any act or feeling the poet describes was hers before she learned that it might seem derivative. Moreover, the phallic formulation, "possess myself . . . at full length," suggests an aggressive role reversal that puts Wordsworth in the subordinate position. This tension between the need to respect and the need to deny a powerful influence—the feeling that what she possesses herself of, she had already possessed—is representative of the attitude toward Wordsworth expressed later on in Eliot's works.

Eliot's ambivalence toward Wordsworth's authority has been magnified for modern readers by a certain critical predisposition. Most readers who identify Wordsworthian features in Eliot have simply demonstrated affinity or resemblance without raising the question of derivation, taking Mary Ann Evans's word for it that Eliot's mind converged spontaneously with Wordsworth's on the same point.[4] Had there been no Wordsworth, Eliot would still have discovered for herself what are commonly taken to be their shared beliefs in the value of childhood and rural life and in the necessity of constant interchange between feeling and knowledge. But while these are freely granted to be Eliot's own beliefs, criticism has nonetheless continued to comment on her Wordsworthian qualities (just as it has sought out her Feuerbachian and Comtean qualities). Perhaps this is because believing her philosophic power imitates male originals (like her pseudonym) allows readers to portion out among various male authors some of the respect Eliot commands, much as the belief that Shelley was a passive reflection of her husband's views has, as we have seen, served to diffuse the impact of *Frankenstein*. It is generally assumed that Eliot's Wordsworthianism is pure, oddly, for two opposing reasons: the respect critics feel for George Eliot's originality is so great that they do not think of calling "him" derivative; but their knowledge that "he" is really only Mary Ann Evans prepares them to find a daughterly veneration that would never tamper with literary authority. Criticism's need to find Eliot derivative not only highlights her own ambivalence but also situates the question of that ambivalence in the question of gender. For critics could not possibly have been so concerned to see authority so docilely obeyed if the genders in the case were reversed.

Despite criticism's collusion with Eliot, there are a number of incongruities between Wordsworth's ideas and Eliot's texts that seem more than simply differences, scenes and passages that Eliot invites her readers to find Wordsworthian while she indicates a significant pattern of divergence from his prototypes. The brotherly instructions that Eliot is most generally concerned at once to follow and to deny are contained in Wordsworth's wish, in the verse "Prospectus" to *The Recluse*, to see "Paradise, and groves / Elysian" be "A simple produce of the common day" (47–48, 55). But when she follows this wish literally, her "common day," the intensely social world of her novels, tests far more strenuously the adaptability of the paradisal vision than does anything Wordsworth wrote. The generic incompatibility between a poet's vision and the form of the novel may account for some of the obvious differences; yet, as I will try to suggest later, it may be that Eliot's choice of the realistic novel as the form for her vision is in part an effect, not a cause, of her ambivalent divergences from Wordsworth (for example, a series of her sonnets, which we will consider shortly, articulates these concerns as much as do the novels). Often seeming to intend to, Eliot neither wishes nor is able, as the good sisters invented in Wordsworth's poems are, always to carry out Wordsworthian instructions verbatim. As in Mary Shelley's revision of romanticism in *Frankenstein*, it is precisely the literalness of Eliot's transposition of Wordsworthian themes—her effort to be a docile student on the model of Wordsworth's implied sister—that constitutes her subversion of them.

The Mill on the Floss is Eliot's "most Wordsworthian novel,"[5] and it is also her novel most concerned both with female education and with the brother-sister relationship. Maggie Tulliver's experience first as a reader and then as a sister may shed light on Eliot's relation to instruction, especially to brotherly instruction. Maggie's existence in the novel is framed by scenes of her reading. She starts out as an accurate reader who distinguishes easily between elucidating a text foreign to her and inventing her own stories, the two kinds of reading that become confused in Eliot's reading of Wordsworth. Having been reprimanded for her very perceptive reading of *The History of the Devil* as "not quite the right book for a little girl" and asked if she has "no prettier book," Maggie defends herself by opposing accurate reading to invention: "I make stories to the pictures out of my own head, you know."[6] At this point in her story, Maggie feels free both to read independently and to imagine freely, but we see her being chastized as a girl for both processes indifferently. However Maggie reads, "a woman's no business wi' being so clever; it'll turn to trouble, I doubt" (1:3).

As Maggie grows up, learning to be feminine, her way of reading changes. As an adolescent in search of spiritual food and guidance, she becomes an overly literal reader of Thomas à Kempis. The eager pupil of two guides, the author and the "quiet hand" that marked certain passages in her second-hand copy, Maggie acts out exactly the text's prescriptions and in so doing radically misreads it in at least two ways. She misconstrues renunciation, not as sorrow, but as an available form of satisfaction, and according to Philip Wakem, she misuses her own gifts: "What you call self-conquest—blinding and deafening yourself to all but one train of impression—is only the culture of monomania in a nature like yours" (5:4). The general effect of her reading Thomas à Kempis is to contribute to her education in femininity. She has turned to Thomas à Kempis in the first place because her brother Tom won't let "*my* sister" work to help pay off the family debt, depriving her of any useful (masculine) occupation. Her docility toward the text, her wish to follow its prescriptions exactly, is repeated both in the self-suppression she learns from the text's preaching and in her willingness to let her mother do with her as she pleases: "Her mother felt the change in her with a sort of puzzled wonder that Maggie should be 'growing up so good'; it was amazing that this once 'contrary' child was become so submissive, so backward to assert her own will" (4:3). Though Maggie does not think of herself as learning how to be feminine—she sees herself as an ascetic—there is a very neat coincidence between her mother's wish for a conventionally good daughter and Thomas à Kempis's message of self-denial.

The more literal her reading, the less accurate and the more feminine. Yet when she attempts, as she used to with the pictures in *The History of the Devil*, her own imaginative departures from Scott's *The Pirate*, which she reads at about the same time, she meets with an equal lack of success that is again part of her education in femininity. Philip offers her his copy of *The Pirate* the first time they meet in the Red Deeps. "O, I began that once," she responds, "I read to where Minna is walking with Cleveland,

and I could never get to read the rest. I went on with it in my own head, and I made several endings; but they were all unhappy. I could never make a happy ending out of that beginning" (5:1).

Maggie is discovering here the inexorable laws of feminine plotting. It is the same discovery she makes later on when she laments that *Corinne* is merely one more repetition of the law requiring the blonde heroine to triumph over the dark heroine. Her invention of optimistic endings for a love story about a dark-haired girl is limited by the conventions both of plot and of social life. In fact, her endeavor to depart from convention only underscores for her both the heroine's and her own entrapment.[7] Her memory of trying and failing to invent happy endings for *The Pirate* is evoked by the fact that Philip has the book with him because he is studying a scene for a picture. His rationale for offering the book is, "I don't want it now. I shall make a picture of you instead—you, among the Scotch firs and the slanting shadows" (5:1). But though she refuses the book, he makes the picture anyway: whether she reads or refuses to read, she will become the static object of a man's vision, in a way that prefigures her final transformation into an object in death.

Maggie enters the novel as a reader, and in her last scene before the flood carries her toward home, Tom, and death, she is reading again, choosing this time between two texts: the letter from Stephen and the words of Thomas à Kempis that would help her resist Stephen's appeal. At this last stage in her growth, her reading is only the passive reiteration of conflicting texts for which she is simply the medium, providing no original words of her own. Ironically, the two texts are really only representations of her own feelings, but she feels that they come from outside her. Stephen's writing is so vivid to her that "she did not *read* the letter: she heard him uttering it, and the voice shook her with its old strange power" (7:5). He asks her "Write me one word—say 'Come!' In two days I should be with you." Her response takes the form of writing to his dictation, a literal repetition of his word provoked by the prospect, not of her own joy, but of Stephen's sorrow and by her self-doubts, which "made her once start from her seat to reach the pen and paper, and write 'Come!'" Maggie knows that her obedient and selfless literal repetition is wrong, but she is so exhausted emotionally that she can only wait passively "for the light that would surely come again." When it comes, the corrective to the reiteration of Stephen's word is her repetition of another word: "The words that were marked by the quiet hand in the little old book that she had long ago learned by heart, rushed even to her lips, and found a vent for themselves in a low murmur that was quite lost in the loud driving of the rain against the window." First an unwilling copier of Stephen's word, now a ready voice for the words of Thomas à

Kempis, Maggie does at last determine what her own words will be, but they "find no utterance but in a sob," and she defers writing them until the next day, which for her never comes.

Maggie's childhood capacity for original invention and for self-expression has by the end of her story quite vanished. Her adult self is a battleground for conflicting texts; when she takes up a pen or opens her mouth, the words that come forth as if they were her own are not hers. And this state of affairs results from, and in turn reinforces, the self-suppressing submissiveness that is identified throughout as feminine. To learn how to read as a repeater of others' words is feminine, and it is also fatal. Her departures from what she reads as an adolescent (her unintentional departure from Thomas à Kempis, her effort to vary the inexorable plot of *The Pirate*) are signs of her vital resistance (willful or unconscious) to feminine submissiveness, even though her efforts fail. When in the last reading scene Maggie gets her texts right, this final docility is a harbinger of her death: her complete passivity as a reader prefigures her succumbing to the flood the next morning.

When Eliot describes her own reading of Wordsworth as a process of possessing herself of what she already possesses, the ambiguous balance of originality and deference prefigures in compressed form some of the features of Maggie's development as a reader. It may be that Eliot is articulating through Maggie the stages of her own education in feminine readership, in how to be a docile or self-suppressing reader. To submit to others' words in Maggie's case is to submit to the law of cause and effect and therefore to reach the unhappy end predicted for all dark heroines. Eliot thematizes both docility and disobedience to instruction through the relation between Maggie's reading and the pattern of her life: disobedient reading is incompatible with Victorian femininity, yet complete feminine docility leads to the self's silence and ultimately to death. I would like to turn now to some instances of that dual reading in *The Mill on the Floss* and elsewhere that may suggest how the balance between docility and disobedience that Eliot thematizes in Maggie appears in her reading of Wordsworth. How is it possible to honor Wordsworth's words yet not die, as Maggie does, of the desire to be Wordsworth's sister and follow silently and involuntarily the wishes of his words? Carrying out Wordsworth's "remember me" in a way that she asks us to think of as literal (as Maggie's later readings are literal), she nonetheless departs radically from her original in passing from poetic and imaginative vision to the novelist's female vision. But the literal reading that for Maggie results in death issues for Eliot in the novelist's originality.

In calling *The Mill on the Floss* Eliot's most Wordsworthian novel, Donald Stone also locates in it "the most serious case of Wordsworthian blight on Eliot's creative imagination," because "the heroine is paralyzed by a myth of the past and a myth of her own childhood."[8] U. C. Knoepflmacher similarly sees "George Eliot's Wordsworthian novel vainly [trying to] enlist the Romantic's power of memory."[9] As he goes on to point out, where Wordsworth restores himself in "Tintern Abbey" through his own memories and through the memory he makes visible in his sister's eyes, Maggie and Tom succumb to the realities of "evil tongues, / Rash judgments," and the "dreary intercourse of daily life" Wordsworth refers to in his poem (lines 128–29, 131). The question that these analyses raise is why the myth of the realistic novelist's growth must diverge so radically from Wordsworth's myth of the poet's growth. "Tintern Abbey" and "Nutting" have only an incidental place for the sister, whereas the poet's accounts of the growth of the imagination picture a solitary, even narcissistic relation between himself and nature's maternal presence in childhood. At its most powerful, too, the visionary imagination can shut out the ordinary, visible world, as Dorothy Wordsworth sees in the "spots of time" and the Simplon Pass passages in *The Prelude*. Eliot's myth of childhood, however, for reasons that I will explore more fully later on, necessarily includes other people and a visible world that can never be ignored. In her revision of the Wordsworthian myth, Eliot's most autobiographical characters pass through what appear to be Wordsworthian childhoods, not to become romantic poets, but to find that their ideal childhood visions are thwarted by circumstances or by social needs. This revision closely resembles the literalizations in *Wuthering Heights, Jane Eyre,* and *Frankenstein,* all of which, in different ways, distort a romantic ideal. Eliot sets her heroines' insatiable need for love, together with her own narrative commitment to realism, against the antisocial implications of what she represents as the introverting power of the imagination. Her heroines' need for love is insatiable because those who can supply it never love as unconditionally as Wordsworth's nature does, and Eliot schools her heroines to choose a love that represents a turning away from disruptive visionary power. In *The Mill on the Floss* and in the lesser-known sonnet sequence "Brother and Sister" (1869), the heroine gives up visionary aspirations (that are perhaps in any case untenable in the world of the novel) in favor of the love of a usually more practical-minded brother that makes childhood last forever and closes off the visionary world. That choice may lead to death, but the loss of vision may also be compensated for by an increase in wisdom ultimately more appropriate to the novel than to poetry.

This ambivalent relation to Wordsworth stands out in one of the moments considered most Wordsworthian in Eliot, the fishing scene in *The Mill on the Floss* and the narrator's subsequent reflections on the value of memories of a childhood passed in nature (1:5). A close look at these passages reveals a willful misreading of the Wordsworthian implications of the scene, and the later consequences of the scene are the opposite of Wordsworthian. Opposing one brother (Tom) to a very different one (Wordsworth, brother of silent sisters), Eliot has Maggie defend against Wordsworth's authority while retaining all the forms of a sister's deference.[10]

As Sandra Gilbert and Susan Gubar point out, Maggie and Tom spend most of their precious time together making each other miserable, and while Maggie, Tom, and their narrator cling to the idea that their idyllic fishing expedition is typical of their childhood, the reader must suspect the effort to generalize from this exceptional scene.[11] The children live in a fallen, gendered world in which they can never escape for very long the pain produced by their social condition. Fishing harmoniously together at "the old favourite spot," "Maggie thought it would make a very nice heaven to sit by the pool in that way, and never be scolded." But this heaven is brief and contingent on absolute physical and mental seclusion. That it cannot be carried over into the common day of their ordinary lives is underscored by the very precise description of its locale. The "old favourite spot" is a pool of unknown depth and mysterious origin that is literally hidden from view, being "framed in with willows and tall reeds, so that the water was only to be seen when you got close to the brink."

Tom supervises the practical business of fishing, but Maggie "had forgotten all about the fish, and was looking dreamily at the glassy water." Hearing Tom's "loud whisper," Maggie is "frightened lest she had been doing something wrong, as usual," and when it turns out instead that she has inadvertently caught a fish, she is "not conscious of unusual merit." Maggie's happiness consists in such accidental absence of wrongdoing and in listening alternately to Tom's whispers and to the "happy whisperings" exchanged between the "light dipping sounds of the rising fish" and the gentle rustling of the willows and reeds. These illusions of reciprocity—for she and Tom communicate no more effectively than the water and the willows—encourage the children's equally illusory idea that their lives will always be like this. The narrator ends her account of Maggie and Tom by generalizing the Wordsworthian principle that the scene has apparently generated: "Life did change for Tom and Maggie; and yet they were not wrong in believing that the thoughts and loves of these first years would always make part of their lives." The narrator then turns to generalize about all human childhoods and finally speaks of her own.

It would seem at this point that "the thoughts and loves of these first years" refers primarily to the children's love for each other, with the mill and the river as setting. But as the passage continues into its larger and explicitly Wordsworthian frame of reference, the reader is given the strange impression that the foregoing scene has instead been solely concerned with the children's love for their natural surroundings.

> We could never have loved the earth so well if we had had no childhood in it,—if it were not the earth where the same flowers come up again every spring that we used to gather with our tiny fingers as we sat lisping to ourselves on the grass. . . . What novelty is worth that sweet monotony where everything is known, and *loved* because it is known?

The child's love of "rural objects" leads here, not to deeper, wider kinds of love, but simply to a renewed love of those identical objects. Even the expected reference to the endurance of Maggie's love for Tom—for which there would in any case be no place in the Wordsworthian paradigm of a solitary childhood in nature—is replaced by this love of objects. Stressing continuity over growth, the passage suggests how the Wordsworthian features of Maggie's childhood will contribute to narrowing her consciousness, not enlarging it. When, seeing all their old possessions taken away after the bankruptcy, Maggie cries to Tom, "The end of our lives will have nothing in it like the beginning!" (3:6), Eliot is presenting us with a version of childhood far more literal than Wordsworth's.

Eliot's ambiguous expression "make part of their lives" suggests, vaguely enough so as not to appear purposely misleading, the Wordsworthian idea that the experiences of childhood seed the ground of character to bear unpredictable fruits, as when Wordsworth's "glad animal movements," remembered later, lead circuitously to the more sober pleasures of the mature poet. He recalls specific incidents from his childhood for their place in his growing awareness, first of nature's presence and then of his own mind's powers. But Maggie's yearnings later are for particular objects—this book, this mill, that river—and in this she is not altogether different from the literal-minded Tom, whose adult energies are devoted solely to repossessing his property, or even from her even more limited mother, whose worship of objects connected with her Dodson past is pathetic and un-Wordsworthian in the extreme. For Maggie, objects loved in childhood remain beloved for their own sakes, or for their place in consecrating her love for her brother, but never for what they teach her about the growth of her own mind. A literal recapitulation of childhood could hardly be further from Wordsworth's aims for himself as a poet; he does portray the dangers of obsessive fixation to a particular spot, but only in characters like Margaret in *The Excursion*, never in images of himself. Within the cultural tradition that can be summarized as the symbolic order, as we have seen, daughters may view objects, or the literal, more favorably than do sons, both through training and through inclination based on early childhood; but where the transcendence of all things is valued, objects are devalued. Eliot, sharing her heroine's love of things, yet recognizing the cost of this love within the symbolic order, identifies growth with transcendence and regression and death with the literal.

The Mill on the Floss's largest plot patterns turn on Maggie's continual need to reaffirm her ties to home. Her conflicting loves for Tom and for Philip are almost equally strong, having taken root in kindnesses conferred in childhood. Among her first sensations on "waking" from "the great temptation" is the urgent need to go home, where she may affirm her identity as a child needing discipline and protection from her wilder impulses and her adult self. The feature of childhood she wishes to repeat is not its illusion of Edenic peace but its pain: "In her anguish at the injury she had inflicted—she almost desired to endure the severity of Tom's reproof, to submit in patient silence to that harsh disapproving judgment against which she had so often rebelled" (7:1). She craves and believes she can return to a pattern, established in childhood by incidents like those with Tom's rabbits or the jam puffs, of harsh judgment, confession, and forgiveness: "I will endure anything. I want to be kept from doing wrong again." Tom, refusing her home and forgiveness, refuses to let her be a child again. But her final attempt to return to the mill (on the flood) does succeed in achieving a restoration both of childhood ties and of cathartic pain. Her death in returning home is thus doubly ensured: what she wants from childhood is its pain, and her wish to turn backward to childhood is, like Cathy's in *Wuthering Heights*, a death wish.

For Wordsworth, the natural objects to which the child feels bonded are always subordinate to the bond itself and to the wider sense of connectedness and vitality engendered by that bond, but Maggie's loyalty does not shift from those primary objects themselves. Wordsworth grows past his love for his mother and even for nature's material presence, but Maggie never transcends her love for Tom. Wordsworth's memories of childhood in *The Prelude* even include "the impressive discipline of fear" (1. 603) brought by nature's "Severer interventions, ministry / More palpable" (1. 355–56). But where Wordsworth's memory transforms that pain into imaginative power, Maggie seeks a literal recapitulation of the identical pain (inflicted in the same home by the same person) in Tom's punishment. The huge fragments of machinery that overtake Maggie and Tom in the flood are literalization itself: the failure of a life's worth of experiences to transcend themselves, remaining instead an agglomeration of things—the very literalness of the novel's revision of the Wordsworthian pattern. The narrator's conclusion to the fishing episode, speaking of the "sweet monotony" of a well-known landscape and of the return of the seasons, offers a seductively beautiful version of the narrative pattern of Maggie's life. In both, what might be self-transcendent turns out to be a return to particularity. Maggie's repetitions transform the beautiful "sweet monotony" into something more dangerous, since to repeat, within the terms of the symbolic order, is to regress, and to regress is to die.

To answer the question of why neither Maggie nor her narrative can go, or even want to go, beyond the literal, it may be useful at this point to suggest the relationship between Maggie's education in feminine reading and her literalizing life. Along with her regressive wishes, her reading prefigures, if it does not actually ensure, her death. When Maggie cries out "the end of our lives will have nothing in it like the beginning," her immediate reference is to the copy of *The Pilgrim's Progress* that she interpreted so acutely for Mr. Riley in the first reading scene. "'Our dear old Pilgrim's Progress that you coloured with your little paints; and that picture of Pilgrim with a mantle on, looking just like a turtle—oh dear!' Maggie went on, half sobbing as she turned over the few books. 'I thought we should never part with that while we lived'" (3:6). Pilgrim "looking just like a turtle" reminds us that this book symbolizes her independent way in childhood of "making stories to the pictures out of [her] own head," a way of reading that is now lost to her. When the book is sold off with all the other books, it is converted into the chief symbol, among the objects that Maggie misses, of her literalization of the Words-worthian sense of the past and thus of the kind of literal reading into which she has now fallen. Furthermore, it is Maggie's sorrow over the loss of the book that indirectly leads her to become a more and more literal reader: it is because of witnessing her sorrow that Bob Jakin later brings Maggie the gift of assorted books among which she finds the Thomas à Kempis. Her docile feminine repetitions, first of Stephen's "Come!" and then of the memorized text of Thomas à Kempis, echo and confirm her desire to repeat her childhood by returning home to Tom and the mill, first after she has left Stephen and finally during the flood, a passive repetition that overdetermines her death. These repetitions of texts represent an abandonment of self that signals the approach of death; and that the repetition is literal prefigures the particular shape that the death will take—her being overtaken by the huge mass of machinery on the flood. This machinery recalls the "machinery of a story" into which Shelley literalizes romantic texts, with monstrous consequences that are no less fatal than those of the machinery that overtakes Maggie. Her reading acts do not themselves cause Maggie's death, but they identify the thematics of return and of love of the literal with rhetorical repetition, and they identify the thematics of death with the lack of one's own word. And as specifically feminine reading acts, they identify learned feminine behavior with return, literal repetition, death, and silence.

Maggie's docility and final silence connect her, then, to the figure Wordsworth projects of his silent, listening sister. Yet her kind of education is also linked to Wordsworth's own. The sonnet sequence "Brother and Sister" presents another version of Maggie's kind of education, one that displays some verbal similarity to a Wordsworthian scene of the poet's instruction. Drawn from the same stock of Eliot's own experience as the dreamy little sister of a practical-minded older brother, the sonnet sequence shares with the fishing scene in *The Mill on the Floss* both its general contours of plot and characterization and its ostensible aim to assert that "the thoughts and loves of these first years would always make part of their lives."[12] The sonnet sequence also revises the rowing episode from book 1 of *The Prelude*, which Eliot had reread at least two years previous to composing the sonnets and perhaps more recently than that.[13] In order to find a paradigm more suitable than that of the silent sister, Eliot considers the future poet; yet she cannot go so far as to portray herself as a brother. Remaining a sister, she makes clear the limits that gender places on what it is possible for a heroine to do or to be.

Like the round pool, the canal setting of the sonnets' fishing episode literalizes the sublime. Where the round pool is both profound and obscure, "Our brown canal was endless to my thought," and barges float into view around "a grassy hill to me sublime / With some Unknown beyond it."[14] While the brother and sister fish together in the canal, the sister tells us that "One day my brother left me in high charge, / To mind the rod while he went seeking bait" (7), with instructions to pull the line out of the way of oncoming barges. Like Maggie fishing in the round pool, the little sister's attention lapses,

> Till sky and earth took on a strange new light
> And seemed a dream-world floating on some tide—
> A fair pavilioned boat for me alone
> Bearing me onward through the vast unknown.
>
> (7)

Her "dreamy peace" is broken by the arrival of a barge and by the sounds of her brother's anger, but the unhappy situation is turned around when it appears that the line she lifts out at the last minute has a fish on it, so that her "guilt that won the prey" is "Now turned to merit" (8). This scene replays very closely Maggie's fishing scene, in which she, too, felt "she had been doing something wrong, as usual," but has instead by pure chance caught a fish. Like Maggie, the little sister here, accidentally rewarded for doing wrong, learns from this event only that "luck was with glory wed." Morally ambiguous, these scenes teach Maggie and the little sister the insignificance of their actions relative to material coincidence.

Like the two fishing scenes, Wordsworth's rowing episode in book 1 of *The Prelude* concerns a child's transgression, but Wordsworth's "act of stealth / And troubled pleasure" (361–62) clearly deserves and as clearly receives punishment, unlike the ambiguous moral situations in which the two little girls find themselves. Having stolen a rowboat, Wordsworth's child enjoys a brief period of wonder that may be identified with what Coleridge and Wordsworth call "fancy." The "elfin pinnance" moves on,

> Leaving behind her still, on either side,
> Small circles glittering idly in the moon,
> Until they melted all into one track
> Of sparkling light.
>
> (364–67)

This part of the episode corresponds to the "dreamy peace" that appears sublime for the sister in the sonnets, a remembered state that includes a vision of "The wondrous watery rings that died too soon" (6), and corresponds also to the moment of transgression before transgression is recognized as such, when "sky and earth took on a strange new light / And seemed a dream-world." The scene turns sinister for Wordsworth's child when, as he rows away from the shore, "the stars and the grey sky" beyond the ridge are replaced by "a huge peak, black and huge" that "As if with voluntary power instinct / Upreared its head" and that appears to grow larger and to stride after him as the boy tries to escape it (372, 378–80). This huge and animated peak corresponds in sonnet 8 to the "barge's pitch-black prow" appearing around the hill that—like Wordsworth's ridge, beyond which is only the sky—has previously screened a sublime vacancy.

Despite the similarity of the two situations, the moral outcome is entirely different for each child. Where Wordsworth senses that nature has arranged this spectacle for his instruction, the looming object is for Eliot an accidental occurrence, not the product of a moral design. The actual barge might be the literalization of the little girl's dream of the "fair pavilioned boat," so that its frightening arrival would be the self-inflicted punishment for daydreaming, as Wordsworth's "huge peak, black and huge" seems to embody the boy's guilt. But the barge in the sonnets is pursuing its own independent, commercial course—unknown to the girl and not therefore a product of her imagination—and does not "str[i]de after" her in the manner of the purposeful "grim shape" of Wordsworth's story. Its arrival is simply bad luck, just as the appearance of the fish on her line at the critical moment is simply good luck. Both are material accidents occurring independently of the girl's psychic growth. Significantly, Eliot's child is stationary on the canal bank, a passive spectator in a world of powerful things that are governed by chance. Of course, if we look at what actually happens in Wordsworth, the appearance of the peak on the horizon is sheer accident too. What is important is that while the girl knows that she is subject to luck, the boy never deviates from his certainty that, because nature regulates her actions according to the needs of his education, nature has in this instance acted for him.

Had the girl been punished for daydreaming, by losing the line, say, she would have received an amply ambiguous moral lesson against imaginative, rather than immoral (as for Wordsworth), actions. As it is, she is even more confusingly rewarded by not being punished for doing something that is considered wrong. Out of this confusion, if there is any lesson for her, it is that daydreaming is inefficacious and irrelevant, too trivial to be either punished or rewarded. Yet it is precisely at this point in the story that Wordsworth's child's imagination is made to grow. One of nature's "severer interventions" on his behalf issues first and almost incidentally in a moral lesson that is both clear and just, a lesson that is, however, subordinate to the deep and troubling indeterminacy he feels in response to his discovery of nature's ministrations:

> my brain
> Worked with a dim and undetermined sense
> Of unknown modes of being; o'er my thoughts
> There hung a darkness, call it solitude
> Or blank desertion.
>
> (391–95)

This "blank desertion" suspends and restructures the boy's total relation to the world around him. Lacking nature's active ministry, Eliot's child learns both to fear and to discount her imagination.

Following the fishing episode, the little sister completes her conversion

from dreaming by entering into her brother's exclusively physical pleasures, such as knocking apples out of trees and playing with marbles and
tops.

> Grasped by such fellowship my vagrant thought
> Ceased with dream-fruit dream-wishes to fulfill
> My aëry-picturing fantasy was taught
> Subjection to the harder, truer skill
>
> That seeks with deeds to grave a thought-tracked line
> And by "What is," "What will be" to define.
>
> (10)

This conversion to the principles of linear plot and realism is presented as
good, supported by and reinforcing the myth of George Eliot as a
contentedly realistic novelist, even though the examples of realistic behavior she adduces are not very persuasive. The next (and final) sonnet's
sketch of the two children's futures confirms the realist's patterning of
"What will be" on "What is," when "the dire years whose awful name is
Change" "pitiless" shapes their souls "in two forms that range / Two
elements which sever their life's course" (11). Eliot is formulating here in
terms that seem applicable to herself as a realistic novelist the same
discovery that Maggie makes when she tries to invent alternate endings
for the heroine in *The Pirate*. "I could never make a happy ending out of
that beginning" is Maggie's recognition that, like Minna, she will succumb to the inexorable laws of cause and effect of realistic plotting.

The sonnets' commitment to linear plotting reverses Wordsworth's
conclusion to the rowing scene. Moving from the actual "huge peak,
black and huge" to the "huge and mighty forms" of the mind, Wordsworth concludes with a disruption between the familiar past and any
possible future, a cleavage that is the signature of the imagination:

> No familiar shapes
> Remained, no pleasant images of trees,
> Of sea or sky, no colours of green fields;
> But huge and mighty forms, that do not live
> Like living men, moved slowly through the mind
> By day, and were a trouble to my dreams.
>
> (395–400)

Wordsworth does value familiar shapes and rural images, but ultimately
because they aid in forming and sustaining the affections of the heart,
which then can survive independently of shapes and images. The imagination casts off, if painfully, precisely those things that both Maggie and

the narrator of *The Mill on the Floss* cling to and affirm to be of highest value in themselves. While Wordsworth moves from actual sight to figurative vision, Eliot moves in the opposite direction, from figure (Wordsworth's text) to thing. The sonnets' turn to realism and the asserted determination of the future by the present reiterates both Maggie's suffocating repetitions of the past and the way in which the novel's narrator, moving at the close of the fishing scene, like Maggie, not from the finite to the sublime but from particular to particular, recalls and celebrates the literal repetition of exactly those "familiar shapes," those "pleasant images of trees, / Of sea or sky," those "colours of green fields" that Wordsworth's young imagination in its most powerful activity discards. For the narrator, love of a natural scene leads beautifully but statically to love of the same natural scene:

> These familiar flowers, these well-remembered bird-notes, this sky, with its fitful brightness, these furrowed and grassy fields, each with a sort of personality given to it by the capricious hedgerows—such things as these are the mother tongue of our imagination, the language that is laden with all the subtle inextricable associations the fleeting hours of our childhood left behind them. Our delight in the sunshine on the deep-bladed grass to-day, might be no more than the faint perception of wearied souls, if it were not for the sunshine and the grass in the far-off years which still live in us, and transform our perception into love. (1:5)

The allusion to the imagination is problematic here, since this love, rich as it is, is not what Wordsworth, whose presence is so clearly invoked, would call the imagination. Human relatedness stands in the place of Wordsworth's solitary perception of nature as the central formative influence on the growing child. Prefatory to the series of related incidents that culminates in the rowing episode, Wordsworth writes: "Fair seed-time had my soul, and I grew up / Fostered alike by beauty and by fear" (301–2). In a comparable position prefatory to the fishing incident, Eliot recalls Wordsworth's lines, but with a crucial difference:

> Thus rambling we were schooled in deepest lore,
> And learned the meanings that give words a soul,
> The fear, the love, the primal passionate store,
> . . . .
> Those hours were seed to all my after good.
>
> (5)

Wordsworth's beauty and fear are nature's ministries, devoted gratuitously and unconditionally to the growing boy, while for Eliot "the fear, the love" are purely human. The love is between the sister and the brother, and the fear is merely of its loss (and also of a gypsy glimpsed in the sonnet preceding these lines). Just as throughout *The Mill on the Floss* Maggie's "need of love had triumphed over her pride, . . . it is a wonderful subduer, this need of love" (1:5), the little sister's allegiance to realism results from a kind of emotional blackmail through which her other needs as an individual are subordinated to the one overwhelming craving to be loved. The sister purchases love through acknowledging the preeminence of the objects that the brother loves. The transformation of perception into love defines the imagination as a binding love (of things and of the brother inextricably) that for Maggie will become obsessive and constricting and that for Wordsworth is antithetical to the imagination.

That "things" should have so privileged a relation to the imagination is troubling, but that things should be "the mother tongue of our imagination" is more problematic still, as the phrase ironically illuminates one source of Eliot's heroines' exclusive need to choose love over the world of imagination. A "mother tongue" in Wordsworth might signify feminized nature's fostering of imaginative growth in passages such as the rowing episode, a fostering made possible by the myth of the mother's early disappearance and replacement by figurative substitutes. But the nature for which Eliot's narrator expresses her enduring love is not at all Wordsworth's maternal nature but rather the nature of objects that signify the brother's realism and the sister's devotion to it. Because of the girl's differing place in and experience of the family configuration, it would be impossible for any female character in Eliot ever to imagine herself in the same relation to the idea of maternal nature that Wordsworth is privileged to feel. As in *Jane Eyre* and *Wuthering Heights*, the mother in Eliot would repeal, not encourage, her daughter's entry into the symbolic order, an entry about which Eliot appears to feel some ambivalence. Mrs. Tulliver's restrictiveness toward Maggie, her partiality to Tom, and her preoccupation with domestic objects reappear in the mother in "Brother and Sister," whose loving overprotectiveness the children try to escape: "Our mother bade us keep the trodden ways," while "the benediction of her gaze / Clung to us lessening, and pursued us still" (3). In a social world in which mothers are not "presences" but socially conditioned beings, these little sisters are unable to assume nature's figuratively maternal love and guidance in the way that Wordsworth's young self can, and no other, more specifically female, relation to the mother can be valued instead.

Wordsworth's introduction to the rowing episode, "One summer evening (led by her)" (357), emphasizes the theme of nature's purposive moral instruction. Introducing her comparable story in "Brother and Sister," Eliot writes, "One day my brother left me in high charge." It is under the brother's responsibility that the girl experiences the moral confusion of luck. The brother can hardly regulate circumstances as nature can, and he cannot be expected to direct the event toward his sister's moral growth. His love, like almost any human love after the myth of maternal love, is conditional, almost as accidental as the motions of barges and fish, and can never be taken for granted by his sister. Lacking the unconditional devotion of the reinvented mother, daughters in Eliot seek for the imagination a *brother* tongue. But because of the brother's fixation on objects that seal him, together with the sister who accepts his values, away from the imagination, that tongue is unobtainable. The transformation of perception into love prevents the transformation of perception into the Wordsworthian, visionary imagination.

In the rowing episode, the boy must violate the law in order to learn of nature's ceaseless attention to his actions, just as in "Nutting" the boy must ravage the virgin bower before he can discover that "there is a spirit in the woods." Such experiences are necessary to the boy's moral and imaginative education, and they are never final because maternal nature always forgives. It is these experiences from which Wordsworth as a brother would protect his sister. Eliot's young sisters are just as much protected from experiencing such enlarging transgressions by their fear of losing the brother's love. The two kinds of brothers (Wordsworth on the one hand and Tom and the brother of the sonnets on the other) share this trait of mediating, or attempting to, between their younger sisters and the sublime. They are linked only in this regard, standing otherwise for opposing values, but this connection suggests the significance of their opposition in Eliot's alignment of them.

Eliot's comments about reading Wordsworth, we have seen, like the change in Maggie's reading, reflect an ambivalent response to the authority of a text that seems both to foster and to subvert her originality. The temptation to silence or rote repetition is an especially feminine one, a temptation to docility and self-supression. Thus though Eliot might like to write in congruence with a revered male authority, conforming as Wordsworth's silent sister might do, or as Maggie does in devoutly repeating the words of Thomas à Kempis, she cannot and does not want to do so in these gendered matters. To defend against being Wordsworth's sister (and perhaps in part also because Mary Ann Evans had such a brother), Eliot represents her heroines as sisters of explicitly anti-Wordsworthian brothers, so that to follow the authority of one is necessarily to contravene that of the other. Excluded from the Wordsworthian paradigm for continuity between a childhood spent with a guiding maternal nature and visionary imagination, Eliot and her female characters seek approval in brothers. But they find that the brother's approval is earned only by turning away from what the other brother, Wordsworth, would approve, the solitary world of the imagination, toward a world governed by the law of cause and effect. When Eliot's heroines are torn between the imaginary world of Wordsworth and the practical world of the other brothers, they thematize the tension between Eliot's desire to listen silently to or repeat Wordsworth and her desire to show that what she reads in his authoritative texts was originally her own. To have the heroine enter fully into the world of imagination would be to concur that there are no truths beyond Wordsworth's, while to have her wholly allied with the brother would be, for Eliot, to deny altogether the values she shares with Wordsworth. Defending herself from one powerful male authority by inventing (or trusting) another, Eliot finds a way to be at once original and deferential.

To repeat Wordsworth literally would in any case be a contradiction in terms. Eliot exploits this contradiction fully: to pay proper homage to Wordsworth would be to have him speak through her, as Maggie lets Thomas à Kempis speak through her; but to do so is necessarily to get Wordsworth wrong and thus to fail to pay proper homage. The more literally Maggie repeats the texts authoritative for her, and the more literally Eliot has her live out what seem to be Wordsworthian notions (in her repetitions of childhood experiences and in her desire for the home objects), the closer she comes both to perfect femininity and to death. But the more literal the repetition, the more divergent from, and subversive of, Wordsworth's aims, for to read Wordsworth literally in a female context is to become a realist. Where the Wordsworthian imagination interrupts or would interrupt between "What is" and "What will be," between material cause and effect, and between the introduction of a dark heroine and the certainty that her end will be unhappy, Eliot's heroines, in submitting to these laws, define a realistic fictional world. The literalizing that characterizes Maggie's adult feelings and actions (her love of the home objects, her desire for literal repetitions of her early life, and her repetitions of texts) is paralleled by Eliot's general turn toward what she persuades us is realism. For Maggie, literalization leads to her death, but it leads for Eliot to something definitively her own—her identity as a novelist of real life and of female experience, an identity that she establishes under cover of seeming to be a docile, feminine reader of her beloved Wordsworth. It is in fact Maggie's death that consolidates Eliot's vital independence from Wordsworth: Maggie dies of choosing social bonds over the self's needs. The scenes of Maggie's reading and instruction are also the scenes of Eliot's reading and instruction; but while Maggie fatally learns the lesson of feminine readership, Eliot fortunately fails.

In later novels, Eliot continues the exploration we have observed in *The Mill on the Floss* of the consequences of literalizing Wordsworthian vision both for her heroines and for her own practice as an author. In the earlier novel, she frames as painfully as possible the price of Maggie's inevitable and female literalizations, and she distinguishes between the fatal effects on Maggie of her passive reading and the critique the author is able to make, through Maggie's suffering, of her own reading. In *Middlemarch*, however, she gives what emerges as the cause of Maggie's suffering a somewhat more comic turn, and she comes closer to identifying her own practices of reading and writing with those of her characters. After emblematically Wordsworthian childhoods, both Mary Garth and Dorothea Brooke give up what are represented as visionary aspirations in favor of the love of (if not a brother, as in Maggie's case) a lover who is like a brother, whose love makes childhood last forever and closes off the visionary world. At the same time, it is as the epigraph to chapter 57 of *Middlemarch* that Eliot writes one of her most important accounts of the relation between her writing and prior texts, an account that suggests both her mastery of concealing subversive reading within apparent docility and her claim that that mastery was always already accomplished, as it is here situated in childhood.

The epigraph consists of a sonnet:[15]

> They numbered scarce eight summers when a name
> Rose on their souls and stirred such motions there
> As thrill the buds and shape their hidden frame
> At penetration of the quickening air:
> His name who told of loyal Evan Dhu,
> Of quaint Bradwardine, and Vich Ian Vor,
> Making the little world their childhood knew
> Large with a land of mountain, lake, and scaur,
> And larger yet with wonder, love, belief
> Toward Walter Scott, who living far away
> Sent them this wealth of joy and noble grief.
> The book and they must part, but day by day,
> In lines that thwart like portly spiders ran,
> They wrote the tale, from Tully Veolan.

Immersed in a copy of *Waverley* loaned to her sister and returned before she could finish it, Mary Ann's response to her loss was to "write out" the part of the story she had read.[16] Neither the sonnet nor the anecdote makes it clear how creative or repetitive this writing was. In the high-toned letter to Maria Lewis in which she repents of her early guilty penchant for novel reading, she says that from her dissatisfaction with the world around her "I was constantly living in a world of my own creation," for which novels supplied "the materials . . . for building my castles in the air" (1:22). Did her reading of *Waverley* provide the impetus for her own inventions, as she suggests in this letter?[17] Or did she, clinging faithfully to memory, literally record the same story that she had read? "Wrote the tale" suggests something that defies the opposition between these two possibilities: she may have so fully internalized Scott as to have been able to reproduce his story feeling that it was her own. Openly venerating Scott, eight-year-old Mary Ann nonetheless retained both her freedom to build castles in the air and her authority over Scott; "wrote the tale" suggests that she wrote Scott as well as Scott himself could have.

This mixture of veneration and independence in one literary act contrasts with the situation of Maggie, for whom there is an abrupt disjunction between reading as invention—as when she "makes stories to the pictures out of [her] own head" as a child, or when later she wishes vainly to change the ending of *The Pirate*—and her reading as rote repetition, as when in a trance of submissiveness at the end of her life she murmurs the words of Thomas à Kempis. The situation in the *Middlemarch* sonnet also contrasts to another act of literary transmission, the acting out with bow and arrows of Scott's archery scene in *Ivanhoe* by Mary Garth's little brother, Ben, in the chapter of which the sonnet is the epigraph. During the reading out loud of the scene, "Ben . . . was making himself dreadfully disagreeable, Letty thought, by begging all present to observe his random shots, which no one wished to do." The little-boy egotism of Ben's reading, which would altogether replace the original text, in its contrast to the more docile listening of the little sister, Letty, suggests that gender matters again in the difference between his awkward aggressiveness and the subtler mastery of the writer in the sonnet. The writing of the tale in the sonnet seems indeed most closely to resemble Eliot's own practice with respect to Wordsworth, in that following open veneration of an authoritative male original, and after dutifully repeating the beginning of his story, both Mary Ann and Eliot change the ending to suit their own requirements, concealing the extent of the change. This is true of Eliot's practice in *The Mill on the Floss*, as we have seen, and it is also true of *Middlemarch*. But while Eliot expresses her sense of the cost and difficulty of such a practice and perhaps protests the necessity of it through Maggie's suffering, the fact that she makes Dorothea's and Mary's inevitably docile female departures from a Wordsworthian original so much less painful than Maggie's suggests that her own departures do not so much protest as accept and even celebrate what can be done within the limits of Victorian womanly duty.

Although we have treated "Brother and Sister" as an adjunct to *The Mill on the Floss*, it was written several years later. Eliot seems to have written "Brother and Sister" in part to revise the use in *The Mill on the Floss* of childhood memories of her brother and of nature, but the more immediate occasion of its composition may have been *Middlemarch*. Memories of her childhood with Isaac may have come back to Eliot with special vividness, as Gordon Haight suggests, because at that time she was beginning to construct the world of Middlemarch in the Warwickshire of her childhood.[18] The writing of *Middlemarch*, as it was first conceived, began in the summer of 1869 with "the Vincy and Featherstone parts"—original versions of all or parts of what are now chapters 11 through 14—and with an "introduction," probably a version of the account of Lydgate's early life, including his "intellectual passion," that the present chapter 15 comprises.[19] Eliot wrote "Brother and Sister" in July 1869; on 19 July she notes in her journal that she is "writing an introduction to 'Middlemarch,'" and on 2 August, she writes that she has begun with the Vincy and Featherstone parts.[20] (This writing all takes place well before the composition of Dorothea's story and the even later integration of that story into *Middlemarch*.) Among "the various elements of the story [that] have been soliciting [her] mind for years—asking for a complete embodiment" (5:16), she notes in February 1869, Fred Vincy and Mary Garth (then named Mary Dove) must have solicited almost the most effectively. "Brother and Sister" recasts the story of Maggie and Tom, and Fred and Mary in turn inherit that theme of a love that because it begins in childhood is unalterable and is associated with an attachment to the land. In developing this relationship, Eliot continues to set the childhood experience of love and of nature in opposition to the growth of what might become the faculty of imagination. As in the brother and sister relationships in *The Mill on the Floss* and the sonnet sequence, although she invokes the authorizing presence of the Wordsworthian pattern, she sees a determining difference between children who grow up in male-female pairs and Wordsworth's specifically male child, whose richest experiences take place in a solitude shared only by the maternal nature of his invention.

Like that of the sisters and brothers, Fred's and Mary's love for each other refers ever backward to an imagined Eden of original, perfect love. They were constant playfellows as children, and "Fred at six years old thought [Mary] the nicest girl in the world, making her his wife with a brass ring which he had cut from an umbrella" (chap. 23). Later when

Farebrother, sent by Fred, is trying to find out the state of Mary's affections, Mary thinks (or the indirect discourse suggests that she thinks) back to that early betrothal, and she explains, "It has taken such deep root in me—my gratitude to him for always loving me best, and minding so much if I hurt myself, from the time when we were very little. I cannot imagine any new feeling coming to make that weaker" (chap. 52). (Maggie and the little sister also value protectiveness, as Mary does here, although the brothers' protection takes more often the form of a painful restraint than the more promising form of "minding so much.")

Fred's "expectations" about Stone Court are a comic version of Maggie and Tom's attachment to their father's mill, but they occupy functionally the same place, in that they demand a return to a specific piece of land, a demand that is fulfilled, if not in precisely the manner Fred had anticipated. Although of all the major characters in the novel Mary alone never forms any wish or plan, she is delighted when her father's new job allows her to refuse a teaching job and stay home. Very early in our introduction to the Fred and Mary plot, before we have even met Mary, a Wordsworthian passage about love for a landscape familiar from childhood established that their story is rooted to the land:

> Little details gave each field a particular physiognomy, dear to the eyes that have looked on them from childhood: the pool in the corner where the grasses were dank and trees leaned whisperingly; the great oak shadowing a bare place in mid-pasture. . . . These are the things that make the gamut of joy in landscape to midland-bred souls—the things they toddled among, or perhaps learned by heart standing between their father's knees while he drove leisurely. (chap. 12)

The passage—whose pool and whispering trees we may recognize from *The Mill on the Floss*—has no direct bearing on the immediate feelings of Fred and Rosamond, who are riding through this landscape on their way to Stone Court. Although Fred is visiting Featherstone to work on his chances for an inheritance, the passage promises that Fred may have a deeper love for the land, a promise fulfilled later by his pleasure in working with Caleb Garth and by his eventual possession of Stone Court as a careful farmer, not as a capitalist. Rosamond's relation to the passage is wholly ironic: her visit to Stone Court is motivated by her wish to meet the new young doctor, who interests her because, as opposed to Fred's attachment to his old playfellow, "She was tired of the faces and figures she had always been used to—the various irregular profiles and gaits and turns of phrase distinguishing those Middlemarch young men whom she had known as boys" (chap. 11).

The variable disjunctiveness between the Wordsworthian passage and the characters to whom it appears immediately to apply is reinforced by manuscript evidence that the passage was written after the scene it precedes. The visit to Stone Court was among those passages written before 2 August 1869, although the extant manuscript may be a later and possibly revised copy, but the introductory paragraph on the landscape belongs to a section added after Eliot had dropped *Middlemarch*, written "Miss Brooke," and then decided to join the two stories.[21] Although the passage may have had an original in the manuscript of 1869, as it now stands it is part of a section added as a bridge, and in fact the chapter does read as though the first paragraph were tacked on to it. Like the Wordsworthian revery at the close of the fishing scene in *The Mill on the Floss*, and despite later intimations of similar themes in Fred and Mary's story (or perhaps because of them), the passage calls attention to itself as not quite fitting its context, as if Eliot were artificially suggesting Wordsworthian possibilities that do not emerge organically from the story.

The same disjunction that occurs between this landscape passage and the story adjacent to it reappears on a larger scale in the relation between Fred and Mary's story and the rest of the novel. Fred and Mary's story was apparently the most difficult for Eliot to interweave with the other plots.[22] In her journal for March 1871, she worried that she had "too much matter" for the novel—"too many 'momenti' " (5:137)—and Jerome Beaty conjectures that only loyalty to her original conception of the book (her own excessive bond to the childhood of the book) kept her from discarding the Fred-Mary plot, which does very little to bridge the separately conceived stories of Lydgate and Dorothea. The introduction in progress in July 1869—if it was the prototype of the present chapter 15—was about Lydgate's "intellectual passion" for anatomy, formed in childhood, resistant to change, and compared (at least in the final version) specifically to romantic passion. Eliot may have originally conceived the novel as the juxtaposition of these two childhood passions. The decision to incorporate Dorothea's story into *Middlemarch* meant a shift in focus from themes shared by Lydgate's story and by Fred and Mary's to themes common to Dorothea's story and Lydgate's—in other words, a change in the central issue of the novel from the course of childhood loves to the course of adult, or symbolic, aspirations. Thus the theme of a disjunction between a childhood in nature and visionary power in adulthood is reflected in the history of the novel's composition, indeed in the final slight disjunctiveness of the form of the novel. Both Dorothea and Lydgate aspire to an ideal synthesis of theory and practice. Dorothea yearns for "some lofty conception of the world which might frankly include the parish of Tipton and her own rule of conduct there" (chap. 1), and as his name Tertius (revised from the more romantic

Tristram, a name more suitable to the original conception of the book) suggests, Lydate's identity is to be the synthesis of a dialectic between a local medical practice and theoretic and scientific research. Aiming too high, too egotistically, without thought for limiting circumstances, both Dorothea and Lydgate have their aspirations revised downward for them, whether happily or not.

Mary and Fred's romance is successful because (after Fred recovers from his disinheritance) they have such moderate aspirations. The aspiration plot circulates around and beyond them, making their situation a comic version of the more profound difficulties experienced by Lydgate and Dorothea. The separation between their story and the two major stories is Eliot's vision of Wordsworth writ large. What Fred and Mary succeed at—the sustaining of a childhood love—seals them off from what most concerns Dorothea and Lydgate, the search for a life adequate to the highest of imaginative needs. As in *The Mill on the Floss*, a childhood that resembles Wordsworthian childhood but that is actually spent in loving someone else leads, not toward sublimity, but toward practical compromises in which larger possibilities for individual growth yield to loyalty to the good of others.

Mary's love for Fred, never really questioned, is at one point defined against higher possibilities consciously and willingly foregone. Having understood in chapter 57 that Farebrother loves her,

> It was impossible to help fleeting visions of another kind—new dignities and an acknowledged value of which she had often felt the absence. But these things with Fred outside them, Fred forsaken and looking sad for the want of her, could never tempt her deliberate thought.

Worded as a restriction, not just of possibility, but of thought itself, this passage follows a restatement of the importance of loyalty to ties formed in childhood:

> Mary earnestly desired to be always clear that she loved Fred best. When a tender affection has been storing itself in us through many of our years, the idea that we could accept any exchange for it seems to be a cheapening of our lives. And we can set a watch over our affections and our constancy as we can over other treasures.

Sympathetic as this passage is, its economic metaphor lends a chilling tone to its endorsement of what amounts to an illusion, even if it is a necessary and a beautiful illusion. Mary repeats this negative reasoning in defending her choice to her father in the last chapter. After saying that she loves Fred "because I have always loved him," her half-joking tone shifts to seriousness: "I don't think either of us could spare the other, or like any one else better, however much we might admire them. It would make too great a difference to us—like seeing all the old places altered, and changing the name for everything."

Such a love is a defense against the fragility of identity and the arbitrariness of language.[23] It provides a clue to life, but it is a choice of feeling that excludes thought. Many readers have found it difficult to share Eliot's interest in and sympathy for Fred, but Fred's value in the story is his lack of admirable qualities.[24] Through him Eliot can test the power of loyalty to childhood loves, without which he would be quite far from what Mary—consulting other faculties besides her loyalty—might wish for in a husband. The entertaining of "fleeting visions of another kind" would shake the very basis of identity, and this love, the getting and providing of security, is a defense against the effects of such visions. Like Maggie and the sonnets' little sister, Mary seeks a secure identity at the price of possibility; she cannot have both (as Wordsworth can). The difference is that while Maggie minds terribly, Mary minds hardly at all; marrying Farebrother would hardly have been for her an experience of the sublime. Still, the danger to her identity threatened by her "fleeting visions" recalls the difference between Wordsworth's experience of imaginative vision as a child and that of Maggie or of the little sister in the sonnet sequence. While for Wordsworth vision leads to further visions, Eliot's heroines must refuse vision in favor of, or convert it by literalizing it into, the machinery of a more prosaic life. That Mary thrives happily on this literalization, while Maggie does not, suggests Eliot's effort to make the impossibility for women of Wordsworthian vision seem as advantageous for her heroines as it is for her own writing. Labeling with Wordsworth's terms for his own childhood the portrayal of a childhood that leads to a happily un-Wordsworthian adult life, Eliot obtains Wordsworth's authority for severing the poet's own connection between childhood in nature and the growth of visionary imagination.

At the very start of the novel, as Eliot finally assembled and rewrote it, Dorothea's plot of revised aspirations begins with a scene involving her mother, a mother whose distant but distinct resemblance to Maggie's mother suggests that, like Mary's, Dorothea's turn away from visionary possibility will resemble, though far less disastrously, Maggie's literalizing life. Much as Mrs. Tulliver's life is wholly absorbed in inert things, all we know of Dorothea's mother is her association with objects and their capacity for distracting women's attention from more visionary or "theoretic" aims. Maggie's mother is alive and therefore not available to the kind of figurative replacement to which Wordsworth's mother yields, but even though Dorothea's mother is dead, her meaning for her daughter is much closer to that of Maggie's mother than of Wordsworth's. In the first scene of the novel, Dorothea and Celia are discussing the division of their mother's silent legacy of jewels in a way that emblematizes the general shift Dorothea makes over the course of the novel from yearning toward theory to accepting available actuality. The sisters' values at first seem polarized: Celia loves jewels and especially her appearance in them, while Dorothea in the light of her religious theories considers them vanities. But when by coincidence "the sun passing beyond a cloud sent a bright gleam over the table," which forces her to see "how very beautiful these gems are" (chap. 1), Dorothea's clear spiritual vision becomes confused, and the scene ends in Celia's concluding that her sister is "not always consistent." Dorothea's confusion results from an accidental resemblance between the worst of female vanity and the highest spiritual value, a resemblance that obliges her to try "to justify her delight in the colours by merging them in her mystic religious joy." Like the accidents of Maggie and the little sister catching fish while doing what is considered wrong, the coincidence here of spiritual and literal is the start of Dorothea's long learning that her "theoretic" mind must bend to circumstances and to the senses, her individual vision to social practice.

That the jewels are all that remain of Dorothea's mother, and that the worldly Celia (who later styles herself as matron) inherits almost all of them, establishes a connection between the dead mother and the world of objects, senses, and circumstances that initially opposes Dorothea's ardent theorizing. Mrs. Brooke's jewels are only a more tasteful version of Mrs. Tulliver's ugly hats, spotted table linens, tippets, and frills. Dorothea's failure to make a convincing coherence between her sensual response to her mother's jewels and her theory about them repeats our sense about Maggie that for a woman there is no "mother tongue of the imagination" (*Mill on the Floss*, 1:5). Unlike the mother Wordsworth reinvents in the form of nature, these heroines' mothers endorse limitation and literal repetition. Where theory and an actual good do not coincide, Dorothea learns to prefer actuality, and this choice is defined as female.

Dorothea's resemblance to Maggie in this scene is carried out in various ways in the rest of the novel. It is clear from the start that Dorothea will find no path, clear or circuitous, from adolescent ardor to a life that will satisfy the demands of theory. In this book "written for grown-up people,"[25] there is no fishing scene, but when Dorothea is "sobbing bitterly" to herself in Rome, in chapter 20, she is at the same turning point where we have seen Maggie and the sonnets' little sister, where what might have been a road to the sublime is barred by the pressure of other needs. (The situation also resembles Cathy's turning back to childhood in *Wuthering Heights*, whereas her author, as well as

Jane Eyre and her author, adopt symbolic ways.) She is in the process of realizing that she has married the wrong man—an utterly innocent error, like Maggie's and the little sister's, yet with far greater practical consequences even than Wordsworth's transgression in stealing the rowboat. She experiences about her marriage a "feeling of desolation" that is heightened by the "stupendous fragmentariness" of Rome with its "gigantic broken revelations," its "ruins and basilicas, palaces and colossi," its "vast wreck of ambitious ideals, sensuous and spiritual." In her innocence and simplicity of heart, she has "no . . . defence against deep impressions," and the epigraph confirms that she is at this point a vulnerable child:

> A child forsaken, waking suddenly,
> Whose gaze afeard on all things round doth rove,
> And seeth only that it cannot see
> The meeting eyes of love.

This scene of a bewildered child whose mind, caught at a moment of moral crisis, is battered by gigantic broken revelations, recalls the way in which Maggie and the little sister of the sonnets revise the child's experience in the boat-stealing scene in *The Prelude*. Just as Wordsworth's vision is blocked by "solitude / Or blank desertion" and turned inward so that he cannot see "familiar shapes" or the "colours of green fields," Dorothea's desolation turns her vision inward so that she blames herself for her marriage and internalizes the vast awfulness of Rome. The "huge and mighty forms" Wordsworth inwardly sees instead are his intimation of the imaginative vision into which he is growing. Wordsworth characteristically figures such visitations in just this way, as the replacement, often very abrupt, of an outer light by an inner one. In the Intimations Ode, the poet is grateful for "Those shadowy recollections, / Which . . . Are yet a master light of all our seeing"; or in the Simplon Pass passage from *The Prelude*, "the light of sense / Goes out, but with a flash that has revealed / The invisible world" (6. 600–602).

For Dorothea, however, the replacement of outer by inner light produces effects opposite to those that occur in Wordsworth. When Will sees her in the Vatican in chapter 19, she seems to be gazing, not at the statues, but at a streak of sunlight on the floor. But after the narrator's long discussion of Rome and marriage we learn that

> she did not really see the streak of sunlight on the floor more than she saw the statues: she was inwardly seeing the light of years to come in her own home and over the English fields and elms and hedge-bordered highroads; and feeling that the way in which they

might be filled with joyful devotedness was not so clear to her as it had been. (chap. 20)

When Dorothea is, like Wordsworth at his highest moments of inward vision, blind to sunlight and to statues, her inner seeing of an inner light reveals to her ironically only the grimmest of realistic pictures. "The light of years to come" represents a light that is closer to the common day into which the clouds of glory in the Intimations Ode fade than it is to the "master light" of visionary seeing. Where Wordsworth's blank desertion supervises the conversion of an actual "huge peak" into "huge and mighty forms" within the mind, Dorothea's desolation signals no creative power. It is that inward vision itself, and its inevitable fulfillment, against which she is in most need of defenses.

It is at the moment of her turning away from romantic vision—which is in any case, not visionary, but a realistic envisioning—that Will visits her, and his visit seals her choice by providing something toward which to turn. What she turns toward in Will is, as is true also for Mary and for Maggie, an imagined past. The narrator says of the change in Dorothea's perception of her marriage that "the light had changed, and you cannot find the pearly dawn at noonday" (chap. 20). Yet the pearly dawn is just what Will offers her: a reversion to innocence and to a metaphoric childhood to accompany her turning away from the desolateness of private consciousness and visionary power. Will and Dorothea are consistently described as children when together or thinking of each other, so that figuratively they become a childhood couple much like Maggie and Tom or Mary and Fred.[26] Each seems younger than the other at their first meeting in Rome. Coming out of her room to greet him,

> there were just signs enough that she had been crying to make her open face look more youthful and appealing than usual. . . . He was the elder by several years, but at that moment he looked much the younger, for his transparent complexion flushed suddenly. (chap. 21)

Later, Will grants himself and Dorothea an Edenic past before the catastrophic misunderstanding occasioned when Dorothea sees him with Rosamond:

> Until that wretched yesterday . . . all their vision, all their thought of each other, had been as in a world apart, where the sunshine fell on tall white lilies, where no evil lurked, and no other soul entered. But now—would Dorothea meet him in that world again? (chap. 82)

This prelinguistic, Edenic past of perfect mutual understanding is of course completely illusory. But, like the narrator's assertion in *The Mill on the Floss* that Maggie and Tom have had an Edenic childhood, and like the disjunctive description of childhood's beloved landscape in relation to Fred and Rosamond—like the whole relation of the Fred-Mary plot to the rest of the novel—their belief in it is what secures the permanence of their love. If Dorothea is the child in the epigraph, waking afraid, she turns from desolate absence to "the meeting eyes of love" of Will, who offers through a return to an imaginary childhood a way out of the impasse into which her vision leads.

In the larger program of the novel, Dorothea's choice of Will represents her final abandonment of her quest for a life of theory, a life as a subject within the symbolic order. Like Maggie's bliss at the round pool with Tom, Dorothea's and Will's vision of the past—their illusion of a shared childhood—demands fulfillment in terms of literal repetition, not of growth or change. Will's way of thinking about recovering Dorothea's love is "But now—would Dorothea meet him in that world again?" In offering a return to the "pearly dawn," Will offers Dorothea an improvement over Casaubon, but a light no more visionary than Casaubon's disappointing noon. She will replace the grim "light of years to come" with the light of hours or years gone by. This loving repetition of an imagined past excludes, with Dorothea's consent, what might remain of her individual vision and aspiration: "'It is quite true that I might be a wiser person, Celia,' said Dorothea, 'and that I might have done something better, if I had been better. But this is what I am going to do'" (chap. 84). For Dorothea, the realm of imaginative vision is always finally what might have been but will never be, not, as for Wordsworth, "something evermore about to be." Where flashes of inward light shift Wordsworth's narrative to a new level and lead to the poet's growth, the lights that Dorothea lives in are all ultimately variants on the light of day, and there is no visionary light that shines inwardly in contrast to an outer darkness or blindness. In Wordsworth, the hope that "Paradise, and groves / Elysian" will become "A simple produce of the common day" remains in the realm of prophecy; for Eliot's heroines, who ultimately dwell only in the light of common day, paradise remains retrospective, at best a saving illusion about the past.

One final light flashes before the close of Dorothea's story, in the scene in which Dorothea and Will finally agree to marry.

There came a vivid flash of lightning which lit each of them up for the other—and the light seemed to be the terror of a hopeless love. Dorothea darted instantaneously from the window; Will followed

her, seizing her hand with a spasmodic movement; and so they
stood, with their hands clasped, like two children, looking out on
the storm. (chap. 83)

The brief scene recapitulates the salient features of the scene in Rome.
Light that seems to be interior usurps the place of inward light and
illuminates a relationship instead of an individual consciousness.
Although the feelings involved are entirely opposite, "the light of years to
come in her own home," which is after all not her own home but
Casaubon's, is not far in kind from this light "which lit each of them up
for the other." This seeing in which vision that seems interior is of the
other, not of the self, is followed in both cases with a turn toward Will
and toward a figurative childhood: "like two children."

The only imaginable happy end for Dorothea, by this point, is the
literalization, or literal reproduction, of that figurative childhood. In
marrying Will, Dorothea may give up her quest for a life of theory,
"feeling that there was always something better which she might have
done," but the "small row of cousins at Freshitt who enjoyed playing
with the two cousins visiting Tipton" literalize and so confirm the happy
childhood in the Midlands landscape that has been only figurative for
their parents. Dorothea's abandonment of the "something better" she
might have done resembles Mary's cleaving to Fred by keeping herself
from thinking of "fleeting visions," and likewise Dorothea's final literalization of a figurative childhood resembles Mary's future, which consists of its happy repetition of the past. Turning from "possibility" back
to the solid reality of her childhood, Mary marries a man who will learn
her father's trade and become almost as much a realist as he. Mary and
Fred's last scene in the story guarantees this reproduction of the past,
through their repetition of each other's words and through their recur-
rence to the original childhood action that has secured their love. Mary
has just told Fred the news that he is to live in Stone Court and earn its
possession:

"Pray don't joke, Mary," said Fred, with strong feeling. "Tell
me seriously that all this is true, and that you are happy because of
it—because you love me best."
"It is all true, Fred, and I am happy because of it—because I love
you best," said Mary, in a tone of obedient recitation.
They lingered on the door-step under the steep-roofed porch,
and Fred almost in a whisper said—
"When we were first engaged, with the umbrella-ring, Mary,
you used to—"

The spirit of joy began to laugh more decidedly in Mary's eyes. (chap. 86)

And the future sketched in the finale is an entirely happy repetition of the past:

> On inquiry it might possibly be found that Fred and Mary still inhabit Stone Court ... that on sunny days the two lovers who were first engaged with the umbrella-ring may be seen in white-haired placidity at the open window from which Mary Garth, in the days of old Peter Featherstone, had often been ordered to look out for Mr. Lydgate.

While Maggie's docilely female repetitions kill her, Mary's bring happiness. Likewise, Mary's relation as a reader and writer to prior texts is a comic version of Maggie's. Mary's "Stories of Great Men, taken from Plutarch," transformations of formal, abstract Latin prose into English and presumably into her lively narrative style, is the literary counterpart of her other docile female repetitions. That its authorship is attributed to Fred, the former classical scholar, reinforces the containment of this writing within Victorian paradigms of female propriety. At the same time, the title, "taken from Plutarch," suggests a daring theft, undertaken under the cover of such propriety. This comically ambiguous situation recalls that of Mary Ann in the sonnet about Scott, in which it is unclear whether "wrote the tale" means authoritative and prior invention or daughterly veneration; and it is the sonnet's ambiguity as to deference or originality that models Eliot's own practice with respect to Wordsworth.

If Mary's fate is a comic version of Maggie's, Dorothea's is likewise a happier version of the abandonment of theory or vision for the literal. And yet that Dorothea nearly dies in giving birth to the first of the "two cousins visiting Tipton," to the literal embodiment of her figurative past, recalls the danger associated with childbirth's reproduction of the self as child in the Brontës' novels. The danger of the literal of which Maggie dies is echoed when Celia, anticipating the news of Dorothea's marriage, thinks "of her sister as the dangerous part of the family machinery" (chap. 84). The dark overtones of the finale's closing account of Dorothea allude particularly to Maggie's fate: the characterization of "her full nature" as a river that "spent itself in channels which had no great name on the earth" recalls the river in which Maggie drowns; and that those like Dorothea "rest in unvisited tombs," in the closing words of the novel, recalls the tomb of Maggie and Tom, visited by Philip, Stephen, and Lucy. If Mary Garth and the little girl writing Scott's novel in the sonnet

offer enactments of Eliot's own myth of female literary transmission—
apparently submissive, yet changing the ending—enactments that suggest Eliot's contentment with that myth, the Maggie-tints in Dorothea
suggest otherwise, that the inevitability of women's variance from the
Wordsworthian model brings, not only power, but also pain.

7

The Author as Mother: Bearing the Word as Nineteenth-Century Ideology

On the maternal bosom the mind of nations reposes; their manners, prejudices, and virtues,—in a word, the civilization of the human race all depend upon maternal influence."[1] It would have been difficult for a woman reading such words in the early Victorian period to have escaped the pressure that they and countless similar exhortations placed on women to embrace motherhood as a vocation—or, at the very least, to define any other vocation in terms of motherhood.[2] Both Eliot and Gaskell attempt to accommodate at once their own desires to write and the expectation that they perform the roles that accumulate around the idea of mother in Victorian England. Gaskell was a mother before she became a writer, and she raised four daughters while writing; Eliot became the figurative mother of George Lewes's adolescent sons at the same time that she began writing fiction. Encomiums about woman's exalted mission as mother, which we would today recognize as characteristically Victorian, indeed do not begin appearing until the 1830s and 1840s, apparently in response to the perception of women's growing independence from the home. Eliot and Gaskell wrote under a pressure much stronger than that experienced by Mary Shelley in the second decade of the century. It is largely in Shelley's 1831 revisions to *Frankenstein* that she attempts most explicitly to bring her writing in line with women's domestic vocation. In order to understand how Gaskell's and Eliot's fictions embody their differing strategies in this endeavor, it will first be necessary, in this chapter, to explicate their more overt discussions of it in letters and other nonfictive prose.

But first, what did it mean to be a mother in mid-nineteenth-century England, and what did motherhood mean for a writer? Why were these vocations perceived as conflicting with one another? In looking for answers to these questions, we will need to review certain aspects of cultural mythology about motherhood, first from medicine and then from religion. It is important to realize how late in the century the physiology of maternity came to be understood, and how resistant to the influences of scientific progress the powerful ideology of motherhood was. Throughout the nineteenth century, arguments for the restriction of women in the home and away from the public workplace were based on male fantasies about women's physiology (for example, many authorities believed that women were completely incapacitated for a full week out of four by menstrual periods),[3] and the socially constructed physiology of maternity is a crucial metaphor for, because fantasized cause of, the restriction of women's minds within certain ideologically determined boundaries.

Aristotle believed that an embryo formed in the uterus only when menstrual blood was activated by semen. The woman's part is thus entirely passive, the man's active; and she contributes only the matter, while he contributes the soul and the form, so that nothing material passes between them.[4] Given Aristotle's hierarchized opposition between matter and spirit, which denigrates matter, this view gives women a decidedly inferior role in reproduction. Aristotle's view constitutes a defense against the obvious visual evidence of women's powerful and active role in childbearing, a defense such as the one that Aeschylus articulates through Apollo in The Eumenides—"The mother is no parent of that which is called / her child, but only the nurse of the new-planted seed / that grows"—or that Freud identifies in patriarchal religion in Moses and Monotheism.[5]

Aristotle's view, as revised and conveyed through Aquinas's view that "the female generative virtue provides the substance but the active male virtue makes it into the finished product," persisted through the late seventeenth century;[6] but the ideological implications of this view were not even then dissipated by two scientific discoveries that might, in a less biased cultural environment, have complicated the perceived opposition between male and female roles. In the 1660s, the egg-producing follicles within the ovaries were first "discovered," but because the ova themselves had not been observed, the function of these follicles was interpreted in line with Aristotelian thinking, as part of the mechanism for incubating the male seed.[7] In 1677, Leeuwenhoek first observed what he described as "animalcula" swimming in semen; but instead of debunking the notion that the man contributes nothing material to reproduction, this discovery gave new impetus to a different theory with the same ideology, the "homunculus" theory that the fetus arrives fully formed from the father and is merely nourished by the mother.[8] (After

Leeuwenhoek, observers claimed to see fully formed, miniature body parts on these animalcules.) Thus it was possible to continue believing that the mother contributes mere matter alone and that the father contributes the form and spirit and constitutes the determining influence in activating the passive womb. The currency of this belief at the time of these discoveries is reflected in Milton's portrayal in *Paradise Lost* of the creation of the earth out of chaos:

> on the wat'ry calm
> His brooding wings the Spirit of God outspread,
> And vital virtue infus'd, and vital warmth
> Throughout the fluid Mass . . .
>   then founded, then conglob'd
> Like things to like . . .
>
> (7. 234–40)

The belief in the activity of the male spirit and the passivity of female matter persists even in "scientific" writing up through the turn of the nineteenth century, in a view such as Erasmus Darwin's that "the real power of imagination, in the act of generation, belongs solely to the male."[9]

In 1827, von Baer first observed an ovum and recognized that it was produced by the ovary, but it was not until 1845 that it was recognized that ova are spontaneously produced every month, and not, as it had still been assumed, called into existence by intercourse.[10] The delay between these two discoveries suggests the reluctance with which researchers yielded up their view of women's unmixed passivity and materiality. Even after the discovery of the spontaneous production of ova, it was a long while again before the discovery that women's fertile periods coincide, not with menstrual periods, but with intervals between.[11] This delay again suggests the desire to retain the belief that menstrual blood is or at least typifies the mother's contribution, a nourishing substance without form.

This fantasy, that the child originates in and belongs to the father and that the mother provides merely the environment in which the child grows, persisted throughout the nineteenth century in ordinary assumptions about maternity, as the evidence of guidance books for mothers suggests. M. L. Holbrook, the author of one such book, comments, "all the best authorities, ancient and modern, agree in saying that the cheerful or sorrowful state of the mother is often gradually, quietly, indelibly transferred to the disposition of the child while yet unborn."[12] This assertion is based on an assumption about the important role played by the mother's blood, which circulates to the child and, according to

Holbrook, carries with it the "habitual states" of the mother's mind. This well-documented "gradual modification" of the child's character by the mother's blood Holbrook carefully distinguishes from the superstition that a mother's ungratified longings, or her reactions to surprises and shocks, might be impressed in the form of birthmarks onto the child's body, for there is "no nervous connection" between mother and child. While these comments would seem to give the mother a primary role in forming the spirit of the child, the concentration on her potential threat to the child assumes that the child has an existence apart from hers, deriving from another source. Moreover, the care with which Holbrook distinguishes between an absence of "nervous connection" but the presence of a connection through the blood asserts his belief in the mother's essentially material role. That her character influences her child's through the blood is an unfortunate by-product of this material connection, and therefore women's activities and feelings ought to be restricted. Because "passionate" women injure fetuses and produce enfeebled children, Holbrook recommends "self-control" and "equanimity" in the mother; a mother's anger or spiritual disorders can make her child "a reproduction of [her] own evil feelings."[13] Indeed, this justification of restrictions on a mother's thoughts appears to be the origin of this author's notion of the mother's spiritual influence; and the view that men have the right to control pregnant women's minds and bodies, because men are the origin and guardian of the fetus, persists today.[14]

That nineteenth-century women shared this conceptualization or myth of maternity, in which the fetus originates in an authoritative male source and passes through a female body that is construed as a potentially dangerous growth medium, is suggested in the letters and other texts by Gaskell and Eliot that we will shortly consider. In order to estimate the effect on women writers of this myth of motherhood, however, it is necessary to look at one more strand in this ideological web. The figure of the Virgin Mary not only represents an exaggerated version of the Aristotelian view of women's passive role in reproduction, but it also specifically articulates this view in terms of language, in the myth of the Virgin's impregnation by the Word.

Although the notion of a virgin birth would appear to suggest the autonomy and power of Mary's maternity, quite the opposite is true: the point of the myth is how little she had to do with it. According to Marina Warner, all interpreters' accounts of the virgin birth emphasize the intactness of the Virgin's body. Not only was she a virgin when she conceived, but she also remained a virgin even during and after giving birth, "a literal epiphany of integrity." Between 1563 and 1964 this notion was dogma, an article of faith.[15] Paradoxically, the point of

Christ's incarnation is that, born of a mortal woman, he unites God's spirit with human flesh; and yet in order to preserve the notion of his holiness, his mother was increasingly depicted as abnormally perfect herself, until in 1854, her immaculate conception (the belief that she too was conceived without sex) became dogma too, effectively neutralizing the idea that the incarnation makes Christ human.[16] Christ as God's word must pass through a mother's body, but in as spiritual and nonphysical a manner as possible, scarcely touching or being touched by female flesh. As Warner points out, the worship of Mary as mother is predicated on a profound hatred for women's bodies. Mary may have been thought to have contributed the matter or substance to the Holy Spirit that passed through her, as medieval theologians following Aristotle believed, but given the denigration of matter by Aristotle and the Church alike, it was important to reduce her role in his birth as far as possible: "It was a deeply misogynistic and contemptuous view of women's role in reproduction that made the idea of conception by the power of the Spirit more acceptable."[17] Mary is worshipped as a mother to the extent that she proves that all mothers should aspire to play as small a role as she in the creation of new beings; and this view recalls the male circumvention and usurpation of the maternal in the *Eumenides*, in Genesis, and also in *Frankenstein*.

Victorian women knew simultaneously that, like Mary's motherhood, their own was exalted as a vocation for women and denigrated relative to men's activities. Although Gaskell's Unitarianism, with its refusal as irrational of the belief in the divinity of Jesus, has no place for Mary at all, and although Eliot's religion in the period of her novel writing consisted of a figurative belief in the beauty and importance of religion as a humanly invented myth,[18] their own portrayals of motherhood in relation to language bear a striking resemblance to the conservative, dogmatic views of Mary we have just reviewed. Gaskell, for example, in a passage we will look at shortly, identifies herself with Mary in relation to a shared problem about their children's language. Eliot's novel *Romola* at least provisionally considers a madonna-like heroine as figure for the novelist's role. The Victorian ideology of the "Angel in the House" denies, as does Catholic dogma, the physicality of women's bodies and of the sexual origin of new life, and substitutes for the maternal body a spiritual presence that presides over but does not seem to touch its family. Martin's argument in "The Civilization of the Human Race by Women," excerpted at the beginning of this discussion, depends on the disembodied spirituality of the "celestial image," "the angel" whom a man marries and whose "maternal love, human love, begins then at the point where animal instinct terminates." He asserts that each of us is born twice, physically and spiritually, and that "our mother owes us that second birth."[19] Although this overly spiritualized view of the mother defined implicitly as Mary would seem to differ greatly from the Aristotelian view of the mother's materiality (and from the nineteenth-century guidebook's emphasis on the mother's blood that reflects this view), these views coexist with and indeed are of a piece with one another through their common assumption that the mother is merely transmitter of a father's (or Father's) word or seed.

What is of particular relevance to Gaskell and Eliot in this nineteenth-century version of virgin birth is not only the myth of Mary as transmitter of God's word but also the interdict on Mary's own manipulation of language that forms a conspicuous part of the myth. Paintings of the girlhood of the Virgin from the Renaissance onward often portray her reading. Annunciations, too, show Mary reading, interrupted by the arrival of the angel Gabriel, whether to convey the Word mystically into her womb or simply to announce the virgin birth. After Mary has become a mother, her relation to books changes: paintings of the madonna and child often include a book, but the book is closed, or she is not reading it. The book Mary reads before the Annunciation is the Bible, open to the prophecy of Isaiah, "Behold, a virgin shall conceive, and bear a son, and shall call his name Immanuel" (Isaiah 7:14). After this prophecy has been fulfilled, the closed book she carries along with the Christ child signifies the closure of her perpetual virginity (an allusion, perhaps, to the vision of a sealed book in Isaiah 29:11, 12). If the book is open, it is the Gospel or the Book of Wisdom, signifying the education of the child.[20] This shift from Mary as a girl reading to Mary as a mother holding a book she does not read has important implications for the history of women's relation to the written word, for it gathers in one continuous image much of the ideology of the notion that women can have children or language but not both. Some of the most recent manifestations of this ideology we have traced in the Lacanian picture of the mother as the silent ground of language whose perpetual absence makes language possible. Or in the Brontë's novels, a girl without a child can be in the position of the writer, but only at the cost of denigration both of literal and figurative childbirth and of any practice or myth of nonsymbolic language.

When Matthew quotes Isaiah's prophecy that "a virgin shall conceive" at the center of his own account of the birth of Christ (Matt. 1:22, 23), he makes it clear that Mary's virginity at Christ's conception is determined by the requirement that prophecy be fulfilled: "Now all this was done, that it might be fulfilled which was spoken of the Lord by the prophet." Although he means that the actual virgin birth verifies the prophecy, his words also suggest that belief in the fiction of a virgin birth is determined by a prior text. He exposes his belief that the words, simply by having been written by Isaiah, have the power to determine the bodily state of the woman. The image of Mary as a girl reading the prophecy thus suggests the causal power of the text to make her enact the words she reads. That she will enact them because she reads them is suggested most clearly by one of the many accounts of what actually happens in the moment of the Annunciation. The word of God, whether carried or merely heralded by Gabriel, enters Mary by the ear and grows in her, merely nourished by her blood. Bizarre as this theory is, it is really only a logical extension of the Aristotelian view of ordinary conception, in which only form and soul pass from father to mother.[21] Although this account is only one of many—in others, something closer to a natural conception occurs—and although Protestant women in mid-nineteenth-century England would have denigrated such a superstition, this theory articulates as directly as possible the power of God's performative word over women readers. According to Justin Martyr, an early interpreter, Mary's conceiving the Word is determined by a text prior to the prophecy of Isaiah: "For Eve, an undefiled virgin, conceived the word of the serpent, and brought forth disobedience and death. But the Virgin Mary, filled with faith and joy, when the angel Gabriel announced to her the glad tidings . . . answered: 'Be it done to me according to thy word.'"[22] Women's obligation to enact the word of God is thus a compensation for the first woman's conceiving the word of Satan.

Thus even as a reader, Mary is preparing to transmit the word she reads. The sealed book she sometimes holds when depicted after the birth of Christ signifies her perpetual virginity, but it is significant that a book should be the figure chosen here: once she has conceived and brought forth the one Word she is allowed to read and transmit, books are closed to her; there is to be no more reading. This situation in the myth is reflected in the nineteenth-century view, which gained increasing currency toward the end of the century, that too much reading (to say nothing of writing) would unfit women for their proper duties, because, on the assumption that there is a finite quantity of bodily energy, the increased demand for blood by the brain during an adolescent girl's education would divert nourishment from the reproductive organs.[23] Herbert Spencer writes in 1867 that educated women are more likely to be sterile than others; moreover, "the reproductive power means the power to bear a well-developed infant, and to supply that infant with the natural food for the natural period. Most of the flat-chested girls who survive their high-pressure education are incompetent to do this."[24] Issues of *The Lancet* for the 1870s and 1880s contain numerous articles detailing the harmful effects of education on girls, including amenorrheoa and chlorosis. After 1870, when university education began to be open to a very few women, this idea seems to have been part of an endeavor to discourage women from taking advantage of new opportunities. But the view of reading's damage to actual organs only lends the authority of the relatively new discipline of medical science to the traditional view, well established, of the masculinity of reading for the purpose of writing, and of the impropriety of women's trespassing on this male domain. Bearing a father's word, women's only acceptable role with respect to language, is incompatible with women's education and with any practice that would enable a woman to write.

Our interest here is not so much with these ideological influences themselves as with the ways in which they shaped myths of language and Gaskell's and Eliot's revisions of those myths. The notion that women's role, both with respect to children and to words or the Word, is to transmit them from their spiritual, paternal origin into embodied form and then out into the world, originates, as we have seen, in the denigration and avoidance of the mother's powerful flesh. This attitude toward the mother is the founding gesture of what has been termed the symbolic order. If in the symbolic order language is constituted as desire for a chain of substitutes for the mother, a translation of her literal body into figures, then we can see this law at work in the denial of her material priority and the replacement of it by powerless figurative substitutes in our founding texts. In the creation story in Genesis and in *Paradise Lost*, the mother is circumvented in the creation of Adam and in her then being recreated, by Adam's imagination, as a derivative of the man.[25] Similarly, in the story of Christ's birth, the avoidance of the mother's flesh is followed by the substitution, for the mother, of the Church as the figurative bride of Christ and by the belief that in heaven, disembodied, Christ marries his equally disembodied mother. As we have seen, sons subscribing to past and present versions of this myth of language understand language to be primarily a matter of representation and to require and enable the distancing of the literal (and of the mother's body) through representation's substitution of signifier for referent.

Daughters living by the terms of this same myth understand language both as representation and as reproduction. If, like sons, they desire to be independent of the mother and enter the symbolic order of the father, they may also remain closely tied to the mother long past their entry into the symbolic order. As Chodorow suggests, they may wish to repeat their early relation to their mother, not as sons do through representations of her in romantic attachments, but through a literal reenactment of the mother-child relation in bearing children of their own. The ideological encouragement to be the mother, to be the literal from which paternal representation absents itself, may coincide with a daughter's wish to literalize through childbirth—not to represent, but to make figures literal again. This coincidence, which amounts to the appropriation of the latter by the former, results in women's taking up a position with respect to language that, however appealing it might be in a less masculinist culture, becomes a trap and yields only silence in a culture that exclusively values the transcendence of the mother. Women's encouragement to desire to repeat the Virgin Mary's reproduction of the Word is thus the advantage their culture takes of a daughter's understanding the literal differently from the way sons do. Bearing or literalizing the word then in turn transforms the mother into the silent ground of representation, the mother as seen from the son's perspective, to make possible androcentric culture's transcending flight from her as representation.

When Gaskell and Eliot, as acculturated women, work to accommodate both their own imperatives to write and their culture's imperative to be a mother and not to write—or if they must write, to mother language as Mary did—it is this complex positioning of women in the myth of language that they are confronting and exposing. Not only do both authors at different points identify themselves as writers with Mary, but both also began their writing careers with culturally legitimate projects to bear men's words. As we saw in chapter 1, in a letter written during her first daughter's infancy, Gaskell associates literary transmission (whatever she is doing when she is "doing" the English poets) with being a mother, and both with the literalization of figures. Eliot's writing career began with translations that she describes in terms that similarly engage a maternal metaphor, a metaphor that reappears in letters written when she became a stepmother. We will begin with a diary written by Gaskell during her first and second daughters' early years, then turn to letters by each author that explore the problem of the mother as author. Gaskell's and Eliot's struggles with the contradiction between mother and author have important implications, not just for their individual sense of their identities as authors, but more important, also for the myth of language that women writers of the nineteenth century so ambivalently accept and contest.[26]

From March 1835, when Marianne was six months old, until October 1838, when she was four and the second daughter, Meta, was a year and nine months old, Gaskell kept a diary that records primarily her children's progress but also her feelings about them. Written before Gaskell began to write for publication, the diary frames, often as explicitly as the letter we looked at in chapter 1, Gaskell's emerging understanding and reinvention of the myth of women's relation to the symbolic order.

Although the title given to the diary for publication, *My Diary: The Early Years of My Daughter Marianne*, is not Gaskell's own, it serves to introduce the the diary's concern with the identification between mother and daughter.[27] At the end of the first entry, she writes, "I had no idea the journal of my own disposition and feelings was so intimately connected with that of my little baby," suggesting that the diary's original subject was herself alone, but that, as the title suggests, "my diary" is for her equivalent to "the early years of my daughter Marianne." The diary's first entry is particularly full of instances of this identification between mother and daughter. She writes, for example, that she cannot tell whether Marianne's "goodness" is due to "the success of my plans" or to the child's own good health. Apparently accidental juxtapositions of pronouns echo this identification in startling ways, as when Gaskell writes, "She lies down on the floor a good deal, and kicks about; a practice I began very early." In the same entry, the mother feels Marianne's feelings as her own: "She goes to bed *awake*; another practice I began early. . . . Once or twice we have had grand cryings, which have been very very distressing to me; but when I have convinced myself that she is not in pain, is perfectly well and that she is only wanting to be taken up, I have been quite firm, though I have sometimes cried almost as much as she has."

Accompanying the mother's identification with her daughter is the writer's assumption that the diary is legible, or worth reading, only if one or the other of its two subjects is dead. Although for Wordsworth language likewise comes into existence to fill the void created by the son's separation from his mother, this eventuality, the entry into the symbolic order, is for Wordsworth generally beneficial, and certainly natural. Gaskell, by contrast, sees the need for language, given her identification with her daughter, as a disaster. In an opening paragraph prior to the entries themselves, Gaskell begins her dedication to her daughter in the following way: "To my dear little Marianne I shall 'dedicate' this book, which, if I should not live to give it her myself, will I trust be reserved for her as a token of her Mother's love, and extreme anxiety in the formation of her little daughter's character." Marianne's readership depends, to a certain extent, on her mother's death; were her mother alive, presumably she could assure her daughter of "her Mother's love" in person, without the mediation of writing. (It is not known at what point Marianne acquired the diary, but it was in her possession at her death, long after her mother's.) Gaskell's readership, too, depends on death, not her own but Marianne's. Within the text of the diary, Gaskell, thinking almost continually of the fear of Marianne's death, defines herself, rather than Marianne, as the reader. In February 1836, she writes, "I sometimes think I may find this little journal a great help in recalling the memory of my darling child if we should lose her."

Paradoxically, then, while writing the diary may link mother and daughter as interchangeable subjects, reading would isolate them. Reading is undertaken only in the absence of the other, on the assumption within the symbolic order that the only value of written language is referential, so that in the presence of the referent words are superfluous. The dedication also ends with a thought of death. Gaskell characterizes "the love and the hope that is bound up in" Marianne as the hope that "however we may be separated on earth, we may each of us so behave while sojourning here that we may meet again to renew the dear and tender tie of Mother and Daughter." They cannot both be readers, as each one's reading assumes the other's death; and the positive value of death for both will be happily to obviate the need for the mediating text, since what has been aimed at all along is an affirmation of the "tender tie of Mother and Daughter."

The situation of the diary with respect to the symbolic order is thus ambiguous. On the one hand, the act of writing the diary reenacts the boundariless relationship of mother and daughter, as well as representing it. This aspect of the diary suggests that it is written partially in what we have called a literal language, or a language of enactment, as exemplified by the passage from *To the Lighthouse* in which Cam's repetition of Mrs. Ramsay's rhythmic words reassures her of her mother's presence. On the other hand, the diary is also written in self-consciously symbolic language, in which "Mother's love" can be represented by a "token," and in which representation assumes the absence of that which is represented.

Indeed, Gaskell seems often to strive for a symbolic language of observation about her daughter and to extricate herself from her sympathetic identification with her daughter in order to make an accurate account of her progress. Moreover, with respect to her daughter, Gaskell becomes a lawgiver, a promulgator of the law of referentiality. Once Marianne has begun to talk, Gaskell's belief in the referentiality of her own account is echoed by one of the chief tenets of her theory of child rearing, that children should learn that language has clear and single referential meanings. These passages (from December 1835 and November 1836), however, which assert that adults have always done what they say, have an air of pure fictiveness about them.

She quite understands me when I gently tell her to be patient about anything. "Wait a little bit, dear little Baby; Betsy will come soon," always makes her still; because, for one thing, I have never allowed her to be told anyone was going to do anything for her unless they *really* were, and have tried to speak as *truly* to her as ever I could.

I am not aware that any promise has been made to her that has not been strictly fulfilled. And the consequence is, she has a firm reliance on our word.

For the same reason, in the same entry in which she writes of promises, the mother treats the child's words as the literal truth: "A few weeks ago she got a habit of refusing her food, saying 'bye-bye,' &c, when a spoonful was offered to her which she did not quite approve. I found the best plan was to take her at her word, and quietly send the plate away." Initial tears yield, predictably in this improbable account of maternal success, to obedience.

Gaskell maintains her belief in teaching Marianne the referential accuracy and potency of words in the face of direct evidence to the contrary from her own experience; indeed, she maintains her own belief in language's "truth" in the face of such contradictions. In the diary's first entry, she has been reading books on child rearing and tries to put them into practice. Problems arise, however, because "Books do so differ," and the subject on which they most disturbingly differ is that of babies' crying—that is, of babies' own language.

One says "Do not let them have anything they cry for;" another (Mme. Necker de Saussure, "Sur l'Education Progressive," the nicest book I have read on the subject) says: "Les larmes des enfants sont si amères, la calme parfaite de l'ame leur est si nécessaire qu'il faut surtout épargner des larmes." So I had to make a rule for myself.

Not only adducing but quoting these conflicting authorities, she makes her text living proof of the inevitable inconsistencies in language and between the cultures these languages express. But the cultural relativity to which her quoting rather than paraphrasing calls attention disappears in the face of the necessity to find an absolute truth, and her desire for truth mirrors and is mirrored by the truth she believes she has discovered, that babies should learn that language is true.

She solves her dilemma by transforming babies' cries into a symbolic sign system: "We must consider that a cry is a child's only language for expressing its wants. It is its little way of saying 'I am hungry, I am very cold,' and *so*, I don't think we should carry out the maxim of never letting a child have anything for crying." Her theory is either to give the child what it wants right away or, if it is an improper desire, to "withhold it steadily;" so that "the child would become aware that *one* cry or indication of a want was sufficient" and therefore so that "the habit of crying would be broken." This system, she claims, works. And yet it is directly following this proud little account that she confesses to confusion about whether this diary is about her own "disposition and feelings" or about "that of my little baby," the mutual identification that complicates her efforts to establish both for herself and for Marianne a linear and referential language. The projection onto the baby of a symbolic sign system is accomplished at the cost of denying the many other functions of the sounds and gestures babies make, functions such as those that Kristeva and others suggest have to do with the baby's connectedness to the mother.[28]

Despite her role as promulgator of the law, which in any case she does not easily maintain, the diary is full of evidences of Gaskell's position, as mother, on the other side of the law. Indeed, it is as a consequence of her strict maintenance of the law of symbolic language that she finds herself effaced. If language's purpose is strictly referential, it is useful for referring only to absent objects, and since this conscientious mother is almost always present, she is left out of her daughter's language. Just as Marianne's reading the diary presupposes Gaskell's death, Marianne's education in language excludes her mother, yet Gaskell doesn't seem to recognize that her own project to teach Marianne symbolic language contributes to this effect. The entry for December 1835 (Marianne is about fifteen months old) reports two episodes about language, both of which in different ways negate the mother. Her first words, Gaskell reports, are "'Papa, dark, stir, ship, lamp, book, tea, sweep,' &c.— leaving poor Mama in the background." Just before this, she has described how Marianne expresses her love for her Papa by "shouting out his name whenever she hears his footstep, never mistaking it, and dancing with delight when she hears the bell which is a signal for her to come in after dinner." Marianne both reads the signs of her absent father and names him, while "leaving poor Mama in the background."

Gaskell as mother is excluded from her daughter's acquisition of symbolic language because of the position of the mother, and of presence, in that language. But she is also excluded for the related reason discussed at the beginning of this chapter. If childbearing is the reproduction of a past relation to a mother's own mother, a reproduction that is appropriated to the requirements of patriliny, the literary equivalent of this reproduction is Gaskell's reproduction of others' words, her quoting and enacting of the words of fathers and of other speakers of symbolic language. In the same entry in which she describes Marianne's affinity, in language, for her father, Gaskell goes on to give another instance of Marianne's acquisition of symbolic language, in this case her ability to understand it: "I was one day speaking of *biscuits*, but fearing, if she understood me, her hopes would be excited, I merely described them as 'things that were on the breakfast-table this morning' (there were none in the room at the time), when immediately she began to dance in Fanny's arms, saying, 'Bis, bis, bis.'" While Gaskell attempts to circumvent Marianne's understanding, Marianne's sense of referentiality seems to be so strong that she can crack the code designed to exclude her. After quoting her own words and Marianne's, Gaskell quotes, turning to her habitual prayer to remember not to idolize Marianne, "The Lord hath given, and the Lord hath taken away. Blessed be the name of the Lord!" and then closes the entry with the words, "I feel weak and exhausted with writing, or I had meant to write more." Her phrasing suggests that not only the energy to write but even the intention of writing left her. Bearing Marianne has been an act of quotation, and here, quoting or being a conduit for religious language leads not just to "leaving poor Mama in the background" but to ceasing to write altogether. Between the name of Papa and the name of the Lord, there is no room for the mother either as name or as writing subject.

If the name of the Lord seems to end her writing one entry, it is a sermon on the words of the Lord that, a month later, gets her started writing the next one. Apparently she has in the interval accepted the mother's role in language not as a writing subject but as a conduit for others' words. "This morning we heard a sermon from the text, 'And his mother kept all these sayings in her heart.' Oh! how very, very true it is—and I sometimes think I may find this little journal a great help in recalling the memory of my darling child if we should lose her." Two kinds of language transmission are being described and enacted here. First, Gaskell is directly applying both a biblical text and the words of a man of God to her own situation ("how very, very true it is"), doing just as Jesus' mother did; second, she is recording Marianne's "sayings" and doings so as to make a kind of permanent record of her.

Both of these transmissions, however, subvert their own apparent passivity, as the context of the sermon suggest. In the reading, when Jesus is twelve, his parents lose track of him on a trip to Jerusalem; having searched for him for three days, they find him talking with the doctors in the temple. To his mother's question, "Son, why hast thou thus dealt with us?" he responds,

> How is it that ye sought me? wist ye not that I must be about my Father's business? And they understood not the saying which he

spake unto them. And he went down with them, and came to
Nazareth, and was subject unto them: but his mother kept all these
sayings in her heart. And Jesus increased in wisdom and stature,
and in favour with God and man. (Luke 2:49–52)

To take up, first, the second of the analogies between Gaskell and Mary
suggested above: out of context, the phrasing "but his mother kept all
these sayings in her heart" suggests that Mary is simply preserving the
memory of Jesus' parables or other holy sayings, with the analogy that
Gaskell is in the diary simply writing down Marianne's doings and
sayings. But the context suggests, especially as the biblical quotation
comes right after Gaskell's quotations from her daughter's first words,
that what each mother is preserving is not simply the evidence of her
child's precociousness, but rather the evidence of the inevitability of the
child's leaving her. "These sayings" about "my Father's business" produce in Mary the same ambivalence that Marianne's "sayings," her
precocious naming of her father, have just produced in Gaskell. They
combine the promise of a brilliant future with a promise of betrayal, a
betrayal constituted of leaving the mother and entering what we would
now call the Law of the Father, "my Father's business," the symbolic
order. Second, Gaskell, by thus skewing the quotation out of its context,
subverts her own apparently passive transmission of the biblical passage.
She intrudes into it her own quiet protest against the symbolic order's
effacement and betrayal of the mother and thus reinserts her own interests where they seem most to have been excluded. Thus in both
regards, Gaskell manages to ironize the passive transmission of others'
words, the mother's ethic of quotation, preserving, just barely, her own
right to write while seeming to yield it up.

I have been suggesting, on the authority of Chodorow's work, that it is
a woman's wish to reproduce the situation of her early childhood that
induces her to wish for children of her own, a wish that collides with the
paternal order's rather different uses for female powers of embodiment.
In an episode toward the end of the diary, about two years later than the
entries discussed above and after the birth of the second daughter, Meta,
Gaskell writes about the relation between her children and her own
foster mother in a way that indicates her fear that the repetition of the
latter in the former does not yield the desired result. By way of introduction to this episode, it is worth mentioning some of Gaskell's own early
history, which, although not mentioned explicitly in the diary, surely
contributes to her sense that motherhood is a process of repetition that
has its dangers, both for mothers and for children. Gaskell's mother,
Elizabeth Stevenson, died about a year after giving birth to her, the last

of eight children. Her father being unable to care for her, the infant Elizabeth was then adopted by her twenty-year-old cousin, Mary Anne Lumb, who lived with her mother (one of Mrs. Stevenson's sisters) in Knutsford. Mary Anne was a cripple because "as an infant she had jumped from her nurse's arms at an open window on seeing her mother approach the house."²⁹ Like Elizabeth's first mother, this adoptive mother died about a year after becoming Elizabeth's mother, and Elizabeth was ultimately raised by Mary Anne's mother, to whom she refers as Aunt Lumb, "my more than mother."

In the episode reported in the diary, Aunt Lumb had been looking after Marianne in her home in Knutsford during Gaskell's "confinement" (in Manchester) with Meta, when she suffered a stroke in March 1837. Gaskell took Meta, by that time about five weeks old, with her to Knutsford, where Gaskell, the two daughters, and the servant Betsy "were confined to two little bedrooms in that unhappy eight weeks" until Aunt Lumb finally died. Narrated at a distance of half a year, and written as part of Marianne's history, the story is concerned not so much with Gaskell's own grief as with the effect of the whole experience on the two girls. "I rather began to fear that the long confinement in small rooms had *told* upon Marianne's temper," she writes, and later in the same entry she turns to consider Meta in the same way: "I sometimes fancy that eight weeks spent day and night in one little close room, may have had some influence on her temper." Thus in the text of the diary, the grandmother's illness appears primarily as the cause of a confinement detrimental to the tempers of the granddaughters, and her death is defined as the release from that confinement.

The word "confinement" holds a crucial place in this narrative, linking children and grandmother. Gaskell repeats the word in connection with the children's quarters during Aunt Lumb's illness, an illness that causes a confinement. Yet the use of the word suggests Gaskell's fear that it is, in reverse, her own confinement that caused the illness, that her shifting the responsibility for Marianne onto Aunt Lumb during her confinement with Meta might have brought on the stroke. The figurative confinement of childbirth is literalized as the real confinement of living in small rooms, in a way that recalls the association in the Brontës' novels between the literalization of figures and the fear that childbirth will destroy the mother—a fear also invoked by the history of Gaskell's first two mothers, and a fear that *Frankenstein's* version of the same thematics suggests derives from the interference of patriliny in childbirth. When Gaskell's children's births are read in connection with the cooptation of Gaskell's writing by quotation, as part of a myth of language, it appears that these births, instead of reproducing her happy daughterhood with

Aunt Lumb, become representations of that early happiness, on the grounds that they do away with Aunt Lumb, just as, in a system of representation, the figure requires the absence of the referent. Reproduction, colliding with and overtaken by representation, disappears and becomes subordinated to a system that effaces mothers, in the same way that we saw the reproduction of others' words become the form in which Gaskell's own words are subordinated and effaced.

Allowing her text to be a conduit for maxims, laws, and biblical quotations, Gaskell at once yields to the paternal order's requirements and finds a strategy for reconciling motherhood and writing, albeit a minimal sort of writing. That Gaskell has in mind a myth of writing and of authorship as she writes her relation to her daughters (and, briefly, to her foster mother) is suggested at the very start of the diary in a series of passages that implicitly compare the "formation of her little daughter's character" to a novelist's formation of literary characters, a comparison that originates in Marianne's being called, in the text of the diary, the "little subject," both of Gaskell's maternal attention and of her text. As we encounter the text of the diary, it is framed by prefatory remarks in which Clement Shorter, the editor, refers to the "material" he assembed in preparation for writing a biography of Gaskell that he never completed. When Gaskell remarks in the first entry that "the materials put into my hands are so excellent, and beautiful," we are given in brief compass one of the operating analogies of the diary. The formation of a child's character on the basis of materials is like the formation of a literary character on the basis of materials. Furthermore, the formation of Marianne's character takes on the attributes of plot and consistency, cause and effect. Gaskell identifies the kind of character she wishes her daughter to have, then sets rationally about producing it through a series of logical and causal steps: "I try always to let her look at anything which attracts her notice as long as she will, and when I see her looking very intently at anything, I take her to it, and let her exercise all her senses upon it, even to tasting, if I am sure it can do her no harm. My object is to give her a habit of fixing her attention." Gaskell sounds exactly like a novelist or biographer setting out to create a consistent character when she writes toward the end of the first entry, "I put down everything now because I have thought a good deal about the formation of any little plans, and I shall like to know their success. I want to act on principles *now* which can be carried on through the whole of her education."

And yet despite the control that Gaskell seems to exert on the formation of character, whether literary or actual, the importance of the "materials" given her always limits the extent of her authorial control. "I sometimes fear there is too much pride in my own heart in attributing her goodness to the success of my plans, when in reality it is owing to her having hitherto had such good health, and freedom from pain, a blessing for which I cannot be too thankful." This ambiguity, as to whether Gaskell creates her daughter's character or whether instead her daughter is simply passing through her hands, ready formed, duplicates the debates about how much the mother contributes to pregnancy and how much it matters. This ambiguity also duplicates the analogous problem of how much a woman attempting to write as a woman within the symbolic order may lay claim to originating words of her own, rather than docilely passing on the words of others. As we turn to Gaskell's letters about the difficulties of being a woman and a writer, we will see that it is precisely the issues that emerge in the diary that dominate her project to reconcile writing and motherhood.

One of the major themes both in Gaskell's account of forming Marianne's character and in the identification between them is that of "wilfullness," or the opposition between feminine selflessness and an inappropriate selfishness. The issue translates into the terms of character the opposition between passive, womanly transmission and original symbolic creation. Gaskell tries in November 1836 to conceal her anxiety about "such little obstinate fits, and whole hours of wilfullness." Earlier, she worries that "impatience will be one of her greatest faults; and I scarcely know the best way of managing it." Gaskell is determined to train Marianne to repress these expressions of desire, it soon becomes clear, because Gaskell's own feminine character is at stake as well. She praises Marianne for acts of selflessness in language and syntax that suggest that selflessness is valuable, not only for the child, but for the mother as well. Again in November 1836, "She gave me a very pretty little instance of unselfishness when we were last at Knutsford which pleased me very much." Someone tosses candy on the carpet for three children, one of whom is so small she is unable to grab for it; "My own dear Marianne, however, did not put one into her own mouth, though as fond of them as could be, but crammed them into little Emily. It made my heart glad."

Gaskell writes in this way of Marianne's willfulness and her unselfishness because it is the intrusion of her own will that, in this culture, Gaskell fears in herself. Directly following the passage in the first entry in which Gaskell initially sketches Marianne's "bursts of passion," she writes, along with her concern to handle her "materials" correctly, of her fear of her own potential willfulness. "If I should misguide from carelessness or negligence! *wilfully* is not in a mother's heart." Willfulness or selfishness is thus opposed to the aims both of the mother and of the writer whose authorship is of necessity modeled on the supervision of children's passage into society. If she herself is willful, she breaks the implicit pact she makes with her society that if she is to write it is only to be as a passive transmitter of God's and others' words. Throughout the diary, she juxtaposes her running account of Marianne's uneven progress in learning unselfishness with anxieties about her own willfulness, especially toward God's dispensations. Typically she writes, "I pray that I may not make her too much my idol, and oh! if thou shouldst call her away . . . may I try to yield her up to him who gave her to me without a murmur."

Marianne, whose early instruction in feminine unselfishness thus became the focus of Gaskell's ambivalence about her own personal as well as literary unselfishness, grew up to write two novels of her own. In her advice to her daughter upon reading the first of these, *The Three Paths*,[30] Gaskell, by now a famous author, formalizes the conciliatory definition of women's writing as passive transmission implicit in the diary. At the same time, she reveals her continuing ambivalence about adhering to this definition. Her comments stress the importance of not dwelling on the self, by way of a criticism of the novel's disproportion of "thought" to plot. "I think you must observe what is *out* of you instead of examining what is *in* you," her commentary begins.[31] She goes on to argue that the formation of a good plot (which *The Three Paths* really does lack) is the first and crucial step in this direction because the novelist's aim is to be on the outside of what she writes about:

> Then set to & imagine yourself a spectator & auditor of every scene & event! Work hard at this till it becomes a reality to you,—a thing you have to recollect & describe & report fully & accurately as it struck you. . . . Don't intrude yourself into your description. If you but think eagerly of your story till *you see it in action*, words, good simple strong words, will come,—just as if you saw an accident in the street that impressed you strongly you would describe it forcibly. (*Gaskell Letters*, p. 542)

This definition of a story, as something that exists that the novelist merely reports, sets plot on the side of selflessness, as opposed to the selfishness of "too great dwelling on feeling."[32]

Gaskell's metaphors reveal her motives for valuing plot over feeling. Earlier in the same letter she writes:

> It is always an unhealthy sign when we are too conscious of any of the physical processes that go on within ɏ us; & I believe in

like manner that we ought not to be too cognizant of our mental proceedings, only taking note of the results. But certainly—whether introspection be morbid or not,—it is not ^{a} safe ~~for a nov~~ training for a novelist. It is a weakening of the art which has crept in of late years. Just read a few pages of De Foe &c—and you will see the healthy way in which he sets *objects* not *feelings* before you. (*Gaskell Letters*, p. 541; alterations and italics in original)

To be healthy is not to be introspective, and not to be introspective is to be a good novelist. The training in feminine selflessness is thus the same as the training of the novelist. Yet the manuscript of the passage suggests that this advice still does not come as naturally as she would like her daughter to think. Thinking that she has finished with the topic of personal health, her revisions show she has not. She begins to write, "introspection is not safe for a novelist" but revises that to "not a safe training for a novelist." The first version carries over the concerns of the first sentence by considering the novelist as an individual who has good or bad health. Revising toward emphasis on the novelist's product, she still retains the idea of safety, which in turn retains a sense of the novelist's personal stake, contradicting the emphasis she seems at pains to place on the novelist's product. This blurring of the very distinction she wishes to make between novelist and novel suggests that she herself in writing about it is caught in the very lack of objectivity, the morbid concern with one's own health, that she seeks to criticize. Furthermore, while she argues that it is introspection that is unhealthy, her example of what the good novelist objectively reports is telling. "Just as if you saw an accident in the street" suggests that dangers lurk in objectivity and passivity just as much as in introspection.

The paragraph on the greater healthiness of objectivity, and on Defoe as an exemplar of it, ends, "I am sure the right way is this. You are an Electric telegraph something or other—" Her recommendation of "good simple strong words" for reporting such things as accidents presumes the complete transparency of the language that conveys the event to the reader. This figure of the writer as electric telegraph puts as strongly as possible the wish for the writer to be without a self, a transmitter of facts who never intrudes her own feelings. That Gaskell closes with the words, "something or other," with the suggestion that she is trying to recall a tag phrase or quotation, would confirm what she is saying. Even in her advice, she is passing on or reporting someone else's idea, not speaking her own heartfelt feeling. Yet at the same time, these words also suggest that as a memorized belief (not confidently memorized at that) the notion of author as telegraph is inauthentic in some way. She passes it on but implies that she does not fully stand behind what she passes on. Like the accident in the street that is paradigmatic of the objective novelist's subject matter, it lets the reader question her ostensible advocacy of selflessness.

The overt intent of this letter, written in 1859, strongly echoes Gaskell's rhetoric about Charlotte Brontë in her 1857 biography, *The Life of Charlotte Brontë*, in which she sets the selfishness of a writer's imagination against the selflessness of realism. The covert ambivalence of the letter to Marianne echoes a similar ambivalence in *The Life*, where Gaskell uses her identification with Brontë to continue working out her own version of this issue. For example, Robert Southey's famous letter on this subject, which Brontë received in 1837 and Gaskell printed in 1857, became central both to Gaskell's portrait of Brontë and, through her identification with Brontë's own conflict between being a woman and being an author, to her own subsequent rhetoric in letters such as the one to Marianne. In his letter, Southey makes explicit an opposition between literature and female duty that maps gender terms onto the issue of selflessness and selfishness:

> The daydreams in which you habitually indulge are likely to induce a distempered state of mind; and in proportion as all the ordinary uses of the world seem to you flat and unprofitable, you will be unfitted for them without becoming fitted for anything else. Literature cannot be the business of a woman's life, and it ought not to be. The more she is engaged in her proper duties, the less leisure she will have for it, even as an accomplishment and a recreation. To those duties you have not yet been called, and when you are you will be less eager for celebrity. . . .
> Write poetry for its own sake; not in a spirit of emulation, and not with a view to celebrity. . . . So written, it is wholesome both for the heart and soul; it may be made the surest means, next to religion, of soothing the mind and elevating it.[33]

Southey's explicitness about the gender of authorship helps us see how gender is implicit in Gaskell's strictures to Marianne. But it also resembles other letters Gaskell wrote before having read it, letters in which she is just as explicit as Southey. Southey's position, that the opposition between selfish writing and a woman's selfless duties is resolved only by her ceasing to write, is one to which Gaskell throughout her career almost succumbs and out of which she tries to argue herself.

Brontë's response in 1837 is to accept Southey's categories, including his definition of writing as selfish, and framing her defense cagily as his idea, to defend herself by arguing that she has time for both without her writing interfering with her duties:

> You kindly allow me to write poetry for its own sake, provided I leave undone nothing which I ought to do, in order to pursue that single, absorbing, exquisite gratification. [As a governess] I find enough to occupy my thoughts all day long, and my head and hands too, without having a moment's time for one dream of the imagination. In the evenings, I confess, I do think, but I never trouble any one else with my thoughts. I carefully avoid any appearance of preoccupation and eccentricity.[34]

By contrast, perhaps because unlike Brontë's her "proper duties" as wife and mother did not end in the evening, Gaskell attempts to elaborate, in response to a criticism like Southey's, a rhetoric in which writing is redefined as a duty, thus eliminating the conflict altogether. In the letter to Marianne, however, as we have seen, this rhetoric is not quite convincing.

Writing much earlier to her friend Eliza Fox, in 1850, at the start of her professional career, Gaskell gets similarly tangled in her theory of the novelist's selflessness. The letter is in two parts, written on two different days. In the first, which is very like Brontë's response to Southey, Gaskell assents to her correspondent's simple opposition between "home duties" and "individual life." She argues for a balance of the two, even while acknowledging that "*Women*, must give up living an artist's life, if home duties are to be paramount."

> I am sure it is healthy for them to have the refuge of the hidden world of Art to shelter themselves in when too much pressed upon by daily small Lilliputian arrows of peddling cares. . . . but the difficulty is where and when to make one set of duties subserve and give place to the other. I have no doubt that the cultivation of each tends to keep the other in a healthy state,—my grammar is all at sixes and sevens I have no doubt. (*Gaskell Letters*, p. 106)

The balancing of two terms and two sets of claims remains syntactically neat while only a conceptual issue; but when it comes to putting this neat symmetry into practice, the difficulty of doing two things at once becomes the difficulty of talking about two things at once ("each . . . the other").[35]

So much does this grammatical tangle seem to have exposed to Gaskell the difficulties of what she proposes, that when she takes up the letter again to finish it two days letter, she continues with the same subject:

If Self is to be the end of exertions, those exertions are unholy, there is no doubt of *that*—and that is part of the danger in cultivating the Individual Life; but I do believe we have all some appointed work to do, whh no one else can do so well; Wh. is *our* work; what *we* have to do in advancing the Kingdom of God; and that first we must find out what we are sent into the world to do, and define it and make it clear to ourselves, (that's *the* hard part) and then forget ourselves in our work, and our work in the End we ought to strive to bring about. I never can either talk or write clearly so I'll ee'n leave it alone. Hearn has been been [*sic*] nearly 3 weeks away nursing her mother who is dying, so we are rather at sixes and sevens upstairs. The little ones come down upon us like the Goths on Rome. (*Gaskell Letters*, p. 107)

The symmetry of the categories in the first part of the letter becomes scrambled here. Earlier, "home duties" were selfless while writing ("the Individual Life") was self-directed if not selfish, and the difficulty arose from seeking a healthy balance between opposing claims. But here, she takes the category that for her includes writing and redefines it, not as the individual life—to cultivate that risks the "unholy"—but instead as its opposite, as another form of selflessness, like home duties, and hyperbolically holy: "*our* work . . . in advancing the Kingdom of God." Like the approach to stories she later recommends to Marianne, this notion of a work that exists for one to discover takes the self out of writing: "forget ourselves in our work." Thus she argues that her writing is of the same kind as home duties, because it is a duty too, and a divinely inspired one at that. By the end of this discussion, she has altogether erased the dangerous category of the individual life.

Yet the turn the passage takes next undermines considerably the effort she has made to identify writing as selfless duty. The absence of Hearn disrupts both the sentence—with the careless doubling of "has been been"—and the household, and this disruption reminds the writer that those home duties are often, in practice, incompatible with writing, however persuasive her rhetoric. She describes the present home chaos with the same expression, "at sixes and sevens," that she used in describing, in the first part of the letter, the effect on her syntax of turning to thinking about how, in practice, to do two things at once. The difficulty of the practice of writing and running a home remains the same in the two parts of the letter. We begin to see what is at stake in Gaskell's definition of the writer as electric telegraph, as selfless transmitter of scenes as observed objects. Even though she reveals that such a version of writing can be as dangerous as its opposite, it is only by persuading herself that writing is a duty as selfless as looking after the home that she can justify writing at all. Yet at the same time, she knows that her "appointed work" takes her away from her home duties just as much as any unholy cultivation of the individual life for the sake of self. She does not fully persuade herself that writing, by being selfless, is compatible with female duty.

A letter written twelve years later, in 1862, to an unknown, aspiring novelist, who had written to her for advice on balancing the demands of writing with those of raising a family, returns to this ambiguity in terms that have not much changed. The entire first page of the two-and-a-half-page letter is devoted to hints about how to run a house more efficiently ("soap & soak your dirty clothes well for some hours before beginning to wash") and how to stay strong ("did you ever try a tea-cup full of *hop-tea* the first thing in the morning?"), so as to have time and energy to write. Then she goes on:

> I do not think I ever cared for literary fame; nor do I think it *is* a thing that ought to be cared for. It comes and it goes. The exercise of talent or power *is* always a great pleasure; but one should weigh well whether this pleasure may not be obtained by the sacrifice of some duty. When I had *little* children I do not think I could have written stories, because I should have become too much absorbed in my *fictitious* people to attend to my *real* ones. I think you would be sorry if you began to feel that your desire to earn money, even for so laudable an object as to help your husband, made you unable to give your tender sympathy to your little ones . . . and yet, don't you know how you,—how every one, who tries to write stories *must* become absorbed in them. (*Gaskell Letters*, pp. 694–95)

Like the letter to Eliza Fox of 1850, the passage begins with a simple opposition between the cultivation of the self (as doing anything for fame and pleasure must be) and "duty". Also like that earlier letter, it acknowledges the possibility of redefining writing to fit the category of selfless duty ("your desire to earn money . . . to help your husband"), while finally acknowledging that this strategy cannot fully work. If writing is to be like woman's duty, then (as in the letter to Marianne in 1859) a woman writer must write realistic fiction, in which events and characters appear as if they were real, and as if she were only reporting on them. At the same time, this strategy of making writing like mothering is precisely what creates a conflict between writing and mothering, for if "fictitious people" are so very like "real ones," then there will always be competition between them for the mother's attention. Mothering fictive characters would seem to resolve the woman writer's dilemma, but it only intensifies it. Gaskell ends her advice with the obverse of the strategy to turn writing into a duty, by urging that duties can be an art: she suggests "making the various households arts into real studies (& there is plenty of poetry and association about them—remember how the Greek princesses in Homer washed the clothes &c &c &c &c)." This string of etceteras suggests that she is hard put to think of any other examples; she is hardly convinced by her own advice. The suggestion shows in another way how the rhetorical strategy of making writing acceptable as a duty can become an even more persuasive version of Southey's prohibition of it.

Like Gaskell, although seemingly under far less pressure to do so, George Eliot, in her early versions of a myth of the woman as writer, adopts a strategy of identifying the writer as a feminine, passive transmitter of others' words, who at the same time covertly asserts her own word. Also as for Gaskell, the inherent contradictions of this myth undermine her project. Like Gaskell's "doing" Coleridge and Wordsworth while covertly criticizing their positioning of the woman speaker, or her diary's subtle twisting of biblical words, Eliot's sonnet in *Middlemarch* on her childish self asserting her mysterious authority over Scott while venerating him offers a model of the ambiguity of the woman writer's position. Like Gaskell, too, in her later letters about writing, Eliot often describes writing in terms of maternity, and for her, this strategy also has its problems that offset the advantage gained. Just as we began this discussion with a text from before Gaskell's literary career, I wish to look briefly at Eliot's essay and some of her comments on translation to see how, as a woman writing who is nonetheless not writing her own words, she explains the appropriateness of her more passive venture.

Before Mary Ann Evans began writing fiction and became George Eliot, she had a long career as a translator, journalist, and editor. During the 1840s and 1850s, she wrote translations of three enormous religious and philosophical works by men, one of which, her translation of Strauss's *Das Leben Jesu*, remains standard today.[36] These translations were made during the period of Eliot's life in which religion and her rejection of Evangelicalism were foremost in her attention. Translation requires, like other kinds of literary transmission, the suppression of self, for the translator writes, not her own words, but someone else's. Although her translation of Strauss followed her rejection of Evangelicalism, the very choice to translate suggests a return to the self-suppression that, in rejecting the discipline of religion, she would seem to have rejected. At the very end of her brief essay, "Translations and Translators" (1855), she writes, "We had meant to say something of the moral qualities especially demanded in the translator—the patience, the rigid fidelity, and the sense of responsibility in interpreting another man's mind. But we have gossiped on this subject long enough."³⁷ By referring to her own meditations as "gossip" and by abruptly truncating her train of thought and the essay, she transfers the self-effacement about which she writes to the very form of the passage itself. Up to this point, she has been writing about other people's translations, but when turning to her own thoughts, she proves her point about the translator's self-suppression by putting it into effect.

The sexual metaphor in this passage is ambiguous. Patience and fidelity seem primarily to be standard feminine attributes, along with gossip, yet "rigid" fidelity seems to be another matter. Moreover, the translator is implicitly male if "interpreting another man's mind" (and in her essays, Eliot normally characterizes the writer as a man). Furthermore, she has previously argued that a good translator cannot simply "cling to the dictionary" but must have "exceptional knowledge" of the subject at hand, and she praises the translator under review for his "real mastery of his author." Like Mary Ann who "wrote the tale" of Scott in the sonnet in *Middlemarch*, the translator's feminine "fidelity" is complicated by a masculine-sounding "mastery." She argues for the superiority of figurative translation, which construes the sense of a passage, over word for word translation on the grounds that figurative translation is more accurate. Yet this preference seems to be a thin if necessary disguise for Eliot's restlessness with the feminine patience and self-suppression required of the translator. In a letter about a good review of the translation of Strauss, she writes, "It is not droll that Wicksted should have chosen one of my interpolations or rather paraphrases to dilate on? The expression 'granite,' applied to the sayings of Jesus is nowhere used by Strauss, but is an impudent addition of mine to eke out his metaphor" (*Eliot Letters* 1:227).³⁸ The pleasure she takes in inserting herself into the text suggests Eliot's discomfort with the selflessly feminine fidelity of this form of literary transmission.

It is significant that her violation of the translator's fidelity should come where it does, for by discounting the element of the miraculous in the gospels, Strauss's aim is to prove Jesus to have been a human prophet, not a conduit for the words of a separate deity. If it takes Evans's "impudent addition" to push the integrity and independence of Jesus's words toward the solidity of granite, then the independence of her own words from Strauss's acquires, paradoxically, the sanction of the weight of Strauss's argument. The content of what she translates counters her pronounced intention to submit to others' words and authorizes her subversion of that fidelity. As she practices it, translation is an art that accommodates the claims both of self and of selflessness.

Like Gaskell, once Eliot begins writing fiction, she transposes this implicit mythmaking about the gender of the author onto explicit questions about the relation between a woman's proper duties and writing in letters written about her novels. She too worries about the selfishness of writing and tries to convert writing into a form of selflessness in order to avoid a conflict between claims. The conflict between writing and family responsibility periodically becomes an overt subject of the letters, and I wish to look at two such periods, the first around the time following the completion of *The Mill on the Floss* and at the start of *Romola* and of *Silas Marner*, the second from the time of the completion of *Middlemarch*.

During the first of these periods (*The Mill on the Floss* was finished in the spring of 1860, whereupon Eliot and Lewes took a trip to Italy; these letters begin after their return), the particular domestic arrangement, the *"solitude à deux"* (3: 449) that had for six years provided Eliot with the support and the tranquility she needed in order to write, underwent a significant change. Lewes's eldest son, Charles, took a job in London, and Lewes and Eliot moved to London from their home in the rural suburbs in order to provide a household for him. Despite her quite sincere love for this "dear, precious boy, worth a great deal of sacrifice for the sake of preserving the purity and beauty of his mind" (3: 449), her letters and journal entries from this period openly record her unhappiness about these sacrifices—chiefly the loss of the country and of her tranquil solitude with Lewes—as well as her view that these sacrifices interfere directly with her writing. During the summer and early fall of 1860, it takes them a long time to find even a temporary home in London.[39] In her journal for 28 November 1860 she writes that "The loss of the country has seemed very bitter to me" and that the resulting "physical weakness accompanied with mental depression . . . has made me despair of ever working well again" (3: 360). In a letter from the same month, she attributes her misery in the city to Charley's moral education, ascribing even the bad weather itself to London:

Here there is almost unintermittent rain and fog—a perpetual blanket over our heads, and I irritate myself with thinking that in the country, though it might rain, I should still see some moving clouds. I languish sadly for the fields and the broad sky; but duties must be done, and Charles's moral education requires that he should have at once a home near to his business and the means of recreation easily within his reach. (3: 362–63)

Throughout this disruptive period, everyone in the family refers to Eliot as the boy's mother. He is to her "our big boy Charley" (3: 324);

Lewes refers to Eliot in the phrase "both his mother and myself" (3: 330); on their second trip to Italy, in April 1861, Lewes and Eliot are "Pater" and "Mutter" in letters to Charles, or "Mater Dolorosa" when in a complaining mood (3: 414). A note of ambivalence slips in when she writes, "Die Mutter thinks of her dear Boy very much and loves him better than ever now she is at a distance from him" (3: 407). To another correspondent, Eliot explains in the severe moral tones of a Victorian matron, "For the last six years I have ceased to be 'Miss Evans' . . . having held myself under all the responsibilities of a married woman. . . . and when I tell you that we have a great boy of eighteen at home who calls me 'mother,' as well as two other boys, almost as tall, who write to me under the same name, you will understand that the point is not one of mere egoism or personal dignity" (3: 396). This peculiar statement makes the ostensible point that the "moral education" of the boys is at stake in creating and maintaining the appearance of a normal Victorian family, but its suggestion that Eliot is doing this from selfless motives— perhaps at the cost of her "mere egoism"—aligns the selflessness of the gesture with the constitutive selflessness of motherhood itself. She proves herself worthy to be a Victorian mother in the very act of naming herself one. "Egoism" and motherhood are as profoundly separate here as writing and motherhood.

When Lewes and Eliot were in Italy the first time, in the spring of 1860, just after the completion of *The Mill on the Floss* and just before the decision to move, Lewes reports Eliot's enthusiastic response to his suggestion that she write a historical novel based on Savonarola (3: 295). In August, however, Eliot writes to her publisher of a change of plan: "Mr. Lewes has encouraged me to persevere in the project. . . . But I want first to write another English story" (3: 339). The syntactic opposition of her desire to what Lewes encourages makes these two novels into figures for the conflict produced by the move, between being an unselfish wife and stepmother and being an implicitly selfish writer. In the same journal entry in which she blames her inability to work on the "bitter" loss of the country, she writes that *Silas Marner* "has thrust itself between me and the other book I was meditating" (3: 360); thrusting itself between her and *Romola*, *Silas* divides the writing of *Romola* in two. If the selfless responsibilities entailed by her relation to Lewes prevent her from working, she gets her metaphoric revenge when her own "want" interrupts what Lewes "encouraged." The apotheosis of selfless motherhood in *Romola*, when it was finally written, confirms this novel's association with Eliot's relations with Lewes; yet, since *Silas* is also a story that recommends the rewards of foster parenting, this book that interrupts Lewes's project is at a deeper level an endeavor to justify the very demands that it metaphorically denies. This figurative suggestion that her duties as mother divide her and her work and divide her work in two reappears in an account of the summer of 1860, when both the move for Charley's sake and the disruption of *Romola* by *Silas* were beginning: "There is so much that I want to do every day—I had need cut myself into four women. We have a great extra interest and occupation just now in our big boy Charley" (3: 324). She goes on to describe her love for him and their decision to let their house and move. This juxtaposition of the figure of cutting herself up with intimations of the things they have to do for love of the child suggests that her double identity as mother and as writer destructively divides her in two (or even in four).

Turning to the correspondence from a later period that also entails conflicts between motherhood and writing, the time of the completion of *Middlemarch* (the latter half of 1872), we see from the start that Eliot has learned to make use of the metaphor of motherhood to generate a complex defense against the violent division of the self found in her letters of 1860. In Gaskell's manner, she redefines writing as maternal and thus attempts to redefine writing as selfless. But also like Gaskell's strategy, Eliot's only partially succeeds. During this time Lewes's daughter-in-law Gertrude (the wife of Charles) was pregnant and gave birth, an event that activated Eliot's thinking about women's duties. The writing of *Middlemarch* itself involves a series of childbirth and baby figures (which we will consider later in greater detail), and her correspondence is colored by implicit and explicit conflicts between being a woman and being an author.

After she has completed the manuscript, she explains the experience of finishing a book by the implicit metaphor of book as child:

> One healthy condition at least for me is that I have finished my book and am thoroughly at peace about it—not because I am convinced of its perfection, but because I have lived to give out what it was in me to give and have not been hindered by illness or death from making my work a whole, such as it is. When a subject has begun to grow in me I suffer terribly until it has wrought itself out—become a complete organism; and then it seems to take wing and go away from me. . . . When a conception has begun to shape itself in written words, I feel that it must go on to the end before I can be happy about it. Then I move away and look at it from a distance without any agitations.(5: 324–25)

The image of the book as something formed within (a "conception" that begins "to grow in me"), and of writing as a painful, inexorable, and curiously passive process of getting it outside ("I suffer terribly until it has wrought itself out"), followed by a sense of detachment from the now "complete organism," suggests an idealized plot of childbirth followed by the mother's healthy acceptance of the otherness of the child.[40]

That Eliot intends a maternal metaphor is confirmed in the next paragraph of the letter when, on a slightly different subject and in a lighter tone, she is explicitly maternal. Responding to her correspondent's "constructing the future of the story" on the basis of the parts already published, she writes, "I felt inclined then to scold you maternally, for your own good." Why is it maternal to object to his appropriation of her story? Her motives are surely not of protectiveness toward him, though that is what she says, but rather of protectiveness toward her not yet fully "wrought out" story. If Eliot compares writing to mothering in defensive response to Victorian England's view that women should mother and not write, her focus in this letter on a mother's possessiveness about her child undermines that defense, for instead of describing writing as being as unselfish as mothering, to the contrary, it describes mothering as being as selfish as writing. Furthermore, as in Gaskell's letters, the effort to see writing as part of female duty flags when it becomes clear that writing conflicts with another female duty, the wife's duty to read the manuscript Lewes has been accumulating while she was writing— and he was supportively reading—Middlemarch. Her letter continues, after her maternal scolding, "I am going now to bathe my mind in deep waters—going to read Mr. Lewes's manuscript which has been storing itself up for me. . . . I easily sink into mere absorption of what other minds have done, and should like a whole life for that alone" (5: 324–25). Indeed, what she is attempting to do is to live two lives: this "whole life" of selfless absorption in others and the life of writing (she remarks of the finished book, "that life has been lived") that she has been hoping a maternal metaphor would prove to be less selfish than it is. These two lives are competing wholes: much as in Gaskell's or Brontë's arguments for balancing writing and duty, the impossibility of the project is revealed in the very stating of it.

Finally the letter closes, in the very next paragraph, "This is an egotistic note. . . . You will not count the I's—which judicious persons make a rule of cutting out from their manuscript, when it is meant for critical readers" (5: 325). There are a good many "I's" in the letter, but the letter has been so occupied with versions of the theme of selflessness—first her maternal production of the novel, then her wifely absorption in George's manuscript—that "egotistic" seems a strange description of it, bringing to light the failure of the maternal metaphor to convince her of the unselfishness of writing. The shape of the letter as a whole recalls that of the 1855 essay on translation. Following a discussion of what is meant to be selflessness, the writer turns to herself but deprecates this turn—there with the pejorative term "gossip," here with the strangely violent notion of "cutting out" the I's—and brings writing to an abrupt halt. What the seemingly misplaced apology for egotism suggests here is, as in the essay, the centripetal force of writing's egotism, such that it alters the metaphors that would alter it.[41]

Toward the beginning of the period of the writing of *Middlemarch*, Lewes offered his perspective on what we have been viewing from Eliot's position, her conflict between being a woman and being a writer. "She is writing—writing—writing!—To parody Garrick's admirer I will say— 'Why, Sir, *away* from the desk she is a perfect woman, but *at* the desk—oh!—my!!——God!!!' " (5: 282). Comic as this description is, it also suggests a certain degree of genuine dismay. After the novel is finished, Lewes guarantees the restoration of his wife to perfect womanhood by insisting on identifying her with her own Dorothea Brooke, despite Eliot's assurance to Harriet Beecher Stowe that, to the contrary, "the Casaubon-tints are not quite foreign to my own mental complexion" (5: 322). Eliot's identification with Casaubon is especially suggestive in the light of the striking figure in the novel of Casaubon's book as "withered in the birth like an elfin child" (chap. 48).[42] If her own covertly egotistical mothering of her novel is like Casaubon's, then the figure of writing as parturition offers her little defense of her attention to woman's proper duties against the charge of egotism. However, Lewes's repeated use of Casaubon as a figure for himself (even if intended merely as self-deprecation) and the identification of Eliot as Dorothea that this identification permits legitimate the demand he makes that she devote herself to his needs. In September (while she is still at work on the novel), he fills out the analogy in this way: "Surely Dorothea is the very cream of lovely womanhood? She is more like her creator than any one else and more so than any other of her creations. Only those who know her (Dodo—or her creator) under all aspects can have any idea of her" (5: 308). It is a large part of Dorothea's "lovely womanhood" that she wants to help her husband. By the time Eliot is actually engaged in her long-postponed Dorothea-like task of reading her husband's manuscript, he writes that she "is suffering now (silently, as Mrs. Casaubon would) under an oppression of marital m.s. with no permission to 'omit the second excursus on Crete' " (5: 332).[43] (His use of the word "suffering" recalls her use of the word to describe the selflessness of mothering her own manuscript, and thus makes the two selflessnesses parallel.)

Giving birth to *Middlemarch* has forced Eliot to put off these wifely jobs, but now writing's egotism, which the metaphor of childbirth has not successfully concealed (whether the book is a great one, able to live on its own, or a withered birth like Casaubon's), must give way to the serious selflessness of Dorothea as dutiful wifely reader. Eliot would hardly wish to choose Casaubon as her model, yet Dorothea is scarcely more useful as a model for a writer. "You are a poem," Will Ladislaw says to her.

One of Lewes's earliest identifications with Casaubon alludes to the figure of Casaubon's books as stillbirths: "I am 'bursting' with ideas—and want to give them birth. The shadow of old Casaubon hangs over me and I fear my 'Key to all Psychologies' will have to be left to Dorothea!" (5: 291) This allusion to a child born dead is followed six days later by Eliot's report of the actual birth of a grandchild, which sadly, oddly, evokes in her grandparents the thoughts of their own deaths: "We have just been saying in our walk, that by the end of this century our one-day-old grand-daughter will probably be married and have children of her own, while we are pretty sure to be at rest" (5: 291). The juxtaposition of the letters suggests an alternative way in which the figure of writing as childbirth becomes problematic for Eliot. When Gaskell, writing of her foster mother's death, implies her fear that it resulted indirectly from her daughter's birth, we saw how this fear and the literalization of a metaphor of confinement with which Gaskell expresses it recall the danger of childbirth in the Brontës' novels, a danger that *Frankenstein* suggests comes from the interference of paternal order in women's experience, the overtaking of reproduction by representation. Mothers and grandmothers do die naturally, of course, yet the mythologization of a mother's or grandmother's death being *caused* by a daughter's birth alludes to the place of women in a patrilineal order, to women's fear that their pleasure in reproduction will be subordinated to the requirements of representation, to the requirements of a chain of symbolic substitutions. The selfishness that Eliot's myth of writing as maternity fails to conceal may be figured as Casaubon's murderous egotism, yet childbirth may also figure the annihilation of the self, through the substitution of baby for mother. Lewes's earlier syntactical conflation of Dorothea and Eliot ("only those who know her [Dodo—or her creator]") is echoed in Eliot's syntactic confusion of the new baby with her mother:

> Gertrude's little Blanche is a charming young lady—fat, cooing, and merry. It is a great comfort to see her with this hope fulfilled—I mean, to see Gertrude with her hope fulfilled, and not Blanche, as the grammar seemed to imply. That small person's hopes are at present easy of fulfilment. (5: 328–29)

Just as Lewes's certainty that his wife "is" Dorothea, with her "lovely womanhood," ensures that she will eventually return to her selfless function as reader of "marital m.s.," the identification between mother and child syntactically enacted in this letter suggests both the pleasures and the dangers of childbirth as a figure for writing. For the same reason that writing and motherhood can be the most egotistical of activities, because there is but one identity in each case, that very singleness of identity poses the greatest threat to the author's, or mother's, identity, because of the possibility that in giving birth to and separating from her books, they will make their author superfluous.[44]

This paradoxical mixture of egotism and selflessness in motherhood takes a comic form in the relation between Celia and her baby, James, in a section of *Middlemarch* written before the letters I have been discussing, although as we have seen, Eliot's writing about the division between writer and mother dates from at least 1860. All of Celia's narrow if charming vanity is displaced onto "that central poising force" whose "remarkable acts" leave her even less attention than usual to spare for Dorothea's mood and feelings. Just after Casaubon's death, Celia calls on the meditative and absorbed Dorothea to notice "his upper lip; see how he is drawing it down, as if he meant to make a face. Isn't it wonderful! He may have his little thoughts" (chap. 50). Celia's enthusiasm for her baby's thoughts prevents her from taking any interest in those of Dorothea, who is merely "brooding." Although her interest in the baby would appear to be a selfless interest in another, her disregard for Dorothea exposes the self-centeredness of Celia's motherhood.

Eliot uses Celia's maternal egotism and Casaubon's selfishness as analogies for each other. Some account of Celia's actual maternity is juxtaposed to every mention of Casaubon's labors over his "elfin child." For example, the narrator describes Dorothea's experience of Casaubon's project using the implicit metaphor of birth: "It appeared that she was to live more and more in a virtual tomb, where there was the apparatus of a ghastly labour producing what would never see the light" (chap. 48). In the very next paragraph, Dorothea "could not have the carriage to go to Celia, who had lately had a baby." Five pages later, in the same chapter, appears the metaphor of the project as "withered in the birth like an elfin child." The announcement of the actual baby's birth serves to make explicit the birth metaphor for "The Key to All Mythologies." In immediate context, it appears that the main effect is of contrast between live and dead births, yet as we see more of Celia's behavior with her baby, we see that the implications of the metaphor are reciprocal. Casaubon dies almost directly after this passage, and in the scene from which I quoted earlier, Celia's self-centered view, as egotistical in its own way as Casaubon's, is that Dorothea is better off with Casaubon dead, and she expresses this view while acting out her own self-absorption in the baby, by speaking to him rather than to Dorothea:

> 'We should not grieve, should we, baby?' said Celia confidentially to that unconscious centre and poise of the world, who had the most remarkable fists all complete even to the nails, and hair enough, really, when you took his cap off, to make—you didn't know what:—in short, he was Bouddha in a Western form. (chap. 50)

Eliot had already written Celia and her baby several months before Blanche's birth (Lewes alludes to Celia in his diary account of Blanche's christening: "all the family present—worshipping *Boudha*" [5: 347]). At the time of the birth, Eliot was working on the final book of *Middlemarch*, in which the comic egotism of Celia's motherhood is replaced by a more tragic image of a mother's egotism. The night after Dorothea witnesses what she assumes to be a romantic scene between Will and Rosamond, the narrator describes her "helpless within the clutch of inescapable anguish." The very moving account includes "waves of suffering [that] shook her too thoroughly to leave any power of thought"; and "she besought hardness and coldness and aching weariness to bring her relief from the mysterious incorporeal might of her anguish . . . her grand woman's frame was shaken by sobs as if she had been a despairing child" (chap. 80). Although Dorothea's anguish is both incorporeal and childlike, the "waves of suffering" and the shaking of her "grand woman's frame" suggest an implicit metaphor of childbirth for her pain. This metaphor becomes explicit in the very next paragraph:

> There were two images—two living forms that tore her heart in two, as if it had been the heart of a mother who seems to see her child divided by the sword, and presses one bleeding half to her breast while her gaze goes forth in agony towards the half which is carried away by the lying woman that has never known the mother's pang. (chap. 80)

Although Dorothea's metaphoric motherhood appears to be far from selfish, an agony of loss, and although it seems callous to accuse Dorothea of egotism at this moment when she is the victim of so terrible a force, the bizarre implication of this retelling of the judgment of Solomon is that the division of Will is the fault of Dorothea's egotism.

In the original story (in 1 Kings 3:16–28), the true mother's generous love prevents the child's being divided, even though the price of his remaining alive is, she believes, the loss of him. If Dorothea is the true mother in the simile, she must have consented to see her child cut in two. In fact, Dorothea has been projecting onto Will her desire that he be ideally understanding and sympathetic (which he is not), and what she has loved and lost has not been Will himself but the emotions he has occasioned: "She could only cry in loud whispers, between her sobs, after her lost belief . . . after her lost joy . . . after her lost woman's pride of reigning in his memory—after her sweet dim perspective of hope." She has failed to perceive his otherness, for example, his inarguable flirtatiousness with Rosamond. Even though she turns out to be wrong about the extent of Will's disloyalty, her needy view of him has in effect divided him in two.

The passionately sympathetic writing of the passage obscures the responsibility Eliot clearly places on Dorothea by adducing the biblical story. "Two living forms that tore her life in two" makes Dorothea appear to be a victim, yet in the biblical story, Dorothea would be the perpetrator. Despite her characterization as the type of unselfish "lovely womanhood," Dorothea is a selfish mother, in much the same way that Eliot's figuring her writing as motherhood only succeeds in making motherhood seem as egotistical as writing. Moreover, in the context of Eliot's figuring her writing as maternity, the figure of the divided child with a divided mother alludes to the division between Eliot's duties as wife and mother and her writing, her "need" in 1860 to "cut myself into four women" and her wish for two "whole lives," one for writing, one for being a wifely reader. Each division of the self, Eliot's and Dorothea's, is the result of a woman's self-punishment for acting on her self's needs. If Eliot wants a whole self for her writing, she must have another whole self for the needs of others; if Dorothea projects her desires onto Will, she must suffer for it. Depicted as a form of selfishness, motherhood doesn't help prove the harmlessness of writing; and yet the egotism that maternity thus fails to correct, far from protecting the self from the claims of others, opens the self to the very loss of self it would have seemed most immune to. Although Eliot's letter about her grandchild suggests her fear of maternity's annihilation of the female self, the compensatory egotism of the mother, in other figures, leads to the same result.

In one of the letters we have already discussed, Gaskell also uses the figure of Solomon's judgment to describe a woman writer's dilemma. Referring in 1850 to the conflicting claims of "home duties" and "individual life" or "the hidden world of Art," Gaskell writes:

so assuredly a blending of the two is desirable. (Home duties and the development of the Individual I mean), which you will say it takes no Solomon to tell you but the difficulty is where and when to make one set of duties subserve and give place to the other. (*Gaskell Letters*, p. 106)

Though this allusion is far less weighty than Eliot's use of the story in *Middlemarch*, the import of the two allusions is similar. Like Eliot, Gaskell has Solomon preside over a division (here, not a division of a child but between children and something else), which, in contrast to the biblical original, suggests that one of the mothers exercised her egotism, rather than unselfishly yielding to the threat of the child's division. Although in context the passage is about the effort to divide time judiciously so as to accommodate both home and writing, the allusion to Solomon suggests that no judicious division is possible, or rather that any division is a murderous one, that the self's needs, in the case of a woman, are always destructive of true motherhood and all that motherhood stands for.

It is worth noting in closing that the very fact of the two writers' using a story from the Bible is part of the same issue of how writing can accommodate the ideology of motherhood. To transmit another's words, especially the words of the Bible, is to subordinate writing to the passivity and docility appropriate to women; and yet, as we have seen in other instances as well, to subvert the quotation, as both Gaskell and Eliot do in the passages about Solomon, to allude but to use the allusion for a purpose opposite to the original one, is to subvert the femininity that allusiveness itself establishes in the first place. Though Gaskell in the near vicinity of the Solomon allusion uses two far more innocuous literary allusions (home duties can become "daily small Lilliputian arrows of peddling cares," while Art is "the land where King Arthur lies hidden"), as if to counteract the subversive effect of her biblical allusion, she sustains, with Eliot, the ambiguity of writing as poised between a woman's proper duty and her desire to write. The chapters that follow will examine the differing complexities of these two authors' articulations of this contradiction in some of their fiction, both through their own transmissions of literary texts and through characters who express various possibilities for bearing language.

8

Figuring the Mother:
Madonna Romola's Incarnation

liot begins *Romola* by remarking on "the broad sameness of the human lot," which justifies the enterprise of writing a historical novel. Despite changes in Florence's language and politics between 1492 and "to-day" (1863), "the sunlight and shadows on the grand walls . . . the faces of the little children" and "the images of willing anguish for a great end" to be found in the same churches— "These things have not changed."[1] Neither, given the "broad sameness of the human lot," is there such a great difference between fifteenth-century Florence and nineteenth-century England. Eliot situates her novel as she does because, among other reasons, fifteenth-century Florence offers a clearer picture of the same ideological forces that work more ambiguously in the England of her day. As the shade of her fictive Florentine of 1492 contemplates the city from the hill of San Miniato but prefers "to be down among those narrow streets and busy humming Piazze," so Eliot moves from a world in which limitations were placed on women largely through cultural myth, and were therefore difficult to criticize, to a world in which these limitations were created and enforced by legal and religious practice. If very little of Anglican or Dissenter England of the 1860s still literally believed in the virgin birth and the power of the Madonna, and imposed its ideology of motherhood in subtler ways, many in fifteenth-century Florence still vehemently believed, in a way that allows Eliot to expose with more certainty the workings of that ideology of motherhood that has made up so much of women's share of "the broad sameness of the human lot." For precisely the reasons that Eliot chose fifteenth-century Florence, *Romola* serves our purposes as Eliot's boldest treatment of the ideology of motherhood.

At the same time, in framing her fiction as the descent of a spirit "down among those narrow streets," in giving historical events together with other works of literature a new life in the vivid drama of her novel, Eliot's own practice of writing takes up the same issues worked out in the novel's story. Making a spirit real, or a figure literal, and allowing her text to be a passageway for others' words, are a woman writer's way of conciliating the very ideological forces the novel exposes. *Romola*, we remember, is the novel Lewes suggested during their trip to Italy but that was interrupted by Eliot's wish to write *Silas Marner* first; thus a woman's bending to the suggestions of her "husband" forms the context of the writing of the novel.[2] As we will see, just as in her letters ambiguously defining writing as mothering, Eliot does not simply follow cultural directions, but she follows them in such a way as to accommodate her own needs as a writer at the same time. It is to the relation between the novel's thematics of female behavior and Eliot's practice that we will turn.

I wish to begin, however, not with Eliot's version of history or of the myth of holy motherhood, but with the novel's altered transmission of Wordsworth, a motif familiar from our reading of *The Mill on the Floss*, "Brother and Sister," and *Middlemarch*. Like these texts, but perhaps even more explicitly, *Romola* presents a sister for whom a visionary career is a possibility but whose female training makes that career impossible and undesirable. Like Mary and Dorothea, Romola's turn away from visionary possibility takes the form of turning toward a substitute brother, who in this case is far more seriously disappointing than in *Middlemarch*. Romola's brother, Dino, is a visionary. He was to have become their blind father's secretary and assistant in his scholarship, but he has instead become a Dominican monk, Fra Luca. Raised by her classics-loving father to scorn Christian visions as dark and sickly superstitions, Romola is further turned against vision by its part in her brother's betrayal of the family, whose claims on her as a daughter are far stronger than on the son. The alternative to her brother's visions takes the form of Tito Melema, the beautiful, Dionysian, shipwrecked scholar from Greece whom she eventually marries and who enters her life explicitly as a substitute for the lost brother. He applies for the job left vacant by Dino; on first meeting him, Bardo asks to touch his hand because "it is long since I touched the hand of a young man," and his further questions confirm that he seeks a substitute son, an improved version of the lost one. When he learns by word and touch that Tito's appearance differs from Dino's, he says, "He must be very unlike thy brother, Romola: and it is the better. You see no visions, I trust, my young friend?" (chap. 6). As if appearing opposite to Dino would guarantee Tito's faithfulness, Bardo accepts him as a son; as a substitute brother and as a representative of all that is opposite to the world of vision—a joyous if thoughtless sensuality—Romola loves him. Even after "her trust" in Tito has been proved "delusive," the narrator says "she would have chosen over again to have acted on it rather than be a creature led by phantoms and disjointed whispers in a world where there was the large music of reasonable speech, and the warm grasp of living hands" (chap. 36). Tito's "warm grasp" turns out to be only the pleasanter side of an amoral pragmatism, but in turning away from her brother's visions, Romola can only turn toward this prosaic alternative. In this her experience is very like Maggie's, Dorothea's, or Mary's. The world of vision does not work for heroines, whether, as in Maggie's or Dorothea's cases, the visions are the heroines' own, or whether, as in Romola's case, the visions belong to a beloved brother. Vision comes from a world alien to that in which heroines must live, and a brother or brother figure—Tom, Will, Fred, Tito—supplies the prosaic alternative.

Why isn't the world of vision available or appealing to heroines? We have seen how, in *The Mill on the Floss* and *Middlemarch*, vision is Wordsworthian and for that and other reasons gender marked, and a similar gender marking takes place in *Romola*, despite the un-Wordsworthian setting. Because the scene is fifteenth-century Florence, the gender arrangements of vision and of its refusal are all the more boldly stated. The conflict between "pagan" or classical learning and Christianity is a political issue of citywide proportions, as compared to the seemingly more purely psychological and aesthetic debate, which conceals its ideological nature, between Wordsworth and his female readers.

The scene of Romola's major confrontation with the visionary world of her brother makes it clear that gender, and not individual temperament, determines her opposition. Dino is dying in the monastery of San Marco, and he sends for Romola, whom he has not seen since he left home, in order to tell her a vision about herself. The scene of vision is literally for men only: "Romola was conducted to the door of the chapter house in the outer cloister, whither the invalid had been conveyed; no woman being allowed admission beyond this precinct" (chap. 15). Eliot, visiting San Marco in May of 1860 to research the settings of her novel, discovered that this exclusion was still in effect. She writes Romola's exclusion only because she first discovered her own (Lewes went inside and made notes for her).[3] This episode brings into focus "the broad sameness of" women's "lot." Researching novels is as much prohibited to a woman in the nineteenth century as witnessing or having visions was to a woman of the fifteenth century.

Dino's vision conveys, in terrifying but abstract terms, a warning against marrying Tito. But Dino also has access to information about Tito of a much more practical sort, which would be of much greater use to Romola, who already distrusts visions. Dino has previously conveyed to Tito, unaware of his connection to Bardo and Romola, a message from Tito's godfather, Baldassare—from whom Tito was separated during the shipwreck—to the effect that he is still alive but in prison. Tito, who had good reason to guess that Baldassare was dead, and who has on that ground decided to give his godfather up for lost, with the incidental advantage that he can keep Baldassare's jewels and make his way unencumbered by an old man, takes the step from passive to active malignity when he disregards this message. Thus Dino, who can easily guess the content of the message he bears, holds the secret of Tito's moral nature. Instead of making the connection between Romola and the Tito Melema to whom he carried the message, a connection he could have made merely by asking the name of Romola's intended, Dino offers her instead the gloomy and insubstantial vision that only propels her back toward the "warm grasp" of Tito.

In the vision itself, Dino identifies the man whom Romola is to marry both with Satan and with Bardo's classical library, because Dino views his father's paganism as Satanic. Dino sees Romola, Bardo, and the faceless lover in the library. They proceed to Santa Croce, where, he tells his sister, "the priest who married you had the face of death, and the grave opened, and the dead in their shrouds rose and followed you like a bridal train" (chap. 15). This part of the vision is strangely framed, before and after, by two figures from the novel's represented action. First, in the previous chapter on the peasants' fair that provides the setting for Tito's mock "marriage," a figurative marriage, to the ignorant contadina Tessa, Tito sees the fair as "a perfect resurrection swarm of remote mortals and fragments of mortals." Second, this portion of Dino's vision is later actualized in the scene of Romola's betrothal, the scene the vision was intended to prevent. Leaving Santa Croce, Romola and Tito witness a "masqued procession" that includes "what looked like a troop of the sheeted dead gliding above blackness." Romola's response is "cold horror," for "it seemed as if her brother's vision, which could never be effaced from her mind, was being half fulfilled" (chap. 20). This sequence, from figure to vision to literal experience suggests that while the figurative and the visionary belong to men, the actualization of them is the woman's lot.[4] Female experience is being limited to the realm of the literal, and the literal or actual consists of the passive reception of men's figurative constructs.

As Dino's vision continues, the dead return to their graves, but they are replaced by another image of death.

> And at last you came to a stony place where there was no water, and no trees or herbage; but instead of water, I saw written parchment unrolling itself everywhere, and instead of trees and herbage I saw men of bronze and marble springing up and crowding round you. And my father was faint for want of water and fell to the ground.

Full of pity though this vision seems to be, it is the furniture of Bardo's library, with its books and its bronze and marble statues, that provides the murderous imagery. The vision's written parchments and bronze and marble men directly recall the opening description of the library, a description in which the deadness of the antiquarian collection, so important when it reappears in the vision, is already emphasized. The marbles include "a beautiful feminine torso; a headless statue, with an uplifted muscular arm wielding a bladeless sword; rounded, dimpled, infantile limbs severed from the trunk, inviting the lips to kiss the cold marble" (chap. 5). The initial description of these marble fragments—which even in their perfect state offered only an illusion of life—places emphasis, not on their intended resemblance to the living, but because of their fragmentation, on their resemblance to the dead. This emphasis increases as the description of the library continues: "the vellum bindings, with their deep-ridged backs, gave little relief to the marble, livid with long burial . . . the dark bronzes wanted sunlight upon them to bring out their tinge of green." The perverse, necrophiliac sexuality of the marbles (the beautiful feminine torso next to the headless uplifted arm with the bladeless sword, their "child" not an infant but a pile of infantile limbs) recurs in the figure of parchment unrolling itself. These parchments recall, not only Bardo's books, but also a series of other parchments that it is a sin to unroll, beginning with the rolled parchment *brevi* containing some sort of sexual secret that the mock bishop at the peasants' fair sells along with his mock marriages, including also the rolled parchment that Baldassare blasphemously tears open to find the valuable amulet that he will exchange for a knife to kill Tito, and alluding also, more distantly, to the sacred virginity of the unseen Madonna whose image is carried through the streets of Florence in a closed tabernacle that symbolizes the sacred closure of her body. As Dino's vision continues, "the man whose face was a blank," who occupies what

Romola recognizes as Tito's place, is revealed to be the Great Tempter as he is in the act of abandoning Romola and Bardo. The bronze and marble figures continue their mocking substitution of their dead artificiality for life, holding out to Bardo cups of water that turn into parchment and turning into demons who snatch Bardo's body away, while the parchments turn into blood and fire.

As Dino interprets it, his vision is a warning to Romola against both "marriage as a temptation of the enemy" and "the vain philosophy and corrupt thoughts of the heathens." With respect to Bardo's beloved classical texts and works of art, Dino's vision seems to focus on the falsity of representation itself, with its gaps between dead matter (bronze, marble, and so on) and the life it claims to represent. Presumably Dino would set representation opposite to the word of God, which is not represented but literally made into flesh. Dino's vision does not quite identify Tito's deceptions with Bardo's heathen philosophy, but it does portray them as complicitous in the same end, the isolation and suffering of Romola. Tito leads Romola and Bardo to the stony place, but it is his own statues that deny Bardo water; and if Romola's husband is the Great Tempter, the statues seem "to turn into demons." Tito's demonic lies and deceptions are somehow equivalent to the representations in the library. In claiming that all representation is demonic, and in seeming to recommend to Romola the literal or real over the representational, Dino intends to distinguish his own vision, like God's word, as nonrepresentational. Yet as a re-presentation of descriptive elements already present in the story, and in contrast to the factual information Romola could put to use, the vision and its contents are clearly figurative and therefore, by Dino's own definitions, dangerously deceptive.

Dino's vision, although it turns out to be quite correct in its assessment of Romola's marriage, is discredited for Romola from the start. Visionary experience never even begins to belong to her as it does to Maggie, to the little sister of the sonnets, or to Dorothea. Much later in the novel, Romola meets a female visionary, Camilla Rucellai, who is even more repellent to Romola than her brother could be. The excessive and physical violence of the encounter, which is peripheral to the plot, seems to mark—beyond Romola's "constitutional disgust for the shallow excitability of women like Camilla, whose faculties seemed all wrought up into fantasies" (chap. 52)—the narrator's reaction to female visionaries as well. Romola "shrank with unconquerable repulsion from the shrill volubility of those illuminated women" and has "a special repugnance towards Camilla" because she is hostile to Romola's godfather, Bernardo del Nero, an honorable man whose position in the shifting sands of Florentine politics happens to place him opposite Camilla. As Camilla's voice rises with her vision that Christ has ordered Bernardo's death, Romola "started up and attempted to wrench her arm from Camilla's tightening grasp. It was of no use. The prophetess kept her hold like a crab. . . . 'Let me go!' said Romola, in a deep voice of anger. . . . The violence of her effort to be free was too strong for Camilla now. She wrenched away her arm and rushed out of the room." If Dino's vision is useless, it is at least authentic; Camilla's is merely the fabrication of a suggestible woman who uses a volatile political climate to gain attention. If San Marco exlcudes women from the scene of vision, so, in this novel, does Eliot, refusing to claim what has been refused to her.

Exposing male visionary power for its incompatibility with female training and possibilities, Eliot alludes specifically to Wordsworth, to a passage that we have already seen is important to her sense of the inadequacy of Wordsworthian vision for female characters. We hear a familiar note behind the phantasmagoria of Dino's vision, particularly these lines:

Instead of trees and herbage I saw men of bronze and marble springing up and crowding round you. . . . The man whose face was a blank loosed thy hand and departed. . . . And the bronze and marble figures seemed to mock thee and hold out cups of water. (chap. 15)

These lines echo lines from Wordsworth that we have seen revised in *The Mill on the Floss* and *Middlemarch*, the passage from the end of the boat-stealing scene in book 1 of *The Prelude* that concludes,

> o'er my thoughts
> There hung a darkness, call it solitude
> Or blank desertion. No familiar shapes
> Remained, no pleasant images of trees,
> Of sea or sky, no colours of green fields;
> But huge and mighty forms, that do not live
> Like living men, moved slowly through the mind
> By day, and were a trouble to my dreams.
> (393–400)

In both visions, trees and herbage are replaced by mighty forms that do not live like living men. Both visions convey the feeling of desertion: in Dino's, Romola and Bardo are literally deserted by Tito; in Wordsworth's, the "blank desertion" of his vision cuts him off from visible nature. Dino's vision may warn against "solitude or blank desertion," but because it is so removed from the ordinary channels of Romola's understanding, it also helps to ensure that desertion. While Wordsworth's vision has the compensatory advantages we have discussed before, Dino's visions are presented from the point of view of the family on whom they have only a destructive effect. When Dino summons Romola, she assumes he wishes to convey through her some message of apology to their father, and she is anguished and shocked that even when dying he has no more thought for his father than when he went away. And if the vision itself is bad, its literalization is if possible even worse. The "real" that Dino recommends to Romola—the trees and herbage that correspond to Wordsworth's "pleasant images of trees" and "colours of green fields"—takes the form of her actual experience of marriage and betrayal.

Despite this particularly violent literalization of Wordsworthian vision, the novel otherwise quite explicitly recommends the virtues of female transmission of men's texts, and it is in this contradiction between a woman's obligation to act as conduit for male words and the pain such a role brings her, the contradiction found in the other novels but framed most acutely here, that Eliot both accommodates and criticizes women's place in androcentric literature. In Eliot's other novels, docile reading and copying are associated thematically with female propriety, but whereas their heroines begin by challenging that propriety, in *Romola* this passive relation to texts comprises the heroine's whole life from the start. And while over the course of the novel the texts and the circumstances of their transmission change, Romola's relation to them does not. At the same time, the novel explicitly connects this relation to textuality to the ideology of motherhood, here in the form of the cult of the Madonna. We will begin by looking at how Romola and others are presented as readers, then at the ways in which the novel's own practice reflects and challenges the maternal transmissions it thematizes.

Romola first appears in the novel reading. Directly after the description of Bardo's somber library, with its vellums, livid marbles, and dark bronzes, the narrator goes on to identify "the only spot of bright colour in the room" as "the hair of a tall maiden . . . who was standing before a carved *leggio*, or reading desk. . . . Her eyes were bent on a large volume placed before her: one long white hand rested on the reading desk, and the other clasped the back of her father's chair" (chap. 5). We soon learn that "the eyes of the father had long been silent, and the eyes of the daughter were bent on the Latin pages of Politian's 'Miscellanea,' from which she was reading aloud the eightieth chapter."

Before going on to look at what and why she is reading, let us look forward briefly to Romola's closing scene, which is also the last scene of the book. It is seventeen years later, both her father and her husband are dead, and Romola has adopted Tessa's and her husband's children. While the daughter, Ninna, weaves flower wreaths to commemorate Savonarola, the son, Lillo, is bored and pretending to read "the finely-printed copy of Petrarch which he kept open at one place, as if he were learning something by heart. Romola sat nearly opposite Lillo, but she was not observing him. Her hands were crossed on her lap and her eyes were fixed absently on the distant mountains: she was evidently unconscious of anything around her." At first, the scene seems quite different from the scene of her first appearance. Her foster son has taken Romola's place as reader. Her hands, instead of making physical the connection between book and listener, are now crossed, making connection only with each other. And where in the earlier scene she was looking at the book and reading, here the absentness of her eyes recalls her father, even though her blindness to outward things comes only from her absorption in memory and thought. Yet the point of the scene is that Romola is teaching Lillo. In having him read Petrarch, whom her father long ago had called "the modern who is least unworthy to be named after the ancients" (chap. 5), but who is also the source of one of her father's most misogynist quotations, she is passing on to Lillo one of the great androcentric literary works.[5] As the scene continues, she passes on more male lore to this son. In response to Lillo's restless question, "What am I to be," she tells him the paradigmatic stories of the three men most important in her life: her father's life as a scholar, Savonarola's life as a prophet, and Tito's life (she doesn't tell Lillo it is his father's story) as a traitor. Though she is not reading to Lillo, the scene shows that her position relative to the patrilineal inheritance of literature and men's stories has not changed since her first appearance in the novel. In both cases, she is the facilitator of textual transmission from one generation of men to the next: in the first scene, from classical authors and scholars to her father, in the second, from a more recent author and the stories of two earlier generations of men to the next generation. In neither case does she get anything for herself; in her life as reader, as transmitter of stories, her desire is always displaced.

Let us return to the earlier scene of her reading to her father, to trace the novel's presentation of her as reader. The scene sets up a pair of differing definitions of men's and women's relations to language. Pausing in his review of the manuscript he wishes to annotate, Bardo complains about the failure of his lifelong ambition to write a great critical work on classical literature (a precursor to Casaubon's great unwritten "Key to All Mythologies"). Because of his blindness and Dino's desertion of him, Bardo is reduced to the lesser ambition of passing on to future generations his collection of classical manuscripts, some of which he himself copied. It becomes clear that he views collecting and transcribing to be essentially feminine activities as opposed to the masculinity of criticism. For example, he uses a metaphor of pregnancy for this lesser scholarly project: "I carry within me the fruits of that fervid study which I gave the Greek tongue." Collection and transcription are also undertaken for the sake of others, and in that sense also feminine. Referring to his disappointment that he now has only Romola to help him, he says that the qualities necessary in a scholar "are still less reconcilable with the wandering, vagrant propensities of the feminine mind than with the feeble powers of the feminine body." Romola protests that she gives him every help he wishes, but Bardo insists on his identification of Romola's mind with his notions about her body: he reminds her that she fainted "in the mere search for the references I needed to explain a single passage of Callimachus." Although she says it was "the weight of the books and not want of attention or patience" that made her faint, he insists on transforming her wholly into a female body, just as, indeed, his original stereotype of the "wandering, vagrant propensities of the feminine mind" recreates women's minds in the image of Plato's myth of the wandering uterus. Although his comparison of his own learning to pregnancy would suggest that he thinks his faculties are not far superior to Romola's, it is at the end of the same speech in which he uses the female metaphor for himself that he identifies the feminine mind with his fantasies about the female body. This identification has the effect of restricting his own figure: the similarity of his mind to the female body is decidedly figurative, in contrast to the inescapable literality of Romola's "feminine mind."[6]

What Bardo wants, instead of Romola's uterine, fainting, material mind, is "the sharp edge of a young mind to pierce the way for my somewhat blunted faculties." His feminine metaphor for his own learning gives way to his certainty that nothing feminine can be considered true scholarship, which is invariably masculine. Furthermore, since Tito, who will become the book's most self-centered character, and who will within a few pages arrive to fulfill Bardo's wish for "the sharp edge of a young mind," is compared to a tool whose handle is smooth but that may prove dangerous to those who use it, the figure of criticism as a knife edge suggests that criticism is self-centered. In fact, unlike transcription, which is done for others, the purpose of a great scholarly work would have been for Bardo to acquire fame: "With my son to aid me, I might have had my share in the triumphs of this century: the names of Bardi, father and son, might have been held reverently on the lips of scholars in the ages to come." Now, limited to the selfless, feminine projects of collection and transcription, with only a female body to help him, bitterly lamenting that other, inferior scholars will be remembered where he is not, Bardo attempts to convert his collecting and transcribing into sources of personal fame. He will "leave them, after the example of the munificent Romans, for an everlasting possession to my fellow-citizens. But why do I say Florence only? If Florence remembers me, will not the world remember me? . . . It is but little to ask . . . that my name should be over the door—that men should own themselves debtors to the Bardi Library in Florence."

Bardo does not use the figure of debt lightly. Although earlier in the scene he has spoken nostalgically of the "scribe who loves the words that grow under his hand" and has inveighed against "these mechanical printers who threaten to make learning a base and vulgar thing," it turns out that his refusal to lend his manuscripts to a printer derives, not from his love of the act of transcription, but from his view of literature as property. Were his manuscripts to be duplicated mechanically, the value of the objects in his collection would decrease, as would his own personal fame: "Some other scholar's name would stand on the title-page of the edition . . . scholarship is a system of licensed robbery. . . . But against that robbery Bardo dei Bardi shall struggle. I too have a right to be remembered."

Bardo's aim as a scholar, then, is precisely opposite to the unselfish transmission of knowledge. Romola's project as her father's amanuensis, however, is constitutively selfless. She reminds Bardo that she reads "anything you wish me to read; and I will look out any passages for you, and make whatever notes you want." The very docility she has been trained into prevents her from having the knifelike mind that Bardo wants in an assistant: all her abilities require Bardo's direction. Hurt by his belittling her help, Romola retains only the hope that because of her own learning some great scholar will marry her: "And he will like to come and live with you, and he will be to you in place of my brother . . . and you will not be sorry that I was a daughter." If for Bardo femininity means only the most minimal contribution to the transmission of texts, Romola's only aim can be to make the connection between her father and some other male scholar.

The passage that Romola is initially seen reading to Bardo confirms this antithesis between feminine, selfless transmission and male, self-centered criticism and bequest. She is reading from the eightieth chapter of Politian's *Miscellanea* a passage about the blinding of Tiresias. The passage begins, however, not with Tiresias but with his mother, the nymph Chariclo, who was "especially dear to Pallas." Tiresias inadvertently sees Pallas naked while she is bathing in the company of Chariclo, and he immediately becomes blind, the punishment for those who behold the gods. However, "Pallas, moved by the tears of Chariclo," endows Tiresias with prophecy and, after his death, with immortality in the form of an oracle that speaks from his tomb. Politian then comments: "And hence, Nonnus, in the fifth book of the 'Dionysiaca,' introduces Actaeon exclaiming that he calls Tiresias happy, since, without dying, and with the loss of his eyesight merely, he had beheld Minerva unveiled, and thus, though blind, could for evermore carry her image in his soul." At this point in her reading, Romola's hand meets her father's, and then Bardo interrupts her to ask her to read from the copy of Nonnus that he himself made. When we see Romola touch her father's hand at the mention of the blind Tiresias's good fortune, it is obvious that both hope that Tiresias's compensations for blindness—memory and immortality—will visit Bardo as well.

It is Nonnus's addition to the story, however, that interests Bardo the most, partly because he has it in his own handwriting but also because it privileges certain aspects of the story over others. In the initial story, the emphasis is on the friendship between the two female figures, Pallas and Chariclo, and on the agency of the two in revising the Saturnian law that decrees the voyeur's punishment. The initial story is about a man's mother getting help for her son from her female friend. It is also a story about a partially successful attempt, by women, to defetishize the female body. A male god has decreed excessive punishment for voyeurism and by doing so has at once made the female body a forbidden object and made it responsible for turning men blind. When the nymph and the goddess seek to mitigate that punishment, they are seeking in effect to defuse these male myths of the magical and dangerous potency of the female body. In the exact same way, in the conversation surrounding her reading of the passage, Romola has attempted to deny her father's attempts to reduce her to merely her body, which, like Minerva's, is seen as subversive to male projects. The commentary, however, in which Bardo is so much more interested, bypasses this aspect of the story, while denying that it does so. Its way of opening, "And hence," conceals the lack of any logical connection to the previous narrative. The commentary stresses what Tiresias saw and characterizes that sight, not as an unfortunate accident, as in the original story, but as a lucky opportunity, which restores the female body to the status as fetish that Chariclo and Pallas, and indeed Romola herself, had attempted to deny.

The commentary also suggests that the detached image of a woman's body in a blind man's memory is preferable to the direct sight of that body, and this prejudice applies to Romola as well as to Minerva. Tiresias's good fortune to have beheld Minerva unveiled and to be able to "carry her image in his soul" bypasses the good actions of Pallas on his behalf and omits his mother altogether; it bypasses the function of women as active agents to identify them as the passive objects of voyeurism. Virtuous woman that she is, Romola is thus obliged to take pleasure in reading out a passage that first proposes and then erases her own importance. The disappearance of Chariclo and of the topic of female friendship from the commentary is echoed later in the chapter in Bardo's mention of Romola's mother, who is dead. Despite Romola's feminine mind, she has, Bardo says, "a man's nobility of soul: thou hast never fretted me with thy petty desires as thy mother did. It is true, I have been careful to keep thee aloof from the debasing influence of thy own sex." Although Romola's mother seems to Bardo to be made of petty desires, Chariclo's desires are as far from petty as possible, but she is banished just the same from the scene of masculine criticism. When mothers are banished (Romola's or Tiresias's), women begin to conform to men's preferred images of them. The commentary and its context in the scene of reading define both Minerva and Romola as goddesses of wisdom but even more as beautiful bodies. As soon as Romola goes to get the copy of Nonnus containing her father's version of the commentary, the narrative calls attention to her "queenly step" and her "tall, finely-wrought frame," which echoes Tiresias's view of the goddess. And again, right after Bardo discusses Romola's lack of her mother's pettiness, he speaks of the almost supernatural beauty that even he can perhaps perceive: "Bernardo tells me thou art fair, and thy hair is like the brightness of the morning, and indeed it seems to me that I discern some radiance from thee." Bardo's blind vision merges with the blind Tiresias's memory of a forbidden sight, as Romola's beauty merges with the goddess's, both as silent objects of vision.

Nonnus's commentary thus both enacts and is about masculine criticism of the sort that Bardo has wished to practice. Centering on what Tiresias got out of his experience, and on a male perspective on the female body, its content repeats the more egotistic, aggressive criticism of which it is an example, in contrast to the initial story, which is presented as a simple transmission of a received story. The matching transformation of Romola from selfless transmitter to object of male vision and criticism is completed in the irony of the speech she later makes about becoming a good scholar so as to get a scholar husband to help Bardo. She thinks her scholarship will be attractive, but of course it is primarily her beauty that attracts Tito.

Romola is thus introduced into the novel submissively bearing the word of women's exclusion from and silencing within literature, which is the same as her being reduced to mere body or to the literal with respect to language. Caught in a circular logic because of the nature of the literary work that her character as a virtuous and docile woman obliges her to perform, and to be happy performing, she herself promulgates the text of her own reduction, her own silencing and exclusion. Her womanly commitment not to be knife-sharp prevents her from doing anything but passively transmitting these erasing words. It is the very fact of her not touching, and being untouched by, the texts she transmits that constitutes her femininity in the book's scheme. Before her engagement, her godfather Bernardo teases her about her idealization of Tito: "Thy father has thought of shutting woman's folly out of thee by cramming thee with Greek and Latin; but thou hast been as ready to believe in the first pair of bright eyes and the first soft words that have come within reach of thee, as if thou couldst say nothing by heart but Paternosters, like other Christian men's daughters" (chap. 19).

After her marriage, Romola continues to serve as her father's reader and amanuensis, for Tito quickly loses interest in "the joint work" and turns to the pleasures of Florentine society. Following Bardo's death (he dies in the very moment of asking Romola to substitute one evening for Tito as scribe), Romola takes upon herself the "sacramental obligation" to fulfill "her father's lifelong ambition" (chap. 27) to have his books and collections transferred to the Florentine state. Tito, however, who wants cash and who is now the legal owner of the library, sells it to the French without Romola's knowledge. As the deeply wounded Romola proposes various plans for undoing the sale, when she learns of it, Tito says, "the event is irrevocable, the library is sold, and you are my wife" (chap. 32), pairing wife and library as properties that came into his possession from the same source. Although Romola's accusation that Tito has "robbed" her father recalls Bardo's comparison of scholarship to "licensed robbery," Tito's view of the library as property is not so very different after all from Bardo's. Tito's use for the library is purely selfish, but then so was Bardo's intention. Similarly, Tito's transformation of Romola from a selfless transmitter of men's words into a piece of property is no different from her situation in the scene of her reading Politian to her father, where she, and the female figures whose stories she reads, are transformed from generous helpers of men into the beautiful objects of male voyeurism. As we have seen elsewhere, it is inherent in a woman's role as the selfless transmitter of culture—which as we will see is here retrospectively identified as maternal—that she also becomes a mere body, the feared and appropriated mother's body, the literal.

Following the sale of the library, Romola contrives and partially executes a plan to leave Tito and Florence, a plan that however solitary still retains at its core her consistent motive to carry out her father's wish for the immortality of his name. She has "an indistinct but strong purpose of labour, that she might be wise enough to write something which would rescue her father's name from oblivion." Despite her selfless motives, Savonarola, encountering her on her road out of Florence, convinces her to return to "her place" in her home and in Florence. From the point of view of the Church he represents, she is "seeking [her] own will," placing her own needs over her duty to "the lot that has been appointed for [her]" (chap. 40). When Romola, thinking of her brother's desertion of the family for the sake of his visions, wonders how he could have been right if she is wrong, Savonarola justifies the difference by an argument from gender: Dino's vocation was to have visions, while Romola's is to be a wife.

Savonarola also appeals to Romola's understanding of her role with respect to language. In leaving her marriage, she is "breaking a pledge," violating her "faithfulness to the spoken word" that undergirds human trust. It is this appeal, to her habitual role as repeater of others' powerful words, that has the strongest effect on dissuading her. When she returns home, she confirms the priority of repeated vows over her own words by tearing up the farewell letters she wrote to Tito and Bernardo, the letters proclaiming her own will through her own language. These letters are the only original writing we ever see her do.

Subsequently, her life is devoted to charitable action at Savonarola's direction, just as her early life was devoted to obeying her father's will. While in the course of her new life she accepts the denunciation of many of her father's loves—along with "rouge-pots" and jewelry, the Dominicans burn on the Bonfire of Vanities copies of "the divine poets," including Petrarch—her participation in suppressing what she so recently devoted herself to preserving is perfectly consistent: a more persuasive and living male voice dictates a higher word. In his mixture of egotism and generosity, Savonarola, as Romola comes to know him, resembles Bardo in his relation to prior words. He stops Romola's flight by "the right of a messenger" with "a message from heaven," and he even uses, as Bardo does, a maternal metaphor for his message carrying in a sermon to which Romola listens: "Listen, O people, over whom my heart yearns, as the heart of a mother over the children she has travailed for" (chap. 24). At the same time, like Bardo, he intrudes his own "need of personal predominance" into his transmission of "divine intentions." His metaphor from the same sermon—"I lifted up my voice as a trumpet. [God's] word possesses me so that . . . it is not in me to keep silence"—is later used against him. Machiavelli remarks, "The Frate wants to be something more than a spiritual trumpet: he wants to be a lever, and what is more, he *is* a lever" (chap. 45). While Savonarola claims to be a messenger from God, the egotism of his message bearing demands, like

Bardo's, a truly compliant bearer of his word in its turn. At the end of the novel, Romola is teaching Petrarch to Tito's son on the day of commemoration for Savonarola. The text may change, but her relation to it stays the same.

Carrying out Savonarola's Christian word, Romola becomes, first, a madonna, then the Madonna, the Christian image of the woman who bears the word. But since in effect she has been acting the part of spiritual mother even in the "pagan" part of her life, by bearing her father's words, her formal transformation into the Madonna now only retrospectively confirms what she has always been (in much the same way that Daniel Deronda "becomes" a Jew half way through his novel). Like the Virgin Mary, who, in so many of the Renaissance paintings of the Annunciation that Eliot saw in Florence, is reading when Gabriel arrives, Romola in her maidenhood was first seen reading. Yet the texts that both Mary and Romola read prophesy their putting away the book and becoming in a much more efficacious way the medium through which the Word, or words, pass. As the Madonna, Romola stops reading her father's pagan books, but that only means that she begins literalizing in a new way.

The "lot" to which Savonarola calls Romola back is to minister aid to those suffering from the plague and famine that afflict Florence during its complicated civil and external wars. Her transformation into the Madonna is gradual. At first, as she patrols the streets tending the sick and feeding the starving, people address her as "madonna," simply a term of respect in Italian that Eliot chooses to leave untranslated. For example, when Romola shames a group of idle workmen out of taking bread from the weak and confused old man she eventually recognizes as Tito's foster father, one of them says, "Madonna, if you want to go on your errands, I'll take care of the old man" (chap. 42). Yet even before this scene, the term has begun to take on its special religious significance in relation to Romola. The beleaguered Florentines believe in the efficaciousness of "the precious Tabernacle of the Madonna dell' Impruneta." If brought into Florence, perhaps "that Mother, rich in sorrows and therefore in mercy, would plead for the suffering city" (chap. 2). When Romola is addressed as "madonna" on the next page, the term resonates with the signification of the Madonna, and during the next pair of chapters, "The Unseen Madonna" and "The Visible Madonna," the arrival of the statue of the Madonna and Romola's ministries are described in parallel. The "unseen" Madonna is the concealed image of the statue, but by the end of that chapter, Romola is an unseen madonna as well: Tito, riding in with news of the French ships, glimpses but does not acknowledge her. The "visible" madonna of the next chapter is Romola, whose deeds of mercy are now explicitly part of the visible effects of the Madonna: when she brings the good news to the people sheltered in her courtyard, they respond, "The Mother of God has had pity on us," and a moment later, as she leaves to bring them food, "'Bless you, madonna! bless you!' said the faint chorus, in much the same tone as that in which they had a few minutes before praised and thanked the unseen Madonna" (chap. 44).

When she meets Romola by accident, Tito's "other wife," Tessa, is certain in her simple faith that Romola is the Holy Mother. At the Bonfire of the Vanities, assaulted by the demand that she too give up her small fineries, Tessa is terrified until "suddenly a gentle hand was laid on her arm, and a soft, wonderful voice, as if the Holy Madonna were speaking, said, 'Do not be afraid; no one shall harm you'" (chap. 50). To Tessa, Romola is "this heavenly lady," and when they part, Tessa whispers, "Addio, Madonna," the term capitalized to indicate Tessa's belief that this is not simply an aristocratic lady but the Madonna she worships. Describing the incident later to Tito, Tessa asks "whether she could be the Holy Mother herself?" When Romola again by accident responds to Tessa's need (she rescues Lillo, who has strayed from home), it is clear that for Tessa "Romola had remained confusedly associated with the pictures in the churches, and when she reappeared, the grateful remembrance of her protection was slightly tinctured with religious awe" (chap. 56).

It is not until later, however, that the novel completes Romola's incarnation as the Madonna. Fleeing Florence a second time, after Savonarola has refused to prevent her godfather's execution and after she has learned the story of Tito's betrayal of his foster father, Romola symbolically dies and is reborn. Drifting away from the shore in a rudderless boat, wishing "that she might be gliding into death," Romola feels "a thirst that the Great Mother has no milk to still" (chap. 61). When she wakes up on the shore of an unrecognized coast, she is like a child. She knows "she was lying in the boat which had been bearing her over the waters all through the night. Instead of bringing her to death, it had been the gently lulling cradle of a new life" (chap. 68). The cove where she lands, "a sheltered nook where . . . she would nestle in the green quiet," is distinctly maternal: "In a deep curve of the mountains lay a breadth of green land, curtained by gentle tree-shadowed slopes leaning towards the rocky heights." But Romola's sense of being herself a trusting child is interrupted by "the cry of a little child in distress," by the demand that she resume her "maternal instinct." As the narrator later comments with a telling verbal juxtaposition, the wish for death "had sobbed within her as she fell asleep, but from the moment after her waking when the cry had drawn her, . . . she had simply lived . . . to do the work which cried aloud to be done" (chap. 69).

She finds the child crying beside the corpse of his mother, a victim of the plague. As Romola walks through the deserted village looking for help, she is wearing a nun's long robes and carrying this baby, and she hopes "a little in a certain awe she had observed herself to inspire, when she appeared, unknown and unexpected, in her religious dress" (chap. 68). It is a measure of her internalization of her religious role that the nun's habit is now her authentic garb; when she fled Florence before, Savonarola detected the inauthenticity of a similar disguise at once. She comes upon a sick woman desperate for water, and as Romola takes the woman's pitcher and walks to the well, her eyes on the church and on a cow in the field above the town, the narrator describes her appearance from the perspective of "a pair of astonished eyes," of one of those who experience that "certain awe":

> Romola certainly presented a sight which, at that moment and in that place, could hardly have been seen without some pausing and palpitation. With her gaze fixed intently on the distant slope, the long lines of her thick grey garment giving a gliding character to her rapid walk, her hair rolling backward and illuminated on the left side by the sun-rays, the little olive baby on her right arm now looking out with jet-black eyes, she might well startle that youth of fifteen, accustomed to swing the censer in the presence of a Madonna less fair and marvellous than this.

The boy observing her thinks to himself, "She carries a pitcher in her hand—to fetch water for the sick. It is the Holy Mother, come to take care of the people who have the pestilence." The boy tells the priest, who is hiding from the plague in his church above the town, that he has seen "the Holy Mother with the Babe . . . : she was as tall as the cypresses, and had a light about her head, and she looked up at the church." The cowardly priest, uncertain as to whether this may really be a vision, nonetheless "trembled at the thought of the mild-faced Mother, conscious that that Invisible Mercy might demand something more of him than prayers and 'Hails.'"

It is important to note that it is primarily as an object of vision that Romola becomes the Holy Mother for the villagers.[7] The "marvellous" way she looks and her fairness are what first strike the boy, and he and the priest imagine that she is "a vision." She is in this scene a holy object of beauty, spied upon by profane male eyes, much as Tiresias spied upon Minerva in the passage from Politian Romola once read to her father. As we have seen, making Minerva a forbidden sight transforms her into an object, a transformation against which she and Tiresias's mother protest. Later in that chapter, Romola becomes, like Minerva, the beautiful object of a blind man's sight, and still later, she becomes an object for Tito, too. To be a mother, even the Madonna, whose body scarcely touches the Messiah who passes through her, is also to be the maternal body so feared by Western culture; and this fear transforms even the Madonna's body into an object. The "awe" mixed in with the adoration the villagers feel is not very far from the horror that attributes to the sight of Minerva's body the power to blind a man.

Although eventually "the suspicion that Romola was a supernatural form was dissipated," to the people she rescues, she remains "the blessed Lady who came over the sea," the "sainted lady" whose eyes "had a blessing in them." As she leaves, "the wailing people, who knelt and kissed her hands, then clung to her skirts and kissed the grey folds," call to her words that children reserve for revered mothers, "Look at us again, Madonna!"

The baby, the "little dark creature" whom Romola initially rescues and who confirms her identity as the Holy Madonna, turns out to be Jewish, but, adopted by this Madonna, he is soon baptized a Christian, with the name Benedetto, "the benediction."[8] Not only does he play the part of the divine infant, the Word incarnate, but he embodies a specific holy word, the blessing. Carrying him through the village on her way to the well, Romola is the Madonna bearing the Word. Furthermore, Benedetto's history alludes to Christ's. Benedetto and his dead mother were "Spanish or Portuguese Jews, who had perhaps been put ashore and abandoned there by rapacious sailors. . . . Such things were happening continually to Jews compelled to abandon their homes by the Inquisition." Three Jewish families had in this way been put ashore, already infected by the plague; the villagers had "refused to give shelter to the miscreants, otherwise than in a distant hovel, and under heaps of straw."

This history of the exiles alludes, not only to the birth of Christ—whose family could not find room at the inn—but also, surprisingly but decidedly, to the history of another character: Tito. Tito, although Greek instead of Jewish, is, like Benedetto, "dark," olive-skinned with black eyes. Also like Benedetto, in his first scene in the novel, Tito is a stranger cast up on the seashore almost destitute, obliged to beg a breakfast of milk from the first woman he meets. Why should Tito, the novel's villain, be thus recalled in the form of a child with such close ties to Christ? At this point in the novel, Tito is dead, although Romola does not yet know it; his death is narrated in between Romola's drifting out to sea and her arrival at the village. Just as Benedetto is the Word, Tito in his death has become an incarnate word, but we will need to look at the history of Tito's relation to language in order to gauge the significance of this transformation, both for Romola's incarnation of the Madonna and for Eliot's fictional practice.

If Romola's incarnation as the Madonna is the apotheosis of the maternal relation to language, the selfless, faithful transmission of men's words (or God's word) into new forms, the most intimate and the most marked contrast to Romola's relation to texts appears in Tito, who as we have seen brings out most malignly the self-centeredness of Bardo's relation to texts. Tito enters the novel as a scholar who appears to wish to aid the literary work of two fathers, not only Bardo, but also his own supposedly dead foster father. He also gets work as a Greek professor. Over the course of the novel, he becomes a professional messenger and translator, but his transmissions are the antithesis of Romola's faithful ones. The messages he carries always change before reaching their destinations, to the benefit of Tito, as for example when he diverts the transmission of Bardo's library from its intended destination into the hands of the French. Both in his personal duplicities and in his increasingly complex political role—he eventually works for all the major factions in Florence—all Tito's activities essentially follow this model. He actively misinterprets the messages he delivers, by spying, forging documents, or delivering real documents to the wrong people, with the effect of betraying each of his employers' secrets to the others.

A year and a half into his marriage to Romola, Tito has proceeded from his jobs as assistant scholar and Greek professor—relatively straightforward forms of language transmission—to a new career that makes more complex use of his skill with languages. As Latin secretary to the "Ten," the ruling body of Florence, he has "become conspicuously serviceable in the intercourse with the French guests" (chap. 22). (At Florence's invitation, the French have become the city's somewhat imperialistic ally against the other Italian states. The French interests are aligned with Savonarola and the popular government, as opposed to the old aristocratic party of the Medici to whom Bardo and Bernardo belong.) In his new role, we first see Tito walking with some covert Medici as well as with a Frenchman, and the narrator intimates that he has already begun his duplicitous political game: his face reveals "the final departure of moral youthfulness." As the group pauses at the barber's shop, the center of male gossip in the novel's Florence, Tito translates for the Frenchman some of the casual talk, astonishing him by translating literally "Piero's pungency of statement. . . . It was a delightful moment for Tito, for he was the only one of the party who could have made so amusing an interpreter, and without any disposition to triumphant self-gratulation he revelled in the sense that he was an object of their liking" (chap. 22). The conspicuous features of this scene recur in almost all of the scenes of Tito's message carrying and translating. He appears, like Romola, not to intrude himself in what he translates (he translates "literally") and not to get anything out of it, but he actually gets a great deal. As he describes to Romola the ceremony directly following the scene of his comic translation, "'a ready-tongued personage—some say it was Gaddi, some say it was Melema, but really it was done so quickly no one knows who it was—had the honor of giving the Cristianissimo the briefest possible welcome in bad French.' 'Tito, it was you, I know,' said Romola, smiling brightly, and kissing him. 'How is it that you never care about claiming anything?'"

Tito never claims anything because he recognizes that saving the credit for others is the surest way of getting something for himself. Soon after, Tito is to be seen "carried above the shoulders of the people" in their joy at the good news he brings of a favorable treaty with the French (chap. 29). Again he refuses credit for himself, conferring it all on the man who worked out the treaty. The scene is repeated almost exactly, but with more sinister implications, nearly two years later when Tito rides into a war-blockaded, desperate Florence bringing the thrilling news that French ships have arrived on the coast with food and arms. Again he hands on the "glory of the messenger," in this case to another rider who broke down just before reaching Florence (chap. 43). Later he says, when teased about his good luck, "I have got nothing by it yet but being laid hold of and breathed upon by wool-beaters." And yet we know that Tito was on the road, and in a position to pick up the dropped message, because he was returning from "a private embassy" to the Pisan government, and that on the same trip he has also done an errand for the Medici, in direct opposition to the interests of those he has so pleased with the news about the French. "He never brags. That's why he's employed everywhere. They say he's getting rich with doing all sorts of underhand work," complains a rival (chap. 45).

The political game Tito plays is to work for all sides—"he could convince each that he was feigning with all the others"—so that he makes plenty of money and so that whoever wins, Tito will end up with those in power. At an aristocratic dinner, two of the leading Medici, Lorenzo Tornabuoni and Giannozzo Pucci, take Tito aside and invite him to serve their cause as envoy to the Medici in Rome, preferring him because of his skill in "hiding his prejudices." Assuming that the "pleasant, service-able" Tito is firmly on their side, Pucci and Tornabuoni encourage him to feign friendships with their enemies, Savonarola on the one hand and the Arrabiati led by Dolfo Spini on the other, in order to spy on them. But in his "triple deceit," Tito cultivates each side, while undermining, for the benefit of its enemies, each side's strategems even as he is employed to create them. The Medici also select Tito as envoy because of his "scholarship, which may always be a pretext for such journeys" (chap. 39). In a figure that confirms the transformation of scholarship's transmissions into the self-interested carrying of political messages, the "sharp edge of a young mind" that Tito initially offered Bardo reappears in this context. "To manage men one ought to have a sharp mind in a velvet sheath," says Pucci, flattering Tito; later, Bernardo, with Romola in mind, thinks, "This husband of hers, who gets employed everywhere, because he's a tool with a smooth handle, I wish Tornabuoni and the rest may not find their fingers cut" (chap. 45). And it is directly following this dinner, in represented time if not in the narrative, that Romola leaves home in response to Tito's betrayal of his remaining responsibility as a scholar. "The sharp edge" that Bardo sought has cut other fingers already.

As the novel proceeds, the politics of Tito's "triple deceit" are intermingled with his domestic deceits. There are three major episodes, in each of which Tito works primarily as a message carrier. In the first of these plots, Tito "had been the bearer of letters to Savonarola—carefully-forged letters; one of them, by a strategem, bearing the very signature and seal of the Cardinal of Naples" (chap. 46). The purpose of these letters is to lure Savonarola outside the gates of Florence where Spini can ambush him. Tito not only carries the letters to Savonarola but also warns Savonarola against the risk that he "guesses" they propose, so that Tito simultaneously challenges Savonarola to take a rash step and gets in favor with him in case the plot fails. "Tito himself did not much care for the result. He managed his affairs so cleverly, that all results, he considered, must turn to his advantage." The evening before Savonarola is to leave the city, the plot is foiled when Romola overhears Spini call Tito "my carrier-pigeon," guesses the plot, and forces Tito to prevent Savonarola's capture.

In the second of these major plots, we learn that Tito, anticipating the eventual exposure and failure of the Mediceans, has continued to work closely with them (as well as continuing to inform against Savonarola and the popular party while "showing subtle evidence that his political convictions were entirely on their side," chap. 57), so as to be able, when they fall (Bernardo del Nero with them) to save himself by informing against them. His work as informer is organized as message carrying. After brokering his immunity from prosecution in return for "acting against his friends, . . . he received a commission to start for Siena by break of day; and besides this, he carried away with him from the council chamber a written guarantee of his immunity and of his retention of office. . . . as Tito galloped with a loose rein towards Siena, he saw a future before him."

After the death of Bernardo and the other Mediceans, Tito's part in his final plot begins with an act of translation and ends with the carrying of a letter. Savonarola, by this time excommunicated by the Pope, has been challenged to prove that God is nonetheless on his side by performing the miracle of walking unharmed through a fire. It is Tito, acting as Spini's agent, who has brought "this little comedy of the Trial by Fire" into reality by getting the Florentine government to "take up the affair" (chap. 63). Just before we learn any of this, however, we see Tito charmingly allowing himself to be pressed into service by a semiliterate crowd to translate from the Latin and read the "unorganized and scrambling" Italian of a large official placard. His first appearance on the political scene was his acute and, because literal, amusing translation of the gossip at the barber's, and in this scene, he will again translate literally. But first, he elaborately paraphrases the Italian part of the placard and says it merely confirms what he already knew, that the government invites anyone who shares his faith to join Savonarola in entering the flames. The crowd, whose discomfiture amuses only Tito, asks him to "favour us by interpreting the Latin." Tito again construes "interpreting," not as literal reading or translation, but as paraphrase, but a shoemaker interrupts him: "'Let us have the Latin bit by bit, and then tell us what it means.' . . . 'Willingly,' said Tito, smiling. 'You will then judge if I give you the right meaning'" (chap. 63). Tito smiles, of course, at his hearers' claim to judge his interpretation if they cannot judge his translation. He does indeed translate word for word the Latin that he reads out, which describes Savonarola's doctrines. However, he neither reads out nor translates, but only paraphrases, the framing language to the effect that these doctrines will be proved or disproved by the trial by fire. Thus his literal translation and his posture of deferential public service mask a wider deceptiveness about interpretation. In secrecy, it is he who has made it necessary that Savonarola's doctrines be interpreted according to the outcome of the absurd trial.

Also concealed within his apparently faithful translation, though concealed in a different way, is another act of treachery. During Tito's performance, Spini walks by and Tito makes a secret sign to him that arranges a meeting. In contrast to Tito's opening his interpretation of the placard up to public judgment, this sign is designed to conceal its meaning. It is during the course of Tito's subsequent interview with Spini, which directly follows the translation scene, that we learn the extent of Tito's role in the trial by fire, and thus that we learn the limitations of his literal translation of the placard. Its real meaning is not in what he reads but in what he leaves out. Thus the contrast with the apparently similar scene of translation at the beginning of the book marks the course of Tito's career. Starting out as a transparent medium of verbal exchange not unlike Romola, by the end he uses this posture to his own ends, although from the start he has always, unlike Romola, "got something out of it." The amount he gets out has increased as the degree of his falsification of translation has deepened.

The plot that this placard introduces is not complete, however, until Tito has delivered his last letter. Guessing that Savonarola in the days before the trial will write to the French king for help, and knowing that the exposure of such a letter would complete Savonarola's ruin, Tito offers to convey a letter to a courier on his way to France. In making this offer, which is really an offer to have the letter intercepted, Tito is already the bearer of an intercepted message, an intimation by a disciple of Savonarola's to the effect that he might need a courier. By implying that he has been sent by this disciple, Tito gains Savonarola's confidence. Savonarola seals his letter in another paper and asks Tito to write the covering address in his own handwriting, better to conceal its contents. Tito, who has portrayed himself to Savonarola, as he has throughout, as a "mere instrument," offers here the illusory possibility of an anonymity behind which Savonarola might hide, a blank sheet of paper written on only by the unrecognizable handwriting of a "cipher." But although Tito duly delivers the letter to the courier of France, he also "had conveyed information in cipher, which was carried by a series of relays to armed agents of Ludovico Sforza, Duke of Milan, on the watch for the very purpose of intercepting despatches" (chap. 64). Florence learns that Savonarola's letter "would soon be in the hands of the Pope" (chap. 65). When a cipher writes in cipher, he is no longer the medium of transmission but its source.

If Madonna Romola's faithful transmission of men's texts is, as we have seen, typical of the way in which a woman's reproduction of language becomes the source of her objectification, if she both literalizes and becomes the literal, then Tito's deceitful transmissions of messages typify the operation of figuration. His view that messages are best delivered, not to the addressee, but instead to another recipient, together with his exposure of secrets and his mistranslations, are grounded on the essential assumption of figuration, that signifiers refer only to other signifiers and not to some literal ground of truth. His figurations have throughout the novel come into conflict with Romola's literalizations, and the novel represents his death as a consequence of literalization. For a life based on the freedom and displacements of figuration, literal meaning would have to mean death. During the night of rioting immediately after the trial and the disgrace of Savonarola, Tito's strategems redound upon him, as if in the infinite circularity of figuration a figure had finally returned to its origin.

Spini learns from Tito's less successful rival in the spying and deceiving business, Cer Ceccone, that Tito was responsible for the failure of the original plot against Savonarola, and he sends in Tito's direction the rioting mob, which has already nearly killed Savonarola and hungers to destroy something new. Trapped on the Ponte Vecchio, Tito becomes a literalization of one of the letters that he has himself misdelivered. He dives into the Arno to escape the mob, and as he surfaces "he ha[s] a sense of deliverance" (chap. 67). His face, all that is visible above the water, is "bloodless" and "pale," "looking white above the dark water." This white face "with the blue veins distended on the temples" recalls most recently the blank sheet enclosing Savonarola's letter, deceptively addressed in Tito's hand. To his betrayed foster father, Baldassare, who seeks revenge and who now sits feeble and bewildered by the river, Tito's face appears "a white object coming along the broader stream." The current casts Tito ashore unconscious at Baldassare's feet. The "deliverance" that Tito first felt in the water, which corresponds to his professional belief that all deliveries remove the letter from its proper destination, turns into this unerring and inescapable delivery of Tito to the one place he belongs, his origin and end. Delivered straight, taken out of the circulation of signifiers his life depended on, he becomes a white object, a word with literal rather than figurative meaning; and because his life depends on figuration, his incarnation of language kills him.

Thus after Tito's death, when Romola has become the Madonna for the plague-stricken village, for her to carry a Word who is both the Logos and the incarnation of Tito is for her to begin symbolically to correct Tito's strayed messages. The form of Romola's maternal virtue has always been to put words in their proper places, in the place of proper or literal meaning; and this she does despite the cost of this project, which is always her transformation into a literal object of male voyeurism. Just as earlier she had put into practice the far worthier words of Bardo and then Savonarola (and the prior authorities that they claimed spoke through them), subordinating her own desires to their demands, her relation to Tito follows the same pattern. Her marriage was the only thing she ever wanted for herself: ("Nothing has ever come to me that I have wished for strongly: I did not think it possible that I could care so much for anything that could happen to myself" (chap. 12). When her desire fails disastrously, she converts it into the likeness of her other relations to men, turning Tito into a word she can transmit. To bear the dead and devious Tito newborn as the true Logos is to bespeak the triumph of self-sacrificing womanly virtue, of literalization and of the literal meaning it both costs and creates, over deceptive and self-centered figuration.

Tito's death is the literalization of another figure, a figure that connects his fear of literalization inversely with Romola's maternal apotheosis of it. His fear most closely resembles the fear we traced in *Jane Eyre* of childbirth as the transformation of self into thing, a fear that Mary Shelley suggests may be not so much of childbirth itself but of the circumvention of childbirth by patriliny. Tito is associated with figures of children, and at the end he becomes at once a child and a literalization, and this simultaneous development signals his death, for he dies as a child at the hands of the father he betrayed. For him as much as for the Brontës' heroines, literalization and the transformation into a child are the same dangerous thing, and this view contrasts sharply, of course, with Romola's view of her history, in which she sees literalization as the only good, and the mothering of children as identical to that good.

Tito's association with figures of children begins with the sale of the onyx ring that betokens his bond to his foster father, a sale that he regrets, as his friends may suspect him of being unfeeling. It is indeed this sale that initiates the train of events leading to his death, for it proves to Baldassare Tito's unforgivable abandonment. The narrator comments,

> But our deeds are like children that are born to us; they live and act apart from our own will. Nay, children may be strangled, but deeds never: they have an indestructible life both in and out of our consciousness; and that dreadful vitality of deeds was pressing hard on Tito for the first time. (chap. 16)

This simile reappears when Baldassare suddenly stumbles into Tito and clutches at him on the steps of the Duomo and Tito speaks the unretractable words, "*Some madman, surely*" (chap. 22). Tito reflects that had he not impulsively spoken these words, he could have saved himself from the consequences of further falsehood (including Baldassare's vengeance), but that now the words are spoken he can only perpetuate the lie: "He seemed to have spoken without any preconception: the words had leaped forth like a sudden birth that had been begotten and nourished in the darkness" (chap. 23).

In between these two similes of words as independent, indestructible, threatening children, there appears, in the main episode of the chapter called "A Florentine Joke," a demonic child who leaps forth uncontrollably, a darkly comic literalization of these figures. The joke represents the barber Nello's effort to rid his piazza of an itinerant quack doctor. When Nello is half way through shaving the doctor, the barber's servant appears, disguised as a contadina seeking help for her baby who suffers from "convulsions." The baby is firmly wrapped, but it "seemed to be struggling and crying in a demoniacal fashion under this imprisonment. 'The fit is on him! . . . It's the evil eye—oh!'" (chap. 16). The "mother" then pulls off the wrappings, "when out struggled—scratching, grinning, and screaming—what the doctor in his fright fully believed to be a demon, but what Tito recognized as Vaiano's monkey, made more formidable by an artificial blackness, such as might have come from a hasty rubbing up the chimney." The monkey claws its way up the mane of the doctor's horse, and horse and monkey take off at full speed, pursued by the lather-covered doctor and the false contadina. "'Il cavallo! Il Diavolo!' was now shouted on all sides."

Although Tito is merely a spectator to the scene, it enacts his concerns. The monkey, appearing as a demonic child and racing diabolically about the streets, resembles as closely as possible the unstranglable children that represent the "dreadful vitality of deeds" in the figure that just precedes the scene. The disguised monkey even more closely resembles the "words [that] leaped forth like a sudden birth," even down to the detail of the darkness in which the words are begotten and nourished, which is actualized as the "artificial blackness" the monkey acquires from his "hasty" transformation into a child. The monkey-child is a visible form of Tito's deeds and words. During this chapter, Tito has good reason to fear these demonic children. He is preoccupied with his fear that Dino will have told Romola about the letter from Baldassare, that his lie about his father will be exposed. Yet at the very opening of the next chapter, Tito learns that Romola knows nothing against him apart from Dino's uncreditable vision of him as the "Great Tempter" and that that has even served to strengthen her love for him. In the moment of discovering that he need not fear his demonic children—"he could only rejoice in her delusion"—he becomes one of them himself; he becomes the tempter that Dino envisions and that his own figures show him becoming. Later, just before the betrothal, Bernardo refers to Tito, teasing Romola about her love for so light-hearted a person, as "one of the *demoni*, who are of no particular country. . . . His mind is a little too nimble to be weighted with all the stuff we men carry about in our hearts" (chap. 19). And on the day that Romola watches the last of her father's books leave the house, she hears the peal of a bell as "little flames" and as "the triumph of demons at the success of her husband's treachery" (chap. 36). At the end of the novel, Spini calls Tito "a good little demon" (chap. 63).

These combinations of littleness or lightness and demonism, the image of Tito as a diminutive demon, link him to the figures of words as a demonic birth and of deeds as children with a "dreadful vitality" that cannot be strangled. They culminate in another literalization of the figure in the scene of Tito's death. Having become one of the messages that he has so continually misdirected, and having become his own deed of treachery against his father, he next becomes the child in the figure and is at last strangled by his parent: "Baldassare's only dread was, lest the young limbs should escape him. He pressed his knuckles against the round throat, and knelt upon the chest with all the force of his aged frame" (chap. 67). Just as the "dreadful vitality of the deed was pressing hard on Tito" in the earlier figure, so now Baldassare literally "presses . . . with all his force" on Tito's body. Unable figuratively to strangle his own deeds, Tito becomes them and is himself strangled. To become a child is to become something literal. Just as the literalization of one of Tito's deviant messages means death for this character who lives in figures, the literalization of figurative language about language means death too. His death is the conjunction of the literalization that is the coming into being of a child together with the literalization of figures.

Thus when Romola appears, in the very next chapter, looking like the Madonna and carrying a child who looks like both the Christ child and Tito, we recognize that Tito in dying has become both a word (a message, a literalized figure) and a child (a stranglable deed-child, a sudden birth from darkness). Yet while for Tito nothing could be more horrifying than these transformations, in Romola's hands, these transformations are decidedly for the good, turning what Tito experiences as a disastrous collapse into the literal into the holy incarnation of the Word as Christ child. There are other children Romola carries as well: on returning to Florence, she adopts Tito's real children, his "word" incarnate in a different way, children to whom she will pass on the word of Tito's history, as well as the words of her father's beloved books, in the novel's final scene. What Romola bears, when she incarnates the Madonna, as much as when she reads about Chariclo and Minerva, is the message of her own exclusion from that position from which language may be manipulated to meet the desires of the self. Yet she nonetheless contentedly accepts her "lot" and performs this womanly duty, transforming the deceits of Tito's figures into the truth of God's literal Word.

If Eliot writes *Romola* on the premise that "the broad sameness of the human lot" makes fifteenth-century Florence not very distant from mid-Victorian England, what is the relation between Romola's lot with respect to language and Eliot's own? As a relation to language that accommodates the myth that woman's proper duty is as a mother, a myth that functions no less decisively in Victorian England than in Catholic

Florence, the myth of women's writing that Romola's relation to language suggests would seem to be enthusiastically endorsed by Eliot, who presents this heroine far less critically than almost any of her other heroines.[9] In contrast to Romola's complete docility with respect to men's words, Maggie Tulliver and Dorothea Brooke both attempt to have their own desires and their own words, and in their early imaginativeness they appear to be artist figures, figures for Eliot's own daring practice. When they become more receptive later on, and give up their own visions, Eliot separates her linguistic practice from theirs. While she does nothing to qualify the goodness of Romola's literalizations, she is overtly critical of Maggie's, for example, in having Maggie die of them. Furthermore, Eliot in Romola identifies deviance from literal transmission with perhaps the most purely evil character in all her fiction. Although like the other heroines, Romola is cheated of her first intentions, her later apotheosis as Madonna is so compelling, and seems so adequate to her revised hopes, that we might pause over the question of how Eliot—for she indeed does—nonetheless separates her own practice from that of her heroine.

We began our discussion of Romola's transmission of male texts with the scene of her reading from Politian and Nonnus to her father, a scene in which both the passage read and the circumstances of its reading are about, and also enact, the exclusion of women in and from androcentric texts and literary practices. It is important to know, for consideration of Eliot's place in the scene, that the translation from Politian's Latin is Eliot's own.[10] The translation is an invisible one that, like Romola's transmissions of others' words, does not call attention to itself, does not intrude its own desires. The passage from Politian is complemented, in the manuscript of the novel, by two epigraphs for the chapter, one for Bardo and one for Romola (these were later cancelled, along with epigraphs for a few other chapters).[11] Like the translation from Politian, which mirrors Romola's unobtrusive style of reading, the epigraph for Romola is an accurate and undisrupted transmission. Quoted verbatim from the original Italian, the lines by Luigi Pulci also offer a reasonable outline of Romola's character. The epigraph begins, "Era tutta cortese, era gentile, / Onesta, savia, pura, e vergognosa." The epigraph for Bardo, by contrast, represents a disrupted transmission. The line, "Novissima omnium cupido gloriae" ("The desire for fame is the last thing to remain"), appears to be a garbled reminiscence of a line from Tacitus's Histories, "Etiam sapientibus cupido gloriae novissima exuitur" ("The desire for fame is the last thing from which even philosophers divest themselves"). Although the sense of the line is not really changed in Eliot's version of it, the very fact of her altering the words (however inadvertently) mirrors Bardo's own approach to the classics, in addition to the way in which the line comments thematically on Bardo's desire for fame after he has lost almost everything else. The "desire for fame," the selfish interest, creates disruptions in the smooth progress of texts from the past to the future. It is as if the desire for fame that Eliot is about to depict enters her own practice of transmission at that point and causes her to intrude her own words—even though in this case, the intrusion accomplishes nothing in the way of selfish interests.

It would seem that the chapter for which Eliot selected these epigraphs presents an uncomplicated paradigm of both the values and the genders of opposing kinds of transmission. Accuracy and faithfulness are associated with Romola, both in Romola's and in Eliot's practice, while obtrusive interruptions by a writer (whether Eliot or someone else) are associated with Bardo's self-seeking idea of masculine criticism and his wish to have his name remembered. By translating Politian in Romola's way, Eliot would seem to side with Romola, calling attention, not to the fabric of the translation itself, but to the intentions of the original. Yet the situation is complicated by the fact that the passage from Politian is a veritable palimpsest of languages. While the base story of Tiresias is written in Politian's original Latin, the passage also includes his paraphrase, in Latin, of Nonnus's commentary on the story, in Greek, from his epic poem "Dionysiaca." While Romola reads to her father in Latin and a Latin paraphrase of Greek, and prepares to read to him from the original Greek of Nonnus (copied by Bardo), the way in which Eliot represents her reading in these different tongues is by writing it all in English. Eliot's translation, unobtrusive and passive as it is, aggressively flattens the complex intertextuality of the passage in order to get an English novel written. Thus the translator's own concerns, the self-interests of the writer, do intrude themselves.

A further ambiguity about translation is that when Eliot writes that Romola reads to her father "to the following effect," the "effect," presumably, is first in Italian, since reader and listener are Italian. Therefore, the narrator is at least theoretically translating first from the Latin (which incorporates translation from the Greek) into the Italian of its reader's understanding, and from there into English. Indeed, all the dialogue is in this way "translated" by the narrator, since the characters are represented as speaking Italian to each other (when they are not quoting classical tags). Eliot exploits this ambiguity when she occasionally uses an Italian word or phrase, such as the term "madonna" for Romola. Because it passes for an ordinary term of respect in "untranslated" Italian, while its English translation has only a religious signification, and because Eliot's frequent use of other Italian words prevents the reader from ascertaining whether the term is being used in Italian or in English, Romola can be at once a dignified lady of Florence and the Holy Mother. Romola's double identity depends on the translator's calling attention to the words of the translation themselves, not just to the intended meaning.

If the entire novel is, fictively, a translation of events transacted in Italian, and yet if this "translation" calls attention to its own fabric, then Eliot as a translator is as close to Bardo's self-centered intrusiveness as to Romola's passivity. Indeed, some of Bardo's comments about being a transcriber sound very like what Eliot herself writes about translation, in the essay and letter on translation we discussed in chapter 7. Bardo says that the scholarly transcriber has "that insight into the poet's meaning which is closely akin to the *mens divinior* of the poet himself" (chap. 5). His identification of his own mind with the poet's "more godlike mind" recalls Eliot's argument that a word for word translation (such as we might imagine Romola would perform) is less successful than that of a translator whose "exceptional knowledge" of the subject at hand and "real mastery of his author" suggest, covertly yet arrogantly, that the translator might have written the original as well as the author himself.[12] Further, in her own translation of Strauss, Eliot's "impudent addition" of a metaphor to vivify his lackluster prose poses a challenge to the translator's "patience" and "rigid fidelity" that suggests that she would indeed be uncomfortable in Romola's role, where the translator's fidelity additionally carries explicitly sexual overtones.[13] Where Romola's idea of transmission is absolute fidelity at the expense of self, Eliot, like Bardo, insists upon the possible insertion of a self into translation.

The fiction of the novel as translation appears to endorse and be endorsed by Romola's passive relation to language, but the novel's practice is actually closer to Bardo's. In the same way, the novel also appears to present itself as a humble vehicle for historical events, and yet it undercuts this apparent passivity, too. As Felicia Bonaparte and others have shown, there are originals, carefully researched by Eliot, for almost all the major and minor characters in the novel, from Savonarola and the political figures who appear on the margins of the book, down to Nello the barber and the young disciple of Savonarola's who helps Romola witness the execution in the last chapter of the book.[14] Eliot gives these real historical personages a new linguistic life, but her research guarantees their derivation from people who really lived. Yet Eliot's version of history is of course no passive transmission at all. In a footnote she herself appended to the long and passionate sermon that she has Romola and

Baldassare hear in the Duomo, Eliot writes, "The sermon here given is not a translation, but a free representation of Fra Girolamo's preaching in its more impassioned moments."[15] With this free representation that is not a translation, Eliot writes Savonarola's words as if she herself were speaking them. She disconcerts the opposition between translation and original invention. This situation is both mirrored and complicated by her having Savonarola claim, in the text of the sermon, to be merely the "trumpet" for God's word, which "possesses" him, a claim that is both true and false, because, like Eliot, he intrudes his private ambition into what he transmits. If his ambiguous transmissions are criminal, so perhaps are Eliot's; if they are virtuous, then perhaps Eliot's are too.

Later on, in discussing Savonarola's "Confession"—his retraction, under torture, of his claims to having the gift of prophecy—the narrator starts out by casting doubt on the text by indicating all the ways in which Savonarola's words might have been misconstrued and mistransmitted. Many of Savonarola's followers believe that "any reported words of his which were in inexplicable contradiction to their faith in him, had not come from the lips of the prophet, but from the falsifying pen of Cer Ceccone, that notary of evil repute, who had made the digest of the examination" (chap. 71). Cer Ceccone, Tito's rival, stands in here for Tito and all that Tito has come to represent about the transmission of language. Yet Eliot stresses that in spite of Cer Ceccone's distortions and additions, Romola and others perceive that most of the text, certainly its general import, is authentic, because much of what is damning is what Savonarola genuinely felt. "Even in this confession, and without expurgation of the notary's malign phrases, Fra Girolamo shone forth as a man who had sought his own glory indeed, but sought it by labouring for the very highest end—the moral welfare of men." Eliot's point is that an interfering transcriber does not harm and possibly helps the authenticity of a strong voice, and she aligns this advantageous interference, not just with Bardo's egotism, but with Tito's far more sinister version of it.

Eliot's novel is itself a "free representation" of the history of Florence; her chief embellishments are the characters of Romola and Tito, the only major characters for whom there are no originals in historical documents. These fictive characters are "additions" in the sense that Cer Ceccone makes malign additions, and also in the same way that Eliot herself as translator once made "impudent additions." Quite early in the novel, when Tito is still relatively uncorrupted, he does something very like what Eliot does. In getting Piero di Cosimo to paint a triptych of himself and Romola as Bacchus and Ariadne, Tito tells Piero that he wants a subject out of Ovid, "but I want it treated in a new way. . . . I want to have the fair-haired Ariadne with him, . . . that is not in Ovid's story, but no matter, you will conceive it all" (chap. 18). Tito adds Romola to a literary text he wishes to have translated into a new medium, and in the same way Eliot adds Romola to the text of history that she translates into the text of fiction. Here is the paradox at the heart of the novel's thematics and practice of linguistic transmissions: Romola, who is the novel's representative of the virtues of faithful, literal, passive transmission, is there in the novel only because she is the novelist's most prominent invention and addition. Eliot seems to approve of Romola's style of transmission, but Romola is herself a figure, dependent for her very existence in the novel on something like Tito's malignant and deviant figurations.[16] I have been assuming for the purposes of argument that Romola is a literalization or incarnation of the Madonna, who is a figure or myth, but it is equally true that Romola is a figure for the Madonna.[17] While the historical Mary actually gave birth to a real child, Romola's bearing of language and of the child is never more than figurative. She is a foster mother, a figurative mother, first for Benedetto, then for Tito's "widow" and her children. Like Eliot herself, she is a mother without ever bearing children of her own.

In these various ways, the figure of Romola disconcerts the opposition and even the difference between literal and figurative. She appears to represent the virtues of the literal, the true, the unswerving, and she comes to life as she literalizes the figure of the Virgin Mary, while Tito would represent fiction, figures, and deviance and dies of being literalized. And it seems that Tito deviates from Ovid while Romola faithfully reads Politian. But the nature of Tito's deviation is Romola, and her bearing of the message of the virtues of the literal can function only within the context of her bearing itself being, not literal, but figurative. Thus while extolling the virtue of direct transmission and of literalization, of bearing the word from language into being, Eliot has Romola do what Eliot says women should do without doing it herself. If "Madonna Romola's" bearing of the word is about women's relation to language, then what Eliot accomplishes here is a superb irony. Thematically endorsing women's traditional vocation, to literalize and to become the literal, she also argues, at the level of her own practice, for the novelist's necessary distance from the literal, the distance created by figuration. Eliot sees women's association with the literal and literalization only in the forms in which they have been appropriated by an androcentric culture, as the silencing of the mother and her transformation into an object of voyeurism. Yet while the figure of Romola is thus a triumph of the Victorian woman writer's effort to accommodate the ideology of motherhood, *Romola* accomplishes this aim only by separating theme from practice, as indeed the novel sets enmity between the characters of the woman and of the artist, between Romola and Tito. The woman writer's dilemma remains intact, or rather, as divided as it has always been; but in this novel Eliot's strategies for concealing, if not healing, that divide are as powerful as they can ever be.

9

Mothers and Daughters I:
Gaskell's Stories of the Mother's Word
and the Daughter's Fate

Central to Gaskell's myth of herself as a writer who put her duties as a woman ahead of her writing is the story of how she began to write seriously. In 1845 her ten-month-old son, William, died of scarlet fever, and "it was to turn her thoughts from the subject of her grief that, by her husband's advice, she attempted to write a work of some length."[1] This work was *Mary Barton*, her first novel, published in 1848 with a preface that encodes her sacred reason for writing: "Three years ago I became anxious (from circumstances that need not be more fully alluded to) to employ myself." Like Mary Shelley in her introduction to *Frankenstein*, Gaskell wishes to demonstrate that her writing begins safely within the bounds of a woman's duty to her family, as behavior that the death of a son might legitimately provoke and of which a protective husband approves. Only when deprived of a woman's proper duties would she consider writing.

Yet the novel also bears an epigraph that encodes a slightly different story of origins:[2]

Nimm nur, Fährmann, nimm die Miethe,
Die ich gerne dreifach biete!
Zween, die mit nur überfuhren,
Waren geistige Naturen.

Two dead children, not one, thus make their ghostly appearance at the start of this novel. The public myth of her writing would make the death of her son be the pivotal moment of her life, yet the other death, the first death, was that of her first child, a stillborn daughter, in 1833. In 1836 she wrote a sonnet "On Visiting the grave of my stillborn little girl." The poem records, and by doing so enacts, the carrying out of the speaker's "vow" never to forget this child, who was "laid beside my weary heart, / With marks of Death on every tender part," even when another is born. "And thou, my child, from thy bright heaven see / How well I keep my faithful vow to thee."[3] As Gaskell's first self-consciously literary venture, though she never published it, the poem marks a different point of origin for the writer's career from that indicated by the story about the death of her son. Written during the period of the diary about Marianne, the "living infant" who the poem asserts does not supplant the dead one, the sonnet precedes her first published work, the Wordsworthian poem "Sketches Among the Poor" (1837), and her sketch of Clopton Hall published in 1840 in William Howitt's *Visits to Remarkable Places*. Most significantly, the first short story she wrote, in 1838, was "Lizzie Leigh" (not published till 1851, after her reputation had already been established by *Mary Barton*), a story about mothers and daughters that hinges on the death of a little girl. The writing of this story suggests that the poem's vow not to forget the dead daughter continues to provide the impetus to write, even if the child is memorialized by a reenactment of her death. Thus, behind the myth of the writer as mother grieving over her son and directed by her husband's wisdom, who writes novels and publishes them immediately, lies hidden another writer who grieves alone over a daughter and writes a poem and a story she is reticent to publish. It is this second writer I wish to uncover.

When Gaskell's living daughter begins to speak, as Gaskell describes it in the diary, Papa's name and the signs of Papa's arrival make up her earliest language, "leaving poor Mama in the background."[4] With this only partially comic exclusion of the mother from the scene of symbolic language, Gaskell's diary begins making its covert myth about the place of women in language, a myth that in the next diary entry offers as compensation for this exclusion women's traditional role as passive medium for the transmission of men's, or God's, words. Though the diary starts out by uniting mother and daughter as its fused "subject," it also acknowledges the premise of symbolic language, that the text will have meaning only if one or the other of its subjects is dead. In these and other ways, the diary yields up to the predominant myths of language and of writing the primacy and tenacity of a mother's relation with her daughter and of the linguistic possibilities that relation might offer.

Briefly to recapitulate my argument in chapter 1 and its development in intervening chapters, the mother's relegation to the background is the result of her being that against which a male subject and speaker must define his difference, defining her as the difference and absence that constitute symbolic language. But furthermore—and this is what is of particular relevance for our discussion of Gaskell—Nancy Chodorow argues that the daughter's original, preoedipal attachment to her mother outlasts the time of the son's separation from the mother and identification with the father, because unlike the son she is never obliged to renounce the mother. Chodorow argues further that it is the desire to reproduce this early situation that causes daughters, and not sons, to grow up to want not only to bear but to rear—to "mother"—children. Whereas sons seek representations of the mother in later romantic attachments, allowing them to keep the mother at a safe distance (and while daughters seek representations of the father in the same way), daughters seek to reproduce literally the same situation they once lived in, without wanting to distance the mother. As a part of a myth of language, this desire to reproduce the mother-daughter relation, with the non- or presymbolic language that both accompanies it and is modeled on it, is the desire to write in what I have been calling a literal language. This literal language is fleetingly exemplified by the rhythmic, cadenced speech Mrs. Ramsay shares with her daughter in Woolf's *To the Lighthouse*, a kind of speech that does not matter because it refers to things but rather because it reassures the daughter of her mother's presence, a presence that is not distanced by the law of the father.

However, women writers of the nineteenth century depend too much for the legitimation of their writing on their acceptance of the symbolic order's codes, codes that would exclude them as the silent objects of representation from writing as women, for them to see value in writing in this way as mother or daughter. Or perhaps it would be more accurate to say that those women novelists who have been accepted within the literary canon are those who have accepted these codes and write according to their identification of writing with masculinity. At the same time, the desire to retain and to reproduce something of, or like, this nonsymbolic language may entice women to value a role as bearers of language (and also as bearers of children). This role has the added appeal of offering an alternative way of accommodating paternal codes. Yet situated as it is in a culture that devalues whatever women do, including motherhood, this role becomes a position of subordination, appropriated, as maternity itself is appropriated, to fill the needs of a paternal order. Women are encouraged to define themselves as mothers, yet are permitted only a narrow and subordinate role when writing as mothers. *Frankenstein* articulates a woman writer's protest against this situation perhaps the most clearly, while the Victorian novelists, especially Gaskell and Eliot, who were personally as well as culturally obliged to subscribe to the cultural mythology of woman as mother, both accede to this situation and find ways to accommodate their own writing to it. Eliot is interested in the manipulation of women's given role as bearers of androcentric language—the role that Gaskell sees as available to her as compensation for Mama's relegation to the background—to see how far women's subjection to a masculinist myth of language can yet be made to afford women speech. Gaskell, perhaps more bold in her claims for writing as a woman, is interested in recovering, however fleetingly and however colored by its situation within the confines of the paternal order, that discourse between mothers and daughters that is lost to most women writers before the twentieth century, given up by daughters and mothers alike as the price of any sort of access to the language of fathers. That Gaskell is the least canonical of the novelists considered in this book is directly related to her claiming, however conditionally, that there might be other ways for women to write, beyond the unsatisfactory alternatives either of adopting what her culture perceived as the masculine position or of accepting the narrow definition of the mother as servant to patriliny.

"Lizzie Leigh," the story Gaskell wrote in commemoration of her dead daughter, is the story of mothers' love for their daughters that is, paradoxically, both destroyed by and dependent upon the intrusion into this relationship of paternal authority. Gaskell does not imagine a mother-daughter relation that is not affected by the father; rather she explores the possibility for such a relation as it exists within a patrilineal culture. As a myth of women's relation to the operation of language, the story suggests not so much that a nonsymbolic language shared between mothers and daughters survives from childhood, or that women's linguistic practices are wholly absorbed within the paternal order, but rather that in the interplay between these seemingly contradictory possibilities exists a language that is specific to mothers and daughters and also, importantly, capable of providing pleasure to them. Gaskell celebrates women's difference without losing sight of its cost.

The story contrasts two kinds of relations between generations, which are also two models of language. Patriliny is the inheritance both of the father's property and of his language, by way of women who (like Romola, or like Brontë's Cathy at the end of her life) facilitate inheritance but are excluded from its benefits. Both against and within patriliny, a matrilineal order acknowledges women's marginal place in patriliny and establishes its own separate principles of intergenerational relations that are more fluid and flexible than those of patriliny. The story opens with the death of James Leigh, who for three years has denied the existence of his "fallen" daughter Lizzie, who nonetheless is mourned by her mother, Anne. Anne's first action on hearing the reading of her husband's will, bequeathing to her for life the farm that "had belonged for generations to the Leighs," is to rent it out in order to go to Manchester in search of her lost daughter.⁵ In "The Crooked Branch," a later "prodigal son" tale that in turn revises Wordsworth's "Michael," the father, Nathan, similarly liquidates some of his farm's assets to pay his erring son's debts. Yet Anne Leigh's readiness to leave the farm to go in search of her daughter contrasts with Nathan's reluctance to leave what remains of his country home, and even more strikingly with Michael's refusal to sacrifice any of his land, preferring that his son should go instead:⁶

> Our Luke shall leave us, Isabel; the land
> Shall not go from us, and it shall be free.

Furthermore, Nathan's strict sense of patriliny in "The Crooked Branch" blinds him to his son's real sins, whereas Anne Leigh is perfectly clear-sighted about her daughter's "fall," and the issue is not whether the sin has occurred but how to rescue Lizzie from further misery. As a mother she unequivocally places human life ahead of property, without any of the conflict experienced by Michael or Nathan. This clear vision appears to derive from her inheriting only a life interest in the farm, which is to be passed thereafter to her eldest son. She is quite aware of her marginal place in patriliny.

James Leigh is a perfect patriarch. Gaskell puts it bluntly: "Milton's famous line might have been framed and hung up as the rule of their married life, for he was truly the interpreter, who stood between God and her." Thus both in form and in content, patriarchal authority flows through him. His God is the unforgiving Old Testament God who authorizes the unforgiving condemnation of female sinners. And his son, Will, inherits his stern attitude, along with his eventual inheritance of the ancestral farm. It is above all Lizzie's illegitimate child who is the source of condemnation by her father, whose participation in patriliny ties him to strict notions of legitimacy of birth. Moreover, his attitude toward Lizzie takes a specifically linguistic form: the family learns of her fall through discovering that a letter has not reached her, since, pregnant, she has been sent from her employer's to the work house. Having deviated from the line that patriliny dictates for a daughter's sexuality, no longer in her "place," she ceases to exist, by the patriarch's act of un-naming. Her father "declared that henceforth they would have no daughter; that she should be as one dead, and her name never more be named."

In contrast to this grim portrait, the story also introduces a maternal vision of the inheritance of property and words that both mimics and conflicts with, as well as being defined by its marginal relation to, patriliny and the patrilineal descent of words. Anne's priorities lie neither with the rigid duplication of patriarchal words, and the linear passage of a letter from sender to receiver that comes to stand for this, nor with the equally rigid adherence to patriliny and to the ancestral way of life that her son insists upon as much as her husband did, but with her daughter herself, whose sin Anne sees only as a cause for sorrow and forgiveness. To begin with, as she takes over possession of the moral categories of the story, Anne provides an alternative to James's interpretation of the Bible, preferring the forgiveness that the stories of the prodigal son and Magdalen articulate to the Old Testament harshness of her husband and son. As Lizzie, later in the story, awakes to the awareness of her mother's presence, Anne asserts God's forgiveness: "'I'll tell thee God's promises to them that are penitent.' . . . Mrs. Leigh repeated every tender and merciful text she could remember." She transmits biblical texts, but texts of her own choosing, thus revising and bending to her purposes, but not wholly rejecting, her given place in patriliny.

Further, the mother's recognition—and therefore eventual restoration and consolation—of Lizzie depends upon the only words and property women can bequeath to their daughters, a first name (as opposed to a patronymic) and a dress. While in Manchester with his mother (against his wishes), Will falls in love with Susan Palmer, a beautiful and silent woman who cares for a "niece," Nanny, and who, Will fears, will reject him if she learns the story of his sister. Anne visits Susan to tell her Lizzie's story and thus test her worthiness of Will by her reaction. Susan, recognizing the name of the mistress who turned Lizzie away when she became pregnant, tells Anne that Nanny is not her niece but was, as a baby, dropped in her arms by a sobbing woman, and she brings Anne the baby clothes that came with her. "There was a little packet of clothes—very few—and as if they were made out of its mother's gowns, for they were large patterns to buy for a baby." With the clothes is a letter that says, "Call her Anne." Anne confirms the identity of baby and mother in part through the name—"'Anne,' common though it was, seemed something to build upon"—but mainly through the clothes: "Mrs Leigh recognised one of the frocks instantly, as being made out of a gown that she and her daughter had bought together in Rochdale."

If James Leigh's letter to Lizzie typifies patriliny's view of language, with its assumption that there is only one line a letter may travel and that the letter's failure to reach its destination means Lizzie's nonexistence, this letter that Nanny carries from her mother to Susan and finally to her own grandmother typifies another, a matrilineal language. Although the letter still must travel in a line in order to have meaning, the line is a far more flexible one than James Leigh's. The letter's first recipient, Susan, can read neither the letter nor the message encoded in the clothes; these signs' correct interpretation must wait for the arrival of the original referent both of the name and of the message of the fabric. It is also important to note that these signs would not have existed in the first place had not a harsh paternal law interfered between mother and daughter. Unlike James Leigh's notion of a straight, one-directional line from father to the future by way of marginal women, which also resembles Bardo's view in *Romola*, and equally unlike Tito's horror at becoming one of his own deviant messages delivered back to his origin, his father, the turning of the line of Nanny's letter back upon itself to reach its source is what constitutes women's pleasure in this story. If a sign signifies only in the presence of what it signifies, especially where that referent is a mother, it undoes and refuses the symbolic economy that stipulates the absence of a referent, especially where the referent is a mother. This kind of sign making suggests that mother and daughter could communicate with one another both as women and within the order of written language. This seeming impossibility contrasts, for example, with the situation in Gaskell's diary in which the words will have meaning only in the absence of one or the other. It also contrasts with the situation of mothers with respect to sons as articulated, for example, in James Leigh's favorite texts, where the mother's absence is said to be the precondition of the son's founding and maintaining of the whole of culture.

This recognition through the dress, bought by the mother, shared with the daughter, made into baby clothes for the granddaughter, takes on another dimension of significance in the light of Victorian critics' assumption that the gender of an anonymous author could be identified by the degree of detailed attention to clothing or other domestic details present in the work.[7] For Gaskell to have Anne recognize Lizzie and the baby by clothing is simultaneously to court recognition of herself—or at least of a woman—as author. Gaskell did not have the powerful motives for anonymity that the Brontës and Eliot had and took no trouble to conceal her identity, yet the story, like *Mary Barton*, was published anonymously as the lead story in the first number of Dickens's *Household Words*. Curiously, though, from its sentimental tone and its honorific position in his magazine, Dickens was commonly assumed to be the author by readers who missed the clue of the clothing, as well as the clue of the intense interest in and positive view of a mother-daughter relationship that distinguishes the story from anything Dickens wrote. The story was as a result first published in the United States under Dickens's name. Despite this accident, Gaskell seems deliberately to have made women's clothing a turning point in the story, to call attention to female authorship by calling attention to the way in which women may send and receive signs in a way that is different from men's and also illegible to

men because overlooked by them.[8] A woman's first name and her clothing thus become models for female authorship as matrilineal inheritance,
a female word or code to compete with the patrilineal word that dictates,
not just the rigid morality within the story, but also the laws of authorship that would prohibit women's writing as women for publication.
Yet at the same time that this women's language is in this way disting-
uished from men's, its existence also clearly depends on the acceptance of
women's marginal place in patriliny. In order to signify, this language
assumes that first names and clothing are the only things a woman can
pass on.

The two major plot-generating events of the story, Lizzie's figurative
fall into sin and disgrace and Nanny's literal fall to her death, can be
described in exactly the same words: the daughter falls because the love
between mother and daughter is in conflict with, and is finally sacrificed
to, the father's wishes. In the first case, Anne, speaking to Susan, gives
this explicitly as the reason for Lizzie's fall: "I had a daughter once, my
heart's darling. Her father thought I made too much on her, and that
she'd grow marred staying at home; so he said she mun go among
strangers, and learn to rough it. . . . That poor girl were led astray."
Anne points out, moreover, that the harm to Lizzie after her fall could
have been mitigated if only James had not forbidden Anne to seek her out
in Manchester right away. The second case, Nanny's fall, repeats this
situation. Susan and Nanny sleep together in an upstairs room. The
night of Anne's visit, Susan's unfeeling and bankrupt father comes home
late and drunk. Will initially became acquainted with this father "for his
father's sake," which suggests a narrative resemblance between the two
fathers; also like James Leigh, Susan's father has always objected to
Nanny's presence because she draws Susan's attention away from him.
Susan, entwined in Nanny's arms, is obliged to "unclose" them to go
downstairs to help her stumbling father with the light. Nanny falls to her
death because she awakes, misses Susan, sees that she is downstairs, and
"dazzled with sleepiness," totters over the edge of the stairs. Thus, like
her own mother, Nanny falls into the gap created by the conflict between
the mother's love for her daughter and her obligations to the father's
authority.

While the two falls stem from the same cause, it is worth noting that
the second literalizes the first. While "fall" is a metaphor for Lizzie's
illicit sexual behavior, on the model of the fall of Adam and Eve, Nanny
literally tumbles downstairs, and while the metaphoric fall brought
mortality to humankind, Nanny really dies on the spot. The daughter's
literalization of the figure used for her mother recalls most immediately
the linguistic situation in Gaskell's account in her diary of the relation

between her second daughter's birth and her own foster mother's death, where Gaskell's figurative confinement in childbirth leads, not only to her children's confinement in small rooms, but also, she fears, to her mother's death. The Brontës' novels, as we have seen, explore the association between literalization and the death of a mother because of childbirth, the fear that in a patrilineal culture a child's birth obviates the life of the mother. We have also seen how this process finds linguistic embodiment in the literalization of figures. But in this story, it is not the mother but the child who dies, and indeed her death and replacement by her own mother exactly reverse the wording of the pivotal episode in *Wuthering Heights*: "About twelve o'clock . . . was born the Catherine you saw . . . and two hours after, the mother died" (chap. 16). Susan's call to the doctor, after Nanny falls, brings Lizzie out of the urban shadows where she lurks, while Susan then fetches Anne to see if Nanny's mother is really Anne's daughter. Within a few lines Susan says to Anne, "Nanny is dead! . . . Her mother is come!" as if Nanny's ceased existence continues in Lizzie.

Lizzie becomes a daughter again through the death of her own daughter. When the doctor arrives intending to help Nanny, Lizzie, overcome by a fit of grief and guilt, has taken her place as the patient. Drugged, she goes to sleep gazing at her dead daughter; she wakes with her eyes fixed on her mother and in a pose—she "lay like one dead"—that duplicates that of her daughter. Lizzie first asks to see her child one more time, but then "she threw her arms round the faithful mother's neck, and wept there as she had done in many a childish sorrow. . . . Her mother hushed her on her breast; and lulled her as if she were a baby." That night, Anne and Lizzie "lay in each other's arms" just as earlier Lizzie goes to sleep holding her dead child and as Susan had used to sleep with Nanny's living arms twined around her. In this part of the story, there is general but not disturbing uncertainty as to who is daughter, who is mother, and of whom. Three mothers contemplate, in grief, the faces of two daughters, one who is dead, one who is "like one dead." After Lizzie falls asleep gazing at and "stroking the little face," Susan too, "gently extricating the dead child from its mother's arms . . . could not resist making her own quiet moan over her darling. She tried to learn off its little, placid face, dumb and pale before her." After this, Anne arrives, recognizes Lizzie, and repeating Lizzie's and Susan's gesture, "stood looking at her with greedy eyes, which seemed as though no gazing could satisfy their longing."

Although the plotting of the story represents a matrilineal inheritance of female experience only insofar as female life is twisted by patriarchal demands, the organizing relations here between mothers and daughters take place notably outside the patriarchal domain. Susan's father, having drunkenly slept through all the commotion, knows only of Nanny's fall; "as yet he was in ignorance of the watcher and the watched, who silently passed away the hours upstairs." Furthermore, the story closes with a telescoped account of their lives afterward, in which mother and daughter continue their stand outside patriarchy and patriliny. Whereas Susan and Will marry and live in the ancestral farm, Nanny is buried on the moor outside the churchyard of the "stern grandfather," and Anne and Lizzie live "in a cottage so secluded that, until you drop into the very hollow where it is placed, you do not see it." Anne, we remember, unnecessary to patriliny once she has borne a son, inherited the farm only for her lifetime, and it is her relative sense of freedom from the obligations of patriliny that allows her to leave the farm to search for Lizzie. The ending confirms her choice in favor of the daughter who was originally excluded by patrilineal property and to live voluntarily outside of it with her. But there is a new "Nanny," Will and Susan's daughter, and the two households love each other, so that exclusion is happily if paradoxically compatible with inclusion.

Indeed, though Anne and Lizzie's happiness was originally ruined by paternal interference, it is now made possible only by the same interference, since Nanny's death, caused by Susan's father's selfishness, was necessary to bring mother and daughter together again. Nanny is the "little, unconscious sacrifice, whose early calling-home had reclaimed her poor, wandering mother." Anne's and Lizzie's happiness, within the scope of the story, depends then, not just on their own love for one another, but emphatically on the situation of that love as something that has been excluded and damaged. The story is thus neither so alarmed by the notion of childbirth and of its consequences for writing as are the Brontës' novels nor so critical of paternal interference in reproduction as is *Frankenstein*. Like Shelley, Gaskell criticizes a father's inappropriate intervention, yet for her the results of such intervention are far from monstrous. At pains to accommodate both a paternal order's view of the proper relations within families and a more gynocentric view of mothers and daughters, the story strangely interweaves these seemingly incompatible strands by making their working out dependent upon each other. The paternal order is satisfied only by excluding Anne and Lizzie, while Anne and Lizzie are satisfied only by the consequences of their exclusion.

A moment we have already looked at typifies this strange interdependence, and also carries it explicitly to the level of language. When Anne Leigh at her suffering daughter's bedside repeats "every tender and merciful text she could remember," she is at once serving as transmitter of biblical words (subordinating her own lovingness to the authority of a higher word), departing from her husband's authority (in choosing these texts over sterner ones), and also speaking in a way of which the distant echo is Mrs. Ramsay's lulling speech at the bedside of her distraught daughter, speech in which sound and presence matter far more than referential meaning. This literal or nonsymbolic speech is very like the fortunate return of Lizzie's letter to its referent, Anne, a situation in which, again, the distancing of the referent in representational language gives way to the presence of the mother. Both the delivery of the letter and Anne's repetitions confirm the literal contact between mother and daughter. At the same time, both the delivery of the letter and Anne's soothing words acknowledge the constitutive presence within them of the exigencies of a paternal order. It is biblical passages that Anne repeats, passages that by preaching the forgiveness of sins define and reify sin in a way that is less forgiving than Anne's own stated wish simply to forget the past. It is Nanny who carries the letter, pinned to her clothes, from her mother to Susan, and although it is only a coincidence that Anne reads the letter the very day of Nanny's death, the narrative sequence suggests a causal relation between the mother's happily correct decoding of a daughter's letter and the child's death, which results from a father's indifference. Carrying a letter from mother to daughter at once affirms and restores that forbidden relationship and brings paternal authority back to intervene again. Nanny is both the agent of the return of the letter to its maternal referent and the embodiment of women's victimization at the hands of men.

A number of Gaskell's other stories turn on the ambiguous consequences of a female character carrying a letter, an action to which Gaskell always calls attention by making its circumstances peculiarly elaborate. For example, in the search for Carson's murderer in *Mary Barton*, the crucial clue that proves to Mary that her father is the murderer is a valentine sent to her by Jem Wilson, onto a partially blank page of which she copies a poem called "God Help the Poor." Mary gives this paper to her father, who tears it in half and uses part as wadding in the gun with which he shoots Carson, leaving the rest in his pocket. Although the police never find any of this paper, as Michael Wheeler points out, in incorrectly pursuing Jem they are pursuing "the line of reasoning symbolically represented by the valentine greeting" (jealousy), while "the motive of the actual murderer is symbolically represented in the Banford poem written on the 'blank half-sheet'" (vengeance for the poor).[9] In this drama among men about men's passions, Mary is merely an intermediary, receiving and copying onto the letter and passing it on.

Yet it is crucial to the novel that both scraps of the paper once given to her father return to Mary, for it is in this way that she can protect her father as long as she does. The way in which it returns is as elaborately detailed, and as fraught with significance, as its transmission. One half Mary finds in her father's coat pocket, and she takes it back. Mary's Aunt Esther, her mother's sister who has unbeknownst to Mary become a prostitute, finds the other half, the gunwadding, on the road where Carson was shot. Reading a fragment of Mary's name and address and recognizing Jem Wilson's handwriting on the paper, Aunt Esther dresses herself to pretend respectability and visits Mary to return it to her. But the scene of Esther's arrival brings an absent figure back and complicates, by foregrounding female relationships, what has seemed to be a purely masculine drama only mediated by women. When Esther knocks on the door, Mary has been dreaming of "the happy times of long ago, and her mother came to her, and kissed her as she lay, and once more the dead were alive again" (chap. 20). She wakes to hear "the accents of her mother's voice . . . which she had sometimes tried to imitate when alone, with the fond mimicry of affection." She opens the door and "there, against the moonlight, stood a form, so closely resembling her dead mother, that Mary never doubted the identity." She exclaims, "Oh, mother! mother! You are come at last?" and falls into Aunt Esther's arms. For her part, Esther recognizes Mary as "so like [her] little girl" who died (chap. 14), yet she does all she can to keep her distance, not wanting the pure Mary to be "shocked and revolted" by her fall, which is never undone.

What matters here is Gaskell's insistent juxtaposition of Mary's reunion with her lost mother (in however illusory a way, for Mary believes it at the time) with the return of a letter that brings men's dangerous, murderous passions closer to home. Very much as in "Lizzie Leigh," a reunion between daughter and mother is dependent upon the intervention between them of men's demands and violent actions. The return of the letter to its female referent both creates the meaning of a mother-daughter reunion and invokes a dangerous paternal power that threatens it. Moreover, Mary associates her mother with a soothing voice, and her way of trying to recall her in the past has been to imitate her accents, "with the fond mimicry of affection." In this repetition of the mother's sounds remains a trace of the literal or presymbolic language that, in the countermyth we have been tracing, mothers and children share and that daughters do not renounce, a language that is connected with the kind of meaning generated by the return of a letter to its referent. The restoration of the mother is equivalent to a language that does not require the absence of the referent. Both kinds of literal, mother-present language suggest a myth of a female language, a language, however, that is always and inextricably bound up with and interdependent upon paternal power and its determination of women's subordinate linguistic role as transmitters of men's words.

Before turning to examine in depth one final story, "Lois the Witch," which offers a particularly striking version of the myth of the relation between women's linguistic subordination and the specificity of their language, we will pause briefly on Gaskell's *Life of Charlotte Brontë*. In this work, written after "Lizzie Leigh" and *Mary Barton* but before "Lois the Witch," a woman's transmission of both men's and women's letters and words is not only one of the major themes but also the organizing principle of the book. The biography contains 350 of Brontë's letters, as well as numerous letters from Brontë's friends Ellen Nussey and Mary Taylor and even from Gaskell herself, together with such authoritative letters as Southey's advice to Brontë on "a woman's proper duties." When not actually transmitting letters, the biography is thematically concerned with transmission as women's duty. A number of people writing on the *Life* have noted Gaskell's way of turning Brontë into a perfect Victorian woman, while at the same time retaining the evidence of Brontë's rebelliousness in her accounts of how hard it was to be good.[10] The use of the imagination has bad consequences, both selfishness and "coarseness" (the accusation often leveled against *Jane Eyre*), while the transmission of truth is both good and selfless. Writing here as a good woman herself, Gaskell reveals Brontë to be only partially successful at her own passive transmissions of others' words (e.g., at acting on Southey's advice not to write for publication). Yet at the same time, through her very docility as transmitter, through her identification of her goodness with Brontë's, Gaskell covertly suggests the drawbacks for any writer (including herself) in such a role.

One example we might select among many instances of Gaskell's working out her own priorities about writing through Brontë is her treatment of the end of the *Life* in relation to her treatment of Brontë's ending to *Villette*. According to Gaskell, Brontë told her that although "the idea of M. Paul Emanuel's death at sea was stamped on her imagination till it assumed the distinct force of reality," her father, who "disliked novels which left a melancholy impression upon the mind . . . requested her to make her hero and heroine . . . 'marry, and live happily ever after.'" Therefore, unable to alter the ending, "all she could do in compliance with her father's wish was so to veil the fate in oracular words, as to leave it to . . . her readers to interpret her meaning."[11] This startling and improbable revelation—that the ambiguity of *Villette*'s ending arises from the circumstances of her father's whim—may be no more than a little allegory of conflicting impulses within Brontë herself: on the one hand, her deep pessimism about the compatibility for women of work and love, and on the other, the patriarchal voice within, which, by way of the seductive fantasy of romantic love, would seal off the implications, disruptive both to the form of the novel and to the social fabric it emerges from, of leaving the heroine single at the end. Yet what matters here is that Gaskell calls attention to this incident as an example of Brontë's goodness; she does not question but endorses the notion of Brontë's putting her father's wishes on a level with the imperatives of her own imagination.

Gaskell's motives soon become clear. Six pages later, when she comes to the question of the last phase of her own story, the marriage of her heroine, she bends her narrative to another but analogous set of patriarchal wishes. Brontë's marriage, Gaskell writes, "requires delicate handling on my part, lest I intrude too roughly on what is most sacred to memory" (2:12). Again, further into her narrative of the marriage, she writes: "Of course, as I draw nearer to the years so recently closed, it becomes impossible for me to write with the same fulness of detail as I have hitherto not felt it wrong to use" (2:13). Although Gaskell hints at her awareness of Nicholls's inadequacy as a spiritual or intellectual match for Brontë, it is possible to accept at its face value her claim to believe in Brontë's marriage as "that short spell of exceeding happiness" (2:12), so strongly would she wish to believe it. Just as Gaskell earlier writes of Brontë's subordination of her imaginative integrity to her father's wishes, Gaskell herself distorts the imaginative truth of her ending, to meet Nicholls's expectations. Obviously editing from these final chapters anything Nicholls or Patrick Brontë would not have liked to see, anything derogatory to the marriage, Gaskell betrays at least part of the truth of Brontë's experience in order to please patriarchal wishes, exactly as she claims Brontë struggled to do with the ending of *Villette*. She identifies her female predicament with Brontë's on the basis of the identical interference in their work by masculine authority.

Gaskell's transmission of Brontë's letters, as well as obeying paternal authority and cementing an identification between the two women, also brought her a considerable amount of real trouble through the scandal caused by some of her allegations about living people, who protested through both epistolary and legal channels and caused Gaskell to withdraw the first and second editions of the *Life* and replace them with a third, revised, edition. In the first of these cases, Gaskell claimed as facts matters that Brontë protected by the decorum of fiction, the conditions of life at the Clergy Daughters' School at Cowan Bridge, the original of Lowood School in *Jane Eyre*. Yet Gaskell claimed only to be doing what she claimed Brontë had been doing, which was to tell the truth. Striving to find the right balance between two equally crucial feminine virtues, truth on the one hand and polite deference to such authorities as run schools on the other, Gaskell tries in her revisions to claim for Brontë both that "she herself would have been glad of an opportunity to correct the over-strong impression" made by her novel and that she had a "deep belief" in the factuality of her portrayal of the school, both of which claims are probably false.[12]

The other case, the one that actually forced the biography's withdrawal and revision, was a threat of libel that originated, like the Cowan Bridge controversy, in Gaskell's aim both to portray Brontë as a good and proper woman and to portray both herself and Brontë as truthful. Doing research for the *Life*, Gaskell discovered that some of the "coarseness" in Brontë's books originated in an actual experience, her unrequited and illicit love for her teacher in Belgium, M. Héger. She wished to exclude it entirely from the *Life*, on the grounds both of sparing Mr. Nicholls and of protecting Brontë's reputation, and therefore she shifted the blame for Charlotte's depression on returning from Brussels onto the dissolute behavior of Branwell Brontë. Branwell's behavior could in turn be blamed on his employer's wife (now the "depraved" Lady Scott), who, "bold and hardened," seduced him "in the very presence of her children" (1:13) and then, when her husband died, refused to keep her promise to marry him. The sexual excesses of another woman thus fill the gap left by suppressing Charlotte's, yet eventually Gaskell's efforts to rectify Brontë's impropriety produce accusations against her own impropriety. The lustful Brontë becomes the adulterous Mrs. Robinson who in turn shifts the burden onto the slanderous Gaskell. Gaskell's efforts to make Brontë over into her own image as a good Victorian woman have the ironic effect of making Gaskell appear to be as "coarse" as Brontë. As in the stories, this identification between two women (although here not mother and daughter) exists in the transmission by one of the other's letters, and yet it also depends upon the appropriation of that transmission by official morality and the interference in that transmission by the law.

I would not argue that the plot of the myth of language is identical in the *Life*, "Lizzie Leigh," and *Mary Barton*, but only that Gaskell repeats a similar scenario often enough to suggest that it represents an important concern. If the sequence of these texts' presentations of this scenario can be read as a progression, it is that of a diminishment of the pleasure to be taken in the reunion of mother and daughter (or identification between two women that I have suggested forms an analogy to this reunion in the *Life*), simultaneous with an increase in the cost of this connection. For example, while "Lizzie Leigh" joyously reunites a mother with a "fallen" daughter, whose fall is as a consequence mitigated, *Mary Barton* embraces only the illusion of her mother and the fallen woman who enables this illusion is never recovered, and Brontë and Gaskell share an identity only at the expense of the tarnishing of that identity. "Lois the Witch," written shortly after the *Life* and its attendant sorrows, restages the earlier stories' peculiar interdependence between the language shared between mother and daughter and the paternal, symbolic order from which it is excluded and by which it is threatened and appropriated. "Lois the Witch," however, in keeping with the gradual darkening of Gaskell's vision, restages the earlier stories only from the point of view of what is lost. That is, rather than being resolved by a reunion of mother and daughter, this story begins with their irrevocable separation and traces the consequences of that separation both for life and for letters. The daughter, still acting on the terms defining her relation to her mother, yet abandoned by her mother's death to unmitigated patriarchal appropriation and interference, experiences as catastrophic the collision between these two orders, the mother's nonsymbolic discourse and the patriarchal law to which she is obliged to submit.

Lois, whose parents die as the story opens, leaves England for Salem in the late seventeenth century and is hanged there as a witch. She travels to Salem by her mother's "dying wish" for her to live with her mother's brother and his family. In this gloomy story, each of several episodes of letter carrying is both unnecessary and peculiarly highlighted by details, so that these episodes stand out as requiring more explanation than is offered by the simple demands of plot and character development. The first of these letters is the letter Lois's mother dictates on her deathbed to her brother, and as she starts her trip, Lois carries not only this letter but also a letter from her dead father to the captain who will give her passage to Boston. Framing the scene of the mother's dying words are two assertions of Lois's faithfulness to the letter. First, "Lois swallowed her tears down till the time came for crying, and acted upon her mother's words."[13] The mother dictates the letter and asks Lois to promise that she will go to Salem at once: " 'The money our goods will bring—the letter thy father wrote to Captain Holdernesse, his old schoolfellow—thou knowest all I would say—my Lois, God bless thee!' Solemnly did Lois promise; strictly she kept her word." The mother's assumption that "thou knowest all I would say" suggests that when Lois "acted upon her mother's words" and "strictly . . . kept her word," she is not simply taking dictation but translating intentions into words.

The letter Lois writes at dictation follows a circuitous course that appears to be unnecessarily particularized. When Lois arrives in Boston, "the letter of her dying mother was sent off to Salem, meanwhile, by a lad going thither," to prepare her new family for her arrival. When Lois reaches Salem, however, she finds that the lad had made an inefficient letter carrier, and that she herself, replacing representation with its referent, arrives before the letter does. Her aunt receives her very coldly. The captain tries to comfort Lois by telling her "if the letter had but been delivered, thou wouldst have had a different kind of welcome," and he takes some pains to recover the letter and punish the boy. The episode, however, is unnecessary, as it is clear that Lois is unwelcome, with or without the letter, for her aunt is not hostile because she doubts Lois's identity but because she hates what Lois represents. Lois's father was an Anglican minister, and her uncle left England and broke from his family as a Puritan. If the straying of the letter is immaterial to Lois's cold reception, why does Gaskell devote such attention to it, to the extent of giving the letter carrier a peculiarly resonant name, Elias Wellcome?

In arriving before her mother's letter and substituting for it, Lois begins a series of literalizations of women's words that prove disastrous. For much the same reasons that Eliot situates *Romola* in fifteenth-century Florence, because that world takes literally what Victorian England takes figuratively, Gaskell uses Puritan Salem as a literalizing version of England. As Lois crosses from the Anglican to the Puritan country, she also crosses from a world of relatively figurative understanding to a world that takes everything literally. (Her ocean passage even literalizes the figure of metaphor, "carry across.") As Lois puts her mother's intentions into practice and as she carries her letter, she literalizes her mother's words, replacing the figures of the letter with their referent, herself. While in "Lizzie Leigh" or even in *Mary Barton*, this co-presence of the letter and its referent signals the happy reunion of mother and daughter, here it points to the absence of the mother and it also, by virtue of the narrative sequence, is arranged to appear to cause the hostility of a patriarchal culture.

Lois also carries two other sets of women's words across the ocean, and in doing so carries them out literally. On her deathbed, directly after dictating the letter to her brother, Lois's mother also expresses a wish: "'Oh, Lois, would that thou wert dying with me! The thought of thee makes death sore!' Lois comforted her mother more than herself, poor child, by promises to obey her dying wishes to the letter." The mother's wish for Lois to die, very strange if taken literally, is quite clearly figurative in context; that is, her words express her love for Lois, her sorrow at parting from her, but not a real wish for Lois to die. Her words are also like Mrs. Ramsay's words at Cam's bedside, which matter not for what they signify representationally but for the love and presence they guarantee. However, Lois's "promises to obey her dying wishes to the letter" have a distinctly ominous ring. In context, "dying wishes" refers back to the letter for the uncle, but to fulfill a wish "to the letter" is to fulfill it literally, and to obey "dying wishes to the letter" is to obey the wish that she will die, that is, to take literally her mother's figurative "Oh, Lois, would that thou wert dying with me." And this ominous suggestion is reinforced a few sentences later by the echo, "strictly she kept her word."

In addition to her mother's words, Lois bears and will carry out another woman's words, the curse of a witch, and the unambiguous negativity of these words helps to clarify the significance of the mother's dying wishes. At a dinner in Boston before Lois reaches Salem, the subject of witches comes up, and Lois tells a story, from when she was four years old, of her own encounter with a witch. Although Lois withholds judgment, she seems half to understand what the reader assumes (but what none of the Puritans sees at all), that this "witch" was nothing but a poor, old recluse, the scapegoat on whom the town chose to blame a series of local illnesses. Out walking with her nurse, Lois says, she saw a silent crowd by the river; they stop and look,

> and I saw old Hannah in the water, her grey hair all streaming down her shoulders, and her face bloody and black with the stones and the mud they had been throwing at her, and her cat tied round her neck. I hid my face, I know, as soon as I saw the fearsome sight, for her eyes met mine as they were glaring with fury—poor, helpless, baited creature!—and she caught the sight of me, and cried out, "Parson's wench, parson's wench, yonder, in thy nurse's arms, thy dad hath never tried for to save me, and none shall save thee when thou art brought up for a witch." Oh! the words rang in my ears, when I was dropping asleep, for years after. I used to dream that I was in that pond, all men hating me with their eyes because I was a witch.

This dream comes true, with the exception that she dies not by drowning but by hanging. Although as a child Lois believed the witch's words and although in England witches were indeed killed, nonetheless, growing up in England, where people understand things relatively figuratively, involves learning that such words deserve pity, not fear or hatred. The curse was effective in frightening the child, but it never to occurs to Lois to believe in it now as a performative that could actually cause her to die as a witch.

Lois's listeners, however, take both the story (the identification of the old woman as a witch) and the curse within it literally, as words that could have literal effects. All such transfers from England to New England involve a similar shift from a relatively figurative understanding of words to a relatively literal one. The New England Puritans, who claim to read the Bible more literally than the "popish" Anglicans, excuse their genocide of the native population by their belief "that these Red Indians are indeed the evil creatures of whom we read in Holy Scripture. . . . Holy Scripture speaks of witches and wizards, and of the power of the Evil One in desert places." One "godly" old man upbraids those who would "speak lightly" of Lois's story and insists, "the hellish witch might have power from Satan to infect her mind, she being yet a child, with the deadly sin."

While the story calls attention to the way in which a woman's words can be taken literally and are literalized, it also calls attention to the distorting presence in these words of patriarchal law. The witch would not be a witch in the first place if a culture fearful of otherness did not brand her peculiarities as crimes, and she would not be cursing Lois in particular if she were not the daughter of the minister of the patriarchal church that excoriates her. Women's words might have power, especially in the relation of presence between mother and daughter, but the intervention of a jealous and disapproving paternal law turns that power into a punishment both of speaker and of listener. The story of the witch makes this intervention explicit and suggests that the same law has intervened as well between Lois and her mother, in the passage from the mother's loving intentions and words to their murderous fulfillment.

After Lois has become a part of her uncle's unfriendly family, she tells her cousin Faith, who grieves over an unrequited love, about another set of supernatural beliefs, the Halloween customs and "innocent ways of divination," such as eating an apple facing a mirror, "by which laughing, trembling English maidens sought to see the form of their future husbands." Telling these stories, Lois is characterized by the narrator as "half believing, half incredulous." That is, she takes these stories at least in part figuratively. But her younger cousin, Prudence, New England born, responds to them as entirely literal compacts with supernatural powers: "Cousin Lois may go out and meet Satan by the brook-side, if she will." Pleased with the attention she receives, Prudence works up a fit of imitation terror:

> "Take her away, take her away!" screamed Prudence. "Look over her shoulder—her left shoulder—the Evil One is there now, I see him stretching over for the half-bitten apple. . . .
> "Faith shall stay by me, not you, wicked English witch!"

It is in this manner that the accusation of witchcraft begins, through New Englanders taking literally what the English girl means at least half figuratively.

It is significant that Lois is first accused of witchcraft in the context of a supposed ability to envision her future husband, for her formal accusation turns on the use of the word "bewitch" to refer both to witchcraft and to ordinary sexual attraction. After Lois has told her story about the witch, unaware of how literally it will be taken, her hostess responds, in an effort to shift the discussion to safer, figurative ground, "'And I don't doubt but what the parson's bonny lass has bewitched many a one since, with her dimples and her pleasant ways. . . .' 'Aye, aye,' said the captain, 'there's one under her charms in Warwickshire who will never get the better of it, I'm thinking.'" While Lois has indeed figuratively bewitched a young man back in England, the case against her develops from two instances in which this figurative kind of bewitching is taken literally, as if she had cast spells on the men who fall in love with her. Two jealous women make use of the witch trial to get rid of Lois as a rival, by enforcing the word's shift to its literal meaning. At a public gathering following the hanging as a witch of an Indian woman servant, Hota, Prudence, jealous of the public attention received by the girls who claim to be bewitched by Hota, stages a convulsive fit that she claims is "caused" by "Witch Lois." But though it is Prudence who thus first formally accuses Lois, she is prompted by her sister Faith, who is jealous of Lois; and the damning fact that their mother, jealous on another score, refuses to speak up for Lois's good character, contributes materially to Lois's condemnation.

Aunt Hickson is jealous because Lois has "bewitched" her son Manasseh, a secretly mad, or possibly visionary, young man who has fallen in love with Lois or, as he puts it, has heard a voice telling him "Marry Lois! Marry Lois!" Aunt Hickson has grander plans for her son, who after the death of Lois's uncle is the head of her prosperous household, and she resents his choice of a poor relation. As Manasseh attempts earnestly but disconnectedly to defend Lois and Aunt Hickson realizes that his madness is now embarrassing public knowledge, she mentally elaborates proofs of Lois's witchcraft, which would excuse his madness, by confusing literal and figurative senses of "bewitch": "How he followed her about, and clung to her, as under some compulsion of affection! And over all reigned the idea that, if he were indeed suffering from being bewitched, he was not mad, and might again assume the honourable position he had held in the congregation and in the town." As a result, Lois is tried for having "bewitched" both Manasseh and Prudence.

Faith's jealousy of Lois's ability to "bewitch" comes from the second of the story's peculiarly foregrounded episodes of letter carrying, this one even more conspicuously fabricated than the first. It is Faith who prompts Prudence to see Lois as "Witch Lois": in the act of purloining Lois's cloak (to attend illicitly the hanging of Hota), Prudence trips and falls, and Faith remarks, "Take care, another time, how you meddle with a witch's things." Faith resents Lois because of a scene she has just witnessed between Lois and the man she unrequitedly loves, Pastor Nolan, a scene, however, that Faith herself inexplicably arranges. The morning of the hanging, Faith has asked Lois to deliver to Nolan a letter that "concerns life and death," implying that the letter contains information that would prove Hota innocent. The story offers no reason why Faith neither delivers the letter herself, nor simply tells Nolan, or why, if Faith can't deliver the letter, Lois must. Lois searches Nolan out, but he, depressed by the sinfulness of the "witch," and infatuated with Lois, is absorbed in his gloom and then in the relief afforded by the sight of her "pure, grave face," and he neglects to open the letter. Just as he is putting his hand on Lois's shoulder, "with an action half paternal," and whispering to her, Faith appears and, furious with jealousy, takes back the unopened letter, with sarcastic allusions to the thematic pun on the word bewitch: "Let [Hota] die, and let all other witches look to themselves; for there be many kinds of witchcraft abroad."

The scene seems almost unnecessary. Though the story does require some occasion for Faith's jealousy, such a need hardly justifies this elaborately plotted and inscrutable scene of letter carrying. It functions in something of the same way as the earlier episode of delivering her mother's letter. Lois herself takes the place of the letter, so that the act of delivering it becomes itself a message, as referent replaces representation. Furthermore, the scene makes clear what we also saw in Romola's transmissions of words, which is that to bear a word is also to be transformed into the object of a man's vision, for bearing a word is a daughter's reproduction of the discourse of her mother, but a reproduction that is appropriated by patriarchal demands and by the androcentric view that any mother is the literal and an object.

What seems to have happened prior to the delivery of this letter is that Faith has been scheming to denounce Pastor Tappan, the rival of Pastor Nolan, whom Tappan has driven out of Salem. Faith and the Hicksons' Indian servant, Nattee, together with Hota, who is Nattee's friend and who works for Tappan, arrange for certain "devilish" accidents, such as crashing dishes, to occur in the Tappan household, presumably in order to pin on Pastor Tappan an accusation of complicity with the devil. The scheme, however, backfires and Hota takes the blame, because Tappan's authority makes it impossible for his community to consider him dangerous, and transformed from potential criminal into victim, he appears even holier than before. Faith's letter to Nolan presumably exonerates

Hota in some way, perhaps also placing the blame back on Pastor Tappan. However, when she sees Nolan's interest in Lois, she abandons her interest in discrediting Tappan, because she has lost her case with Nolan anyway. In carrying Faith's letter, Lois is continuing to literalize her mother's and the English witch's "dying wishes," in that her delivery of the letter, when she "bewitches" Nolan, will contribute materially to her eventual execution. She is also literalizing the intentions of the letter's sender, if not in precisely the manner Faith had in mind. Though at first it seems that Faith's intentions (to capture Nolan) are reversed, ultimately she does accomplish her aim of ridding herself of a rival, Lois instead of Tappan.

Lois's transformation into the object of a man's vision is a necessary part of her execution as a witch, for it is precisely the passage from figurative to literal that makes her a witch; and her being an object is inseparable from her being perceived by Salem as an other. It is no accident that the three witches accused and executed in the story are not only all women but also foreigners, outsiders, doubly other with respect to the Puritan majority. That Lois is British-born and popish puts her in the same category with the Indians Nattee and Hota. Lois's ability to "bewitch" young men derives from her otherness, the contrast her pink and white English charm makes to the sober grey tones of New England. Part of the function of witch-hunting as Gaskell depicts it is the removal of anomalies; Pastor Tappan, for example, is constitutively not a witch because he is part of the definition of the community that defines itself in opposition to others.

Ironically, Lois's feminine otherness, with its dangerous charms, derives from her loyalty to patriarchal men. Her loyalty to the king stems from her love for her father, preacher at Barford, and the Hicksons' hatred is properly for that father, who split with Ralph Hickson when he rejected these hereditary loyalties. It is because of the religious differences of two men that Lois's mother led a divided, unhappy life, and Lois inherits her mother's position as the ground on which their dispute is enacted. And the dying English witch curses Lois because of her father's role in her persecution. The syntax of the story seems to equate her being other than patriarchal figures like Tappan with her being other because of a patriarchal figure like her father, because she is merely the medium through which their hatreds work. Though she seems, in dying as a witch, to be literalizing her mother's and the English witch's dying wishes, by carrying their letters and words to a place that takes everything literally, what lies behind these curses, what makes them curses, and what she is really carrying out, is the patriarchal prohibition of female difference that victimizes them as much as it does her. In a culture like that of Salem, a culture in which women's speech is suspect, women's words are constitutively curses. Patriarchal authority lies behind the cursedness of women's words and the tendency of women's words to each other to be distorted into curses. They are not cursing each other so much as trying to speak to each other, yet with a speech that is appropriated to do the work of patriarchal words. And not only are women's words distorted in this way, but even their thoughts. Lois begins to fear, after her accusation, that she may indeed be a witch, because of the chance that her unhappy feelings about her foster family may "have had devilish power given to them by the father of evil, and, all unconsciously to herself, have gone forth as active curses into the world." A woman is made to feel that for her feelings to matter at all, in a culture that views them as illegitimate, would be for them to have satanic powers.

This situation is underscored by the one quotation from romantic poetry in the story, the narrator's words for Nolan's feelings for Lois at the crucial moment of their meeting over Faith's letter, under Faith's gaze. Depressed by his view of Hota's otherness as "pollution" and gazing at Lois's "pure, grave face," "faith in earthly goodness came over his soul in that instant, 'and he blessed her unaware.'" Why, to depict this moment, which combines elements of erotic attraction and religious confirmation, does Gaskell choose these words from Coleridge's "The Rime of the Ancient Mariner"? Nolan's blessing contributes to Lois's curse: the scene leads to Faith's betrayal of Lois. Even more immediately than its effect on Lois's life, Nolan's "bless[ing] her unaware" leads directly to Hota's death, for it is because his attention has shifted from Hota to Lois that Nolan neglects his opportunity to exonerate the Indian. The transformation of a blessing into a curse or curses exactly reverses the process to which the line originally refers in "The Ancient Mariner," where the Mariner's outgoing love for the sea snakes brings about his release from the curse brought on by shooting the albatross.[14] Morally complex as "The Ancient Mariner" is, Gaskell reverses its temporary exoneration of the Mariner in order to condemn covertly what speaks through the pastor. In the largest sense, the blessings of a patriarchal religion can never be more than curses for women who are outsiders, and in this sense Nolan—kind, innocent, and himself eventually victimized—is no different from the tyrannical Tappan.[15] The beneficial effect of the blessing of the sea snakes depends on the challenge to human sympathy created by an inherent ugliness. Not only are they at first "slimy things" on a "slimy sea," but also the rotting sea in which they swim "like a witch's oils, / Burnt green, and blue and white."[16] These blessed witch's oils are recalled in Nolan's blessing of Gaskell's witch, Lois, and remind us that in the androcentric logic of Coleridge's poem or in that of the

Puritan ministers that Gaskell criticizes here, the purpose of the blessing has a beneficial effect, not on what is blessed (with its female associations of witches and sliminess), but on him who blesses. Nolan's blessing, by way of Coleridge, blesses only himself, while it obligates Lois to be a witch.

In the same way, Lois's being the object of Manasseh's half erotic and half divine vision hurts rather than helps her case. Manasseh's divinely inspired vision hurts Lois even more directly than Nolan's "blessing," for his crazed and seemingly blasphemous defense of Lois contributes to turning the congregation against her. His final vision makes blessing and condemnation dependent upon each other. He sees angels carrying an unspecified "her" to the beautiful land of Beulah; the vision closes, "I hear her pleading there for those on earth who consented to her death. O Lois! pray also for me!" (His public defense of her rests on the argument that, if divine visions foretell her execution as a witch, she can't be a witch, because she is part of God's plans.) Like the Coleridge quotation, this divine word, carried into the story, brings with it only Lois's further victimization. Likewise, Lois's own religious utterances bring her only increased trouble. Her understandably pausing slightly over the words, "as we forgive those who trespass against us" in a recitation of the Lord's prayer confirms the proof of her witchcraft. Visited in her jail by Aunt Hickson, who is now firmly convinced of her guilt, Lois prays, "God have mercy on you and yours," but Grace cries out, "Witches' prayers are read backwards. I spit at thee."

Just before the execution, Lois comforts her new cellmate, Nattee, and herself by reciting "the marvellous and sorrowful story" of the crucifixion, but the "blessed words" have only an ironic relation to her situation as victim of an entirely purposeless sacrifice. Indeed, the scene is a dark parody of a familiar one. When Nattee is first thrown into her cell, Lois "held her in her arms" and "tended" her, and her recitation of biblical passages recalls Anne Leigh's repetitions to Lizzie, in which the soothing sound of the motherly voice is more important than what is repeated: "As long as she spoke, the Indian woman's terror seemed lulled; but the instant she paused, for weariness, Nattee cried out afresh. . . . And then Lois went on." The next day, at the gallows, when "they took Nattee from her arms" to hang Lois first, "she gazed wildly around, stretched out her arms as if to some person in the distance, who was yet visible to her, and cried out once, . . . 'Mother!'" Like the reunion in "Lizzie Leigh," this reunion of mother and daughter is indeed made possible through the intervention of patriarchal authority. The exorbitant cost, however, suggests that Gaskell now views with pessimism her desire to accommodate that authority as well as women's pleasure. The scene recalls, too, the dedication of Gaskell's diary about her daughter, where she suggests that their earliest and closest relation, marred by the symbolic order's requirement that language have meaning only in the absence of one or the other, can be recovered only in heaven, where "we may meet again to renew the dear and tender tie of Mother and Daughter." If mothers' and daughters' love and the nonsymbolic or literal language it includes and thematizes require this severe intervention by the Law of the Father, their accomplishment holds out little promise to those who read and write as mothers or daughters. As the carrying of the mother's words from figurative to literal, not inherently harmful, becomes distorted into a curse by patriarchal law and by subordination to the task of carrying the letter of men's texts, Gaskell exposes her own discomfort at the habitual subordination, which a Victorian woman cannot help but impose upon herself, of her own word to androcentric ones.

As a part of this criticism, just as she reverses the meaning of Coleridge's line when putting it into her story, she also reverses the usual meaning of the patriarchal "line," that a woman's virtuous behavior is rewarded, a line that many of her other stories and most of her novels apparently promulgate. The most conspicuous feature of "Lois the Witch" is that Lois, despite her virtue, is not only not rewarded but is punished. The story makes no sense, morally speaking, and that *is* its sense.

Yet despite Gaskell's anger, or perhaps in keeping with its covertness, the story ends on a conciliatory note, both in terms of its characterization of the patriarchal witch-hunters and in terms of its relation to the female author's duty to transmit others' words. The story ends with long quotations from actual documents, the declarations of confession and regret signed by the Salem witch-hunters many years later. The reader is reminded that, not unlike *Romola* or even, in a way, *The Life of Charlotte Brontë*, this story is historical fiction. Although the protagonists are invented, the events are authentic. Cotton Mather himself appears in the scene of Lois's public accusation, and at least two central characters, the two rival pastors, are "taken" from Gaskell's main historical source.[17] Despite the invention of Lois's story, much of the story is arguably devoted to translating history into terms that make learning pleasurable. In the manuscript, the long verbatim quotations from historical documents, which themselves include scriptural quotations, were, like some of Brontë's letters in the manuscript of the *Life*, copied out by another writer, probably Marianne or Meta. This situation not only defines the story as a good woman's passive transcription but also suggests that Gaskell trained her own daughters to value copying men's words over speaking for oneself, or with one's mother. Although this ending raises the possibility of many of the same ambiguities we found in Eliot's balancing of the claims of fiction and history and of invention and transmission in *Romola*, it does seem to apologize for the rest of the story's resentment of the consequences of women's transmission of men's words, and it restores the author to a safer position as bearer of a patriarchal word.

The story's ambivalence as to whether the daughter is the father's or the mother's reappears in another story written about the same time, and while this second story does not substantially change our picture of Gaskell, it is worth looking at very briefly, if only to show how pervasive are the issues I have been presenting, and also because it introduces an image central to *Wives and Daughters*. "The Poor Clare," set like "Lois" in a day and place of a more literal religious belief than Gaskell's own, also centers on a woman's curse that harms her daughter by way of the interference between them of powerful men. Like "Lois" too, in contrast to "Lizzie Leigh," it begins with a daughter's separation from her mother and ends, not with their reunion, but rather with the mother's silence. The central figure of the story is the mother, Bridget Fitzgerald, a respected servant at a manor house in Ireland. Although both Bridget and her daughter Mary are "the ruling spirits of the household," against her mother's will Mary "not unfrequently rebelled. She and her mother were too much alike to agree. There were wild quarrels between them, and wilder reconciliations."[18] This rebellious daughter finally leaves home for a job abroad, unsure to the last whether she wants to leave her mother. Predictably, Mary's letters stop just at the point when she says she is about to marry a "gentleman" of "superior . . . station and fortune." Bridget devotes her life first sorrowfully to waiting for her daughter's return, then to searching for her in Europe. On her return, alone, to England, she earns "the dreadful reputation of a witch" for her half-crazed manner and for her ability to affect people's fortunes by her words and wishes. Knowing that her "wishes are terrible," she fears that her wish "that [Mary's] voyage might not turn out well," which she meant only as a wish for Mary to return home, has been fulfilled. Of her wishes she says, "their power goes beyond my thought." One day a "gentleman" riding by her home shoots Mary's dog, now Bridget's only companion. She curses him: "Hear me, ye blessed ones! . . . He has killed the only creature that loved me—the dumb beast that I loved. . . . You shall live to see the creature you love best, and who alone loves you . . . become a terror and a loathing to all, for this blood's sake."

At this point, the story shifts to several years later and a different scene. The narrator, a young land agent sent to locate Bridget because of an unexpected inheritance, not only finds Bridget and learns her story, but also, in a nearby town, meets and falls in love with Lucy, a beautiful and melancholy woman who has a terrible secret. Lucy turns out to be Bridget's granddaughter, Mary's daughter, and her father turns out to be the man Bridget cursed. Mary has since died through this man's "wilful usage," and Lucy, the creature her father loves best, has become the victim of the curse. "Pure and holy" as she is, Lucy has a monstrous double who impersonates her to do "wicked" things "such as shame any modest woman." This "loathsome demon," whose relation to Lucy resembles that of Bertha Mason to Jane Eyre, is clearly as sexual as Lucy is "pure," for it has "tried to suggest wicked thoughts and to tempt wicked actions; but she, in her saintly maidenhood, [has] passed on undefiled." And when the narrator sees the double, his "eyes were fascinated" and he finds her expression "mocking and voluptuous." When they visit Bridget to seek a release from the curse, this powerful woman is herself terrified by Lucy's double, for the power of her wishes "goes beyond [her] thought."

The story exemplifies the literal power of a woman's word, a power beneficial when inherent in a mother's and daughter's presymbolic relation, but a power that is twisted to evil ends by the intervention of paternal authority between mother and daughter. Mary leaves Bridget ambivalently seeking relief from the intensity of their identification, a relief promised by marriage, but it is because of the man who holds out this promise to her that Mary dies and that Bridget's powerful words have their devastating effect on her own granddaughter. Her horror when she learns that she has cursed the "flesh of my flesh" is the emotional center of the narrative.

The curse takes the form it does because a doubling, or splitting, of a daughter's self makes concrete her ambivalent view of her parents once she has been invited to leave her mother and enter the father's law, the symbolic order. That Lucy first sees her double in a mirror recalls those frequent occasions in the Brontës' novels when the heroine sees herself in a mirror divided from herself and forshadowing her own death. It is a mother's curse on her daughter to divide her daughter's loyalty between herself and the father, between love of and identification with the mother and the desire to separate and enter the father's law. The figure of the mirror, as the agent through which this division is revealed, suggests the helplessness of the mother, who, in patriarchal culture, has already been frozen into a passive reflector of male selves.[19] (In this story, it is not Bridget but Mary who plays the role of the mother killed by male vanity and therefore helpless to save her daughter.) That the daughter is split, or doubled, along the lines of her present or absent sexuality marks the point at which the daughter responds to the father's appeal: it is through her own desire for difference that the father seduces the daughter to leave her mother and enter his law. It is not so much that Lucy is one parent's child while her sexualized double is the other's, but rather that the splitting itself is determined by the antithetical appeal of mother and father.

But the story is not over: Bridget, seeking to release her granddaughter from the curse, travels to Belgium to enter the penitent order of the Poor Clares, hoping, by piety, self-abasement, and good works, to earn forgiveness for "the sin of witchcraft." All along, Bridget has held the belief that the Virgin Mary helps her. She has a shrine to the Virgin in her home and is seen praying to it first for Mary's return and later for the double's disappearance. But Mary is clearly the goddess only of more docile mothers, mothers who more willingly subordinate their wishes and their motherhood to men's requirements. Although for the narrator, as for the New England Puritans of "Lois the Witch," witchcraft and popery go hand in hand, witchcraft as a form of female power is a sin in Catholicism. For Bridget, the significant feature of the Poor Clares must be the vow of silence they take: only if dying of starvation may these women communicate a need, and then only by ringing a little bell. Yet even after so totally yielding her voice up to the father's law, Bridget cannot save Lucy until she subordinates herself even further, to the man she has most reason to hate, Lucy's father, who is conveniently wounded in a riot in Antwerp and whom Bridget tends in her own dying moments. Only then is the curse lifted.

Like Lucy, the heroine of *Wives and Daughters* has a sexual double, and for similar reasons, yet in the novel this double, while somewhat dangerous, is in no way as sinister as Lucy's. As we turn now to this novel, Gaskell's last work, we will see how in a more spacious design she continues to work out the daughter's ambivalent and often painful choice between the mother's word and the father's law, but with a conventionally happy result that is more cheerful even than the optimistic treatment in "Lizzie Leigh" of the coexistence of mother-daughter love and the father's prohibition. Yet the novel ends happily only by covering up the conflicts it not so much resolves as displaces.

──10──
Mothers and Daughters II:
Wives and Daughters, or "Two Mothers"

efore she started writing *Wives and Daughters*, Gaskell proposed
to her publisher, George Smith, a long story (to head a collection
of stories) to be called "Two Mothers," but she soon "threw
overboard the story of the 'Two Mothers' because I thought you
did not seem to like it fully" and replaced it with a sketch of *Wives and
Daughters*. *(Gaskell Letters*, p. 731).[1] Gaskell probably invented, or
exaggerated, Smith's lack of interest, as her stories and novels sold so
well as to make anything she might propose acceptable. The incident
suggests both that Gaskell was defensive about such a topic and that
Wives and Daughters conveys the concerns of the unwritten story, but in
a way calculated to be liked more "fully." "Two Mothers" would be just
as accurate a title for this final novel as *Wives and Daughters*, for while
the actual title reflects the novel's overt thematic concern with the transformation of daughters into wives and with the multiplicity of wives—
the way one wife can come to substitute for another in the symbolic
order's economy of desire—the earlier title exposes the hidden structure
of the novel, the difference between two mothers, one living and one
dead, which is also the difference between two kinds of signification.
"Two Mothers" also points to the relation that is prior to the circulation
of daughters as wives, a relation that is almost always hidden from the
representational purview of a literary work.[2]

As in the stories considered in chapter 9, this novel's plot turns on a
series of curiously foregrounded episodes in which a daughter carries a
letter, episodes that thematize different kinds of language use. Also like
earlier texts, this novel explores various kinds of interdependence between a presymbolic language shared between mother and daughter and
the father's symbolic order. In the two kinds of language modeled by

daughters' relationships with the two mothers, the father's requirements are felt, yet to differing degrees and in differing ways. The mother of the heroine, Molly Gibson, is dead before the novel begins; her father remarries, and this stepmother has a daughter Molly's age who lives with them. Molly's language is at first governed by her dead, real mother, who comes to stand for truth and literal meaning, although this language is always, like Romola's, at the service of the father's needs for passive transmission. But when the father remarries, the sexualization of all the familial relationships brings about a shift in the kind of influence the father has on women's language, so that the new family members speak a language wholly identified with figuration and the substitutions that constitute symbolic language, and Molly's language begins intermittently to resemble theirs as well as remaining partially as it was. Molly is thus a fuller and more credible Lucy from "The Poor Clare," the ambivalent daughter torn between loyalty to the literal language shared with the mother and the enticements of the father's difference. But the fact that Molly's own mother is dead from the start weights her eventual choice and suggests that all daughters' choices, in that culture, are similarly weighted, even when the mother is present. At the same time that Gaskell explores thematically through her characters varying kinds of language use, her own quotations from and allusions to prior authors, both male and female, reflect the stages and the divisions of Molly's linguistic practice. The novel closes with an allusion that suggests the weighting of Molly's choice is the same as Gaskell's own.

An early episode of letter carrying serves as the point of departure for the novel's presentation of women's language. Molly's father, a doctor, keeps apprentices who live in the Gibsons' house. When Molly is fifteen, one of them, Mr. Coxe, sends Molly a love letter through a female servant, a letter that Mr. Gibson intercepts and reads. Thinking of his own first love, "poor Jeanie," Mr. Gibson admonishes Mr. Coxe lightly and sympathetically and fires the servant. The episode is important to the plot because it provokes Mr. Gibson to consider remarrying for the sake of Molly's upbringing. More immediately, it causes him to send Molly away on a visit to friends. For women to deliver and to receive an illicit letter are, it seems, more serious offenses than for a man to send one. When the cook "chose to say it was Mr. Coxe the tempter who ought to have 'been sent packing,' not Bethia the tempted," Mr. Gibson thinks, "'I wish I'd a five-pound house and not a woman within ten miles of me! I might have some peace then.' Apparently, he forgot Mr. Coxe's powers of making mischief; but indeed he might have traced that evil back to the unconscious Molly."[3] (Mr.Gibson is irritated with women also because Molly's governess, a Miss Eyre, has just quit, leaving Molly's sexuality even more unguarded.) The situation is not unlike that in "Lizzie Leigh," "Lois the Witch," and "The Poor Clare," in which a verbal transaction between women is dangerous to them, not because of their own actions, but because of the men who interfere in such exchanges or who are the real sources of the letters carried.

Until the letter, Molly and her father have lived together in a way that is compatible with a girl's first relation with her mother, even though her mother is missing. But the transformation this letter effects in Molly, sexualizing her, causes her father to send her away as much from himself as from Mr. Coxe. He sets between them the distance of desire that is the beginning of a girl's entry into the symbolic order. Yet the transition is gradual, for it is not Molly but her father's view of her that has changed. The innocent Molly, who never learns or guesses the contents of Coxe's letter, continues to conduct herself as always. At the Hamleys', where her father send her, Molly's linguistic behavior closely resembles those moments in Gaskell's stories that come closest to a mother's and daughter's nonsymbolic language, even though this language includes within it a father's words. Obedient to her father's plans for her, Molly finds the closest approximation of a mother in the gradually fading Mrs. Hamley, who "had given her the place of a daughter in her heart" (chap. 13). But this mother's favorite child is her eldest son, Osborne, the patrilineal heir who is himself secretly a father.

One of Mrs. Hamley's favorite texts for reading aloud to Molly is her son's manuscript book of poems, and one of Molly's ways of affirming her tie to this substitute mother is to take an equal pleasure in these poems. The day that Roger, the second son whom Molly will be about to marry at the end of the novel, is expected home from Cambridge, a lazy, still, summer afternoon, Molly is copying out and attempting to memorize some of them:

> 'I asked of the wind, but answer made it none,
> Save its accustomed and solitary moan'—
> she kept saying to herself, losing her sense of whatever meaning the
> words had ever had, in the repetition which had become mechanical. (chap. 8)

As she recites, signifiers detach from signification and become pure sound, like "the bomming buzz of the blue flies" or the "humming of bees" whose sounds pleasantly deepen "the present silence." Like Anne Leigh's repetition to her daughter of "every tender and merciful text she could remember" from the gospels, or Lois's reiteration to Nattee of the Passion story, Molly's repetitions of Osborne's verses matter, not for their signification, but for their lulling sound, which confirms Molly's connection to a mother figure. Like those other repetitions, too, it is only through the mediation of a male text—the writings of a man whom both women view as superior to them—that this linkage is affirmed, for these women speak a mother-daughter language only within the frame of an androcentric order.

But just as Molly's voice is merging with the nonsymbolic sounds of bee and fly, new noises intervene:

> Suddenly, there was the snap of a shutting gate; wheels crackling on the dry gravel; horses' feet on the drive; a loud cheerful voice in the house, coming up through the open windows, the hall, the passages, the staircase, with unwonted fullness and roundness of tone. . . . Molly heard the Squire's glad 'Hallo! here he is!' and Madam's softer, more plaintive voice; and then the loud, full, strange tone, which she knew must be Roger's. (chap. 8)

Not only do sounds return to being signifiers with interpretable signifieds, in contrast to the revery of pure sound into which she has drowsed, but also the new sounds are loud, in contrast to the previous silence, penetrative, almost invasive, and decidedly masculine. Having already decided to let the family greet Roger first, Molly responds to this masculine invasion by continuing with her private repetitions, yet her withdrawal, which would seem also to be a sign of resentment, does not suffice to protect her nonsymbolic discourse from transformation back into the symbolic. That "this time she had nearly finished learning the poem" suggests that representational meanings have returned, if their lack was what made it unnecessary previously for her to get beyond the first two lines. In a general sense, too, Roger's arrival, with its associations of symbolic as opposed to nonsymbolic discourse, interrupts the mother-daughter relation Molly is presently enjoying, for he will eventually occasion Molly's departure altogether from such early relations and from the language they include, a departure similar to Mary Fitzgerald's when she leaves her beloved mother for the promise of a man's alternative discourse.

As a daughter whose relation to someone she loves as a mother is both dependent on and violated by the insertion between them of a man's "strange tone," Molly acts particularly in the early part of the novel as the selfless intermediary between speakers and writers. Her training in feminine selflessness begins when Roger finds her weeping in a "selfish passion" over the news of her father's engagement to a woman she dislikes. When Roger exhorts her to think of her father's feelings ahead of her own, she weeps again, but now not "for the fact that her father was going to be married again, but for her own ill-behaviour" (chap. 10). She views "her new-born desire of thinking for others" as "giving up her very individuality," and she thinks "it will be very dull when I shall have killed myself, as it were, and live only in trying to do, and to be, as other people like" (chap. 11). But this death of the self, which recalls also Romola's surprise "that [she] could care so much for anything that could happen to [her]self," is precisely what is required of the mother's daughter who becomes a passive transmitter of male words and who gets nothing out of it for herself. Her own mother's death, and the death of Mrs. Hamley that follows shortly, model the selflessness of the daughter who repeats these mothers' way with words. Molly can identify herself with these dead and dying mothers only by dying, in a way, herself.[4]

On Molly's second visit to Hamley Hall, Mrs. Hamley is dying of a wasting illness exacerbated both by the news that Osborne is in debt and failing in his studies and by her husband's angry response to this news. Molly's role, as the one who takes "the place of a daughter in her heart," is to withhold herself—for example, she refuses to complain to Mrs. Hamley of her own unhappiness with her stepmother—and instead to function as a stand-in and messenger for others. The squire brings her in to his wife with the glad news, "here's the doctor's daughter, nearly as good as the doctor himself" (chap. 17). Molly's first duty, after Mrs. Hamley becomes suddenly much weaker, is to convey to the squire the telling news that her father has sent for the two sons to come home, a message about messages whose message is impending death. Afraid of the squire's likely anger at the bearer of such news, Molly nevertheless does her job and discovers that as a messenger she has become transparent; the squire's anger turns, not on her, but on Osborne. Molly's message carrying requires a removal of her self, in order for the words to have their meanings.

Soon after, Mrs. Hamley, in her delirium, not only gives Molly "the place of a daughter in her heart," but also calls her "Fanny," the name of an actual daughter who died. Molly has already become the dead daughter of the house, for her invisibility, her transparency, is more and more called into service for the bearing of messages. In the same conversation in which Roger explains to Molly the meaning of his mother's calling her Fanny, he also asks Molly to give Mrs. Hamley a diluted report of the mysterious truth about Osborne, a message that Roger refuses to give himself: "I am so involved by promises of secrecy, Molly, that I couldn't satisfy her if she once began to question me" (chap. 18). It is precisely because Molly is of no immediate consequence to the family, because she suppresses any personal interest in the family's secrets, that she is best fitted to convey messages between its members. As Mrs. Hamley drops further and further out of consciousness, "only occasionally appearing to remember [Molly's] existence," Molly's position becomes more and more marginal. She continues as selfless messenger, however: when Osborne reaches home, he is asking for a report on his mother's condition just as the squire walks in "seeking Molly to ask her to write a letter for him" (chap. 18). The day before she is to leave, she thinks back to the day when her father told her about his engagement and wonders, "Could she ever be so passionately unhappy again? Was it goodness, or was it numbness, that made her feel as though life was too short to be troubled much about anything? Death seemed the only reality." Having "killed" herself, goodness, numbness, and personal death are equivalent for her, as they are again equivalent with the death of this second mother, whose goodness also was inextricable from her feebleness. When Molly takes her last farewell, "her very existence seemed forgotten by the poor lady." Paradoxically, she is closest to this mother, most identified with her, when forgotten by her.

Directly following her revelation about goodness and numbness, Molly receives one of the two messages that are most central to the novel's plot and that most fully test her abilities as selfless message bearer. Sitting in her cloak on a ladder in the library, invisible, "crouched up in her corner," she hears Roger (who doesn't know she is there) tell Osborne (who does), "Here's a letter from your wife" (chap. 18). Having overheard this secret, Molly must seem not to have been there. As Roger and Osborne discuss the matter, alluding to her "as the third person before whom conversation was to be restrained," she says, "I'm going away. Perhaps I ought not to have been here. . . . I'll try to forget what I've heard." Although she can't help being "a third person," Osborne asks her to promise "to act and speak as if [she] had never heard it."

As receiver of secrets, and as selfless mediator and "third person" who erases her own presence, Molly has inherited Mrs. Hamley's own role in the family. Shortly after his mother's death, Roger asks Molly to visit Hamley Hall again, for the squire and Osborne are at odds with each other over Osborne's secrecy, and Roger expects that Molly would be able to "put us a little to rights." He continues, "It is just what my mother would have put right very soon, and perhaps you could have done it—unconsciously, I mean" (chap. 21). Unconsciously, indeed: the final way in which Mrs. Hamley brought the family together was by her literal unconsciousness, and it is to the strain of mediating between Osborne's silence and the squire's rage that the novel attributes her death. Her role as the selfless spirit of communication between men finally requires her death, as the same role figuratively requires of Molly, and for Molly to inherit Mrs. Hamley's role is to confirm the death of her self. Molly is caught between the claims of two conflicting selflessnesses. The only way to put the squire and Osborne "to rights" would be for her to tell the squire his son's secret and mediate the inevitable dispute, but she is prevented from performing this selfless task by her previous vow not to have a self.

At the same time that Molly is being defined as intermediary and carrier of messages, a role defined as the daughter's reproduction of the mother's selflessness, and a role in which language is transmitted without the messenger's interference, the novel is also developing another model of language, one that depends upon the daughter's more complete entry into the symbolic order and more complete departure from the dead mother's language. This new language is presided over by the new Mrs. Gibson, the second of the "two mothers," who enters the novel as a substitute along the chain of the father's desires. During the period of Mrs. Hamley's dying, the new Mrs. Gibson is being installed in Molly's home, and her arrival both reasserts the death of Molly's own mother and initiates Molly's entry into a new world of desire and representation. For the arrival of the new mother, the house is being redecorated, including Mr. Gibson's room, which for Molly contains the memory of "being taken . . . to bid farewell to her dying mother." In this room, Molly can still see "in vivid fancy that same wan, wistful face lying on the pillow, . . . and the girl had not shrunk from such visions, but rather cherished them, as preserving to her the remembrance of her mother's outward semblance" (chap. 13). Now, however, the changes in furniture banish these "visions" of her mother, and Molly especially notes and is hurt by an exchange of mirrors: "There was a grand toilette-table now, with a glass upon it, instead of the primitive substitute of the top of a chest of drawers, with a mirror above upon the wall." Since it is this mirror that in particular held for Molly the remembrance of her mother's "outward semblance," it is no surprise that on the next page Molly, dressed for the first time in a really elegant dress (her new mother's choice for the wedding), looks in the mirror and sees herself changed. Her stepmother's taste transforms Molly's outward semblance as it appears in the mirror, just as it has transformed the mirror itself: "She was almost startled when she looked into the glass, and saw the improvement in her appearance. 'I wonder if I'm pretty.'" When she shows herself to the Brownings, the friends she is staying with, "she [is] greeted with a burst of admiration," and Miss Browning says, "I shouldn't have known you."

Molly's difference from herself in her stepmother's mirror recalls mirror scenes we have considered earlier, both in the Brontës' novels and in Gaskell's "The Poor Clare," in which a mirror proves the female self's radical disunity, as for example when Lucy looks in the mirror and sees her monstrous double beside her. The "pretty" self Molly sees in the mirror, herself as desirable object, appears only after her father has begun to see her as a sexual being—as he does after the episode with Mr. Coxe's love letter—and only after her father has himself become an actively desiring subject, a man who seeks out and then marries the new and attractive wife whose arrival occasions the change in mirrors and the change in the mirror. Molly's earlier relation to language included her love for her father and for the subordinate role women like her own mother assume in patrilineal culture and language, but this new relation is based on her awareness of herself as, and her desire to be, an object of sexual interest who would fit entirely within the symbolic's economy of desire. As we have seen in "The Poor Clare," a splitting or doubling of the self is the consequence when the daughter divides her loyalty between, on the one hand, her mother's literal language and her old relation to the mother and, on the other, the father's symbolic order and the new relation it represents. Also as in "The Poor Clare," the heroine's division from herself takes the concrete form of a sexualized double. While Molly for the most part has been and remains a sheltered girl, her new stepsister, Cynthia, has lived most of her life dependent on her attractiveness to men. Raised by a vain and unloving mother, she lacks Molly's moral sense; she is fully within the economy of desire when Molly meets her. Again, in this story, the heroine is pure, sober, modest, and moral, while the double is something of a sinner whose deceitful behavior (here, far less sinister) has sexual overtones. That the two girls are doubles is suggested by the way Molly's old bedroom is redecorated (with the loss of Molly's mother's girlhood furniture) to match Cynthia's new one exactly, and by a number of scenes in which their looks and manners are paired and contrasted, most notably in the mirror.

Cynthia and her mother introduce into the novel a language in which words do not tell truths or accurately convey messages but, rather, enter into a free play of signifiers as figuration. This language is identified, not with Molly's dead mothers, but with women's place in the chain of substitutions that makes up the economy of male desire, a place that the new Mrs. Gibson knows well and has just successfully exploited in maneuvering Mr. Gibson to propose. In direct contrast to Molly's faithful and literal conveyance of messages, Mrs. Gibson typically misquotes people to each other and uses others' words for her own selfish ends, as when she discusses "London topics" with Osborne (whom she plans to snare as a husband for her daughter), in such a way as to suggest that she has recently been there, skillfully arranging "her words, so as to make it appear as if the opinions that were in reality quotations were formed by herself from actual experience of personal observation" (chap. 16).

Osborne, Mrs. Gibson, and Cynthia are especially skilled at this kind of talk, and the first time the two brothers visit the Gibsons' together we see these adepts in action, differentiated from Molly, who takes everything seriously, as do, to a slightly lesser degree, Roger and Mr. Gibson. Osborne and Mrs. Gibson "prattled on with all the ease of manner and commonplaceness of meaning which go far to make the 'art of polite conversation'" (chap. 24). Cynthia is even more skilled than her mother. Detecting Roger's infatuated gaze on her, she uses her skill at detaching words from meanings to turn his potential seriousness into a joke by pretending that his stare is a rebuke for inattentiveness: "It is quite true! . . . I don't even know the ABC of science. But please don't look so severely at me, even if I am a dunce!" Her mother, catching up Cynthia's words without fathoming her intentions, denies that Cynthia is a dunce and privately rebukes her for presenting herself so unfavorably. Cynthia, whose intelligence is demonstrated by her ironic and figurative use of language, defends herself:

'But, mamma,' Cynthia replied, 'I am either a dunce, or I am not. If I am, I did right to own it; if I am not, he's a dunce if he doesn't find out I was joking.'
    'Well,' said Mrs. Gibson . . .
    'Only that, if he's a dunce, his opinion of me is worth nothing. So, any way, it doesn't signify.'

The values of figurative and literal uses of language clash again when Cynthia, ignorant that Osborne is married and to a French woman, sings at her mother's request a French song, "a pretty, playful little warning to young men" of which the refrain closes, "Car, si tu prends une femme, Colin, / Tu t'en repentiras." As Cynthia "carrolled the saucy ditty out," playful because the song is meaningless to her, Osborne, Roger, and Molly look very grave and embarrassed, because the song is as full of meaning for them as it is empty for Cynthia and her mother.

The conflict between Cynthia and her mother's language on the one hand and Molly and her dead mothers' on the other, which is really a conflict within Molly herself, appears most acutely in the events leading up to Roger's engagement to Cynthia. Molly's role as messenger, identified as it is with mothers who are dead, has always required a kind of death of the self, but it has at least offered the satisfactions both of doing good for others and of gaining her identification with her mother. But in this episode the death of Molly's self is so complete that she has stopped even being a messenger. Though in a general sense Molly is responsible for bringing Roger and Cynthia together—she is the link between the two families—at the scene of their first meeting, Molly experiences the invisibility to which her role as "a third person" inevitably leads. Molly begins at this point to see the limitations of her messenger's role: identified with the daughter's presymbolic relation to the mother, it is decidedly prior to, and thus in conflict with, the daughter's entry into heterosexuality, desire, and the symbolic exchanges these entail.

Gaskell uses the scene of Molly' reaction to news of the engagement for one of her own most significant and extended quotations from romantic poetry. Just as Molly's situation begins to expose the limitations of women's bearing words, Gaskell complicates the question by faithfully transmitting a passage that has the effect, in context, of exposing the dangers for women in their other possible compromise with the father's language, their entry as tokens of exchange into the symbolic order. Returning from a walk, Molly learns that Roger, who is to be away for two years on a scientific voyage, has come to say goodbye. Consistent with her role as the excluded third person, her absence has made it possible for him to propose to Cynthia. Mrs. Gibson, having cagily kept out of the way, tells Molly she has overheard him say to Cynthia "that the temptation of seeing her alone" had overcome his resolve not to speak to her until his return to England. Molly's response includes and depends on Gaskell's quotation from Wordsworth:

> Molly did not hear these last words. She had escaped upstairs, and shut the door. . . . She felt as if she could not understand it all; but as for that matter, what could she understand? Nothing. For a few minutes, her brain seemed in too great a whirl to comprehend anything but that she was being carried on in earth's diurnal course, with rocks, and stones, and trees, with as little volition on her part as if she were dead. (chap. 34)

Molly here becomes Wordsworth's Lucy, from "A Slumber Did My Spirit Seal," which begins with the speaker's explaining that "She seemed a thing that could not feel / The touch of earthly years," and ends with his acknowledging that nonetheless she has died:[5]

> No motion has she now, no force;
> She neither hears nor sees;
> Rolled round in earth's diurnal course,
> With rocks, and stones, and trees.

What does it mean to equate Molly with this unnamed "she"? ("She," though called "Lucy" by convention, should properly remain unnamed, as Shelley's demon is unnamed, and for the same reason.) "She" is the quintessential poetic object, a "thing." The speaker has so little clue to her subjectivity that he does not know, sealed as he is in "a slumber" that suggests his unconsciousness of anything outside him, whether she is dead, alive, or immortal. Although her death or vanishing in the second stanza would seem to defy the speaker's desire, it is also a measure of his desire's power to obliterate otherness that she disappears in the first place. As the object of representational language, the referent of symbolic speech, she must disappear for the speaker's language, which is his desire, to operate. Disappearing from the realm of language, she joins the immense "round" of that original of all objects, all referents, Mother Nature, who is also always elsewhere. Both the mother and "she" remain hovering on the edge of nonexistence, however, for it is not their entire absence but rather an absence for which substitutions can be found that constitutes the referent's place in language.

Just as Lucy's very existence depends on the consciousness of the poet, so too Molly's existence seems at this moment to depend on Roger's consciousness of her, for it is being forgotten by Roger, being overlooked as that object for which a substitution has been found, that makes Molly feel "that she was being carried on in earth's diurnal course." To be the referent is to be, or to be identified with, the (dead) mother. And just as Lucy returns to and merges with Mother Nature, so Molly thinks at this moment of one of her dead mothers: "He could not have gone without even seeing her. . . . her, whom his mother had so loved, and called by the name of his little dead sister. And, as she thought of the tender love Mrs. Hamley had borne her, she cried the more, for the vanishing of such love for her from off the face of the earth." This last figure links Mrs. Hamley to the "diurnal round" of nature in "A Slumber" and further connects Molly, through her identification with Mrs. Hamley and her dead daughter, with those female referents who, in the erotics of symbolic discourse, desiring male subjects neessarily forget. Even though her identification with Mrs. Hamley has been subordinate to the linguistic needs of men, as their messenger, Molly would vanish even further in symbolic discourse.

Although Gaskell could not have known it, Dorothy Wordsworth too alludes to "A Slumber Did My Spirit Seal" and in effect identifies herself with Lucy, on the occasion of the marriage of the man she loves, whose marriage in a sense makes her vanish. As William Wordsworth and Mary are returning from the church, Dorothy writes in her journal, "I threw myself on the bed where I lay in stillness, neither hearing or seeing any thing"; obliged to get up and greet the couple, she says, "I moved I knew not how straight forward, faster than my strength could carry me."[6] Dorothy's identification with Lucy's fate also identifies her with the real object that must drop out for the chain of desire to begin. While Words-worth's speaker's sorrow is for himself, these women's rewritings of Lucy from her point of view direct the reader's sympathies to her.

At the same time that Molly's scene alludes to Wordsworth, it also alludes to the earlier scene of her memorization of Osborne's poems, which not only introduces the theme of quotation into the characters' action but also includes another of Gaskell's own quotations, from Tennyson's "Mariana." In that scene, Molly is sitting at a window and "losing herself in the dreamy outlooks." Gaskell writes, "The house was so still, in its silence it might have been the 'moated grange'; the bomming buzz of the blue flies, in the great staircase window, seemed the loudest noise indoors" (chap. 8). Though "moated grange" comes from Shakespeare's *Measure for Measure*, it is most familiar as part of the epigraph to Tennyson's poem, and the other elements of Gaskell's description are allusive too:[7]

> All day within the dreamy house,
>   The doors upon their hinges creaked;
> The blue fly sung in the pane; the mouse
>   Behind the mouldering wainscot shrieked . . .
>   ("Mariana," 61–64)

Molly's repetitions of Osborne's poems in this scene, which drain them of their meaning and transform them into sound like the "humming of bees," are like that nonrepresentational speech that confirms the bond between a mother and a daughter. In the context of the allusion to "Mariana," that buzzing sound seems also to allude to Mariana's erotic self-containment, which is expressed in the poem especially through Mariana's repetition of her refrain ("He cometh not") and through her hallucinatory imaginative power ("Old footsteps trod the upper floors / Old voices called her from without"). Although for Tennyson, Mariana's refrain is far from soothingly maternal—her frustrated sex-uality makes her restless and resentful of intrusions—in Gaskell's hands, a woman's solitary imagining and repetition of words becomes both a healthy self-containment and a bond to the mother. Gaskell herself repeats Tennyson in such a way as to make her repetition seem obedient, but she actually alters Tennyson's sense.

In this earlier scene, "the bomming buzz of the blue flies" and the "humming of bees" model Molly's nonrepresentational repetitions in a positive way, but in the scene in which she reacts to Roger's engagement, she experiences a very painful deafness and inability to "understand it all" and a "buzzing confusion." (The moment also recalls a scene a few pages earlier when Molly first learns that Roger is to be away for so long: "There was a buzzing in her ears . . . the words [the others] uttered seemed indistinct and blurred.") If the earlier "buzzing" betokens a happy connection both to the mother and to Mother Nature, here the identification with the dead mother that the buzzing indicates suggests only Molly's unhappy exclusion from the system of substitutions through which Roger proposes to Cynthia and that Molly now, it seems, would like to enter. If as Mariana she is no one's erotic object and does not miss it, as Lucy she is the object that has vanished through the necessities of an eroticized language.

In her use of both of these quotations, we might note, Gaskell appears to be behaving like Molly herself, repeating accurately the words of a father figure (she quotes and does not simply allude). Yet because the contexts in which Gaskell situates these quotations alter their significa-tion, her behavior is really more like that of Mrs. Gibson, who misquotes, not only other people's conversations, but lines from poetry in order to make the original serve her own selfish purposes. For example, when later in the novel Mr. Gibson unexpectedly sends Molly home from Hamley Hall with a fever, Mrs. Gibson says, "I am sure he thought directly of giving me this surprise, this pleasure. You're looking a little— what shall I call it? I remember such a pretty line of poetry, 'Oh, call her fair, not pale!' So we'll call you fair." Mr. Gibson responds, "You'd better not call her anything, but let her get to her own room" (chap. 54). Nothing could be less appropriate, or reassuring, than this quotation from Coleridge's "Christabel," but Mrs. Gibson clearly has no idea where her line comes from, or even that lines of poetry might have their own meanings apart from her self-centered purposes. As a model for Gaskell's own acts of quotation, Mrs. Gibson's are both disturbing and liberating. Somewhat like Eliot's use as an artist figure of the villain Tito, who also and far more dangerously liberates words from their meanings for his own gain, Gaskell's use of Mrs. Gibson to model some of her own linguistic practice on the one hand exposes some of Gaskell's anxiety about the novelist's necessary departure from the simple transmission of prior meanings and, on the other hand, helps expose the limitations of the kind of language used by her saintly heroine, limitations she is also exploring thematically.

Following the scene in which Molly is identified with Wordsworth's Lucy, Gaskell has Molly gradually shift her position in the symbolic order from the referent that must vanish to the eroticized substitute (and from identification with her dead mothers to an increasing similarity to her figurative mother and to her eroticized double, Cynthia), a shift that occurs both in the love plot and in the developing story of language.[8] Or rather, from here on, Molly occupies both positions simultaneously, as if she were both her girlhood self and the eroticized self who appears in the mirror, the child of both kinds of mother. Molly continues in her role as the bearer of others' words: the plot now turns to the gradual exposure of two dangerous secrets, Osborne's and Cynthia's, and it is Molly who guards both secrets and who uses her role as intermediary to help resolve them. Yet secrecy itself is part of the linguistic order foreign to Molly, for whom language is for telling the truth. Moreover, the nature of these secrets—both turn on the interchangeability of money and language— places them squarely within the symbolic order's system of substitutions. Molly's role as selfless intermediary thus involves her in a series of linguistic and symbolic exchanges that teach her both the disadvantages and eventually the advantages of this language.

Osborne, who has intermittently been grouped with Mrs. Gibson and Cynthia as a skilled practitioner of "polite conversation," keeps his wife a secret from his father because she is a Frenchwoman and, worse, has earned money as a governess. She therefore cannot yet be introduced to the squire. Osborne hopes to raise Aimée to respectability by selling a volume of poems about her, proving his own worth in the process. He recognizes that in order to turn his words into money (to make one set of signifiers refer to another, more universal, currency of exchange), he will have to translate "Aimée" into the more conventional "Lucy" for publication. But in that case, the figure in the poems will no longer be the wife he wishes to elevate. His poems can either sell or remain autobiographical, but not both. A mother herself, Aimée is, like Mrs. Hamley and Molly's first mother, prior to language's capacity for exchange. Later in the novel, after Roger has left and his own health is deteriorating, Osborne tells Molly his wife's name and address. This secret Molly will later participate in exposing.

But Molly's linguistic involvement is chiefly with the other secret she negotiates, the secret of Cynthia's engagement to the shady Mr. Preston, who holds old letters from Cynthia as blackmail. Molly stumbles upon Cynthia's secret when she is out walking on a lonely path in the country. Recognizing Cynthia's tones in a "passionate voice of distress" she hears through the bushes, she locates Cynthia in Preston's grasp. In an echo of Osborne's words on discovering that Molly has overheard his secret, Preston says, "The subject of our conversation does not well admit of a third person's presence" (chap. 42). The secret of Cynthia's engagement to Preston parallels Osborne's, not only in the matter of an illicit love affair, but also in the relation of letters and money. Cynthia's promise to marry him, words with determinate meanings, she sees instead as negotiable currency, because the promise was originally exacted in exchange for twenty pounds borrowed from Preston. Thinking that repayment of the loan will release her from her promise, Cynthia discovers that Preston refuses to accept money in exchange for the cancellation of words. She operates on the principle that language is a medium of exchange, infinitely transformable, while he does not.

Explaining later to Molly, Cynthia, typically referring one set of signifiers to another, attributes the "scrape" over her letters to another set of letters. Cynthia's mother, having gone on vacation leaving Cynthia alone at her boarding school, had written Cynthia her permission to make a holiday visit of her own, without sending her either any money for the trip or a return address where she could be reached. Mrs. Gibson's irresponsibility as a mother takes here its usual form of a proliferation of pointless words, words that "don't signify" (she "descanted largely on the enjoyment she was having"), but also the form of her unanswerability. With no return address, Mrs. Gibson becomes herself a shifting signifier. For Cynthia to write to her at the place she has left would be equivalent to attempting to pin down any meaning of hers, especially her meaning as a mother. The word "mother" cannot signify this woman, because she has always just moved to another place, and the impossibility of signifying her is confirmed by the number of names she has in the course of the novel. She is Hyacinth Clare to her original employers, Mrs. Kirkpatrick as wife and widow, and finally Mrs. Gibson. Unable to "refer to" her mother, Cynthia borrows from Preston the money she needs for her trip, and on this trip she discovers the pleasures of society: "I did look pretty in my fine new clothes, and I saw that other people thought so too" (chap. 43). After her success, Preston proposes, she says, with "a reference to my unlucky debt, which was to be a debt no longer, only an advance of the money to be hereafter mine if only—"

Cynthia's discovery of her prettiness, like Molly's earlier in the novel, takes place in relation to her mother, but the relation is very different in the two cases. Molly's prettiness amounts to a difference from her usual self in the mirror, a change of self that parallels the changes also being made in the house to erase the memory of her dead mother, so that Molly's self becomes associated with her mother, and social prettiness with the erasure of her. Even though her mother is dead, the memory of her and the loyalty to that memory constitute Molly's identity, so that the shift from the dead mother to the new one amounts to a shift from the realm of the real to the realm of appearances. For Cynthia, however, there never was a mother, only a correspondent with no return address. The discovery of her prettiness is not of a difference from herself or from her mother but rather a deeper entry into her mother's world of shifting signifiers, where for twenty pounds of new clothes prettiness can be bought and then itself turned into a medium of exchange, a way of purchasing the cancellation of a debt. For both girls, prettiness involves the separation of signifier from referent, but for Cynthia this means moving toward the values of her mother, while for Molly it means moving away.

Having bought Cynthia this way, Preston believes he can remove her from the realm of negotiable currency and install her in a realm where words can be held to their meanings: "I don't despair of making her love me as much as she ever did, according to her letters" (chap. 44). He refuses to acknowledge that for Cynthia there are no values apart from exchange values. Cynthia attempts to break the engagement when she hears a rumor that her mother is interested in Preston for herself, and she is now determined to retrieve the love letters with which Preston would blackmail her into keeping her promise. He wants the letters to "mean," by insisting that once they have reached their linear destination their travel is over; she wants to change their meaning and believes that meaning can be cancelled by reversing their trajectory. Thus Molly, volunteering out of love for Cynthia to get them back, becomes involved in assumptions and practices about language that are fundamentally in conflict with her own belief in the irrevocable and literal sanctity of words, a belief that has up to now kept her from deceit of any kind. Promising not only to get the letters back but also to do it in secrecy, without enlisting her father's authority, "Molly was compelled to perceive that there must have been a good deal of underhand work going on beneath Cynthia's apparent openness of behaviour; and still more unwillingly she began to be afraid that she herself might be led into the practice" (chap. 43).

Ominously, the metaphor through which she expresses this intention not to engage in "underhand work" is a figurative revision of the scene with which the project began. In order to locate the source of Cynthia's voice in the woods, she "left the path, . . . plunging through the brown tangled growth of ferns and underwood" (chap. 42). Now, "she would try and walk in a straight path; and, if she did wander out of it, it should only be to save pain to those whom she loved" (chap. 43). This shift reverses the usual course of Molly's (and of other fictive heroines') dealings with language, in which the virtuous path is from the figurative to the literal, what we have been calling literalization. The process of figuration here, the shift from literal to figurative, mirrors Molly's shift from true speech with single meanings to a language of displacements, exchanges, and other slippages from signifier to signifier.

Molly becomes Cynthia's messenger, the translator to Preston of Cynthia's intentions, a role in which she has excelled up to now because of her selflessness and her belief in the literal transmission of words. But in keeping with her learning Cynthia's "underhand" style, in which words lose their fixed meanings, she succeeds in her mission, not by transmitting Cynthia's words directly, but by exchanging Cynthia's words for another language, another currency, by getting Cynthia's words to refer to another set of words. Molly starts by assuming that language based in a code of honor will work: she tells Preston he has "no right at all, as a gentleman, to keep a girl's letters when she asks for them back again." He denies her report that Cynthia hates him by reference to the relativity of Cynthia's language: "Young ladies are very fond of the words 'hate' and 'detest'" (chap. 44). Where her truth telling fails in its intended effect, Molly ultimately succeeds by referring instead to another set of signifiers, Preston's economic interests. Molly threatens to tell this embarrassing story to her friend Lady Harriet Cumnor and ask her to tell it to her father, Lord Cumnor, who is Preston's employer. If Preston's interest in Cynthia was originally that of a purchaser, the threat that other and larger economic interests will be endangered through this one is effective, and his response exposes the fact that his interest in Cynthia remains ultimately at the level of her exchange value.

Preston, defeated, admires Molly for so cleverly finding out his weak spot. However, Molly understands the world of exchange (and therefore just what it is that she has done) only insofar as it overlaps with the world of paternal authority. She thinks of Lord Cumnor as a substitute for her own father, in whose power she entirely believes. Molly is therefore not yet really touched by her use of language as exchange, because her knowledge of it is accidental; she thinks she is using language from her own more stable and moral world. The danger to Molly's character is that, as letter carrier, she will change from being a faithful copyist to being part of a chain of signifiers, to being that mechanism by which words refer to other signifiers rather than to fixed meanings. Worse, she may discover that the two functions are the same, because to carry Cynthia's letters is to transmit words that are inherently untrustworthy. Cynthia, who remains blind to the profound moral consequences of language, doesn't see the potential for hurt to Molly, and she demands of her one more labor of transmission, the return of Preston's money, plus interest, so that the exchange of words for money will be complete.

Molly encounters Preston in the local bookstore that doubles as circulating library and, informally, as "the center of news, and the club, as it were, of the little town" (chap. 46). Here, where words, both books and news, are put into circulation, in full view of one of the town's most fluent gossips, Molly gives Preston the envelope containing the money. Putting the money back into circulation (Preston wanted Cynthia to take it, like herself, out of circulation), Molly simultaneously puts herself into circulation as the subject of gossip. The censure of Molly connects her to the servant Bethia who delivered Mr. Coxe's love letter to Molly: "Going out at dusk to meet her sweetheart, just as if she was my Betty, or your Jenny. And her name is Molly, too— . . . she might as well be a scullery-maid at oncest." It doesn't matter that rather than perpetrating an illicit liaison Molly is working to end one; what counts is the appearance of things, and when the letters are viewed as tokens of exchange rather than as words with meanings, the circulation of letters in one direction is equivalent to their circulation in the other. Gossip, like money, is a chain of signifiers that can easily operate without referring to anything.

Circulated among the Hollingford gossips, this story is referred to two other stories: Preston and Molly, but not Cynthia, were seen entering the woods where Molly first came upon Preston and Cynthia, and again Molly and Preston were observed discussing Cynthia's letters. These stories are in turn given meaning only with reference to other entirely conjectural clandestine meetings and correspondence. The circulation of the gossip provides that words, once they have been made part of a system of exchanges, can never be removed from circulation; they just change their form. Indeed the very grounds for Cynthia thinking that words can stop signifying once returned to the writer are, ironically, precisely the reason that they never stop signifying, their exchangeability, even if what they signify is only another set of empty signifiers. And Cynthia does learn this when eventually the story she thought she had stopped comes back to her as rumor. Attempting to take her words, promises, and letters out of circulation, assuming that their return will make them cease to signify, Cynthia buys them back. Yet the exchange itself, as performed by Molly, only becomes a new subject of circulation, a substitute for what was removed, in an economy that demands a constant quantity of currency. Cynthia's illicit secret now becomes Molly's; even the content of the story is the same, a secret engagement to Preston. As Mr. Gibson says later when the story inevitably circulates back to him, "Scandal has been resting on Molly, and ought to have rested on you, Cynthia" (chap. 50).

Acknowledging her underhandedness, Cynthia writes to Roger in Africa to break off the engagement, wishing instead for a lover without so high a moral standard as his. She is then "stung with a new idea: . . . 'Molly, Roger will marry you! See if it isn't so!'" Molly is shocked by this vision of Roger's character: "Your husband this morning! Mine to-night! What do you take him for?" But Cynthia goes on, "If you won't let me call him changeable, I'll coin a word and call him consolable!" (chap.

51). Though Roger is as good a character as Gaskell could invent, Cynthia is exactly right in her assessment of him, and her proliferation of a new term to accommodate that assessment matches Roger's actions more accurately than does Molly's strict sense of fidelity to vows. Were Roger as faithful to his words as Molly thinks, she would continue to be left out. By contrast, Cynthia's understanding of Roger's ability to seek out substitutes, which, as she seems intuitively to know, constitutes the basis of all desire, allows for Molly's inclusion as the next in that series of substitutes. Although up to now Molly's participation in Cynthia's linguistic exchanges has harmed her, here the novel suggests that if Molly is to be happy she must participate for herself in this substitutive language, a participation that her negotiation of Cynthia's secret has trained her for. Molly begins to shift from the language of one kind of mother to that of the other. While her identification with her dead mothers grounds her faithful and accurate transmissions of words, it also places her within the symbolic as the absent referent. The new Mrs. Gibson, the figurative mother with whom neither Molly nor Cynthia ever identifies as the daughter of a mother, authorizes, precisely by not being a stable referent, a different place in the symbolic order, the place of the shifting signifier that constitutes women's existence on a chain of substitutive objects of male desire. Gaskell presents this shift from one mother to the other both as a fall—Mrs. Gibson is after all an unappealing character—and as an adult woman's only chance for pleasure.

So ambivalently is this shift presented—or rather, so minutely does Gaskell follow the twisting path of its arrival—that directly after this conversation between Cynthia and Molly, Molly is drawn back into a repetition of her old role as transparent and selfless carrier of messages, in seeming contradiction of the future Cynthia outlines for her. Their conversation is interrupted by the news of Osborne's sudden death, which distracts Molly from her interest in Roger and sends her back to the stable world of Hamley Hall and her linguistic function there. Entering "with the softest steps, the most hushed breath" the nursery where the squire sits alone by his son's body, Molly, "silent and still," becomes an attendant spirit with no self of her own. With Roger in Africa, she is the only one who knows the secret, and the address, of Osborne's wife and child. She tells her father, under whose direction she tells the squire and then writes to Aimée. But Molly's function as a selfless messenger has been altered, both by events and by the more complex sense of language she has developed as a result of her entanglements. That is, the change in her that Osborne's death seems to interrupt and arrest takes place anyway. Although she tells the squire all she knows about Aimée, in a simple narrative, her letter to Aimée is a deceit: benign, of course, and invented and legitimized by her father, but a deceit nonetheless. She waits three days before writing, so that Aimée, who will be expecting a letter every day, will be prepared for bad news; then she writes that Osborne is very ill; finally she writes of his death. Moreover, it turns out her letters are superfluous. Though Molly alone in Hollingford holds the key to Osborne's secret, and stands as a link between the dead and the living, Aimée doesn't wait for the second letter, much less for an invitation, to travel to Hamley on her own. If the absence of Osborne's letters and the one about his "illness" are enough to bring her there, it is clear that a sufficiently long break in Osborne's letters would alone have been enough to bring her.

If Molly's function as selfless transmitter of messages has in some respects been made superfluous, she has also improved it by means of the other language she is learning. Molly spots Cynthia's letter to the squire, telling of her broken engagement to Roger, lying among the other un-opened mail delivered since the death. Molly pleads with Cynthia to be allowed to bring the letter back unopened, to make it cease to signify. Though originating in her selfless love for others, this suggestion obviously recalls Molly's earlier agency in the return of Cynthia's other letters, an agency that initiated her into a world of linguistic and mone-tary displacements. She has learned something of the value and possibili-ties of a language more flexible than her own. Also during this period she is occupied in reading aloud to the squire her translations of letters they have discovered from Aimée to Osborne. In these translations, Molly's own abilities, not merely her transparency, play an important part in conveying a moving impression: "Perhaps, if Molly had read French more easily, she might not have translated them into such touching, homely, broken words. . . . that went home to the Squire's heart" (chap. 53). Like Mary Ann Evans translating Strauss, Molly discovers that what the translator adds is often the best part. When Molly reads the letters again at other times, the squire's insistence that she repeat verbatim her own first translation shifts the emphasis from Aimée's original text, which could be translated in a variety of ways, to the text of Molly's translation itself.

After Aimée and her child arrive, Molly spends the next few weeks in her old way, sympathizing with Aimée and worrying over how to medi-ate her eventual struggle with the squire over possession of the child. Molly becomes ill, and her illness makes her, like Mrs. Hamley, appear to be "fading." Like Mrs. Hamley's gently wasting disease, this one results from the demands of mediation, and, appropriately, it also succeeds in removing Molly from the circulation of the gossip that began with Cynthia's letter. As she convalesces, her role of selfless intermediary continues to come into conflict with her developing sense of her new place in the chain of desire. It is she who has to tell Roger, who hopes to get Cynthia back again on his return from Africa, that Cynthia is already engaged to another man. Cynthia is visible in the garden with Mr. Henderson; in the sitting room with Molly, Roger "could see over her into the garden." Though he thus can see for himself, his view is mediated by Molly's presence, and as soon as she gives him the explanation he asks for, she "faint[s] away utterly" (chap. 56).

After Cynthia leaves to get married, the plot returns to the point, which the announcement of Osborne's death interrupted, at which Cynthia was in the act of handing Roger over to Molly and, with him, some of the value of her kind of language. Still considered too ill to go to London with the wedding party, Molly completes her convalescence at Cumnor Towers, where she repeats her earlier discovery of her difference from herself in a mirror. The maid "dressed her in some of the new clothes prepared for the [London] visit, and did her hair in some new and pretty way, so that, when Molly looked at herself in the cheval-glass, she scarcely knew the elegant reflection to be that of herself" (chap. 57). This difference from herself recurs in various ways. When Roger arrives as a dinner guest, he "hardly recognised her. . . . He began to feel that admiring deference which most young men experience, when conversing with a very pretty girl . . . in a manner very different to his old familiar friendliness" (chap. 58). Her perceived difference from herself echoes clearly Cynthia's discovery of her own prettiness, which included an account of men treating her differently. And she is moving here, as Cynthia predicted, into Cynthia's position as the object of Roger's desires.

At the same time that Molly continues to replace Cynthia, entertaining the positive possibilities of Cynthia's figurative language, she is still called upon to act in her old role as mediator, as literal translator and substitute for Mrs. Hamley. At Cumnor Towers, Roger tells her that Aimée and the squire still quarrel. Although Roger, who has the love and respect of both, is well situated to help them, it is clear that the job requires something he lacks, the feminine selflessness shared by Molly and his mother. But Molly discovers that she cannot visit Hamley Hall "as simply now as she had done before" (chap. 59), because of the new way in which Roger and the Hollingford gossips see her, as erotic object. Removed from gossip's circulation by her illness, she reenters it as soon as she begins again to resemble Cynthia. Receiving hints from several quarters that she is seen as a candidate for Roger's affections, Molly feels self-conscious about the "impropriety" of the visit. In her self-conscious "resolve . . . to ignore Roger," Molly, as in her moment before the mirror, "was so different from her usual self that Roger noticed the change in her, as soon as she arrived." And her erotic self-consciousness prevents her from being an effective mediator. The conflict between the two kinds of self and of language makes her miserable.

It is, however, through her ability to manipulate and to accept being the object of symbolic discourse that Molly comes to something like a happy understanding with Roger. Presenting her with a bouquet of flowers on her departure from Hamley Hall, Roger asks Molly to select one flower and give it back to him, and this exchange of such a conventional token of love serves for Molly as a sign of their "friendship." And her father confides to Roger, "I'd rather give my child . . . to you, than to any man in the world!" (chap. 60), making Molly an object of exchange between the two men. Nevertheless, Molly's innocence about the symbolic and erotic exchange in which she has just taken part makes her last sight of Roger (before he leaves on another lengthy scientific expedition), not an erotic one, but rather a repetition of her very earliest, and unrepresented, relation to her mother. Molly remains divided, as she has been for so much of the novel, between her dead and her living mothers' languages, between the literal and the symbolic order.

At the close of the novel, having been exposed to scarlet fever, Roger is forbidden to visit the Gibson's house, but he appears outside to wave goodbye to Molly. Molly waves back, but with difficulty, because Mrs. Gibson fills the entire window. "Molly could only peep here and there, dodging now up, now down, now on this side, now on that, of the perpetually-moving arms. She fancied she saw something of a corresponding movement on Roger's part" (chap. 60). Roger can signal that his message is for Molly only by mirroring her waves with an active, lively response to her that at once alludes to a mother's mirroring her child and marks a distinct contrast to both of the maternal mirrors we have seen up to now.[9] In chapter 13, when one mirror is exchanged for another, Molly's own mother has already died and been reduced to a memory in a motionless mirror. The second Mrs. Gibson as figurative mother is associated with a mirroring in which a daughter sees only her difference from herself. By making Roger, the origin and goal of Molly's entry into the symbolic order, into a figure for the mother who precedes and resists that order (and Roger has been depicted as acting maternally toward Molly earlier in the novel), Gaskell seems to allow Molly both mothers at once. Placed in this final scene between the figurative mother who epitomizes the liberation of signifiers from any determinate meaning and a figure who promises Molly both the advantages of that freedom (adult heterosexual love) and the values of the prior relation to the mother, Molly would seem to be slated to get everything that it is within the power and position of a nineteenth-century daughter to get, all the possibilities combined that for Gaskell's other ambivalent daughters are mutually exclusive alternatives.

Yet this resolution of a daughter's conflict, the "everything" she seems to get, is not as rich or full as Gaskell would have it appear. That it is a man, Roger, who represents the values of the presymbolic mother emphasizes painfully that that mother is dead from the beginning of the novel, her function assumed first by another dying woman and then by Molly's father. Although I have been arguing for an important distinction between Molly's own mother and her stepmother in relation to the languages they each give to Molly, we have also noted that the traces of a presymbolic or maternal language have been found only, as in all Gaskell's writing, in a daughter's transmission of paternal words. Indeed, the fact that Molly's mother, no less than her stepmother, has been transformed into a mirror suggests that with respect to a patriarchal culture's appropriations of them, they do not differ from each other as much as they differ together from the lively, responsive, maternal mirroring to which Roger's and Molly's final gestures so tantalizingly allude. Moreover, the fact that Molly's mother was herself (as we learn in the episode of Coxe's letter) a substitute for Mr. Gibson's first love, Jeanie, makes her only one more in the chain of substitutive objects of desire that end with Cynthia's mother. This resemblance between the two mothers also compromises the opposing values I have been claiming for them, since the literal, presymbolic language of the dead mother is thus contained within the frame of the living one's symbolic language. Thus while it seems that Molly is an ambivalent daughter who nonetheless need not feel torn between her loyalties, this potential conflict is resolved only by its having been displaced and covered up. The mother to whom Molly's final gesture expresses its loyalty was never really there to begin with. She had already left Molly to a life in one place or another within a symbolic order emptied of her consoling and troubling presence.

The scene of Molly's waving out the window to Roger is still more complex than at first appears, however, for it forms a part of Gaskell's consideration of her own relation to prior texts. As we have seen, Gaskell appears to take up Molly's role as selfless messenger when she herself quotes male poets, although her twisting these quotations to her own ends resembles more closely Mrs. Gibson's free way of detaching quotations from their original meanings. If Molly's way with language is that of a father's good daughter (even if her repetition of the father's words is also her way of affirming her tie to her mother), then Mrs. Gibson's practice suggests a way of turning the patrilineal order against itself. And yet the very liberties Mrs. Gibson takes with language place her all the more squarely within the frame of the symbolic order. She is a man's woman, constructed as an object of desire, and her sense of the slippage of meaning along a chain of signification, however much it irritates Mr. Gibson, is precisely what placed her before him to begin with as a substitute along the chain of his desire. Within the thematics of the novel, she stands for women's accepting, if not a daughter's, a wife's place in a patrilineal order. Thus any form of quotation from male texts, whether by a daughter or by a wife, reaffirms women's place somewhere within the requirements of androcentric writing.

Yet Gaskell alludes frequently in *Wives and Daughters*, not only to male poets, but also to the works of Charlotte Brontë, especially to *Jane Eyre*. In her literary practice in the *Life of Charlotte Brontë* and in the thematics of her stories, for a woman to carry another woman's letters, especially her mother's, is both to identify with her and to incur intervention and punishment from patriarchal authority, to affirm a relationship that is inextricable from the threat of its own denial. Brontë is not strictly speaking a mother figure for Gaskell—Gaskell was six years the elder—in the way that Wordsworth or Milton stand in the place of a literary father, yet Brontë's literary fame preceded and always exceeded Gaskell's. Brontë, for example, delayed the publication of *Villette* by a month so as not to interfere with the sales and reputation of Gaskell's *Ruth*, which appeared in January 1853. How do Gaskell's allusions to Brontë reflect the thematic situation of mothers and daughters in this novel, and how do they reflect the myth of the daughter's language that the novel articulates?

The scene of Molly's waving to Roger echoes very distantly Jane Eyre's dream of climbing the crumbling battlements of Thornfield Hall to catch a final glimpse of vanishing Rochester (*Jane Eyre*, chap. 25). We would probably not recognize the similarity if the scene did not also recall an earlier scene in *Wives and Daughters* that more directly alludes to the same scene in *Jane Eyre*. After saying goodbye to Roger the first time he leaves (after his proposal to Cynthia), "numb to the heart" and "stunned," Molly runs up to an attic window facing the street to get one last sight of him. She has to tug hard at the window to open it, and in her frustration she sounds very much like the passionate Jane (and also, distantly, like the ghost of the Cathy who "will get in!" in *Wuthering Heights*): "'I must see him again; I must! I must!' she wailed out, as she was pulling." She sees him turn to look at Cynthia, at a downstairs window, but she herself "had drawn back when he turned, and kept herself in shadow; for she had no right to put herself forward as the one to watch and yearn for farewell signs" (chap. 34). Her desire for Roger is almost as explicit as Jane's for Rochester, and equally illicit, but unlike Jane she recognizes and acts on the impropriety of her feelings. When Molly waves to Roger from the drawingroom window, in her own right this time, and waves at him in a way that makes him a mother figure, it is as if Gaskell were signaling to the literary mother she constructs for herself in Brontë, but a version of Brontë that has been made morally more acceptable. Gaskell begins correcting Brontë and her heroine at the start of the novel. It is Molly's governess, the very proper Miss Eyre, who teaches Molly to read and write, though Mr. Gibson asks her not to "teach Molly too much," for "many a good woman gets married with only a cross instead of her name" (chap. 3). This new Miss Eyre, as servile to paternal law as any governess could be, "tried honestly to keep her back," although Molly reads endlessly on her own. Moreover, the novel's central plot, the consequences of Mr. Gibson's marrying to get a chaperone for Molly, takes its start from the fact that this Miss Eyre, unlike Jane, never considers marrying her employer.

Although Molly's Miss Eyre is as unlike the original one as possible, as a child Molly herself behaves as rebelliously as Jane Eyre, but with an important difference. When Miss Eyre either timidly or decorously puts up with the jealous abuse of Betty, the servant who has mothered Molly until her arrival, "the girl flew out in such a violent passion of words in defence of her silent trembling governess, that even Betty herself was daunted" (chap. 3). The description recalls the opening episode of *Jane Eyre*, in which Jane, having defended herself against her cousin's violent assault, is called by her aunt "a picture of passion" and "a fury." The character of Molly is thus constituted as a defense of this new and obedient Miss Eyre, for Molly herself, unlike Jane, will learn to restrain her "violent passion." Gaskell thus transmits and reforms Brontë's plot and Brontë's heroine in her own text, exploring the consequences of such a governess acting properly. Her heroine and the heroine's governess divide the task of presenting a far milder version of Jane's passionate character.

That it is Miss Eyre who teaches Molly in so limiting a way to read and write encodes the idea that *Jane Eyre* taught Gaskell to write *Wives and Daughters*. Paradoxically, however, the *Jane Eyre* that instructs Gaskell is a *Jane Eyre* of Gaskell's own devising, the more conservative rendering of the novel Gaskell writes into her own. Yet there really is no contradiction in saying that it is Gaskell's revision that teaches Gaskell, for her adaptation of *Jane Eyre* exposes, rather than invents, the paternal law within it. Jane's seemingly revolutionary spirit, Gaskell suggests, is really only the servility of Miss Eyre. If all that Miss Eyre teaches is what the father permits her to teach—and if Molly must get most of her education from her own reading—Gaskell is suggesting that the *Jane Eyre* that taught her is that aspect of Brontë's writing that has already made its compact with the father's law, its agreement to subscribe to the father's view of women and the feminine. For example, *Jane Eyre* shares the symbolic order's distaste for literal reproduction. Gaskell repeats the farewell dream scene from *Jane Eyre* three times (the third occurs when Cynthia waves goodbye to Molly from the attic before Cynthia leaves to get married), a repetition that above all affirms the connection between two women writers, as if between mother and daughter, apart from patriarchy. Yet this is superseded by the subordination of all Gaskell's quotations to paternal requirements. Inviting Victorian morals to intervene between them, Gaskell repeats Brontë in the way that daughters carry their mothers' words and letters in Gaskell's stories, with dependence upon the paternal intervention that both joins and separates them. And yet that intervention had already taken place, the father's word was there from the start, and the revised Brontë is revealed to be the real Brontë, if Miss Eyre, or a novel called *Jane Eyre*, was teaching Gaskell only according to the father's law. Gaskell's stories affirm the dependence of any language shared by a mother and a daughter on its containment within patriarchal power, and from this author we would not expect a relation to a literary mother of any other sort. If a daughter's ambivalent division of loyalty between the mother's literal and father's symbolic order reflects a woman author's ambivalent division of loyalty between matrilineal and patrilineal inheritances, what Gaskell inherits from Brontë is already part of the paternal order. When Molly waves out the window at the novel's end, the sense of a choice collapses. Gaskell waves lovingly to Brontë as a daughter mirrors herself in her mother, but only when and because that mother has silently been replaced by a man.

Postscript:
Mother and Daughters in Virginia Woolf's
Victorian Novel

Arriving late for Mrs. Ramsay's dinner party, having just become engaged to be married and having at the same time lost her grandmother's brooch, Minta Doyle finds herself called a goose by Mr. Ramsay. The narrative continues, explicating the moment's sexual code:

> The first night when she had sat by him, and he talked about George Eliot, she had been really frightened, for she had left the third volume of *Middlemarch* in the train and she never knew what happened in the end; but afterwards she got on perfectly, and made herself out even more ignorant than she was, because he liked telling her she was a fool. And so tonight, directly he laughed at her, she was not frightened. Besides, she knew, directly she came into the room that the miracle had happened; she wore her golden haze. Sometimes she had it; sometimes not. . . . Yes, tonight she had it, tremendously; she knew that by the way Mr. Ramsay told her not to be a fool. She sat beside him, smiling. (*To the Lighthouse*, pp. 148–49)

To be called a fool by a man like Mr. Ramsay is to have achieved the only power—temporary and illusory at best, deriving from self-denigration—that, in Woolf's analysis, a woman can expect to enjoy within the conventions of Victorian heterosexual relations. For Mr. Ramsay, sexual attraction requires an imbalance of power, and Minta intuitively knows that her foolishness—feigned or genuine—helps to confer on her the "golden haze" of desirability. But why should losing her grandmother's brooch and leaving the last volume of *Middlemarch* in the train be the particular acts of foolishness with which Minta purchases so compromised a success? These details suggest that a woman must deny, not only her rationality and intelligence, but also her maternal heritage. Though she perhaps did not intend to leave the last volume of Middlemarch on the train, this event appears to have taken place in an indefinite past prior to her visit to the Ramsays, and we are to assume that she might at some later point have replaced her loss. She does not take herself seriously as a reader, and she does not take Eliot seriously. Her obligatory coyness with Mr. Ramsay requires that she deny her own intelligence and, as well, that of Woolf's literary ancestress.

The juxtaposition of Middlemarch with a grandmother's brooch recalls the opening scene of that novel, in which, as we have seen, Dorothea's confused response to her mother's jewels introduces the compromise that she—like other Eliot heroines—will have to make between unwomanly aspirations and the limited scope available to her because of her gender. Where the mother is reduced to her things, to things themselves, her daughter is induced to reject that heritage in favor of the father's, and Woolf appears to regret this situation. But the abandonment of the volume of Middlemarch equally recalls Maggie Tulliver's refusal of a loan of the second volume of The Pirate; she had begun the novel once but stopped at the point where it seemed inevitable that the dark heroine, Minna, would lose out to the blonde one, just as in Corinne, which she also refuses to finish. As U. C. Knoepflmacher has pointed out, Woolf disparages the last volume of Middlemarch for similar reasons: she writes that Eliot characterizes Dorothea as "seeking wisdom and finding one scarcely knows what in marriage with Ladislaw. . . . There is no doubt that [her heroines] bring out the worst of her, . . . make her self-conscious, didactic, and occasionally vulgar."[1] With its celebration of conventional marriage, the end of Middlemarch, like Corinne and The Pirate, offers its female inheritors a debilitating training in the kind of costly bargain Minta makes. Minta's gesture, then, embodies Woolf's ambivalence about the idea of a maternal heritage. On the one hand, Woolf disapproves of Minta's devaluation of mothers— especially of one of Woolf's literary mothers—in the interest of gaining the father's approval. On the other hand, Minta's abandonment of the end of Middlemarch suggests that Woolf celebrates the abandonment of the mother as purveyor of the conventional female fate.[2]

In A Room of One's Own, celebrating the value of a women's literary tradition and of her own heritage of strong ancestresses, Woolf exhorts women writers to "think back through our mothers."[3] And yet as Jane Marcus points out, the women in Woolf's family were "collaborators in their own oppression."[4] Woolf's literary ancestresses, too, offered her at best an ambiguous heritage, whose drawbacks she if anything exaggerates. In *A Room of One's Own,* Woolf's account of literary women in history does as much to take away their accomplishments as it does to celebrate their courage. In "Professions for Women" she writes of how, in order to write, she herself had to kill the "Angel in the House," that Victorian matron who "excelled in the difficult arts of family life," "sacrificed herself daily," and insisted that women "must charm, they must conciliate, they must—to put it bluntly—tell lies if they are to succeed."[5] Minta Doyle, lying about her intelligence in order to please Mr. Ramsay, has learned the Angel's lesson. The Angel in *To the Lighthouse,* who presides over Minta's engagement and thus also over the novel's other heterosexual contracts, is Mrs. Ramsay, but Mrs. Ramsay also embodies the enormous positive value Woolf finds in "think[ing] back through our mothers." Mrs. Ramsay is Woolf's summary of nineteenth-century ideologies of motherhood, and the novel embodies Woolf's ambivalence about Victorian mothers. At the same time, as the daughter of a Victorian mother and of a Victorian tradition of literary women, Woolf uses the novel to speculate about what it means to write as the daughter of such mothers. The novel raises in a new and more explicit way the questions we have been tracing about the place of a mother-daughter relationship in literary discourse. Does the daughter need to imitate the son, as Nelly Dean does, and distance the mother in order to speak? Or is a different paradigm possible, one that would acknowledge the value of a mother-daughter relation outside the law? Does Woolf's idea of a woman's art require the death of the mother? Or does it rather depend on her continued life? In particular, Woolf asks, does representation require the mother's death, making nonrepresentational art preferable? Or can representation be reclaimed for mothers and daughters?

Like Romola, Mrs. Ramsay is an ideally beautiful madonna figure. For Mr. Bankes, watching Lily paint them, she and her son amount to "mother and child then—objects of universal veneration" (p. 81). Like Romola reading to her father and to her stepson stories endorsing the exclusion of women, she reads to James a story about the dangers of women's desires. She selflessly tends her family and the poor and sick, and she too serves an egotistical scholar. In this role, Mrs. Ramsay arouses both skepticism and admiration, just as it is both appropriate and inappropriate for Minta to leave *Middlemarch* on the trian.

As a mother, however, Mrs. Ramsay also embodies both Western culture's fear of the mother who is identified with nature and the literal and some daughters' rebellious love of this mother. Her civilizing work—the creation of the house and of the social relations that thrive there—is destroyed by nature in "Time Passes," yet she is also "a rosy-flowered

fruit tree laid with leaves and dancing boughs" (p. 60). As Maria DiBattista argues, she is identified, through "this mania of hers for marriage"
and reproduction (p. 261), with the vitality and the relentless forces of
nature.[6] And as Gayatri Spivak points out, Mrs. Ramsay sees the marriages she sponsors as specifically continuing her maternal line.[7] Paradoxically, her matchmaking and her association with nature make her
both the Angel in the House and her reverse, someone like the "withered
hag" Cathy imagines Nelly will become in fifty years. The history of her
daughter Prue most succinctly exposes the ambiguity of the appeal for
her daughters of Mrs. Ramsay's alliance with nature. Aspiring to repeat
her mother's life, Prue reproduces only a reduced version of her mother's
reproductive history, because for Prue, as for Cathy, childbirth leads
directly to death. As a figure for Mother Nature, Mrs. Ramsay summarizes both the nature that Cathy suicidally loves and remains loyal to and
the nature that Lockwood and Jane Eyre fear. She is both the loved body
of a daughter's mother and the feared body of a son's (or male-identified
daughter's) mother.

Through this woman with her "core of darkness," Woolf reconsiders
the Victorian novel's ambivalence about the possibility that the mother is
beyond or prior to language. This is clear, for example, in "The Window," which ends with her triumphant resistance to speech:

> He wanted something—wanted the thing she always found it so
> difficult to give him; wanted her to tell him that she loved him. And
> that, no, she could not do. . . . As she looked at him she began to
> smile, for though she had not said a word, he knew, of course he
> knew, that she loved him. He could not deny it. And smiling she
> looked out of the window and said (thinking to herself, Nothing on
> earth can equal this happiness)—
> "Yes, you were right. It's going to be wet tomorrow. You won't
> be able to go." And she looked at him smiling. For she had tri-
> umphed again. She had not said it: yet he knew. (pp. 184–86)

Perhaps, like Minta, she deludes herself in thinking that by depriving
herself of language she has gained her power over him, for she
"triumphs" only while speaking words that concede his real authority
over nature and over her. On the other hand, Woolf makes it equally
possible that this is a genuine triumph. If words distance their referents,
then not to represent her love is to keep it present and alive. Her
inconsequential words, which bear so slight and tangential a relation to
her thought, operate like the words she shares with Cam after the dinner
party: they resist representation and instead create a present relation. She

stands for both the danger and the value of a woman's adherence to the literal. Like Molly Gibson's dead mother and Mrs. Hamley in *Wives and Daughters*, she initially authorizes a daughter's nonsymbolic discourse yet offers her a deceptive promise, for the mother-daughter relation was from the beginning incorporated within the law. Mrs. Ramsay talks Cam to sleep as movingly and subversively as she does only because she has yielded to James's fetishization of the horned skull, just as the first Mrs. Gibson and as Mrs. Hamley authorize a language whose function is to transmit men's words.

The novel constructs its paradigms of the relation of a daughter's art to the mother on all these ambiguous aspects of Mrs. Ramsay. We will begin by looking at Cam's relation to language as a story about the daughter as artist, since it was with her exchange with Mrs. Ramsay that we initially posited a mother-daughter language existing outside the law of representation. Because "she and James shared the same tastes" (p. 86), Mrs. Ramsay welcomes the departure of "that wild villain, Cam" (p. 83) when she is reading to James. Yet although Mrs. Ramsay, like Romola and Nelly Dean, in this way identifies her interests as a narrator with those of patriarchy, she also understands and sympathizes with her daughter: she invites Cam to leave, "knowing that Cam was attracted only by the word 'Flounder'" (p. 86). Like other daughters who live outside the law—notably the first Cathy, the second Cathy as a child, and Lizzie Leigh—she loves the sounds of words for themselves, especially insofar as they guarantee the mother's presence. It is this understanding that Mrs. Ramsay again displays when she talks her daugher to sleep after the dinner party. Another scene recalls and reverses the scene of the second Cathy's entry into the law: Cam "was picking Sweet Alice on the bank. She was wild and fierce. She would not 'give a flower to the gentleman' as the nursemaid told her. No! no! no! she would not! She clenched her fist. She stamped" (p. 36). Cathy Linton at age seventeen won't pick a flower because she has learned to read nature symbolically; Cam picks flowers but, herself interchangeable with flowers bearing a girl's name, refuses to bend either nature or herself to a man's will.

"That wild villain, Cam, dashing past" reincarnates, not only one of "the Kings and Queens of England; Cam the Wicked" (p. 37), but also Virgil's Camilla, the warrior whose history is recounted and who dies fighting against Aeneas in book 11 of *The Aeneid*. Camilla's most striking feature is her speed:

> If she ran full speed
> Over the tips of grain unharvested
> She would not ever have bruised an ear, or else

She might have sprinted on the deep sea swell
And never dipped her flying feet.[8]

Of her own speeding outlaw Woolf writes,

> Cam grazed the easel by an inch; . . . she would not stop for her
> father, whom she grazed also by an inch; nor for her mother, who
> called "Cam! I want you a moment!" as she dashed past. She was
> off like a bird, bullet, or arrow, impelled by what desire, shot by
> whom, at what directed, who could say? What, what? Mrs. Ram-
> say pondered, watching her. It might be a vision—of a shell, of a
> wheelbarrow, of a fairy kingdom on the far side of the hedge; or it
> might be the glory of speed; no one knew. (pp. 83–84)

When the motherless Camilla was a child, her father saved her life by
binding her to a spear and hurling her across a river; Woolf continues,
"But when Mrs. Ramsay called 'Cam!' a second time, the projectile
dropped in mid career, and Cam came lagging back, pulling a leaf by the
way, to her mother." Both Cam and Camilla are "projectiles," yet where
Camilla is hurled by her father, Cam is impelled by an unrepresentable
force, and ends with her mother. Reluctant to join a mother who represents the law, Cam also knows her mother's sympathy with female
outlawry.

Virgil has his Camilla die of "a girl's love of finery": she is distracted in
battle by her desire for an enemy's beautiful clothes, succumbing like
Dorothea Brooke to the beauty of her mother's jewels, as if the mother's
heritage were only the trivia of decoration. Woolf, by contrast, values
and so redefines the mother's heritage, allowing Cam's return to her
mother to be played out at the end of the novel in a highly favorable way.
Toward the end of the voyage, Cam, looking back at the distant, small
island, sleepily repeats to herself the words her mother spoke after the
dinner party:

> All those paths and terraces and bedrooms were fading and dis-
> appearing, and nothing was left but a pale blue censer swinging
> rhythmically this way and that across her mind. It was a hanging
> garden; it was a valley, full of birds, and flowers, and ante-
> lopes. . . . She was falling asleep. (p. 303)[9]

Cam has not lost her childhood "parrot-like instinct" to repeat words "in
a colourless singsong" (p. 85). This reproduction of her mother's words
marks a turning point in the voyage, for it is when Cam wakes up in the

next paragraph that Mr. Ramsay has changed from mournful romantic quester to distributor of sandwiches. Although she earlier in the voyage also repeats her father's words—"she murmured, dreamily half asleep, how we perished, each alone" (p. 284)—and although she yields to her father's demand for her sympathy, the mother has the last word. In the masculine, military world of *The Aeneid*, to choose the mother is to die (as it would be also in *Jane Eyre*, when Jane is tempted to seek the embrace of Mother Nature), while in Woolf's novel a girl can choose to remain the daughter of her mother, to repeat her, and stay alive.

What does it mean for Cam to repeat her mother's words in this way? When we considered the original passage, we saw how "valleys and flowers and bells ringing and birds singing and little goats and antelopes" did not signify referential objects (either the antelopes they seem to denominate or the boar's skull for which they appear to be metaphors) but rather constituted a link, through nonrepresentational sounds, between the mother's body and her daughter's. That Cam repeats these words with reference to an entirely different object, the distant island, confirms that they are nonrepresentational: they have as little to do with an island as with any other referent, for their function is instead comfortingly to recall the mother. And Cam succeeds, for the spirit of Mrs. Ramsay now appears to enter the boat and join her husband.

But Cam is not the artist in the novel, and it is not her relation to language and the mother that the novel adduces as its principle paradigm for its own practice. We will want to consider why, after taking a look at the complex relation between Lily Briscoe's art and the life and death of so ambiguous a mother as Mrs. Ramsay. While Mr. Bankes sees Mrs. Ramsay as the Madonna, Lily shocks him by reducing "the significance of mother and son" to a purple shadow, to an effect of "how a light there needed a shadow there" (p. 262). Compared to Mr. Bankes's notion of art, Lily's picture does not victimize Mrs. Ramsay through representation: "But the picture was not of them, she said" (p. 81). It takes the mother and child as its pretext, but it does not freeze them as a representational painting would, and especially it does not subordinate Mrs. Ramsay to the Christian denial, through the notion of Mary's virginity, of the mother's body. After Mrs. Ramsay's death, Mr. Ramsay will accept almost any woman as a substitute for her: indiscriminately, he demands sympathy from all the women in his vicinity, even from Lily, who resembles Mrs. Ramsay solely in gender. Women are for Mr. Ramsay, as they are for Lockwood, a signifying chain, and one will do almost as well as another. His loss only confirms and darkens his role as romantic quester ("we perished, each alone"). By contrast, Lily responds to Mrs. Ramsay's death by really wanting her, and only her, back again.

For her, Mrs. Ramsay is irreplaceable, and representation is wholly inadequate for the purposes of recovering her.

> Little words that broke up the thought and dismembered it said nothing. . . . Words fluttered sideways and struck the object inches too low. . . . For how could one express in words these emotions of the body? express that emptiness there? (She was looking at the drawing-room steps; they looked extraordinarily empty.) It was one's body feeling, one's mind. The physical sensations that went with the bare look of the steps had become suddenly extremely unpleasant. To want and not to have, sent all up her body a hardness, a hollowness, a strain. And then to want and not to have—to want and want—how that wrung the heart, and wrung it again and again! Oh, Mrs. Ramsay! she called out silently. (pp. 265–66)

That Lily, in contrast to Mr. Ramsay, experiences Mrs. Ramsay's loss with such particularity and as a physical sensation exemplifies the difference we have hypothesized between a daughter's and a son's relation to the mother: Lily wants to reproduce her, and wants to reproduce a relation to a present body, while Mr. Ramsay wants to replace or represent her.

This difference leads us to expect that Lily's art would seek not to represent but rather to reproduce Mrs. Ramsay. But Lily's paintings are as different from Cam's reproduction of her mother's nonrepresentational words as they are from the Raphael madonnas that Mr. Bankes has in mind. The shapes on Lily's canvas do not represent Mrs. Ramsay in any conventional sense, but they do represent the shapes of light and shadow made by Mrs. Ramsay's body. Quite possibly, Woolf wants us to see that Lily's painting is representational, if only in a subtler way than Raphael's. She does not simply create abstract patterns on her canvas; she paints out of doors and she is irritated if something or someone changes the composition that she is painting. Moreover, when Lily paints in Mrs. Ramsay's presence, she is unable to complete her painting; only after Mrs. Ramsay's death does she manage to finish successfully. What most tellingly distinguishes Cam from Lily is that Lily's art still depends upon memory. While Cam in her inability to remember the points of the compass reproduces Mrs. Ramsay (Mr. Ramsay thinks, "It had been so with her—his wife. They could not keep anything clearly fixed in their minds" [p. 249]), Lily's second painting does require the memory of the mother and therefore her absence. Just as Lily must reject Mrs. Ramsay's Victorian values and her beauty, it is only through her efforts to remember Mrs. Ramsay that she can solve the problem of her picture. "She went on tunnelling her way into her picture, into the past. . . . So much depends, she thought, up on distance" (pp. 258, 284). In the course of remembering Mrs. Ramsay, Lily thinks, "she did not want Mrs. Ramsay now" (p. 290), for her memory substitutes fullness for emptiness. When Lily sees the phantom kitchen table lodged in the fork of the pear tree at the beginning of the novel, she does, as I have claimed, restore the mother's presence, but only relatively. Her vision in a different sense depends on the referent's absence, for like the hero of *Alastor* or Brontë's Heathcliff, she superimposes her projection onto the present reality of the tree. When the phantom Mrs. Ramsay, "a sense of some one there," appears in response to Lily's crying out her name, as much as it may inscribe a new and female kind of restoration, it may equally reinscribe the romantic pattern, the return as figuration of "someone like the mother." If Lily's art is modeled on a son's, then Lily's version of Mrs. Ramsay is indeed madonna-like, for the final form of her angelic selflessness is her death, which makes possible the completion of a work of art.[10] Having coaxed the daughter by the seductive promise of her own presence into serving instead the father, Mrs. Ramsay vanishes, leaving an absence on which a work of art may be constructed. Cam's repetition of her mother's words reproduces her by placing Cam in her mother's place, speaking with her words, while Lily's project inevitably courts the dangers of representation. As in *Wuthering Heights*, the daughter who is most fiercely loyal to the mother is also the least likely to be or to stand for the artist.

Woolf's own practice in writing the novel shares the ambiguities of Lily's art. Although *To the Lighthouse* seems to favor the possibilities of nonrepresentational art and holds out the possibility that Lily's painting avoids at least some of the pitfalls of representation, we cannot see the painting. (Did Woolf make her artist figure a painter and not a poet so as to make it impossible for her art to enter the boundaries of the novel?) What Woolf provides instead is a representational account of the painting, together with Lily's reconstruction of Mrs. Ramsay through the representational words of her memory. And Lily's long retrospect occupies far more of the novel's time than does the account of her painting. Moreover, her retrospect is synonymous with Woolf's: writing an elegy for her parents, Woolf, like Lily, creates a fullness with memory that depends upon the parents' deaths. It is well known that in a quite literal sense Woolf felt her becoming a writer at all depended on the deaths of parents whose lives told her, in different ways, as Charles Tansley tells Lily, "Women can't paint, women can't write" (p. 75).

Why does Woolf persist in the representational project? Why doesn't she go beyond the linguistic practice that she criticizes? Why can't Cam's way with words, instead of Lily's, model the novelist's own practice? Perhaps the situation is a consequence of her writing a novel about the Victorian family. It may be that Woolf embodies her criticism of the Victorian family—and of its effects on its daughters—in the effect it has on her own practice, by having such a family produce such a relation to language. Although in *The Waves* Woolf's language does become more like Cam's, when Woolf writes about the fate of Victorian life she typically writes about, not in, a voice like Cam's. For example, at the end of *Between the Acts*, Miss La Trobe recovers from her play and begins to envision the next one:

> She raised her glass to her lips. And drank. And listened. Words of one syllable sank down into the mud. She drowsed; she nodded. The mud became fertile. Words rose above the intolerably laden dumb oxen plodding through the mud. Words without meaning— wonderful words.[11]

Like *To the Lighthouse*, *Between the Acts* is largely concerned to critique Victorian England. If La Trobe's last play has been composed of the "scraps, orts and fragments" of English literary history, perhaps the next one will break free altogether from history and from representational language, and liberate words from meaning. "Words without meaning— wonderful words" comes closest to describing the language of Mrs. Ramsay's lullaby, the language that Cam recalls at the end of the voyage: a language that embodies the maternal ("the mud became fertile") and makes it present by reproducing it, not by representing it. Yet such a language is imagined as coming into being only beyond the frame of the text, just as Cam's language never materializes as a paradigm for the novelist's language. Given the dilemmas of Victorian daughters, even such powerfully marginal ones as Lily, La Trobe, and Woolf herself, representation remains the given medium.[12]

Perhaps, alternatively, Woolf would redefine representation to reappropriate it for female experience, just as Lily, adopting some of the son's strategies, yet creating an art that at least refuses to victimize the mother actively, extends the limits of what a daughterly artist can do. To adhere at least in part to representational language is Woolf's way of honoring the father and the mother at once.[13] But it is also a symptom of the reasonable scepticism Woolf conveys about the value of throwing her lot entirely in with her maternal inheritance. After all, for Cam to repeat her mother's words may embody a revolutionary and potentially antipatriarchal way of using language, yet the mother who is re-presenced in this way is highly problematic from the point of view of Woolf's social criticism. For Cam to repeat her mother as she does also means for her to repeat her mother's submissiveness toward Mr. Ramsay: Cam, as a number of readers have pointed out, takes Mrs. Ramsay's place as the mediator between James and Mr. Ramsay.[14] Repeating her mother's gestures in "The Window," she gives her father what he wants, to James's dismay. If Cam's ability to reproduce her mother tongue ends only in her becoming an Angel in the House, then the promise for liberating women's language that this mother-daughter language seemed to hold out will not, after all, have been fulfilled. As when she has Minta Doyle leave *Middlemarch* on the train, Woolf resents and distances the mother's Victorian legacy, while she also attempts to revalue and recover a different maternal heritage, the mother's body and the new relations its presence makes possible.[15]

This book has attempted to show that the representational project, inevitable for Victorian women novelists, brings with it what all of these writers in one way or another acknowledge to be inherent limitations for the evocation of female experience. Woolf, like the nineteenth-century novelists considered here, but more self-consciously, experiments with a different literary practice that would value women as the literal and as bearers of words, a literary practice associated with the early experience of daughters with their mothers. Yet this literary practice too has its limitations because androcentric culture controls, not merely the daughter's perception of the mother, but also her very construction. The questions remain for Woolf as I believe they remain for us: is it, at the very least, possible to stop excluding and killing the mother for the sake of representation's projects? And can the mother and the linguistic practices she and her daughters can share, tainted as they are by the patriarchal culture with which they are intertwined and by which they come into being, be recuperated for gynocentric, perhaps even for feminist, projects? I end this book with H.D.'s promise that a book borne by a woman can be used for writing something new:[16]

> She carries a book but it is not
> the tome of ancient wisdom,
>
> the pages, I imagine, are the blank pages
> of the unwritten volume of the new;
> . . . .
> I grant you her face was innocent
>
> and immaculate and her veils
> like the Lamb's Bride

but the Lamb was not with her,
either as Bridegroom or Child;

her attention is undivided,
we are her bridegroom and lamb;

her book is our book; written
or unwritten . . .

Notes

Preface

1. Elaine Showalter, "Feminist Criticism in the Wilderness," *Critical Inquiry* 8 (1981): 197 (the essay discusses this concept throughout, pp. 179–205). I am using "North American" and "French," it should be clear, as tropes for two general categories of feminist literary criticism that are by no means restricted to their respective nations of origin and that by no means divide the totality of feminist literary criticism, but that seem to me to generate between them one of the most interesting debates in literary criticism of any sort. For a fuller discussion of this critical debate, see Elaine Marks, "Women and Literature in France," *Signs* 3 (1978): 832–42; Mary Jacobus, "The Difference of View," in *Women Writers and Writing about Women*, ed. Mary Jacobus (Totowa, N. J.: Barnes and Noble, 1979), pp. 10–21; Alice Jardine, "Pre-Texts for the Transatlantic Feminist," *Yale French Studies* 62 (1981): 220–36, and *Gynesis: Configurations of Women and Modernity* (Ithaca: Cornell University Press, 1985).

2. In a fuller account of "French" feminism, it would be important to distinguish among many, very different positions, critical and uncritical. Luce Irigaray, for example, has devoted much of her writing to critiquing Lacan, Freud, and the phallocentric tradition of which they are part, in which "any theory of the subject has always been appropriated by the 'masculine'" (Irigaray, *Speculum of the Other Woman* (1974), trans. Gillian C. Gill [Ithaca: Cornell University Press, 1985], p. 133). And she has also written of the need to resurrect the mother. For the purposes of the simple distinction I am making here, however, it would be fair to say that all the "French" feminists agree with Lacan's analysis that gender is a construction of language, and wish (to varying degrees) to see what he analyzes change; whereas "North American" feminists would disagree with that analysis itself.

3. For Peggy Kamuf, for example, the "signature" is unimportant and even misleading (see "Writing Like a Woman," in *Women and Language in Literature*

and Society, eds. Sally McConnell-Ginet, Ruth Borker, and Nelly Furman [New York: Praeger, 1980], pp. 284–99).

4. Patricia Meyer Spacks, "The Difference It Makes," in *A Feminist Perspective in the Academy,* ed. Elizabeth Langland and Walter Gove (Chicago: University of Chicago Press, 1981), p. 14.

Chapter 1

1. Virginia Woolf, *To the Lighthouse* (New York: Harcourt Brace, 1927), p. 38. Subsequent quotations are from this edition and are cited in the text by page number.

2. Christine Froula summarizes her argument thus: "Milton's nativity scenes . . . reveal that the repression of the mother is the genesis of Genesis" ("When Eve Reads Milton: Undoing the Canonical Economy," *Critical Inquiry* 10 [1983]: 337). Mary Jacobus's speculations about the "appropriation" or "elimination" of women in literary and psychoanalytic theory helped to shape my argument here. See "Is There a Woman in This Text?" *New Literary History* 14 (1982): 117–41.

3. Luce Irigaray, *Le Corps-à-corps avec la mère* (Ottawa: Pleine Lune, 1981), pp. 15–16; translations from this text are mine.

4. Ibid., p. 17.

5. Aeschylus, *The Eumenides,* trans. Richmond Lattimore (Chicago: University of Chicago Press, 1953), p. 158.

6. William Wordsworth, *The Prelude: 1799, 1805, 1850,* ed. Jonathan Wordsworth, M.H. Abrams, and Stephen Gill (New York: Norton, 1979); quotations in this chapter are from the 1850 text, book 2, cited by line numbers.

7. John Milton, *Paradise Lost* 7. 281. Shakespeare draws on the same set of associations when he has Hamlet ask, "Mother, what's the matter?" (*Hamlet* 3. 4. 9), with the suggestion that it is precisely his mother's (and all women's) "matter" or physicality that is "the matter." (I am grateful to Margaret Ferguson for pointing this out.) On the traditional association of women with nature, see for example Sherry Ortner, "Is Female to Male as Nature is to Culture?" in *Women, Culture, and Society,* ed. Michelle Zimbalist Rosaldo and Louise Lamphere (Stanford: Stanford University Press, 1974), pp. 67–87.

8. In her discussion of using psychoanalysis to understand prejudices about women's writing prior to the invention of psychoanalysis, Susan Suleiman helpfully puts the matter thus: "Psychoanalysis lent scientific prestige to a widespread cultural prejudice, reinforcing it and elevating it to the status of a 'natural' law" ("Writing and Motherhood," in *The (M)other Tongue: Essays in Feminist Psychoanalytic Interpretation,* ed. Shirley Nelson Garner, Claire Kahane, and Madelon Sprengnether [Ithaca: Cornell University Press, 1985], p. 360).

9. Luce Irigaray has also explored the implications of a feminist view of mother-daughter relations for Lacanian language, and vice versa, in *This Sex which Is Not One* (1977), trans. Catherine Porter with Carolyn Burke (Ithaca: Cornell University Press, 1985), as well as in "And the One Doesn't Stir without

the Other," trans. Hélène Vivienne Wenzel, *Signs* 7 (1981): 60–67. However, I privilege Chodorow here because in Irigaray's view, the mother is so wholly appropriated by androcentric culture that any relation to her daughter consists mainly in provoking the daughter's flight away from her to the symbolic. Right or wrong, Chodorow explores a terrain closer to that inhabited by the writers considered in this book.

In my argument, Chodorow—with her training as a social scientist—could be said to stand in for "North American" feminist critics, with their assumption that experience can be referentially represented, while Lacan and Lacanians share the opposite, "French," set of assumptions about language. Thus it is through this cross-mapping that I will specify what I consider to be the area of fruitful concatenation in the critical debate sketched in the Preface.

10. For the sketch of Lacanian language that follows, I am relying particularly on Lacan's essays "The Mirror Stage" and "The Signification of the Phallus," in *Ecrits: A Selection,* trans. Alan Sheridan (New York: Norton, 1977), pp. 1–7, 281–91, as well as on the essays collected in *Feminine Sexuality: Jacques Lacan and the école freudienne,* ed. Juliet Mitchell and Jacqueline Rose, trans. Jacqueline Rose (London: Macmillan, 1982). I am also relying on the following works by interpreters of Lacan, listed here because not all will be cited for quotations: Jacques Derrida, "The Purveyor of Truth," in *Yale French Studies* 52 (1975): 31–113; Terry Eagleton, *Literary Theory: An Introduction* (Minneapolis: University of Minnesota Press, 1983), pp. 151–93; Jane Gallop, *The Daughter's Seduction* (Ithaca: Cornell University Press, 1982); Luce Irigaray, *This Sex,* especially the essay "Cosi Fan Tutti" (as well as other texts by Irigaray, cited below); Julia Kristeva, *Desire in Language,* ed. Leon Roudiez, trans. Thomas Gora, Alice Jardine, and Leon Roudiez (New York: Columbia University Press, 1980); Anika Lemaire, *Jacques Lacan,* trans. David Macey (London: Routledge and Kegan Paul, 1977); Juliet Mitchell, *Psychoanalysis and Feminism* (New York: Random House, 1975), pp. 382–98; Joseph H. Smith and William Kerrigan, eds., *Interpreting Lacan*: vol. 6 of *Psychiatry and the Humanities* (New Haven: Yale University Press, 1983). These works are as important to this chapter as the works of Lacan himself, for my interest is not so much in Lacan himself as in the reception of his theories within the literary cultures of France, England, and the United States.

11. Kristeva, "From One Identity to Another," in *Desire in Language,* pp. 124–47.

12. Eagleton, *Literary Theory,* p. 166.

13. Ibid., p. 166.

14. Serge Leclaire, "Les elements en jeu dans une psychanalyse," *Cahiers pour l'Analyse,* no. 5 (1966); translated and quoted in Lemaire, *Jacques Lacan,* p. 145.

15. Lacan, *Ecrits,* pp. 287–88.

16. Eagleton, *Literary Theory,* pp. 167–68. See also Suleiman's account of Melanie Klein's theory of artistic creation, which also presupposes the mother's loss: "The creative writer . . . is impelled by the 'desire to re-discover the mother of the early days, whom [he] has lost actually or in [his] feelings.' The work of art

itself stands for the mother's body, destroyed repeatedly in fantasy but restored or 'repaired' in the act of creation" (Suleiman, "Writing and Motherhood," p. 357; she quotes Melanie Klein, "Love, Guilt, and Reparation," reprinted in *Love, Guilt, and Reparation and Other Works, 1921–1945* [New York: Doubleday, 1977], p. 334).

17. Lacan, "Du *Treib* de Freud et du désir du psychanalyste," in *Ecrits* (Paris: Seuil, 1966), pp. 851–54; this passage translated and quoted in Lemaire, *Jacques Lacan,* p. 164.

18. On this question see, most recently, Jardine, *Gynesis,* pp. 159–77.

19. Lacan, quoted in Irigaray, *This Sex,* p. 87; original in *Seminar XX: Encore* (Paris, 1975).

20. Nancy Chodorow, *The Reproduction of Mothering: Psychoanalysis and the Sociology of Gender* (Berkeley: University of California Press, 1978), p. 192 (italics hers). Future quotations from this book will be cited parenthetically by page number within the text. Jacobus suggestively analyses the substitution of a represented for a real woman in one of Freud's texts in "Is There a Woman in This Text?"

21. *Alastor,* line 206, in *Shelley's Poetry and Prose,* ed. Donald Reiman and Sharon Powers (New York: Norton, 1977). Other quotations from this work will be cited by line number within the text.

22. See Judith Herman, *Father-Daughter Incest* (Cambridge: Harvard University Press, 1981), especially chap. 4, pp. 50–63, where the condoning of incest is placed in a psychoanalytic framework.

23. Ellie Raglund-Sullivan, "Jacques Lacan: Feminism and the Problem of Gender Identity," *Sub-Stance* 36 (1982): 16. Because the daughter does not put a gap of difference between herself and her mother, she never experiences the loss and absence that would allow for full entry into the symbolic order. Jane Gallop also argues for the daughter's horror at entrapment within the mother's identity and the appeal of the father's difference and of the symbolic as relief from that entrapment in "The Monster in the Mirror: The Feminist Critic's Psychoanalysis," paper delivered at the English Institute, September 1983. A related point is Lacan's view that psychosis is the result of the excessive prolongation, for a child of either sex, of the "symbiotic union with the mother" (see John P. Muller, "Language, Psychosis, and the Subject in Lacan," in Smith and Kerrigan, *Interpreting Lacan,* pp. 21–32).

24. For Irigaray, it is precisely this "facelessness" of the mother that makes the daughter wish to flee identification with her and turn toward the father. ("And the One Doesn't Stir," p. 63).

25. On this danger Jane Gallop perceptively writes: "Belief in simple referentiality is . . . politically conservative, because it cannot recognize that the reality to which it appeals is a traditional ideological construction, whether one terms it phallomorphic, or metaphysical, or bourgeois, or something else. The politics of experience is inevitably a conservative politics for it cannot help but conserve traditional ideological constructs which are . . . taken for the 'real'" ("*Quand nos lèvres s'écrivent:* Irigaray's Body Politic," *Romantic Review* 74 [1983]: 83).

26. On the possibility that any appeal to truth only reinscribes androcentric

humanism and for a defense of the opposite view, see Peggy Kamuf, "Replacing Feminist Criticism," and Nancy Miller, "The Text's Heroine: A Feminist Critic and her Fictions," *Diacritics* 12 (1982): 42–47, 48–53. For related feminist considerations of deconstruction, see Barbara Johnson, "Gender Theory and the Yale School" *Genre* 17 (1984): 101–12, and Gayatri Spivak, "Love Me, Love My Ombre, Elle," *Diacritics* 14 (1984): 19–36.

27. Gayatri Spivak mentions that Woolf saw in Cam "a kind of pre-Oedipal girlhood," and she argues that Cam and James together "go through an Oedipal scene that involves both father *and* mother as givers of law and language," so as to revise Freud ("Making and Unmaking in *To the Lighthouse*," in *Women and Language in Literature and Society*, ed. Sally McConnell-Ginet, Ruth Borker, and Nelly Furman [New York: Praeger, 1980], p. 319.) I would agree that Woolf uses Cam to revise Freud, but not in the way that Spivak suggests; rather than offering Cam an oedipal scene to match her bother's, Woolf fills in the gaps in female psychohistory left by Freud's masculinist account. Spivak's general line of inquiry, however—about the relation between the languages of male philosopher and woman artist and the female object they both attempt to capture—was very suggestive for my own.

It is worth mentioning that this scene is usually read as being about Mrs. Ramsay's attempt to transform death (the skull) into life (a garden). See, for example, Avrom Fleishman, *Virginia Woolf: A Critical Reading* (Baltimore: Johns Hopkins University Press, 1975), pp. 119, 127; or Nancy Topping Bazin, *Virginia Woolf and the Androgynous Vision* (New Brunswick: Rutgers University Press, 1973), p. 133.

28. Kristeva, *Desire*, pp. 136, 142.

29. For example, responding to D. W. Winnicott's suggestion that in the analytic situation the analyst does well to recapitulate the reassuring "holding" the infant experiences with the mother, Kristeva writes that this project would only "repair" the "patient's narcissistic image." A better project is for the analyst to see "his own discourse as the *solder* of the signifying function in its logical, syntactical dimension." If he does so, "he can avoid making the cure a sinking into dependence (a reduction of the subject to the egoic or imaginary dynamic of the mother-child relation)" ("Within the Microcosm of 'The Talking Cure,' " in Smith and Kerrigan, *Interpreting Lacan*, p. 46).

30. Kristeva, *Desire*, pp. 34, 142.

31. This is the case in "And the One Doesn't Stir." Irigaray's text most compelling written both in (as much as possible, within the bounds of comprehensibility) and about a nonsymbolic discourse between two women who are each present to the other and who are both the same and different is "When Our Lips Speak Together" (*This Sex*, pp. 205–18), and in this text she specifically excludes the mother-daughter relation as a model for women's relations to language because of the mother's absorption within the androcentric and symbolic culture to which these women seek an alternative: "So let's try to take back [*reprenons*] some part of our mouth to speak with" (p. 208). If this new, mutual language does originate in the presymbolic mother-daughter relation, this origin must be denied in order for its history not to make the new relation and new

language merely a repetition of women's old bondage: "If we keep on speaking sameness, if we speak to each other as men have been doing for centuries, as we have been taught to speak, we'll miss each other, fail ourselves" (p. 205). This aspect of Irigaray's writing is clarified in Harriet Chessman, "A Lesbian Dialogic: Speculations," manuscript, Yale University, 1984.

32. Elaine Showalter, *A Literature of Their Own: British Women Novelists from Brontë to Lessing* (Princeton: Princeton University Press, 1977), p. 19; see also pp. 57–60. Showalter's extensive discussion of the contradiction of writing and being a woman, especially in chapters 1–3 (pp. 3–99), provides the historical grounding and a historical parallel for my discussion of how this conflict takes place at the level of myths of language.

33. From Charlotte Brontë's "Biographical Notice of Ellis and Acton Bell," included with the 1850 edition of *Wuthering Heights* (New York: Norton, 1972), p. 4.

34. Irigaray, criticizing Lacan's notion presented in "The Mirror Stage," writes, "[For them], any move toward the other means turning back to the attraction of one's own mirage. A (scarcely) living mirror, she/it is frozen, mute. More lifelike. The ebb and flow of our lives spent in the exhausting labor of copying, miming. Dedicated to reproducing—that sameness in which we have remained for centuries, as the other" (*This Sex*, p. 207). "And the One Doesn't Stir" suggests that the mother's congealing into a mirror is in large part responsible for her daughter's rejection of her, and it expresses the hope that she will "lose your mirror reflection," and "thaw" and "melt" (p. 63). *Glace,* meaning both ice and mirror, suggests puns that aren't as effective in English, though as we shall see in chapters 4, 9, and 10, both the Brontës and Gaskell make effective use of the image of the mother killed into the form of a mirror. For Irigaray's original discussion of women as mirrors in patriarchal culture, see *Speculum,* pp. 133–46.

35. See, for example, Nancy Friday, *My Mother/Myself* (New York: Dell, 1977), and Irigaray, "And the One Doesn't Stir."

36. On this point see also Suleiman, "Writing and Motherhood," p. 357. Suleiman's essay also asks the question I ask here: "Does the mother who writes write exclusively as her own mother's child?" (p. 358). But by this question she has in mind an inquiry rather different from mine, as she is not concerned with the differences between a son's and a daughter's writing, but only about the differences between the writing of children (who in one way or another elegize the mother) and the writing of mothers.

37. Elaine Showalter's discussion of the nineteenth-century contradiction between being a woman and writing, in *A Literature of Their Own,* includes discussion of motherhood and writing, both the common perception of their incompatibility and women writers' efforts to reconcile them (see especially pp. 65–72). For examples of the pressure on women to define themselves as wives and mothers, see, for example, Walter Houghton, *The Victorian Frame of Mind* (New Haven: Yale University Press, 1957), pp. 341–57; or John Ruskin, "Of Queens' Gardens," in *Sesame and Lilies* (1863). For fuller discussion of these issues, see chapter 7.

38. From Lewes's 1850 review of Brontë's *Shirley, Contemporary Review* 67 (1938): 370. Quoted in Showalter, *A Literature of Their Own,* p. 68.

39. Southey's 1837 letter is quoted in Elizabeth Gaskell, *The Life of Charlotte Brontë* (1857; reprint, Harmondsworth: Penguin, 1975), p. 173.

40. For example, following Lacan (*Ecrits,* 179–225), Muller assumes that the mother's desire is for the phallus: "In psychotic development castration is foreclosed: the child remains in a dual, symbiotic union with the mother in which the child identifies with being the all-fulfilling object of the mother's desire" (see Muller, "Language, Psychosis, and the Subject in Lacan" p. 23).

41. Irigaray, *Le Corps-à-corps,* p. 20.

42. Ibid.

43. Ibid., p. 21. The dictionary translation of *corps-à-corps* is "hand-to-hand," with the implication of combat. By using this expression as she does, however, Irigaray simultaneously points out how strange it is that almost all body-to-body contact between men in our culture is represented as agonistic, and recuperates this expression for a nonagonistic body-within-body-next-to-body contact between mother and daughter. I am indebted to Hélène Wenzel for this point.

44. Kristeva, *Desire,* pp. 241–42. Kristeva elsewhere suggests that the mother is situated uniquely well for participation in the symbolic order, since for the mother, "the Other is not [only] an arbitrary sign, a necessary absence: it is the child, whose presence and whose bodily link to her are . . . material facts." This material presence of the child is precisely, however, what according to Lacanian thinking would prevent the mother from seeking to manipulate symbols, and much of the rest of Suleiman's essay, from which I quote this useful paraphrase, analyzes the high cost of combining writing and motherhood. See Suleiman, "Writing and Motherhood," p. 367; she is referring to Kristeva, "Héréthique de l'amour," *Tel Quel* 74 (1977).

45. George Eliot, *Adam Bede* (1859; reprint, Harmondsworth: Penguin, 1980), p. 379.

46. Reverend Hugh Hughes, *Female Characters of Holy Writ* (London: Frederick Warne, 1890), pp. 37, 196.

47. Elizabeth Gaskell, *The Letters of Elizabeth Gaskell,* ed. J. A. V. Chapple and Arthur Pollard (Manchester: Manchester University Press, 1966), pp. 6–7.

48. "Ode: Intimations of Immortality," lines 19–21, in *The Poetical Works of William Wordsworth,* ed. E. de Selincourt and Helen Darbishire (London: Oxford University Press, 1947), 4:279.

Chapter 2

1. Quotations from *The Prelude* are (unless otherwise indicated) from the 1850 text as it appears in the Wordsworth, Abrams, and Gill edition; quotations will be cited hereafter by line numbers and by book, where necessary.

2. It is worth noting that Wordsworth's later portrayal of (Mother) Nature,

which takes over the mother's role, teaching the boy to go beyond her to vision and imagination, is analogous to the Lacanian view of the mother's obligatory self-effacement in the acculturation of her children. Referring to the child's discovery of the gap within himself and between himself and the world, Julia Kristeva writes, "The 'good enough' mother is perhaps the one who hears this 'void,' supports it, plays with it, but . . . directs it toward the father—in other words, towards the Symbolic" ("Within the Microcosm of the Talking Cure," p. 44). My discussion of Wordsworth in a Freudian context is indebted to Richard Onorato, *The Character of the Poet: Wordsworth in The Prelude* (Princeton: Princeton University Press, 1971).

3. Thomas Weiskel, *The Romantic Sublime: Studies in the Structure and Psychology of Transcendence* (Baltimore: Johns Hopkins University Press, 1976), p. 172. Further quotations from this book will be cited parenthetically within the text by page number. Although I will be pointing to what I believe this book leaves out, it would of course not be possible to make such an argument without it.

4. Although Weiskel throughout uses the oppositional pairing signifier/signified as a general designation for all instances of language's difference, in certain instances (such as this passage) the term "referent" seems to designate more accurately the second part of this opposition, and in commenting on this and other passages below I substitute referent for signified. The referent is the thing a word denotes (such as a natural object), while the signified is the (constitutively absent) idea a signifier constitutes (as in Weiskel's formulation, "the death which has been signified," p. 179). See Oswald Ducrot and Tzvetan Todorov, *Dictionnaire encyclopedique des sciences du langage* (Paris: Seuil, 1972), pp. 132–34.

5. *The Two-Part Prelude of 1799,* in Wordsworth, *The Prelude,* part 1, line 309. But see also *The Prelude, 1798–1799,* ed. Stephen Parrish (Ithaca: Cornell University Press, 1977), for more complete information on the manuscripts and background of this early version, on which I draw in this and the following paragraph. I am grateful to Alan Bewell for pointing out to me the complexity of Wordsworth's use of the murder story.

6. Just to document briefly that Dorothy's writing is sufficiently independent of William's both to influence and to alarm him, quite often when he borrows from Dorothy's journal to write a poem, he seems to be in flight from her. For example, she records that he is unable to write his poem "Beggars" because he cannot lose the sound of Dorothy's account of them. Wordsworth occasionally removes Dorothy (and sometimes others) from scenes in which, from her accounts, written either before or after his, we know she participated. Examples are "I Wandered Lonely as a Cloud," which follows her account of encountering a mass of daffodils at lakeside but leaves out her special emphasis on their seeing this together and indeed focuses on the rewards he will reap in solitary reflection; or their accounts of their first trip to Grasmere: Dorothy includes William, whereas he, at the start of book 1 of *The Prelude,* omits her. See *Journals of Dorothy Wordsworth,* ed. Mary Moorman (London: Oxford University Press, 1971), entries for 13 March 1802, p. 101; 15 April 1802, p. 109; October 1802, pp. 158–60. Quotations from this edition, which prints the Alfoxden and Grasmere journals, will be cited hereafter within the text by page number.

7. Rachel Brownstein discusses something like this aspect of Dorothy's writing in "The Private Life: Dorothy Wordsworth's Journals," *Modern Language Quarterly* 34 (1973): 48–63.

8. Mary Shelley, *Frankenstein* (1817; reprint, New York: New American Library, 1965), p. 53.

9. Jane Austen, *Persuasion* (1818; reprint, Harmondsworth: Penguin, 1965), pp. 107–8.

10. *Journals of Dorothy Wordsworth*, ed. E. de Selincourt (Macmillan, 1941; reprint, Hamden, Conn.: Archon, 1970), 2: 86. Future references to the *Journal of a Tour on the Continent* will be from this edition and volume, cited by page number within the text, except where otherwise noted.

11. *Journals of Dorothy Wordsworth*, ed. William Knight (1897; reprint, London: Macmillan, 1924), p. 478. Because neither de Selincourt's edition nor this one is complete, but because they are incomplete in different ways, it will occasionally be necessary to correct de Selincourt's lacunae from Knight's edition. Quotations from this edition are cited in the text by page number.

12. Susan Levin discusses Dorothy's echoing of "A Slumber" in "His Bitten Apple: Revisionism in British and American Romanticism," manuscript.

13. "A Slumber Did My Spirit Seal," in *The Poetical Works of William Wordsworth* 2: 216.

14. *The Letters of William and Dorothy Wordsworth: The Middle Years: 1806–1820*, ed. E. de Selincourt and Mary Moorman (London: Oxford University Press, 1969), 1: 454. The narrative was eventually published as *George and Sarah Green: A Narrative*, ed E. de Selincourt (London: Oxford University Press, 1936).

Chapter 3

1. This chapter is based very loosely upon my article "Repression and Sublimation of Nature in *Wuthering Heights*," *PMLA* 93 (1978): 9–19; the argument here, however, is quite different.

2. Emily Brontë, *Wuthering Heights* (1847; reprint, New York: Norton, 1972), chap. 1. All subsequent references to the novel will be from this edition, cited by chapter number for those using other editions.

3. Although Brontë's narrators might have had doubts about referring to anything, it is only with respect to nature that their language draws back. Lockwood's and Nelly's accounts of their protagonists' violent passions suggest that the narrators are not disturbed by any general belief in the fictiveness of language, and Brontë's use of characterized narrators indicates her assumption that language can be transparent. For any nineteenth-century writer, nature is the archetype of the literal and thus brings out anxieties about writing's relation to the literal that remain unprovoked elsewhere.

4. The character who is most devoted to staying indoors, Linton Heathcliff, appears in two extensive outdoor scenes during his meetings with the second Cathy, who also both talks about and is seen in nature; yet all that is shown of her most significant foray into nature, her excursion to Penistone Crags at the age of

thirteen, is the encounter inside Wuthering Heights after Nelly arrives to take her home. Dorothy Van Ghent's classic study of house and threshold imagery provides a useful confirmation of my observation that the narrative itself is housebound (see *The English Novel: Form and Function* [New York: Holt, 1953], pp. 160–63). The closed, locked house generally represents the psychic or social entrapment of the characters: for example, the open doors and lattices Lockwood finds on his last visit to the Heights, after Heathcliff's death and Cathy and Hareton's engagement, contrast with the locked door he encounters on his second visit, when the same characters are all prisoners of Heathcliff's vengeful hatred. Building on Van Ghent's reading, I would suggest that the narrative as well as the characters are imprisoned in a locked house.

5. I am indebted to J. Hillis Miller for pointing out the importance of this scene for any discussion of reading in the novel (see *Fiction and Repetition* [Cambridge: Harvard University Press, 1982], pp. 55–60). My discussion of Brontë's use of figures to make nature intelligible does not disagree with Miller's conclusions about the unreadability of the novel's figures for itself, since I focus on the meaning of the process of reading, not on the possibility of an all-encompassing interpretation.

6. Although strictly speaking, all language is figurative in a novel obeying nineteenth-century conventions of representation, in a reader's experience of the novel, there are degrees of figuration. In this discussion, we will use the term "figurative language" to refer to what is overtly figurative—metaphors, similes, and the like—as opposed to language that is less self-consciously figurative, for example, the representational naming of natural scenes and objects. The novel contains no truly literal nature because to write of it at all is to deny its literality.

7. A number of critics have assumed that the novel is informed by the immediate presence of the Yorkshire moors; see, for example, Arnold Kettle, *An Introduction to the English Novel* (London: Hutchinson, 1951), 1: 139–40, or Mark Shorer, "Fiction and the 'Matrix of Analogy,'" *Kenyon Review* 11 (1949): 544–50.

8. *Peni*stone Crags, after all, dominates this landscape. Sandra Gilbert and Susan Gubar have asserted that the "hellish nature" of *Wuthering Heights* "is somehow female or associated with femaleness, like an angry goddess," but I do not find their evidence or argument for this reading to be convincing (see *The Madwoman in the Attic* [New Haven: Yale University Press, 1979], pp. 262–63).

9. I am indebted to Leo Bersani's chapter on *Wuthering Heights* in *A Future for Astyanax: Character and Desire in Literature* (Boston: Little, Brown and Co., 1976), pp. 189–229, for the suggestion to read the novel with special attention to relations between self and other, though his concern is primarily with the sharing of identity between Cathy and Heathcliff. He reads their deaths as the final act of transference from self to other. Concurring with this reading, I would nonetheless add other kinds of otherness into which Cathy merges as she dies.

10. For a more complete discussion of the issues raised by Heathcliff's orphanhood, see Wade Thompson, "Infanticide and Sadism in *Wuthering Heights*," *PMLA* 78 (1963): 69–74.

11. As we have seen in chapter 1, readers of Lacan argue that the failure to repress the presymbolic tie to the mother is the origin of psychosis.

12. Her terror is magnified here by a superstition that to see oneself in a mirror at midnight is a portent of death; see Jacqueline Simpson, "The Function of Folklore in *Jane Eyre* and *Wuthering Heights*," *Folklore* 85 (1974): 57. Gilbert and Gubar discuss the alienation represented by Cathy's mirror image in the context of her earlier dressing up like a conventional lady to impress Edgar Linton as continuous parts of her "fragmentation of self" (*The Madwoman*, pp. 278–86).

Chapter 4

1. Charlotte Brontë, *Jane Eyre* (1847; reprint; New York: Norton, 1971), chap. 1. All references to the novel will be from this edition, cited in the text by chapter number.

This chapter is a revised and abbreviated version of "Dreaming of Children: Literalization in *Jane Eyre* and *Wuthering Heights*," in *The Female Gothic*, ed. Juliann Fleenor (Montreal: Eden Press, 1983), pp. 257–79.

2. *Jane Eyre* was begun just a few months after the completion of *Wuthering Heights*, and we know that the sisters read their ongoing work aloud to each other.

3. It is this sort of feminine objectification, brought about by the pressure to conform to socially acceptable notions of femininity, that concerns Sandra Gilbert and Susan Gubar in their readings of *Jane Eyre* as well as of *Wuthering Heights*. See in particular their discussion of Jane's various mirror images (*The Madwoman*, p. 359).

4. This reading is indebted to Mary Poovey's interpretation of the gothic mode as the novel's way of incorporating the romantic period's privileging of subjectivity and imagination ("The Novel as Imaginative Order," Ph.D. diss., University of Virginia, 1976). See also G. R. Thompson, "Introduction: Romanticism and the Gothic Tradition," in *The Gothic Imagination: Essays in Dark Romanticism*, ed. G. R. Thompson (Pullman: Washington State University Press, 1974), pp. 1–10.

5. Coleridge, "Dejection: An Ode," lines 54–55. The question of the literalization of prior texts will be considered in a more systematic way in chapter 5.

6. The term "female gothic" was first introduced by Ellen Moers in her reading of Mary Shelley, Emily Brontë, Christina Rossetti, and others in her chapter "Female Gothic" in *Literary Women* (New York: Doubleday, 1977), pp. 137–67. This reading enables our inquiry into Charlotte Brontë's particular version of the female gothic.

7. Although both Charlotte and Emily Brontë use gothic elements in their novels, and although the structure of gothic literalization is essentially the same in *Wuthering Heights* and *Jane Eyre*, *Jane Eyre* is more skeptical than *Wuthering Heights* about gothic literalization and about its implications for women, for Emily envisages the possibility of reclaiming the literal and literalization for an original female power in a way that Charlotte does not.

8. In a reading of the female gothic that in some respects thematically parallels my own, and that like mine draws on the work of Nancy Chodorow,

Claire Kahane argues that the female gothic (defined mainly by Anne Radcliffe's works) represents the daughter's struggle to separate from the boundariless preoedipal mother, who is typically figured in gothic fiction both as nature and as a gloomy, mysterious castle. She writes: "the female child, who shares the female body and its symbolic place in our culture, remains locked in a . . . tenuous and fundamentally ambivalent struggle for a separate identity. This ongoing battle with a mirror image who is both self and other is what I find at the center of the Gothic structure." My argument about the complex results of Charlotte Brontë's ambivalence about the cultural identification of woman with the literal and with nature investigates, with respect to myths and structures of language, something like what Kahane explores thematically and with particular emphasis on the reader's experience. See Kahane, "The Gothic Mirror," *Centennial Review* 24 (1980): 43–64; revised and reprinted in *The (M)other Tongue*, pp. 334–51 (quotation p. 337).

9. At least two commentators on the novel have argued that Brontë modifies the gothic elements she introduces, testing them against the reality principle so that they will deepen her novel's emotional realism rather than making it too fantastic to be believed. I am adding to, not disagreeing with, these arguments. See Robert Heilman, "Charlotte Brontë's 'New Gothic,'" in *From Jane Austen to Joseph Conrad: Essays Collected in Memory of James T. Hillhouse*, ed. Robert C. Rathburn and Martin Steinman, Jr. (Minneapolis: University of Minnesota Press, 1958), pp. 118–32; Ruth Bernard Yeazell, "More True than Real: Jane Eyre's 'Mysterious Summons,'" *Nineteenth-Century Fiction* 29 (1974): 127–43.

10. The Brontës' mother died when they were young children, probably of complications resulting from bearing six children in seven years. Helene Moglen discusses Charlotte's response to the deaths of her mother and of her maternal older sister, Maria (see *Charlotte Brontë: The Self Conceived* [New York: Norton, 1976], pp. 21–32). She argues that Charlotte's fears about childbirth (actual and metaphoric, her own and her mother's) constrained both her life and her literary production (pp. 21, 241). Although Mrs. Brontë's death may well have left her daughters with a powerful nostalgia for mothering, a nostalgia that can be traced in what is known of Charlotte's life, the response to the mother's death within the literary text is an overriding drive to dissociate the writing self from the idea of the mother because of the various threats she poses to writing. Emily's representation of a lost mother, as we have seen in chapter 3, tends to balance the writer's defensiveness with the daughter's nostalgia.

For discussion and documentation of maternal and infant mortality in the nineteenth century, see, for example, Adrienne Rich, *Of Woman Born* (New York: Norton, 1976), pp. 30, 143–45, 161; Roy P. Finney, *The Story of Motherhood* (New York: Liveright, 1937), pp. 191–223: or A. J. Rongy, *Childbirth Yesterday and Today* (New York: Emerson Books, 1937), pp. 176–88. Susan Gubar summarizes the history of views of childbirth and suggests their implications for more recent women writers in "The Birth of the Artist as Heroine: (Re)production, the Kunstlerroman Tradition, and the Fiction of Katherine Mansfield," in *The Representation of Women in Fiction*, ed. Carolyn Heilbrun and Margaret Higonnet (Baltimore: Johns Hopkins University Press, 1983), pp. 19–59.

11. Helene Deutsch, *Motherhood*, vol. 2 of *The Psychology of Women: A Psychoanalytic Interpretation* (New York: Grune and Stratton, 1945), p. 215. It is important to stress that Deutsch's conservative and pessimistic view is not the only one, but that it seems to describe the mood of the Brontës' novels better than does, say, Nancy Chodorow's interpretation discussed in chapter 1.

12. Charlotte Brontë apparently had dreams of this kind herself and shared Jane's belief in them, based on an actual superstition: see Lucile Dooley, "Psychoanalysis of Charlotte Brontë, as a Type of the Woman of Genius," *American Journal of Psychology* 31 (1920): 242. Like much genuine folklore, whatever logical origin the belief may once have had has been obscured and now seems arbitrary. Freud's translation of small children in dreams as the genitals could point to a hypothetical origin for the actual superstition, but the novel avoids offering any explanation of whatever sort.

13. There has been much debate over the interpretation of the child in Jane's dreams, and almost all readings are justifiable; but there can be no single interpretation. See, for example, William R. Siebenschuh, "The Image of the Child and the Plot of *Jane Eyre*," *Studies in the Novel* 8 (1976): 304–17; and Moglen, *Charlotte Brontë*, pp. 125–27. Gilbert and Gubar read the dreams of children and the Mrs. Rochester passage as representing the "fragmentation" of Jane's self, the major thesis of their reading of the novel, although the aim of their discussion is different from mine (*The Madwoman*, pp. 357–59).

14. If the passage from symbol to metaphor moves in the direction of relative literalization, the sequence is finally completed much later on (though not with reference to the mother and child figure that concerns us here) by the uncanny literal repetition of Jane's vision in the object world. The shelllike battlements that she climbs in the second dream, burdened with the child, are precisely realized in Thornfield's ruin by fire. Typical of *Jane Eyre*'s handling of the gothic, when the dream picture of Thornfield comes true so literally, Jane very casually relegates to a subordinate clause her acknowledgment of the uncanniness of the situation, as if the gothic's turn from visionary fear to the world of substance were a demystification, and not a further mystery: "The front was, as I had once seen it in a dream, but a shell-like wall, very high and very fragile looking."

15. See Adrienne Rich's more positive acount of Jane's relations with a series of surrogate mothers: "Jane Eyre: The Temptations of a Motherless Woman" (1973), reprinted in *On Lies, Secrets, and Silence: Selected Prose 1966–1978* (New York: Norton, 1979), pp. 89–106.

16. Of course, to say that the white cross, or Jane's lack of money, figures Jane's reduced state, and to remember that while the white cross may not signify a town it does signify in a different way by pointing to four destinations, is already to acknowledge that literal meaning is never quite representable, yet this is as close as a written text can come to literality.

17. Readers using the Penguin edition find this point made even more strongly by a misprint: "black, where the dry soil bore only death." There is no authority for this reading in any of the editions supervised by the author.

18. Indeed, Lockwood's "dream" of Cathy is itself prophetic in something of the same way that dreams of children are in *Jane Eyre*. It "comes true" in the gothic sense that Heathcliff knows the objective reality of what Lockwood takes

to be "imagination," and in the literary sense that it prefigures the novel's actual violence, its scenes of exiled wanderers, and its orphans. Numerous writers have considered this latter aspect of the dream: for example, Edgar F. Shannon, Jr., "Lockwood's Dream and the Exegesis of *Wuthering Heights*," *Nineteenth-Century Fiction* 14 (1959): 95–109; and Ronald E. Fine, "Lockwood's Dream and the Key to *Wuthering Heights*," *Nineteenth-Century Fiction* 24 (1969): 16–30.

Chapter 5

1. Mary Poovey, *The Proper Lady and the Woman Writer* (Chicago: University of Chicago Press, 1984), 114–42. Hereafter I will refer to Mary Shelley as Shelley (except where her unmarried name is necessary for clarity) and to her husband as Percy.

2. Sandra Gilbert and Susan Gubar's reading of the novel focuses on its "apparently docile submission to male myths" and identifies it specifically as "a fictionalized rendition of the meaning of *Paradise Lost* to women" (*The Madwoman*, pp. 219, 221). Although my interest in Shelley as a reader of prior, masculine texts, as well as some of my specific points about the novel's reading of Milton, overlaps with theirs, I am putting these concerns to uses different from theirs.

3. For example, Robert Kiely writes that Frankenstein "seeks to combine the role of both parents in one, to eliminate the need for the woman in the creative act, to make sex unnecessary" (*The Romantic Novel in England* [Cambridge: Harvard University Press, 1972], p. 164). Marc Rubenstein remarks on "the series of motherless family romances which form the substance of Frankenstein's past" ("'My Accursed Origin': The Search for the Mother in *Frankenstein*," *Studies in Romanticism* 15 [1976], 177). The general argument of his psychoanalytic reading of the novel is that the novel represents Shelley's quest for her own dead mother. U. C. Knoepflmacher, in the course of arguing that the novel portrays a daughter's rage at her parents, mentions "the novel's attack on a male's usurpation of the role of mother" ("Thoughts on the Aggression of Daughters," in *The Endurance of Frankenstein: Essays on Mary Shelley's Novel*, ed. George Levine and U. C. Knoepflmacher [Berkeley: University of California Press, 1979], p. 105). Mary Jacobus writes that "the exclusion of woman from creation symbolically 'kills' the mother" ("Is There a Woman in This Text?" p. 131). Barbara Johnson suggests that the novel focuses on "eliminations of the mother" as well as on "the fear of somehow effecting the death of one's own parents" ("My Monster/My Self," *Diacritics* 12 (1982): 9). Christine Froula's argument about the maternal in Milton, although it focuses on the author's appropriation of the maternal for masculine creativity (as differentiated from its circumvention or elimination) helped to stimulate my thinking. See Froula, "When Eve Reads Milton," pp. 321–47.

4. I am following, in this reading, the 1831 revised text of the novel; in the 1818 version, Elizabeth is Frankenstein's cousin. All quotations from the novel

will be from the Signet edition (Mary Shelley, *Frankenstein, Or The Modern Prometheus* [New York: NAL, 1965]), which prints the text of 1831. Future references will be cited in the text by chapter number or by letter number for the letters that precede the chapter sequence. See also James Reiger's edition of the 1818 version, with revisions of 1823 and 1831 (Chicago: University of Chicago Press, 1982).

5. Rubenstein notes the sexual nature of Walton's quest, as well as the maternal associations of those aspects of nature on which Frankenstein carries out his research ("My Accursed Origin," pp. 174–75, 177). Kiely notes the necrophilia of the passage from *Alastor*'s invocation to Mother Nature (discussed here in chapter 1), and suggests its similarity to Frankenstein's "penetrating the recesses of nature" (*The Romantic Novel*, pp. 162–63).

6. Quoted p. 149; Frankenstein quotes lines 76–83 of the poem, altering the original "haunted *me* like a passion" to fit a third person.

7. In the context of arguing that the novel critiques the bourgeois family, Kate Ellis shows that Frankenstein's mother passes on to Elizabeth her "view of the female role as one of constant, self-sacrificing devotion to others," and she suggests that "Elizabeth's early death, like her adopted mother's, was a logical outgrowth of the female ideal she sought to embody" ("Monsters in the Garden: Mary Shelley and the Bourgeois Family," in *The Endurance of Frankenstein*, p. 131). My argument would explain why what created this "female ideal" also determined the interchangeability of mother and daughter.

8. Harold Bloom suggests the resemblance between the demon and Blake's emanations or Shelley's epipsyche, in his afterword to the Signet edition of the novel, p. 215. The essay is reprinted in *Ringers in the Tower* (Chicago: University of Chicago Press, 1971), pp. 119–29. Peter Brooks makes a similar point when he writes, "fulfillment with Elizabeth would mark Frankenstein's achievement of a full signified in his life, accession to plenitude of being—which would leave no place in creation for his daemonic projection, the Monster" ("Godlike Science/ Unhallowed Arts: Language and Monstrosity in *Frankenstein*," *New Literary History* 9 [1978]: 599). Ellis also suggests, though for different reasons, that the demon is a representative for Elizabeth ("Monsters in the Garden," p. 136). Jacobus writes that Frankenstein "exchang[es] a woman for a monster," and she discusses Frankenstein's preference for imagined over actual beings ("Is There a Woman in This Text?" p. 131).

9. Gilbert and Gubar suggest first that "the part of Eve *is* all the parts" and then discuss at length the demon's resemblance to Eve (*The Madwoman*, pp. 230, 235–44. However, in describing this resemblance, they focus primarily on the patriarchal rejection of women's bodies as deformed and monstrous, as well as on Eve's motherlessness, but not, as I do here, on Eve as Adam's imaginative projection. Joyce Carol Oates also suggests the demon's resemblance to Eve, also using the scene I am about to discuss, in "Frankenstein's Fallen Angel," *Critical Inquiry* 10 (1984): 547.

10. Quotations from *Paradise Lost* are from *Complete Poems and Major Prose of John Milton*, ed. Merritt Hughes (Indianapolis: Bobbs-Merrill, 1957), and are cited in the text by book and line numbers. Other critics have noted

Shelley's allusion to this Miltonic scene; see, for example, Brooks, "Godlike Science," p. 595.

11. Froula writes, "Through the dream of the rib Adam both enacts a parody of birth and gains possession of the womb by claiming credit for woman herself." Milton, she goes on to argue, reenacts Adam's solution to his "womb envy" by analogously repressing female power in his account of the origin of his poem: "The male Logos called upon to articulate the cosmos against an abyss of female silence overcomes the anxieties generated by the tension between visible maternity and invisible paternity by appropriating female power to itself in a parody of parthenogenesis" ("When Eve Reads Milton," pp. 332, 338; and see passim pp. 326–40).

12. Ibid., pp. 326–28.

13. All quotations from Shelley's verse are from the Reiman and Powers edition of his works.

14. Gilbert and Gubar also discuss narcissistic love in the novel, although with reference only to the potentially incestuous relation between Frankenstein and Elizabeth, not with reference to the demon (*The Madwoman*, p. 229). My reading would suggest that Frankenstein's relation to Elizabeth is far less narcissistic than his relation to the demon; in his descriptions of Elizabeth, he focuses on her difference from him, which is what I believe makes her like the mother and therefore threatening.

15. Jaya Mehta pointed out to me the significance of this aspect of Walton, in a seminar paper at Yale in 1984.

16. Kiely discusses "the sheer concreteness" of the demon, though his concern is with the mismatching between ideal and real in the novel (*The Romantic Novel*, p. 161).

17. *The Diary of Dr. John William Polidori*, ed. W. M. Rossetti (London: Elkin Matthews, 1911), pp. 128–29, entry for 18 June 1816. Cited also by Rubenstein, who reads it as a story about "maternal reproach" and connects it with Frankenstein's dream of his dead mother ("My Accursed Origin," pp. 184–85). I am grateful to Marina Leslie for her discussion of this episode in a seminar paper at Yale in 1984.

18. Peter Brooks's essay on *Frankenstein* also connects the plot of desire with the plot of language in the novel, but to a somewhat different effect. Brooks argues that the demon's acquisition of the "godlike science" of language places him within the symbolic order. Trapped at first, like any baby, within the specular order of the imaginary, the demon is first judged only by its looks; it is only when it masters the art of rhetoric that the monster gains sympathy. But, Brooks continues, despite the promise that the symbolic seems to hold, the monster's failure to find an object of love removes its life from the signifying "chain" of human interconnectedness and makes of it instead a "miserable series," in which one signifier refers always to another with "no point of arrest." Thus Brooks sees the monster as a dark and exaggerated version of all life within the symbolic, where desire is never satisfied and where there is no transcendental signified. Although I agree with much of what Brooks writes, I would argue that in its materiality and its failure to acquire an object of desire, the demon enters the

symbolic primarily as the (dreaded) referent, not as signifier. The negative picture of the demon's materiality is a product of its female place in the symbolic, and not of any lingering in the realm of the imaginary (which Brooks, with other readers of Lacan, views as tragic). I would also argue that the novel presents, not a vision of the condition of human signification, but a targeted criticism of those in whose interests the symbolic order constitutes itself in the ways that it does.

19. Ellen Moers, *Literary Women* (New York: Doubleday, 1977), p. 140.

20. Ibid., pp. 145–47.

21. This is the general tendency of Rubenstein's argument, carrying the material Moers presents into a psychoanalytic frame.

22. See Rubenstein, "My Accursed Origin," pp. 168, 178–81; Poovey, *The Proper Lady*, pp. 138–42.

23. Deutsch, *Motherhood*, p. 215.

24. One of the central tenets of Poovey's argument concerns Shelley's endeavor in her 1831 revisions to make the novel more conservative, more in keeping with a proto-Victorian ideology of the family (see *The Proper Lady*, pp. 133–42). Poovey argues, however, that both versions of the novel oppose romantic egotism's assault on the family.

25. Gilbert and Gubar assert as part of their argument that everyone in the novel is Eve that "Frankenstein has a baby" and that as a consequence he becomes female (*The Madwoman*, p. 232). I would argue, to the contrary, that Frankenstein's production of a new life is pointedly masculine, that it matters to the book that he is a man circumventing childbirth, not a woman giving birth.

26. Letter of 22 November 1817 to Benjamin Bailey, in *Letters of John Keats*, ed. Robert Gittings (London: Oxford University Press, 1970), p. 37.

27. I am indebted to Suzanne Raitt for her discussion of this point in a seminar at Yale in 1984.

28. Rubenstein also argues that Shelley deliberately created the impression that she merely recorded Percy and Byron's conversation as part of a project to make her creativity seem as passive and maternal as possible. He discusses at length the analogy she sets up between conceiving a child and conceiving a book, and he specifically suggests that the men's words in conversation are like men's role in procreation, which was, in the early nineteenth century, thought to involve the man actively and the woman only passively: "She is trying to draw for us a picture of her imagination as a passive womb, inseminated by those titans of romantic poetry" ("My Accursed Origin," p. 181). I would agree with everything Rubenstein says, although I am using this idea for a somewhat different purpose: he is using it to show how the novel is about Shelley's effort to make restitution for her dead mother.

29. Mario Praz, *The Romantic Agony*, trans. Angus Davidson (London: Oxford University Press, 1933), p. 114. Cited by Moers and also by Rubenstein in support of his argument discussed in note 28 above.

30. Harold Bloom, "Afterword," *Frankenstein*, p. 215. It is worth noting that *Frankenstein* preceded *Prometheus Unbound* and was of course written in ignorance of the *Book of Urizen*.

31. Oates, "Frankenstein's Fallen Angel," p. 552.

32. Gilbert and Gubar, who focus much of their argument on Shelley's reading of *Paradise Lost*, connect that reading to the demon's reading of the poem, as well as connecting Shelley's listening to her husband and Byron with the demon's listening to the DeLaceys.

Chapter 6

1. The discussion in this chapter of *The Mill on the Floss* is a revised version of an essay of the same title in *Critical Inquiry* 8 (1981): 223–41; reprinted in *Writing and Sexual Difference*, ed. Elizabeth Abel (Chicago: University of Chicago Press, 1982), pp. 223–42.

2. All quotations from Wordsworth are from the de Selincourt and Darbishire edition of *The Poetical Works* and from the Wordsworth, Abrams, and Gill edition of *The Prelude*. Quotations from *The Prelude* are from the 1850 version. All further references to these works will be included in the text.

3. *The George Eliot Letters*, ed. Gordon S. Haight (New Haven: Yale University Press, 1954), 1: 34. Letters cited hereafter by volume and page number.

4. There are far too many articles and parts of books about Eliot's Wordsworthianism to cite them all here. Among the excellent recent essays are Henry Auster, "George Eliot and the Modern Temper," in *The Worlds of Victorian Fiction*, ed. Jerome H. Buckley (Cambridge: Harvard University Press, 1975), pp. 75–101; Deborah H. Roazen, "*Middlemarch* and the Wordsworthian Imagination," *English Studies* 58 (1977): 411–25; Jay Clayton, "Visionary Power and Narrative Form: Wordsworth and *Adam Bede*," *ELH* 46 (1979): 645–72; and U. C. Knoepflmacher, "Genre and the Integration of Gender: from Wordsworth to George Eliot and Virginia Woolf," in *Victorian Literature and Society*, ed. James R. Kincaid and Albert Kuhn (Columbus: Ohio State University Press, 1983), pp. 94–118. Of value also is Robert Dunham, "Wordsworthian Themes and Attitudes in George Eliot's Fiction," (Ph.D. diss., Stanford University, 1972).

5. Donald D. Stone, *The Romantic Impulse in Victorian Fiction* (Cambridge: Harvard University Press, 1980), p. 194.

6. *The Mill on the Floss*, vols. 14 and 15 of *The Works of George Eliot* (1860; Cabinet Edition, Edinburgh and London: William Blackwood and Sons, 1877), book 1, chapter 3; while I have quoted from this edition throughout, I will hereafter include in the text only book and chapter numbers, for the convenience of those using other editions.

7. I am generally indebted to the recent work of Nancy K. Miller for my understanding of the issue of feminine plotting; see especially her reading of the *Corinne* scene in "Emphasis Added: Plots and Plausibilities in Women's Fiction," *PMLA* 96 (1981): 36–48.

8. Stone, *Romantic Impulse*, p. 194.

9. U. C. Knoepflmacher, *George Eliot's Early Novels: The Limits of Realism* (Berkeley: University of California Press, 1968), p. 175.

10. Mary Ann Evans's beloved older brother, Isaac, seems to have provided the model for many of Eliot's fictive brothers, including their dictatorial distaste for reading and for the pleasures of the imagination. Apparently Evans was so anxious as a child to please her brother, whose only pleasures were physical, that she learned to read with difficulty and did not become an avid reader until he abandoned her to her own amusements (the story comes from her half sister, Fanny Houghton, in *George Eliot's Life as Related in Her Letters and Journals*, ed. J. W. Cross [Edinburgh and London: William Blackwood and Sons, 1885], 1:15). However, the brothers in Eliot's fiction seem to be generated not so much to immortalize him as to justify the novelist's choice of realism and of the novel, to justify her affirmation of love over the visionary imagination.

11. See Gilbert and Gubar, *The Madwoman*, p. 492.

12. "Brother and Sister" and *The Mill on the Floss* have always been taken to be generally autobiographical, but it is of course both impossible and unnecessary to tell how accurately they record the actual events of Eliot's early life. It is possible that these works have been taken tautologically as the source of biographical information. See Ruby Redinger, *George Eliot: The Emergent Self* (New York: Knopf, 1975), pp. 44–65, for an extensive reading of "Brother and Sister" as autobiography; see also Gordon S. Haight, *George Eliot: A Biography* (New York: Oxford University Press, 1968), pp. 5–6, 421.

13. See Thomas Pinney, "George Eliot's Reading of Wordsworth: The Record," *Victorian Newsletter* 24 (Fall 1963): 20–22.

14. Eliot, "Brother and Sister," in *The Legend of Jubal and Other Poems, Old and New* (Edinburgh and London: William Blackwood and Sons, 1874), sonnet 6, p. 202; all further references to the sonnets will be cited in the text by sonnet number.

15. *Middlemarch*, vols. 11–13 of *The Works of George Eliot* (1871–72; Cabinet Edition, Edinburgh and London: William Blackwood and Sons, 1877), chap. 57. Hereafter, all quotations are from this text and are cited by chapter number.

16. The story was told for the first time by Edith Simcox, in *Nineteenth Century* 9 (1881): 779; there is no other corroboration for it except in the sonnet itself.

17. Her first known short story would support this reading. Heavily influenced by the novelist G. P. R. James and by a history of Monmouthshire, the story is still Mary Ann Evans's' own. See Haight, *Eliot*, pp. 15–18, 554–62.

18. Ibid., pp. 420–21.

19. See Jerome Beaty's account of the origins of *Middlemarch* and of what remains of the earliest version of the story in *Middlemarch from Notebook to Novel* (Urbana: University of Illinois Press, 1960), pp. 3–42.

20. The relevant passages from Eliot's journals are printed in Cross, *Eliot's Life* 3:95, 97.

21. Beaty, *Middlemarch from Notebook to Novel*, pp. 13–14; my own reading of the manuscript in the British Museum confirms this conjecture, as far as it can be confirmed.

22. Anna T. Kitchel has drawn this conclusion from the evidence of the

changing chapter outlines. See *Quarry for Middlemarch* (Berkeley: University of California Press, 1950), pp. 15–16, 46ff.

23. J. Hillis Miller makes essentially the same point about the security of naming and Mary Garth in an unpublished paper on *Middlemarch*.

24. See, for example, Henry James, review of *Middlemarch*, *Galaxy* 15 (1873): 424–28; reprinted in *A Century of George Eliot Criticism*, ed. Gordon S. Haight (Boston: Houghton Mifflin and Co., 1965), pp. 80–87; the comment on Fred is on p. 82.

25. Virginia Woolf, "George Eliot," *The Common Reader: First Series* (New York: Harcourt Brace, 1925), p. 172.

26. Gilbert and Gubar, p. 529, point out that Will is presented as a brother figure. Knoepflmacher ("Genre," p. 101) points out that Will and Dorothea are given the names of that prototypical sister and brother, William and Dorothy Wordsworth, which would confirm my argument that Will and Dorothea are granted an honorary childhood in Wordsworthian nature.

Chapter 7

1. Louis Aimé Martin, *The Education of Mothers of Families, or, The Civilization of the Human Race by Women*, trans. Edwin Lee (1840; London, 1842), p. 19.

2. Mary Ann Evans records having read the book in 1840, although her response is to another aspect of the book (see *Eliot Letters* 1:70). But see the speculative discussion of Eliot's more general response to Martin in Bonnie Zimmerman, "'The Mother's History' in George Eliot's Life, Literature, and Political Ideology," in *The Lost Tradition: Mothers and Daughters in Literature*, ed. Cathy N. Davidson and E. M. Broner (New York: Frederick Ungar, 1980), pp. 81–94, esp. pp. 90–91. Other early Victorian books about motherhood are less interested than Martin in its political ramifications, but they assume no less that motherhood is woman's true vocation. See, for example, the works of Mrs. Sarah Ellis, such as *The Women of England, or The Mothers of England: Their Influence and Responsibility*, published and reprinted many times in the 1840s.

3. See the discussion of this subject in Elaine Showalter and English Showalter, "Victorian Women and Menstruation," in *Suffer and be Still*, ed. Martha Vicinus (Bloomington: Indiana University Press, 1972), pp. 38–44. They cite primarily Dr. Edward Clarke's *Sex in Education* (1873) and the writings of Henry Maudsley in the *Fortnightly Review* based on Clarke. George Henry Lewes also writes in 1852 of the "precarious" and "broken" health of women during "twenty of the best years of their lives" as evidence for women's incapacity for writing novels (from "The Lady Novelists," *Westminster Review*, n.s. 2 [1852]: 133; cited in the Showalters' article, p. 43).

4. In *On the Generation of Animals*, Aristotle compares the process to the coagulation of milk when mixed with fig juice. Ambiguities in this text also, however, authorized an extensive debate in the Middle Ages over the question of the presence and the efficacy of female semen. Galen believed that women's semen contributed both form and matter but that it was "colder and less active

than that of the male." See Ian Maclean, *The Renaissance Notion of Woman* (Cambridge: Cambridge University Press, 1980), pp. 35–37. Although the attribution of semen to women might seem to place them in a less passive position in procreation, it seems to have served the function of construing women as imperfect copies of men. For an excellent brief discussion of various ancient and medieval theories of conception, see Marina Warner, *Alone of All Her Sex: The Myth and the Cult of the Virgin Mary* (New York: Knopf, 1976), pp. 39–41. On Aristotle, see also Joseph Needham, *A History of Embryology* (New York: Abelard-Schuman, 1959), pp. 37–55. Susan Gubar reviews much of the history I discuss in this and the following paragraph, with emphasis on a different aspect of its implications, in "The Birth of the Artist as Heroine," pp. 21–23.

5. Freud argues that "the compulsion to worship an invisible God" who is also a father "signifies above all a victory of spirituality over the senses—that is to say, a step forward in culture, since maternity is proved by the senses whereas paternity is a surmise based on a deduction and a premiss" (*Moses and Monotheism*, trans. Katherine Jones [1939; reprint, New York: Knopf, 1967], pp. 144–46). The quotation from Aeschylus is from *The Oresteia*, trans. Richmond Lattimore (Chicago: University of Chicago Press, 1953), lines 658–60.

6. Aristotle, *Summa Theologica*; cited in Needham, *A History of Embryology*, p. 93.

7. See ibid., pp. 162–63; see also Harold Speert, *Obstetrical and Gynecological Milestones* (New York: Macmillan, 1958), pp. 10–15; and Shirley Green, *The Curious History of Contraception* (London: Ebury Press, 1971), p. 137. On medieval through seventeenth-century accounts of procreation and their ideological impact on women, see Hilda Scott, "Gynecology and Ideology in Seventeenth-Century England," in *Liberating Women's History*, ed. Berenice A. Carroll (Urbana: University of Illinois Press, 1976), pp. 97–114.

8. See Green, pp. 132–34; Needham, *A History of Embryology*, pp. 205–9.

9. Erasmus Darwin, *Zoonomia* (Dublin, 1794); cited in Rubenstein, "My Accursed Origin," p. 180.

10. See Speert, *Obstetrical Milestones*, p. 15; Showalter and Showalter, "Victorian Women and Menstruation," p. 39.

11. See ibid., p. 39; the Showalters cite the twenty-fifth edition, published in 1886, of George R. Drysdale's *Elements of Social Science*, first published in 1854, which states that menstrual periods are like heat in animals. See also Gubar, "The Birth of the Artist as Heroine," p. 23.

12. M. L. Holbrook, *Parturition without Pain: A Code of Directions for Escaping from the Primal Curse* (New York: published by the author, 1871; reprinted 1889), pp. 68–69.

13. Ibid., pp. 70–72. For a discussion of other superstitions about the danger of the mother's feelings to the fetus, see Edward Shorter, *A History of Women's Bodies* (New York: Basic Books, 1982), pp. 49–50.

14. For a recent review of drastic legal and medical efforts to appropriate pregnant women's bodies on the assumption that the fetus belongs to others, see Janet Gallagher, "The Fetus and the Law—Whose Life is it Anyway?" *Ms.* 13 (1984): 62–66, 134–35.

15. See Warner, *Alone of All Her Sex*, pp. 45, 73.

16. See ibid., pp. 236–54.

17. Ibid., p. 47. See also Kristeva, "Héréthique de l'amour"; in Suleiman's paraphrase, the myth of Mary offered women a variety of compensations ("fulfillment of the female desire for power [and] of the fantasy of deathlessness") in return for "one condition: that the ultimate supremacy and divinity of the male be maintained in the person of the Son, before whom the Mother kneels." Suleiman goes on to suggest the similarity between this myth and that of psychoanalysis. "In both cases the mother is elevated precisely to the extent that she prostrates herself before her son" (Suleiman, "Writing and Motherhood," pp. 368–69).

18. For an account of Gaskell's religion, see Angus Easson, *Elizabeth Gaskell* (London: Routledge and Kegan Paul, 1979), pp. 4–13. The many accounts of Eliot's version of religion include U. C. Knoepflmacher, *Religious Humanism and the Victorian Novel* (Princeton: Princeton University Press, 1965), pp. 24–59; Bernard Paris, *Experiments in Life: George Eliot's Quest for Values* (Detroit: Wayne State University Press, 1965); and Felicia Bonaparte, *The Triptych and the Cross* (New York: New York University Press, 1979), pp. 203–4, 235–39. Bonaparte perceptively writes of Eliot's view, "Christianity does not require . . . belief in Jesus's divinity. It requires only the imagination that can perceive it as poetry, as a historical force, that is, and as a symbolic meaning" (p. 237).

19. Martin, *The Education of Mothers*, p. 19.

20. Anna Jameson, *Legends of the Madonna* (Boston: Houghton Mifflin, 1895), pp. 35–36, 125, 216–25. For example, among the many Italian Renaissance paintings Eliot would have looked at in Florence (and in London and in books, in preparation for writing *Romola*) are many Annunciations in which Mary turns away from a book held in her hand or lying in her lap. Among them are Donatello's relief in Santa Croce, in which Mary holds the book open against her waist as she turns to the angel, and Fra Filippo Lippi's painting in San Lorenzo, in which Mary turns away from a bookstand to listen to the angel (although the viewer cannot see what is on the stand). About two paintings of Mary by Gaskell's and Eliot's contemporary, Dante Gabriel Rossetti—portraits of his sister Christina in "The Girlhood of Mary Virgin" (1849) and "Ecce Ancilla Domini" (1850)—Sandra Ludig has argued that the same sequence occurs. Although in neither painting is Mary reading or holding a book, in the first, she is making a symbol of herself (she embroiders a lily on a red cloth, symbol of her virginity); while in the second, this embroidery hangs finished on a stand while Gabriel, announcing the virgin birth to the terrified girl, holds a lily exactly as a painter would hold a brush and points it at Mary's womb. Ludig argues that the two paintings chart a shift from Mary as symbol maker to Mary as the object of others' symbol making, her powers as an artist usurped by Gabriel. Especially since these are portraits by another Gabriel of Christina Rossetti, who was herself an aspiring artist as well as poet, these paintings are indeed significant for nineteenth-century women artists' and writers' identification with Mary and the particular form of silencing that her history emblematizes for them (see "D. G. Rossetti's Paintings of Christina Rossetti as Mary" [manuscript, Yale University, 1982]).

21. For this account of Mary's relation to the Word, I am relying on Warner, *Alone of All Her Sex*, pp. 34–49; for the myth of her insemination by the ear, see Warner's quotation of a sixth-century hymn, still used, that translates, "The centuries marvel therefore that the angel bore the seed, the virgin conceived through her ear, and, believing in her heart, became fruitful" (p. 37). See also Joyce's use of this myth in the "Sirens" section of *Ulysses*, where the men in the bar joke about sex, religion, and singing: "Sure, you'd burst the tympanum of her ear, man, Mr. Dedalus said through smoke aroma, with an organ like yours. . . . Not to mention another membrane, Father Cowley added" (*Ulysses* [New York: Random House, 1961], p. 270).

22. Justin Martyr, *Dialogue with Trypho*, trans. A. L. Williams (London: SPCK, 1930), p. 21; quoted in John A. Phillips, *Eve: The History of an Idea* (San Francisco: Harper and Row, 1984), p. 133. Justin is quoting Luke 1:38.

23. See Joan N. Burstyn, *Victorian Education and the Ideal of Womanhood* (New Brunswick, N.J.: Rutgers University Press, 1984), pp. 84–98.

24. Herbert Spencer, *The Principles of Biology* (London, 1867), 2: 485; quoted in ibid., p. 94. Burstyn cites some of the same sources used by Showalter and Showalter, "Victorian Women and Menstruation," including Maudsley, whose *Sex in Mind and Education* (1874) Burstyn argues was written in response to women's entering universities in England.

25. See Froula, "When Eve Reads Milton," and my somewhat different reading of this moment in chap. 5.

26. Elaine Showalter has argued that some of the "feminine" novelists of the early Victorian period, needing to reconcile the duties of motherhood and the will to write, attempted to define writing as "motherly" (see *A Literature of Their Own*, pp. 65–72). Her chief example is Gaskell. Likewise, Bonnie Zimmerman takes seriously Eliot's consideration of motherhood: "motherhood was a *political* concept to her, as it was to the nineteenth century in general" ("The Mother's History," p. 82). By contrast, other recent critics have disparaged the notion that a woman's writing might be identified with motherhood because it has been used to trivialize women's writing especially as compensation for childlessness. I wish to stress that, in what follows, in considering women writers' use of metaphors of motherhood and of women's "duties" to describe their writing, I am not arguing that this is either good or bad but rather that these writers are attempting strategies for making their peace with the culture in which they live. Nina Auerbach contrasts women writers' metaphors of their books as children—such as Austen's remark when *Sense and Sensibility* was in proof, "I can no more forget it, than a mother can forget her sucking child" or the fact that Eliot "repeatedly defined her own sense of moral mission in the imagery of motherhood"—to their highly negative remarks about actual childbirth and its effects on women's minds (see "Artists and Mothers: A False Alliance," *Women and Literature* 6 (1978): 3–15. Auerbach cites, as an example of the reductive assumption that writing fiction compensated for Eliot's lack of her own children, U. C. Knoepflmacher, "Mr. Haight's George Eliot: 'Warheit und Dichtung,'" *Victorian Studies* 12 (1969): 420. While I would agree with the general tendency of her argument about Eliot, just as I would agree with the general tendency of

Showalter's argument about Gaskell, I am in both cases offering a more complex account both of these authors' motives for using maternal metaphors and of the contradictions within these metaphors. Rachel Brownstein has recently sounded Auerbach's note in a footnote about Eliot in *Becoming a Heroine: Reading about Women in Novels* (1982; reprint, Harmondsworth: Penguin, 1984), p. 319. Susan Stanford Friedman has argued persuasively and exhaustively for the difference between the use of maternal metaphors for men's and for women's creativity. Men, she suggests, compare their own creativity to childbirth with emphasis on the difference between vehicle and tenor, and they can disparage women authors by means of the same comparison precisely because maternity is not a metaphor for so many women. This emphasis on the literality of childbirth for women is very close to my own investigation of the ways in which maternity is used against women (see Friedman, "Creativity and the Childbirth Metaphor: A Case Study for Gender Difference in Literary Discourse," *Feminist Studies*, forthcoming.

27. Elizabeth Gaskell, *My Diary: The Early Years of My Daughter Marianne* (London: privately printed by Clement Shorter, 1923). Because the diary is only forty pages long, quotations will be identified only by context. I am grateful to Mrs. R. Trevor Dabbs for supplying information about the title and the manuscript of the diary, which belongs to her mother, Mrs. M. Trevor Jones of Cardiff, Wales.

28. See chapter 1, and Kristeva, *Desire*, pp. 124–27.

29. Winifred Gérin, *Elizabeth Gaskell: A Biography* (Oxford: Oxford University Press, 1980), p. 8. On the subject of biography, it is worth pointing out that although like all the other writers discussed in this book Gaskell lost her mother at an early age, she was raised entirely by women (see ibid., pp. 6–22). Her foster mother was a widow, and moreover, most of her mother's relations living nearby in Knutsford were single or widowed women (much as in the female world of *Cranford*). Showalter argues that the early deaths of the mothers of the nineteenth-century women novelists (the Brontës, Eliot, and Gaskell, and we might include Shelley as well) led to their strong identification with their fathers and hence, in my terms, with the symbolic order (*A Literature of Their Own*, pp. 61–64). But although Shelley, the Brontës, and Eliot were raised by strong fathers, Gaskell rarely saw her father. While individual biography is not likely to have as determinative an effect on a writer's writing as are patterns prevalent in the culture at large, this biographical difference offers, if not an explanation for, certainly an analogy for Gaskell's interest in writing as a woman and mother, which exceeds that of Shelley and Eliot as well as of the Brontës.

30. The novel was published in 1859 under the pseudonym "Herbert Grey, M. A.," the name under which Gaskell addresses her daughter as author. The second novel is *The Voyage of the Lady* (London, 1860).

31. *The Letters of Elizabeth Gaskell*, ed. J. A. V. Chapple and Arthur Pollard (Manchester: Manchester University Press, 1966), p. 541. Quotations from this volume will be cited parenthetically within the text by page number.

32. Showalter discusses the contradictions between the selflessness expected

of Victorian women and "the self-centeredness implicit in the act of writing" (*A Literature of Their Own*, p. 22; see also pp. 3–99, *passim*). While her discussion is a necessary starting point for this investigation, my conclusions as to the outcome of this contradiction for particular authors differ from hers.

33. Gaskell, *Life of Charlotte Brontë*, pp. 172–73.

34. Ibid., pp. 174–75.

35. Showalter uses this letter to demonstrate women writers' hope for "a balanced life in which the domestic role enriched the art, and the art kept the domestic role spontaneous and meaningful," a balance that would refute male critics' view of the contradiction between writing and women's duties (*A Literature of Their Own*, pp. 69–70). My reading of a longer selection from the letter reveals that ambiguity and contradiction underlie and partially undermine this optimism about women's turning contradiction into balance.

36. David Friedrich Strauss, *Life of Jesus*, trans. Mary Ann Evans (1846; reprint, Philadelphia: Fortress Press, 1973). She also translated in the 1850s Feuerbach's *Essence of Christianity* and Spinoza's *Ethics*.

37. *Essays of George Eliot*, ed. Thomas Pinney (New York: Columbia University Press, 1963), p. 211.

38. As in previous chapters, future quotations from Eliot's letters will be cited in the text only by volume and page numbers. Redinger also discusses this episode (see *George Eliot*, p. 145).

39. See *Eliot Letters* 3: 331, 344, and 364, where Eliot complains about the nuisance of moving, including the loss of the pen with which she had written for eight years. In December, they finally moved to 16 Blanford Square, where they stayed for six years.

40. Auerbach points to two letters (ibid., 3:382, 5:214–15) as examples of Eliot's ability to separate herself from her books once finished (they became part of "the non-ego"), a separation that Auerbach argues differentiates writing from motherhood; but the letter I discuss here suggests that such detachment is part of Eliot's maternal metaphor.

41. For another instance of a letter following the same train of thought, see ibid., 6:246–47. In this letter, Eliot moves from describing her "cares" for one of her "spiritual children" (in this case *Daniel Deronda*) at the beginning of the letter to worrying about her familial duties: "My studies have lately kept me away from the track of my husband's researches and I feel behindhand in my wifely sympathies."

42. Sandra Gilbert and Susan Gubar discuss the significance of Casaubon's book as "elfin child": "Textuality has been substituted for sexuality in [Dorothea's] married life" (*The Madwoman*, p. 505).

43. See *Eliot Letters* 5:350, 352, for other instances of Lewes's identification of himself and Eliot with Casaubon and Dorothea.

44. A letter of 1866 moves similarly from the metaphor of book as child (*Felix Holt* has "been growing slowly like a sickly child") to the thought of real grandchildren immediately to the thought of her own death: the same Gertrude is

expecting her first child (eventually born dead), a "joy" that leads Eliot, however serenely, to "think of old age and death as journeys not far off" (4:236–37).

Chapter 8

1. George Eliot, *Romola*, vols. 1 and 2 of The Works of George Eliot (1863; Cabinet Edition, Edinburgh and London: William Blackwell and Sons, 1877), proem. All citations will be from this edition, cited parenthetically in the text by chapter number for the convenience of those using other editions.

2. *Eliot Letters* 2:295, 339.

3. Haight, *Eliot*, p. 345; Haight quotes from Lewes's travel journal (Yale University Library).

4. That this masque represents a procession that the historical Piero di Cosimo actually staged in Florence adds a further layer of complexity to the question of literalization: Eliot as (woman) writer literalizes the work of a prior male artist (though unlike her literalization of Wordsworthian vision, this one does not alter the original significantly). See Giorgio Vasari, *The Lives of the Painters, Sculptors, and Architects*, trans. A. B. Hinds (London: Everyman, 1963), 2:178–79. (Vasari was Eliot's chief source of information about Piero.)

5. The quotation is a misquotation from Plautus, via Petrarch, to the effect that "no woman is really good, though one may be worse than another." Felicia Bonaparte points out about this moment that, as a borrowing of a borrowing (and Plautus was in turn relying on the Greek dramatists), it represents "a sequence of cultural inheritance that traces the evolution of Western civilization," and that Bardo's quotation of these earlier authors' sentiments is ironic, "since it is a woman, Romola, who carries, and even pioneers, civilization" (*Triptych and Cross*, pp. 48–49). I would argue that what Bonaparte identifies as an irony here is actually central to the transmission of culture as it is represented in the novel, and much of this chapter will be devoted to exploring how and why this is so. Bonaparte's argument focuses on Romola's passage through the various stages of Western culture, from classical paganism through Christianity to Protestantism and a mythic understanding of religion.

6. See Friedman, "Creativity and the Childbirth Metaphor."

7. Bonaparte argues that what distinguishes Romola as a forerunner of Protestantism from the Madonna of Renaissance Christianity is that she is not an icon but rather a woman who has internalized the values of Christianity (*Triptych and Cross*, p. 237). This may be so from Romola's perspective, but taking into consideration the totality of the novel's views of her, I would have to argue that Romola is very much what other eyes make of her.

8. Bonaparte points out the many parallels between Romola and the Virgin Mary in this episode, including the similarity between Benedetto and the Christ child (ibid., pp. 235–36). I am providing a different context and interpretation for the same parallels.

9. Indeed, as Elaine Showalter suggests, "Romola's dedication to the pres-

ervation of her father's library is a paradigm of the feminine novelist's veneration for male culture" (*A Literature of Their Own*, p. 44).

10. See Andrew Saunders's note in his edition of *Romola* (Harmondsworth: Penguin, 1980), p. 697.

11. The cancelled epigraphs are printed, translated, and discussed in the Penguin edition, pp. 682–85.

12. *Eliot Essays*, p. 208.

13. *Eliot Letters* 1:227; *Eliot Essays*, p. 211.

14. Many commentators on the novel have noted that Eliot's research seems to have been excessive; Avrom Fleishman attributes Eliot's zealousness for historical accuracy to her Comtean belief in the need to recreate historical milieu. I would not disagree but suggest that another motive might underlie her having adopted this principle in the first place. See Fleishman, *The English Historical Novel: Walter Scott to Virginia Woolf* (Baltimore: Johns Hopkins University Press, 1971), p. 158.

15. Eliot's footnote added in the Cabinet edition.

16. I am indebted here to J. Hillis Miller's reading of realism as catachresis, that is, as the naming of something that can be named only figuratively, despite realistic fiction's claim to present something that really happened (see Miller, "Narrative and History," *ELH* 41 [1974]: 455–73).

17. The same could be said of the other female figures Romola enacts: Antigone, Ariadne, Aurora, Boccaccio's Gostanza, and others. These figures are mythic or literary, with even less grounding in historical fact than Mary. But in the transfer from one literary text to another, it is just as likely to be true that the second version is a figuration of the first, as that the second literalizes the first.

Chapter 9

1. A. W. Ward, introduction to *Mary Barton* (1848; reprint, Knutsford Edition, London: Smith and Elder and Co., 1906), 1: xxvii–xxviii. Although I have not been able to trace Ward's source for this story—all Gaskell's letters from the time of William's death to 1847 were destroyed at her wish—it has been accepted as fact by Gaskell's readers. Gaskell's most judicious recent critic, Angus Easson, repeating the story, states that "whatever part the children played in her writing . . . only one seems responsible for starting her writing, and that, tragically, her only son, William" (*Elizabeth Gaskell* [London: Routledge and Kegan Paul, 1979], p. 36). Quotations from *Mary Barton* will be from the Knutsford edition, cited by chapter.

2. Gaskell gives the epigraph in the original German of J. L. Uhland; the translation is from the Knutsford edition, p. xlix:

> Take, good ferryman, I pray
> Take a triple fare to-day:
> The twain who with me touched the strand
> Were visitants from spirit-land.

3. Printed in the introduction to the Knutsford edition, pp. xxvi–xxvii.

4. Gaskell, *Diary*, p. 19. For detailed discussion of this passage in the context of the diary, see chapter 7.

5. Elizabeth Gaskell, "Lizzie Leigh" (1850); reprinted in *Cousin Phyllis and Other Tales* (Oxford: Oxford University Press, 1981), pp. 1–32.

6. "Michael," lines 244–45, in *The Poetical Works of William Wordsworth* 2:88.

7. See Showalter, *A Literature of Their Own*, p. 92. The example she gives is the debate over the sex of the author of *Jane Eyre*.

8. I am indebted to Karen Matthews for her account of this publication history and for her analysis of this issue in "Lizzie Leigh," in a paper written for a seminar at Yale in 1978. Annette Kolodny discusses a woman writer's use of the secret female code of domestic detail in "A Map for Rereading; or, Gender and the Interpretation of Literary Texts," *New Literary History* 11 (1980): 451–67.

9. Michael Wheeler, *The Art of Allusion in Victorian Fiction* (London: Macmillan, 1979), p. 50.

10. For example, Inga-Stina Ewbank writes of Gaskell's idealization of Brontë (*Their Proper Sphere: A Study of The Brontë Sisters as Early Victorian Female Novelists* [Cambridge: Harvard University Press, 1966], p. 47). Margaret Ganz writes, "her material would be made subservient to her desire, to present Charlotte's life to the world as a moral exemplum," yet Ganz also points out that by quoting Brontë's letters at such length, Gaskell preserves the evidence of Brontë's less conventional side (*Elizabeth Gaskell: The Artist in Conflict* [New York: Twayne, 1969], pp. 182–97; quotation p. 187). Showalter writes of Gaskell's portrayal of Brontë as a "tragic heroine" (*A Literature of Their Own*, p. 106). Brownstein writes of the "smugness" and "slyness" of the revelation of Brontë's struggles to be good, which reveal a discrepancy between Brontë the perfect woman and Brontë the improper and visionary rebel (*Becoming a Heroine*, pp. 160–62).

11. Gaskell, *Life of Charlotte Brontë* 2:11. Quotations from the *Life* are from this text of the first edition, cited by volume and chapter numbers.

12. These quotations are from the third edition's revised version of vol. 1, chap. 4, included in the appendix to the Penguin edition.

13. Elizabeth Gaskell, "Lois the Witch" (1859); reprinted in *Cousin Phyllis and Other Tales*, pp. 105–93. All other quotations will be from this edition.

14. See Geoffrey Hartman's reading of the interchangeability of blessing and cursing in "The Ancient Mariner," in *Saving the Text* (Baltimore: Johns Hopkins University Press, 1981), pp. 99, 131, 164–65.

15. In the manuscript from this point on, Gaskell continually mistakes one pastor's name for the other's and has to go back and make corrections. The manuscript is in the Houghton Library at Harvard University. Though the Oxford text prints Tappan's name as Tappau, it is clear from the manuscript that this is a misreading.

16. "The Rime of the Ancient Mariner," lines 125–26, 129–30, in *The Complete Works of Samuel Taylor Coleridge*, ed. E. H. Coleridge (London: Oxford University Press, 1912), p. 191.

17. Rev. Charles W. Upham, *Lectures on Witchcraft* (Boston, 1831).

18. Elizabeth Gaskell, "The Poor Clare," in *Round the Sofa* (1859; Knutsford Edition, London: Smith and Elder and Co., 1906), 5:329–90.

19. For a brief discussion of a feminist critique of the mirror as the form into which women are objectified (most recently in Lacan's figure of the "mirror stage"), see chapter 1, note 34.

Chapter 10

1. See also page 712, where she writes to Smith, "'Two Mothers' in my head very clear," but does not describe the story; Smith's own response to the story proposal is lost.

2. For an interesting introduction to the thematics of mothers and daughters in the novel, see Jacqueline Berke and Laura Berke, "Mothers and Daughters in *Wives and Daughters:* A study of Elizabeth Gaskell's Last Novel," in *The Lost Tradition*, pp. 95–109. My concern is only tangentially with this theme.

3. Elizabeth Gaskell, *Wives and Daughters* (1864–1866; Knutsford Edition, London: Smith and Elder and Co., 1907), 8:7. For the convenience of those using other editions, quotations will be cited in the text by chapter only.

4. Discussing the themes of female selflessness and the duty to "take care" of others instead of the self, Patricia Meyer Spacks writes, "Mrs. Hamley perseveres in self-suppression to its natural conclusion in death," and suggests that while Molly models herself after Mrs. Hamley for a period, she "finds the course finally impossible" (*The Female Imagination* [1975; reprint, New York: Avon, 1976], p. 117). My reading of this theme in the novel is no different from Spacks's, but I situate it in the context of Gaskell's mythmaking about language.

5. "A Slumber Did My Spirit Seal," in *The Poetical Works of William Wordsworth* 2:216.

6. Moorman, *Journals of Dorothy Wordsworth*, p. 154.

7. Quoted from *The Poems of Tennyson*, ed. Christopher Ricks (London and New York: Longman and Norton, 1969), pp. 187–90. Angus Easson points out the rich allusiveness of *Wives and Daughters* generally, mentioning this allusion as an example (*Elizabeth Gaskell*, p. 189).

8. In terms of female thematics, Spacks points out that despite all the stepmother's unappealing traits, as a model, "Molly can see in her the advantages that selfishness brings" (*The Female Imagination*, pp. 114–15).

9. In her critique of the Lacanian "mirror stage," Luce Irigaray makes an important distinction between the frozen mirrors women are obliged to become in patriarchal society, passively reflecting men's desires and thus repelling their daughters, and a more active, playful "mirroring" that seems closer to what Roger acts out. In the voice of the presymbolic daughter, Irigaray writes, "I would like us to play together at being the same and different. You/I exchanging selves endlessly and each staying herself. Living mirrors" ("And the One Doesn't Stir without the Other," p. 61; see also chapter 1, note 34).

Postscript

1. Virginia Woolf, "George Eliot," in *The Common Reader: First Series* (New York: Harcourt Brace, 1925), p. 173. See Knoepflmacher, "Genre and the Integration of Gender," p. 112. Bazin points out that Mrs. Ramsay has unfulfilled philanthropic plans that resemble Dorothea's (see Bazin, *Virginia Woolf*, p. 128).

2. We might note here an inverse similarity between Woolf's allusion to *Middlemarch* and Gaskell's allusion to *Jane Eyre*. Gaskell acknowledges her female predecessor only to transform her into an even more male-identified mother than she is; Woolf acknowledges her female predecessor while wishing that she were less male-identified.

Sandra Gilbert's analysis of a similarly ambivalent relation between Eliot and Edith Wharton was very suggestive for my argument about Woolf (see "Life's Empty Pack: Notes toward a Literary Daughteronomy," *Critical Inquiry* 11 [1985]: 355–84).

3. Virginia Woolf, *A Room of One's Own* (New York: Harcourt Brace, 1929), p. 79.

4. Jane Marcus, "Liberty, Sorority, Misogyny," in *The Representation of Women in Fiction*, ed. Carolyn G. Heilbrun and Margaret R. Higonnet (Baltimore: Johns Hopkins University Press, 1983), p. 71.

5. Virginia Woolf, "Professions for Women," in *The Death of the Moth and Other Essays* (New York: Harcourt Brace, 1942), pp. 237, 238.

6. Maria DiBattista, *Virginia Woolf's Major Novels: The Fables of Anon* (New Haven: Yale University Press, 1980), p. 75. Geoffrey Hartman also points out that Mrs. Ramsay is associated with "the will of nature," both with natural vitality and with nature's destructiveness (see "Virginia's Web," in *Beyond Formalism* [New Haven: Yale University Press, 1970], p. 82). Fleishman likewise sees Mrs. Ramsay as an ambiguous queen, with powers both benign and sinister (*Virginia Woolf*, pp. 109–10, 157).

7. Spivak, "Making and Unmaking in *To the Lighthouse*," p. 315.

8. Virgil, *The Aeneid*, trans. Robert Fitzgerald (New York: Random House, 1983), p. 225.

9. I am grateful to Maria DiBattista for pointing out to me the significance of this passage for my argument.

10. As DiBattista writes in *Virginia Woolf's Major Novels*, *To the Lighthouse* "concerns itself with the death of the beloved queen mother and her resurrection through art" (p. 93). She also argues that "the novel is an elegiac narrative that treats its subject—the dead mother and father—exclusively in terms of the surviving daughter, the implied, anonymous narrator of the novel" (p. 68). Agreeing with DiBattista, I place these insights in a different context to give them an added significance. Susan Dick also argues for the importance of memory in the novel, and particularly in Lily's painting, in "The Tunnelling Process: Some Aspects of Virginia Woolf's Use of Memory and the Past," in *Virginia Woolf: New Critical Essays*, ed. Patricia Clements and Isobel Grundy (London: Vision Press, 1983), pp. 190–95. John Mepham discusses Woolf's own comments about the novel as the completion of her mourning for her mother and

as an elegy in "Mourning and Modernism," also in Clements and Grundy, *Virginia Woolf*, p. 142.

11. Virginia Woolf, *Between the Acts* (New York: Harcourt Brace, 1941), p. 212.

12. Critics have ordinarily assumed that Lily alone (and not Cam) is Woolf's figure for the artist. Bazin, moreover, asserts that Lily's "painting is . . . an abstract equivalent of the novel itself" (Bazin, *Virginia Woolf*, p. 126). Woolf, I argue to the contrary, is considerably ambivalent about Lily as a figure for Woolf's own art, and we can see this ambivalence at work in Lily's penultimate thought in the novel: "It would be hung in attics, she thought; it would be destroyed. But what did that matter?" (pp. 309–10). On the one hand, Woolf may be dismissing Lily's painting as third-rate, and thus distancing herself from it as a paradigm for her own art; on the other, she may be suggesting that it is precisely those artists whom their audiences fail to appreciate who are most likely to be the creators of a genuinely new vision. The latter interpretation would apply to La Trobe, as it would also to Woolf herself, who, celebrating her view of women as a "Society of Outsiders," preferred being locked out to being locked in.

13. It would be possible to discuss Woolf's hopes for the idea of androgyny in this context. Bazin discusses Woolf's argument for androgyny in the novel, citing among other features Lily's desire in her painting to balance the left and the right sides. See Bazin, *Virginia Woolf*, p. 45.

14. See, for example, Josephine O'Brien Schaefer, "Mr. and Mrs. Ramsay," in *Critics on Virginia Woolf*, ed. Jaqueline E. M. Latham (London: George Allen and Unwin, 1970), p. 73.

15. It is worth noting that Woolf's recent feminist critics are among the most powerful voices in the "maternal," "North American" school of criticism I sketched in the Preface. Following out in relation to Woolf as mother Woolf's exhortation to "think back through our mothers," critics and editors such as Jane Marcus, and textual scholars recovering the boldness and anger Woolf censored in revising her manuscripts for publication, have shown us a Woolf who may be the most powerful, political, thematically feminist writer of the modern period. This Woolf has become central to the maternal legacy that those feminist critics who believe in the possibility of representing female experience would recover. It is quite possible that this Woolf will enable a still more powerful, and less self-censoring, feminist writing in a way that her own mothers could not, following out Lily's lead in the direction of a representational practice that does not victimize the mother (because she is not perceived to victimize us). For a review of recent Woolf criticism, especially its separatist tendencies, see Bonnie Kime Scott, "Review Essay: Virginia Woolf: Access to an Outsider's Vision," *Tulsa Studies in Women's Literature* 4 (1985): 125–36.

16. H. D., "Tribute to the Angels," *Trilogy* (1945; reprint, New York: New Directions, 1970), from sections 38 and 39, pp. 103–5.

Index